# OPERATION JEDBURGH

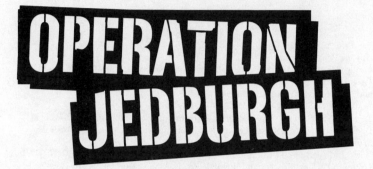

# OPERATION JEDBURGH

## D-DAY AND AMERICA'S
## FIRST SHADOW WAR

### COLIN BEAVAN

VIKING

VIKING
Published by the Penguin Group
Penguin Group (USA) Inc., 375 Hudson Street, New York, New York 10014, U.S.A.
Penguin Group (Canada), 90 Eglinton Avenue East, Suite 700, Toronto, Ontario, Canada M4P 2Y3
(a division of Pearson Penguin Canada Inc.)
Penguin Books Ltd, 80 Strand, London WC2R 0RL, England
Penguin Ireland, 25 St. Stephen's Green, Dublin 2, Ireland (a division of Penguin Books Ltd)
Penguin Books Australia Ltd, 250 Camberwell Road, Camberwell, Victoria 3124, Australia
(a division of Pearson Australia Group Pty Ltd)
Penguin Books India Pvt Ltd, 11 Community Centre, Panchsheel Park, New Delhi–110 017, India
Penguin Group (NZ), Cnr Airborne and Rosedale Roads, Albany, Auckland 1310, New Zealand
(a division of Pearson New Zealand Ltd)
Penguin Books (South Africa) (Pty) Ltd, 24 Sturdee Avenue,
Rosebank, Johannesburg 2196, South Africa

Penguin Books Ltd, Registered Offices:
80 Strand, London WC2R 0RL, England

First published in 2006 by Viking Penguin,
a member of Penguin Group (USA) Inc.

ISBN 0-670-03762-1

Printed in the United States of America
Set in Minion Display with Gazz
Designed by Daniel Lagin

*For my family:*

*Michelle, Isabella, and Frankie*

# CONTENTS

# MAPS

War is love's response to a neighbor threatened by force.

—Saint Augustine

War may sometimes be a necessary evil. But no matter how necessary, it is always an evil, never a good.

—Jimmy Carter

It is just as sentimental to pretend that war does not have its monstrous ugliness as it is to deny that it has its own strange and fatal beauty.

—Bernard Knox, former Jedburgh

There's just one thing I think you ought to know before you take on this job. And don't forget it. If you do well, you'll get no thanks and if you get into trouble you'll get no help. Does that suit you?

Perfectly.

Then I'll wish you good-afternoon.

—W. Somerset Maugham, *Ashenden;
or, The British Agent*

## A NOTE ON DIALOGUE

Throughout the text, quotation marks are used only when a living or published source exists for the exact words spoken or written. In cases where sources provide only the contents of a conversation, but the author has reconstructed it as dialogue, no quotation marks are used.

# PREFACE

Back when intercontinental missiles scared the world more than suicide bombers, when radiation worried us more than bioterror, before duct tape to seal our windows replaced shovels to dig our fallout shelters, back in those days when the United States waged war against Communism rather than Terrorism, from the 1950s to the 1970s, my maternal grandfather, Gerry Miller, was a spy.

Every morning, in the later years of his career, when I was old enough to remember him, he wrestled his stout body behind the wheel of his blue Chevy Impala, dropped his broad-brimmed hat into the passenger seat, and drove from his McLean, Virginia, home to the CIA's headquarters at Langley. His heels echoed across the granite floor of the restricted building; he flashed his ID at the guards. When the doors to the executive elevator slid closed and sent him upward, he disappeared from my family's world. Eight, ten, or fourteen hours later, the elevator doors split open again, my grandfather reappeared, and he ambled back to his Chevy.

About the Beltway traffic jams, about the species of birds his wife had seen in the backyard that day, about his college years at Yale, about any other trivial aspect of life you brought up, my grandfather would talk. About his part in fascinating affairs of state, about his role in creating or alleviating international tensions with the Russians, about the worldwide chess match he played in the hours between the Langley elevator doors' swallowing him up and spitting him out, he never told any of us in his family a single thing. Literally. Not one single thing. My mother and her siblings never even saw his office.

All that my family could divine about my grandfather's CIA career came from a very few, poorly detailed family stories. During the Cuban missile crisis, as one family anecdote goes, a phone call to my grandparents' vacation home in Westport Point, Massachusetts, sent my grandfather racing the eight hours back to Washington for a meeting at the White House. On the indictment of Howard Hunt, the architect of the Watergate burglary and a former CIA employee, another story goes, my grandfather furiously admitted to my father having tried several times to have the renegade Hunt fired from the agency. Last, an old family friend and senior-ranking CIA colleague of my grandfather's once said that "Gerry Miller is one of the ten most powerful men in the United States." Not much to go on.

We also have the guest books my grandparents foisted upon every dinnerparty companion with the expectation of some witty doggerel or snippet. Inscriptions by former CIA directors Allen Dulles, Richard Helms, and William Colby all appear in the leather-bound books. "Proud to be second to a great mentor, boss and friend," Colby wrote in 1978, two years after being fired by President Gerald Ford. Colby, according to his book *Honorable Men,* originally joined the cloak-and-dagger society when he "accepted Gerry Miller's invitation to join CIA."

I mention all this not out of a sense of grandiosity, but to offer a glimpse of how my grandfather's career came to arouse such curiosity in my family. Why was he summoned to the White House as the Soviets steamed their shiploads of missiles toward Cuba? With whom did he meet? What was his relationship with heads of the CIA? An unstated rule forbade my mother from asking. But in a bout of enthusiasm after seeing some spy movie, when I was ten or eleven and too young to understand the family mores, I begged my grandfather to tell me about his career while my mother tensely stood by. "Forget all the James Bond stuff," my grandfather said. "It really wasn't very interesting." He changed the subject.

My family accepted my grandfather's secrecy about the CIA and his career—at least in the beginning. In those times, when writers from Ian Fleming to John Le Carré romanticized the espionage game, to be in the secret service was seen as patriotic, exciting, and glamorous. Even after the CIA's botched attempt to invade Cuba at the Bay of Pigs, few people really questioned the agency's nobility, not in our family and not in the country.

But then, in the late sixties and early seventies, came the Vietnam War and news that the CIA had infiltrated agents onto university campuses across the

United States; that former agents participated in the Watergate break-in; and that the CIA bugged the phones and broke into the homes of American citizens involved in the antiwar movement. Was the CIA more concerned with fighting the Russians or with controlling Americans? people began to ask. Was it the secret police force of some sort of Big Brother–style invisible government?

On February 28, 1975, CBS reporter Daniel Schorr appeared on our TV screens announcing that the CIA might have been involved in the assassinations of foreign leaders. Over the next two years, a select committee led by Senator Frank Church of Idaho investigated the agency and confirmed Schorr's allegations—and much more.

The CIA, the Church committee discovered, had plotted assassination attempts against the leaders of Cuba, the Congo, and the Dominican Republic. The agency had run a program of mind-control experiments, which included dosing unsuspecting subjects with LSD and other drugs, resulting in at least one death. And the CIA had assisted the 1973 military coup against Salvador Allende, Chile's president, even though he had been democratically elected. That action ended in the installation of General Augusto Pinochet, arguably the most vicious and murderous dictator in South American history, who was only in 2005 nearing trial for his atrocities.

The Church committee's report of the CIA's highly questionable activities, as journalist Thomas Powers wrote, "was like a crash course in political realism for reporters, scholars, historians and the general public." No one could take comfort anymore in official denials and proclamations that the United States did not stoop to secret murders. Congress began enacting legislative curbs on the CIA's activities and powers.

Meanwhile, the Church report was a crash course in realism for the families of CIA agents, too. "What am I going to tell my children?" agents asked my grandfather's friend and then CIA Director William Colby. My grandfather had come up with an answer all his own: he would tell his children absolutely nothing.

My grandfather died in 1987. In 1994, my sister tried to find out as much as she could from our grandmother, who lay on her own deathbed, wasted by lung cancer. Grannie told my sister that she knew nothing about my grandfather's work. "I always knew I just wasn't supposed to ask," Grannie said. My grandfather, as the family story goes, fell in love with Grannie the first time he saw her, at a hockey game, sitting a few seats away from her. "I'm going to marry that girl," he whispered to a friend. And he did. But even to her, about his CIA work, my grandfather said nothing.

Like a good spy, he left behind few clues. So, in 1997, ten years after his death, I began my investigation of his espionage career.

Down in my grandparents' cellar, I rolled up my sleeves and dug through cardboard boxes containing a lot of old checkbooks and bank statements and a very few old papers and artifacts relating to my grandfather's work. Most of them dated back to World War II, which he spent in the Office of Strategic Services (OSS), the first centralized American secret service and the precursor to the CIA.

I dusted off a leather shoulder holster that contained a World War II .32 caliber Colt automatic with the words "U.S. Government" etched on the barrel. I found my grandfather's Presidential Medal of Freedom, America's highest civilian honor, presented to him at the end of the war. The accompanying citation read, in part: "for exceptionally meritorious achievement which aided the United States in the prosecution of the war against the enemy in Continental Europe." (The same medal was awarded in 2004 by President George W. Bush to General Tommy Franks, commander of the invasion of Iraq; L. Paul Bremer III, chief civilian administrator of the U.S. occupation there; and former CIA director George Tenet.)

I next pulled from the boxes a short stack of brown-edged index cards with notes for what seemed to be a speech my grandfather once gave. "The OSS has been labeled the cloak and dagger society," the cards said. "I was in the dagger end of the business." By this, he meant that he worked not for OSS Secret Intelligence, which spied on the Germans, Italians, and Japanese, but for OSS Special Operations, which attacked, sabotaged, and killed them. This was my first real clue into my grandfather's work. He was not the gentleman spy whose agents merely skulked in dark doorways; he worked much more lethally on what was called "making bangs."

I then went to the huge greenhouse-like National Archives complex at College Park, Maryland, where I shuffled through yellowed papers and discovered that my grandfather probably never pulled from its holster that .32 I found in the basement. He was too senior. It turns out that, in the summer of 1944, as the Allied forces crawled over the Normandy beaches and into France, my grandfather was first the executive officer and then the overall chief of Special Operations (SO) at the OSS London branch. In cooperation with the

British government and European governments-in-exile, my grandfather and his senior SO colleagues parachuted saboteurs, assassins, and guerrilla fighters, together with the weapons and explosives they needed, into Nazi-occupied Europe.

One group of those agents, known as the Jedburghs, became the subject of this book. My grandfather and the other spy chiefs consulted with Eisenhower's D-Day planners and commanders to determine what behind-the-lines actions would most effectively defeat the Germans. The Jedburghs, and other agents, led Resistance forces on sabotage operations or paramilitary raids against the Germans. So successful was the agent-led skulduggery of the Resistance that Eisenhower himself said, "[W]ithout their great assistance the liberation of France and the defeat of the enemy in western Europe would have consumed a much longer time and meant greater losses to ourselves."

Allied victory came, the war ended, and despite concern over Soviet expansionism, President Truman disbanded the OSS. The United States was once again without a secret service. My grandfather shipped home from London and returned for a couple of years to his investment banking firm in Detroit, Michigan. What would sadly turn out to be the most clearly noble period of his espionage career had already come to an end, as had the paper trail I'd so far followed.

The Soviet army occupied Eastern Europe. Communist regimes took power in East Germany, Albania, Yugoslavia, Poland, Hungary, Romania, Bulgaria, and Czechoslovakia. Civil war, fomented by Soviet-backed Communists, raged in Greece. Democratic parties in France and Italy faced the danger of electoral defeat by the Communists. Politicians, statesmen, and former OSS spies alike harbored the very real fear that Stalin would invade Western Europe. On top of all that, in September 1949, a radioactive cloud floating across the northern Pacific alerted the United States to the fact that the Soviet Union had performed a nuclear test and now had the atom bomb.

That year, as my mother remembers it, without warning, my grandparents suddenly packed their possessions, sold their house, and uprooted themselves to Washington, D.C. My grandfather, as far as my mother or anyone else was told, had taken a job with the "government." In fact, thanks to the frenzied war scare, a throng of old OSS shadow warriors like my grandfather now converged on Washington to build on their wartime successes at a fledgling new espionage organization, the Central Intelligence Agency.

From the CIA's beginning, former OSS men held its reins. To carry out their plans and intrigues, they seduced their old derring-do OSS wartime parachute agents back into the game. The CIA, one-third staffed by former OSSers, adopted the same structure and functions as the OSS. No one really knew anything about peacetime espionage, nor did they feel they needed to. War with the Soviets had become a matter not of "if" but of "when." For the next thirty years, World War II spies, including my grandfather, would justify their warlike footing on the grounds that they continually either prepared for or prevented imminent war with the Soviets. Clandestine operations, my grandfather's line of work, quickly became the CIA's preeminent activity.

I found precious few papers from this period to help with my investigation of my grandfather's career. Instead, old colleagues I discovered by digging through my grandfather's address books told me that his résumé read like the history of the CIA's dirty tricks department, through the agency's better times and worse.

When the CIA concerned itself mainly with preparing for a blitzkrieg of Soviet tanks toward Paris and Rome, my grandfather, drawing on his OSS experience, oversaw the organization, training, and arming of a series of top secret "sleeper" or "stay-behind" networks across the Continent. These units would rise up and fight Soviet invaders just as my grandfather's World War II agents had fought the Germans. My grandfather had taken the job of chief of the Western European section of the Office of Policy Coordination (OPC), the precursor to the CIA's most highly secretive Directorate of Operations.

In the 1950s, when the CIA's attention turned to the Soviets' effort, financed by hundreds of millions of dollars, to get Communist governments peaceably elected across Europe, my grandfather packed up his family again and moved to Italy, where he became CIA station chief. Working with his protégé, William Colby, my grandfather fought the Soviet efforts by pumping CIA money into Italy's centrist parties, planting anti-Communist stories in the press, and busting Communist trade unions. My grandfather and Colby ran what Colby wrote was "by far the CIA's largest covert political-action program." They prevented any further Communist incursion into the Italian government.

Finally, in the sixties, when the CIA fought furiously to overthrow Fidel Castro's Communist regime in Cuba and opposed Ho Chi Minh's Communist government in North Vietnam, my grandfather moved back to Washington, where he whooshed his way to work every day in Langley's executive elevator. My grandfather became chief of operational services. He chose the senior team to run operations around the world and, with his staff of thousands, made sure that operations, both small and large, had weapons and anything else needed.

For thirty years, the old OSS men like my grandfather ran the CIA as though they were still at war. When planning or seeking approval for new operations, they used a top secret official history of the OSS as a sort of playbook. These veterans of World War II espionage and their students would claim that by doing so, they both kept the United States prepared for World War III and helped prevent it. But it's difficult to verify the accuracy of their claims: the United States never went to war with the Soviet Union. In fact, Soviet tanks never even rumbled outside their Eastern bloc territory—at least, not until 1979.

That year, the Soviet army invaded Afghanistan. In 1980, President Jimmy Carter ordered the CIA to support Afghan resistance to the Soviet occupation. In 1981, President Ronald Reagan brought on board as director of Central Intelligence an old colleague of my grandfather's, William Casey. Casey had been chief of Secret Intelligence in London while my grandfather was chief of Special Operations. Now the OSS veteran presided over a huge CIA operation in Afghanistan, a dream come true for OSS men and their followers and perhaps the last big showdown between the United States and the Soviet Union.

The CIA, in what seemed like a brilliant propaganda ploy at the time, revived the idea of the jihad, a holy war to protect Islam, which had been largely forgotten since the tenth century. CIA agents and their allies spun their jihad sales pitch everywhere from northern Africa to the Philippines, where they sold it to all manner of Muslim activists. This was in the days when the United States and Osama bin Laden were on the same side—he was one among a number of wealthy Arabs who recruited and raised funds for the jihad. From around the world, Islamic fighters streamed into Afghanistan, like the International Brigades who had gone to Spain to fight Franco forty years earlier.

Working in parallel with Saudi intelligence, bin Laden, and others, the CIA gave the insurgents hundreds of millions of dollars' worth of arms and the world's best training in hit-and-run guerrilla warfare. The CIA even built with them a network of hidden caves near the Pakistan border called Tora Bora (the same one where bin Laden would later hide after 9/11). This operation harked straight back to the OSS work with the Resistance during World War II, and so was the legacy of old OSS men like my grandfather, though he had by now retired. "Afghan freedom fighters have made it as dangerous for a Russian soldier or Soviet convoy to stray off a main road as it was for the Germans in France in 1944," Casey said.

The operation seemed a complete success. The Soviets withdrew from Afghanistan in February 1989. In May, the Hungarians bravely opened their border with Austria without Soviet intervention. The next month, Solidarity gained a majority in Poland's parliament, ending half a century of Communism. In November, East Germans breached the Berlin Wall and surged west. A month after that, the entire leadership in Czechoslovakia resigned, ending Communist rule there. Two years after my grandfather died, the cold war had ended, and the CIA and all its old OSS leadership and their aggressive covert antics seemed to be exonerated.

There was a problem, however: by bringing together Islamic fighters from around the world in Afghanistan, the CIA had inadvertently participated in the creation of a network of extremists who now looked for the next target for their jihad. While the United States basked in the glow of its cold war victory, battle-torn Afghanistan fell into the Taliban's hands, and Osama bin Laden shaped the network of extremists into al Qaeda. Appalled by the fact that five years after the Gulf War the United States still stationed its troops in Saudi Arabia, bin Laden made America his prime target. First came the 1998 car bombings of the U.S. embassies in Kenya and Tanzania; then, in October 2000, a hole was blasted in the side of the USS *Cole* as it refueled in the port of Aden; and, most horrifically, three thousand people died in the 9/11 attacks.

With such mixed results, how can the United States assess the history of its covert action capability first established during World War II by men like my grandfather? How do my family and I assess my grandfather's life?

Take the Afghanistan example. The OSS-style covert operations that helped weaken the Soviet Union also helped give momentum to bin Laden's terrorist movement. But after sanctions by the Church committee and other investigations following the Iran-Contra affair, according to the 9/11 Commission, the CIA's leadership was reluctant to pursue operations of questionable legality against al Qaeda. Strangely, the failure of the United States to prevent 9/11 came from both its enthusiasm for and its reluctance to use the covert operations capability established during World War II by the OSS.

As I write, the American intelligence service, including the CIA, is under the most severe scrutiny since World War II. In December 2004, President George W. Bush signed into law the National Security Intelligence Reform Act, presaging the most sweeping changes since Truman established the CIA along OSS lines in 1947. Meanwhile, the Department of Defense has established its own covert action capability, partly in the hope that it will not be subject to the legislation and congressional oversight that so ties the CIA's hands.

Just as in the 1950s, when covert operations seemed to prevent war with the Soviets, the national mood once again favors them if they will prevent attacks on American soil. Going forward, shadow warriors will be more independent and subject to less oversight than they have been at any time since World War II's OSS and the early years of the CIA. In the world of "black operations," history is repeating itself.

The question, in gauging the proper use of covert operations in the future, is: Where did they work in the past—and where did they fail? Such a survey of wins and losses will be complete only if it reaches back to the origins of the American intelligence service: World War II's OSS. The emphasis on covert operations, the bellicose approach, the assassination precedent all followed from it.

The CIA took its moral authority from the successes of the OSS. Operations staff often looked to a secret official history of the OSS, written in the late 1940s, as a sort of playbook to support claims of past accomplishments and the correctness of taking shadow warfare opportunities. But were OSS operations truly successes? Did they contribute to the winning of the war or at least the shortening of it? Did my grandfather base his later questionable activities on a firm foundation?

From a historian's point of view, to understand much of what the CIA did after World War II, from the laying of stay-behind networks to putting weapons into the hands of men like bin Laden, one has to understand what was done by the OSS in Europe. From a personal point of view, it was also the high point in my grandfather's life. My grandfather's Presidential Medal of Freedom testified to his being a hero. This was the unquestioned time of victory in the careers of both my grandfather and the American intelligence service from which so much else followed, which is why I wrote this book.

One day, when my grandfather was about eighty, long before my research into his career began, I came home on a visit from college. I stopped by his house and sat on the sofa. As I looked out the window over the harbor, he sat in the same red upholstered chair where he had spent most of his old age napping and reading. I asked him to show me his World War II medals. It had been ten years since the whole CIA–Church committee blowup. My grandfather had ceased to be a spy in anyone's mind. He was just "Grandfa."

He struggled out of his chair and took me upstairs to his bedroom, opened his closet door, and began shoving his suit jackets aside. He pointed to a hatch in the back of the closet, in the true fashion of a spy. I crawled toward the hatch, opened it, and dragged out a gray metal safety-deposit box.

I picked up the box and handed it to my grandfather. I noticed that his hands were shaking, and not from age. He had a loud, booming voice that now went very quiet, as though he had a frog in his throat. One at a time, as though they were made of glass, he gingerly pulled out the medals he had won for his World War II OSS service. They had been awarded to him personally by the kings of Denmark and Norway and the leaders of other formerly Nazi-occupied countries. Then he pulled out his Presidential Medal of Freedom. By this time, tears dripped slowly from his chin.

As I held the medal, I knew it was full of meaning, but I wish now that I had thought to ask my grandfather why he cried. Did he feel regret, pride, nostalgia? Since then, I have always imagined that he felt nostalgia for the World War II years, when his espionage career with a clearly defined enemy could not be misconstrued. I wish I had asked, but at the time what I really wanted was to get out of the room as quickly as I could because I felt so awkward seeing my grandfather cry.

Later, downstairs, when the spell had broken, I did ask him what he had done in the war to win the medals. He just shook his head. "Oh, hell," he said, "all I ever did was hand the suicide pills to them before they got on the airplanes." He never said who "them" referred to; never said where the airplanes went. Family members told me that it was a stock answer he had always given. Only through my research did I discover that "them" meant the agents he dispatched to be parachuted into Nazi-occupied Europe. As part of his duty, he gave them cyanide pills in case of capture.

My grandfather died only a few years after he showed me his medals, at the age of eighty-four. A good ten years passed after that before I began looking into his work and realized how central World War II had been to both his career and the history of American espionage and covert operations. As part of my readings, I learned in William Colby's memoir about a cooperative venture my grandfather was involved in with British, American, and French secret services called Operation Jedburgh.

In 1943, the British realized that the Gestapo was catching British agents in France at such a rapid rate that by the time of Eisenhower's invasion there might be very few left to give their behind-the-lines assistance, just when the

Allies would need them the most. The Gestapo would round up every other remaining agent they knew of once the invasion started. The British conceived of the Jedburgh idea to train a three-hundred-strong group of British, Free French, and Americans and drop them in three-man teams into France, just as the invasion started. These "Jeds," as they came to be called, would take up the reins and lead the French Resistance's delaying actions against the Nazis as they converged on Normandy from all over France and Europe.

Operation Jedburgh, I discovered in my research, had such stature within the OSS that the Jedburgh name came to be used for just about any agent who "made bangs" behind the lines, even in the Far East. The Jeds represented by far the largest number of American agents in France. Operation Jedburgh became the prototype for large-scale covert action in enemy-occupied territory, not just for the OSS but for the CIA. The Jeds set an example in France for what the CIA would do much later in Afghanistan.

Operation Jedburgh is central to, if not the literal beginning of, the history of U.S. covert operations. It also, as it turns out, made the first proving ground for a group of men whose careers, in their own fields, were as conspicuous as that of William Colby, himself one of the Jeds. Aaron Bank became the father of the Green Berets. Jack Singlaub commanded the U.S. forces in Korea in the seventies and then went on to be a central figure in the Iran-Contra affair. Stewart Alsop, with his brother Joe, became one of the nation's most important columnists. Bernard Knox was arguably the most important classical scholar of his generation. Similar accomplishments are found among the British and French participants in Operation Jedburgh.

My first interest in the operation came after reading Colby's short chapter on his Jedburgh experience, especially because Colby referred to my grandfather, Gerry Miller, as "our London Jedburgh chief." But there was little to read. Perhaps a half-dozen Jeds had published any sort of memoir, and little else existed on the swashbuckling exploits of these men, or on how they were deployed to assist with the main military invasion and how their work dovetailed with that of the soldiers in Normandy. Fortunately, I discovered that an informal alumni organization of former Jedburghs existed, and I was able to find many of the French, British, and Americans who took part.

It took some doing to get them to talk to me. They had been told never to speak of their exploits. Some opened up when I showed them that the American records of the operation had been declassified in 1979 and that the British records were declassified in 2002. Over the course of time, I managed to find and speak to some thirty of the men who took part in the organization, in addition to a couple of senior officers who worked in the London OSS. With many of them, I had conversations that lasted as long as six days.

I have chosen, in writing the story of these former Jedburghs, to re-create their experiences in narrative rather than academic fashion. I have written much more about the excitement, the fear, and the moral dilemmas faced by these men than the headquarters documents that swirled around them, and as the source notes will attest, there are mountains of those documents. As fascinating as they may be, to both me and other historians, including lengthy quotations in the text would only serve to disturb the narrative for the general reader. Where I consider the exact wording of a documentary source important, for the sake of either credibility or interest, I have quoted it in the notes.

During the writing of this book, I wished over and over that I could also have talked to my grandfather about these events. Though my grandfather said almost nothing about his espionage work to me or the rest of my family, one thing I'd understood was that he thought that the men to whom he handed the suicide pills in World War II were some of the real heroes of the United States' clandestine work. Twenty years after I first asked my grandfather the questions about them, in the course of writing this book, I finally found out why.

—Colin Beavan
New York City

# PART I
# DANGEROUS BEGINNINGS

# CHAPTER ONE
# SHADOW WAR SETBACK

When Odette Sansom entered, Sergeant Hugo Bleicher, a counterintelligence officer of the Abwehr, stood up from his little wooden table, as if he were a gentleman, and offered her a cigarette. Odette took it, this time, and held it to the flame. She exhaled a cloud of smoke.

"I still have nothing to say," she said.

The sentry who had escorted her from her cell, one of the women whose gray uniforms closely matched the stone walls of the Maison de Correction de Fresnes, sidled out of the interrogation room. *Les souris,* the inmates called the female guards, the mice. *Les souris* had scampered into Fresnes, outside Paris, three years earlier, when the Nazis first unfurled the huge swastika between the legs of the Eiffel Tower, proclaiming, in brazen red and black, the German conquest of France.

Bleicher assembled his features into a contrived look of sadness.

"The Gestapo will send for you," he said in a gentle and quiet manner.

He affected a tone of kind warning, as though his mentioning the Gestapo was not really a threat. The Nazi war effort could go to hell, he had told Odette in previous interviews, but he wished she would give him just a little information with which to protect her. He pretended concern for the three potentially motherless daughters Odette had left in a Somerset convent, away from their London home and the German bombs that pounded around it.

Odette took another drag from her cigarette.

Outside the interrogation room, the wooden-soled shoes of Odette's fellow prisoners clopped the corridor floors; only the Germans could still get leather shoes in France. Guttural Aryan orders echoed from the courtyards. Odette held her cigarette between long, thin fingers. Bleicher watched her.

Since 1940, the organizations to which Bleicher and Odette owed their loyalties had been locked in a shadow war. Back in London, for the last three years, Odette's bosses had tried to parachute enough agents and weapons into France to organize and lead the Resistance in an uprising that would give crucial assistance to the eventual Allied invasion. Meanwhile, in France, both Bleicher's Abwehr, the intelligence branch of the German army, and its rival organization, the Nazi Party's Sicherheitsdienst (SD)—often referred to by the name of another organization, the Gestapo—urgently tried to round up the agents and Resistance fighters before they could organize their secret armies.

This was why Bleicher so cunningly tried to get Odette to talk. In this behind-the-lines shadow war, her capture by him had been a major setback for the Allies. If Bleicher could pry Odette's secrets from her, the Germans could arrest more agents and Resistance fighters, perhaps even capture their radios, and the damage would be much worse.

Odette's cigarette smoke rose through the air while she and Bleicher sat in silence.

A mop of curly brown hair framed Odette's round forehead and baby-fat cheeks. They made her look more like twenty-five than thirty. She had almond-shaped eyes. Odette had married a British hotelier and settled in England, but she was born in France. Her father had been killed by the Germans in World War I. She took her duties personally.

One last puff of her barely smoked cigarette and Odette stubbed it against her heel, careful to preserve what remained. Since her arrest, Odette had not accepted Bleicher's offers of either extra food or excursions outside the Fresnes gates. Satiation of her cravings, even for this cigarette's tobacco, would only clear the way for pangs that might more seriously undermine her resolve. Odette tucked away the cigarette stub.

"Why do you do that?" asked Bleicher.

"For a friend," Odette said. She did not bother to lie about her intended flouting of Fresnes's rules. Through an inmate who pushed the food cart, she would pass the cigarette to her unseen companion, a woman who conversed with Odette from the other end of her cell's heating duct.

Bleicher perceived the other, deeper signal of intention in the ember of tobacco Odette had so easily put out. He ended the interview and ushered her out of the room and along the labyrinthine corridors. He stopped at cell number 108. Odette had told him nothing.

"There is no point in my coming anymore," Bleicher said, as he closed her cell door. He meant, of course, that the Gestapo would come instead.

A couple of weeks earlier at Station 53, a top secret radio base hidden in Grendon Hall, a stately manor in the flat English farmlands near Grendon Underwood, a twenty-year-old member of the First Aid Nursing Yeomanry, a FANY, twisted the dials to tune in her radio to an agent secretly transmitting from the southeast of France. The FANY tapped a few times on her Morse key to confirm she was listening. Suddenly, the high-pitched chatter of dihs and dahs flooded her headphones and she began rapidly jotting down nonsensical groups of letters.

Five minutes later, the FANY radio operator ripped the page off her pad and handed it to a clerk. In a room nearby, another young FANY quickly decoded the urgent transmission. It was a message about the Allies' most important shadow war network in France. Quickly, a dispatch rider climbed onto his motorcycle, kick-started it to life, and roared off with the terrible news.

Lieutenant Colonel Maurice Buckmaster took the back door and rode the lift to the musty offices in the top floors at 64 Baker Street, London, above Marks & Spencer's corporate headquarters. Buckmaster's colleagues, some wearing uniforms, others avoiding them, bustled between walls covered with maps of France and the rest of Europe and the world. As for what this busy crowd did, hidden secretly in the forgotten corners of Marylebone, passersby might deduce from a sign on a building entrance that read "Inter-Services Research Bureau." But that, of course, was just a cover.

Buckmaster tucked himself behind his desk. Things had been particularly tense of late. The British chiefs of staff had recently ordered "The Firm," as Buckmaster and his colleagues called it, to prepare for the Allies' most ambitious operation of the war—the much-awaited cross-Channel invasion of the Continent.

Already, the Special Operations Executive (SOE)—The Firm's official, unmentionable name—had scored many successes: the 1942 assassination of Gestapo chief Himmler's deputy in Czechoslovakia by grenade; the 1942 destruction of a Greek rail bridge that carried supplies vital to General Rommel's

German desert army; and the 1943 destruction of the Nazis' heavy-water plant in Norway, effectively ending their atomic bomb program. In fact, the SOE, established by Prime Minister Winston Churchill himself to organize and arm secret, underground armies throughout the enemy-occupied territories, employed nearly thirteen thousand people. It had agent-agitators working around the world, from Norway to Burma.

But now, the stakes were raised. A massive Allied operation was planned to invade the Continent, and the chiefs of staff would soon want to know specifically what help to expect from the SOE's secret armies in France. The SOE had begun organizing, dropping arms to, planning for, and communicating with the Resistance there in 1940. Since France would be the battleground of this final showdown with Hitler, sections of the SOE that sent agents to France were now the most important. Their job was to prepare for a massive Resistance uprising that would hopefully hobble Hitler's ability to defend the French beaches.

As the Allied strategists finally turned their attentions away from North Africa and Italy and toward France, Buckmaster and his colleagues traded an anxious flurry of top secret memos and huddled together in urgently called meetings to make their behind-the-lines plans for the invasion. Today, April 17, 1943, the day the urgent message from France was dispatched from Station 53, must have been no less tense as Buckmaster began leafing through his phone messages and unread memos.

He had been thirty-seven when war broke out. Before that, the tall, thin Oxford graduate had worked in peacetime France for over a decade, first as a journalist and then as the Paris manager of the Ford Motor Company office. He was a natural fit for the SOE. In the autumn of 1940, he heard Winston Churchill's voice crackle from a radio in French: "Those Frenchmen who are in the French Empire may see their way from time to time to useful action. I will not go into details. Hostile ears are listening. . . . *Vive la France.*" Ever since hearing that broadcast, Buckmaster searched for a job that would put him to work assisting the French in their "useful action."

Recently, a group of pesky American spies-in-training from the United States' fledgling espionage outfit, the Office of Strategic Services (OSS), had begun arriving at the SOE's offices. They planned to apprentice themselves in the dark arts of clandestine warfare, but none of the naive Americans had even an iota of regular warfare experience. In contrast, Buckmaster, like most of his senior SOE colleagues, already had substantial experience in battle with the regular army. He had fought with the British Expeditionary Force in France, staggered home defeated with them from the northern French port of Dunkirk, and participated in the ill-fated Allied attempt to grab the strategic Atlantic port at Dakar, Senegal, in September 1940.

It was not too long after Dakar that Buckmaster at last found his place among this group of London-based Francophile Brits. These were the types of traveled gentlemen who never needed a map to ride the Métro and who smoked Gauloises by preference. Together, here at Baker Street, they comprised the French, or "F," Section of the SOE. By September 1941, a year after Buckmaster heard Churchill's broadcast, he found himself at F Section's helm as chief. It was toward him that the dispatch rider from Station 53 at Grendon Hall now urgently raced.

"Buck," as some of his agents called him, made a habit of seeing his operatives off at the airfield, or at least visiting with them one last time in his office, when they left for France. It won't be held against you if you change your mind, he sincerely told them. To Odette, he had shyly proffered a gift, an elegant silver compact. "You can always hock it if you run out of money," he said to avoid embarrassment when he gave his agents such gifts. He felt a personal attachment and responsibility for those he sent into harm's way, which is why the radio message, now brought in by the dispatch rider, must have hurt him personally as well as militarily.

Odette Sansom had been arrested, the message said. So had Peter Churchill, the more senior agent, of no relation to the prime minister, for whom Odette worked. The message had been sent by Adolphe Rabinovitch, code-named Arnaud, an F Section radio operator who worked with Sansom and Churchill in the Savoy mountains in the southeast of France. Officials as high-ranking as the British chiefs of staff had placed extraordinary hope in the Resistance network, code-named Carte, with which Churchill, Sansom, and Rabinovitch worked.

Carte, the SOE had believed, would inspire hundreds of thousands of Resistance fighters to rise up and attack the Nazis from behind as the Allies began their invasion. The lives of thousands of Allied soldiers might be saved by the effort. Indeed, if the invasion did not go well, such a Resistance effort might make the difference between victory and defeat. Carte, therefore, had been F Section's major focus for over a year. Now, of its three agents working with Carte, only Rabinovitch remained. He had barely escaped capture himself.

The radio report made Buckmaster's heart sink. It was likely that he had lost two friends. More important for the British war effort, their arrests confirmed the collapse of Carte. With little more than a year until D-Day, this threw into disarray the SOE's crucial plans for a mass uprising of its secret armies in France on the day that the Allied invasion of the Continent finally began.

A police van, the sort that the French called a *panier à salade* (salad basket) because of the wire cages inside, carried Odette toward central Paris and the headquarters of the Gestapo, at the notorious 84 avenue Foche, where handpicked inquisitors specialized in extracting answers.

Odette forced her reluctant legs up the stairs. She eventually found herself in a room with an interrogator and a clerk behind a typewriter, but not before the arrival of an unexpected meat and gravy feast, her first opportunity for a decent meal in weeks. She understood the Gestapo interrogation technique, and knew better than to eat more than a few bites. Too large a meal can disorient a starving person. Instead, hoping she might live to return to her prison cell, Odette hid a potato in her clothes to pass to her friend at the end of the heating duct.

The typewriter clerk wore the uniform of an enlisted man. The interrogator dressed in a suit. He looked healthy and fresh, as though he had just put on his clothes after a cool bath. He smelled, not unpleasantly, of cologne.

The interrogator asked Odette her full name. She spelled it. He asked her rank. The typewriter clacked out her answer. Branch of service? More smacks of metal keys on paper. Dull, routine questions, an interrogator hoped, would lull a subject into inattention. It did not. When the young inquisitor asked Odette for her home address in England, the sounds of the typewriter stopped.

The Geneva convention required POWs to answer only certain questions, and nothing more. Prisoners interrogated by the Gestapo soon faced the dilemma of whether to adhere to propriety, and hasten the coming of the torturer for the sake of something as trivial as their street number.

I am not required to answer that question, Odette said.

All the same, you will answer it.

I will not.

Where is Arnaud?

I have nothing to say.

They went around in circles, but even after hours, the meaningless repetition did not tire Odette into making a mistake.

Who is Arnaud? She told them nothing of Rabinovitch, her team's two-way radio operator, or his ability to relay Allied orders and call for supplies and personnel. Where is he? The address of the safe house she had sent him to did not pass her lips. Who is Roger? They would never hear from her that this newly arrived agent, whose real name was Francis Cammaerts, would be working, already, to reorganize her broken network of southeastern Resistance, preparing for the new agents to come and again distributing arms dropped from black-painted airplanes in the middle of the night.

Each defiant refusal to answer their questions ratcheted Odette, with cold mechanics, one notch closer to torture and perhaps death. On this occasion, however, she was returned to her cell at Fresnes. That night, through the heating duct, a thank-you came for the potato. "Can you bring me another one if you go tomorrow?" Odette's jailmate pleaded. "I am so hungry."

Some of Carte's Resistance workers would talk; others would become double agents. SOE networks around France and even the survival of agents yet to parachute into the country were in terrible danger. The good news was that Odette had given the man with the cologne less than a page of notes, typed by the clerk, to put in his file.

She had told him nothing about Britain's scheme to arm and organize the Resistance of Europe into hidden armies, nothing about the resulting mob of angry Frenchmen who would rise up to assist the Allied landings on D-Day, nothing about how London communicated its orders to them by two-way radio, and, most especially, nothing about how to capture the coming wave of replacement agents and radio operators. But the Germans had not yet begun to use their most efficient methods of extracting Odette's secrets. When she returned to avenue Foche the next day, they would not be giving her any more potatoes.

## CHAPTER TWO
# RESISTANCE? WHAT RESISTANCE?

It was out of sheer desperation that three years earlier, in May 1940, Prime Minister Winston Churchill and his war cabinet first hatched the scheme to arm and organize into secret armies the Resistance of Nazi-occupied Europe.

Hitler had launched his blitzkrieg into France, his tanks rumbled virtually unopposed through the countryside, and the defeated British Expeditionary Force scurried to the northern French port of Dunkirk. Nearly 340,000 exhausted men slowly drifted across the Channel in a hastily assembled armada of fishing dinghies, lifeboats, and sailboats. The British navy still had too few warships to save the men by itself.

Masses of French civilian refugees, meanwhile, fleeing from the approaching Germans, clogged northeastern France's roads with wooden wagons and baby carriages filled with everything they owned. Retreating French soldiers had no choice but to abandon their vehicles in the traffic jam and join the walking crowds. The once proud army of France disintegrated into a disorganized rabble of retreating foot soldiers, showered by machine-gun bullets fired by the merciless Messerschmitt pilots above.

Hitler had marched easily into France. The Allies suffered crushing defeat. In London, the British government secretly panicked.

The Americans had not yet entered the war, and Churchill and his war cabinet, in highly confidential meetings, debated whether their armed services had the strength to continue the fight without the French. Not only caught short with an undernourished navy, Britain, if attacked, had barely the troops, tanks, and airplanes to stop Hitler's armies from marching over the beaches.

Should we admit defeat and sue for peace? Churchill's war cabinet wondered. The British chiefs of staff told them there might be one slim chance of eventual victory—if the German war machine could somehow be starved and weakened.

A naval blockade, said the chiefs, would deprive Hitler of supplies. Strategic bombardment would wreak havoc on his country's economy and sap its will to fight. And the "creation of widespread revolt in the occupied territories" would keep the German army overextended. In time, these three methods, the chiefs of staff told Churchill, might weaken the Nazi goliath to the point where an Allied attack could be successful. Since Britain had yet neither sufficient ships to blockade nor planes to bombard, the chiefs particularly urged Churchill to devote what resources could be spared to the third method and to establish a secret organization to "stimulate the seeds of revolt."

The idea itself was nothing new. Agents provocateurs and secret armies had operated behind enemy lines in every major war before and after the wooden horse rolled into Troy. By 1940, however, the development of long-range bombers and efficient parachutes meant that agent-organizers could be infiltrated behind the lines in the hundreds and weapons supplied to their Resistance organizations by the ton. Also, communication by two-way radio would allow the high command to order sabotage operations and attacks in line with grand strategy.

If all went well, the mobilization of Resistance armies might even mean that a reduced conventional force would be needed to launch the eventual Continental attack. The loss of British soldiers in the Second World War, the war cabinet and chiefs of staff hoped, might not be as devastating as in the First. In July 1940, therefore, two months after the Nazi invasion of France, Churchill established the brand-new Special Operations Executive to pursue Britain's program of sabotage, subversion, and secret armies.

Churchill gave charge of the new SOE to his minister of economic warfare, Hugh Dalton, launching, for spy chiefs like Maurice Buckmaster and agents like Odette Sansom, a long and dangerous secret, behind-the-lines battle. "And now," Churchill said to Dalton, "set Europe ablaze," as though, with such little provocation, the people of the occupied territories would enthusiastically rise up in rebellion. Churchill had not counted on how completely defeat can destroy the will to revolt.

"I make a gift of myself to France to lessen her misfortune," said France's eighty-four-year-old World War I hero Marshal Henri-Philippe Pétain on the radio in French. While Churchill and his cabinet had worked on strategy, Pétain had, on June 16, 1940, taken over the government of France. German soldiers crawled across the country, chasing whatever remained of the French army.

*"Il faut cesser le combat,"* Pétain declared on June 17: The fighting must stop. Neither Pétain nor most of his countrymen had in mind to join Churchill's rebellion. All over the country, without ceremony, French soldiers disrespected their uniforms by stripping them off, putting down their weapons, and drifting back to their girlfriends, wives, or parents.

As the logic went, France had been roundly defeated. For all Churchill's posturing, Britain would soon be, too. European domination by the Reich seemed an imminent fact of life, and the main point was to try to win some concessions. Pétain opened negotiations with Hitler.

The most important thing for France was not to rebel but to avoid the terrible military dictatorship imposed on Poland and to try to retain as much sovereignty for itself as possible. This was Pétain's reasoning when he agreed to an armistice that required France to demobilize all but one hundred thousand of its army's men, pay nearly 60 percent of its national income to the Reich, leave French prisoners of war in German hands, and allow German forces to occupy the country's northern two-thirds along with the Atlantic coast. At least France would be left with her honor, most French citizens felt. But there were a precious few who would never be willing to surrender.

Among them was General Charles de Gaulle, who had escaped to London during the German onslaught. Enraged by Pétain's capitulation, de Gaulle, though he had never been more than a junior minister in the French government, intended to command a continued battle for France. He proclaimed himself leader of the "Free French." On June 18, the day after Pétain's broadcast, de Gaulle, over the airwaves of the BBC, asked, "Has the last word been said? Must we abandon all hope? Is our defeat final and irremediable? To those questions I answer—No!"

He invited French soldiers around the world, particularly those in Britain and in the as yet unoccupied French colonies, to join him. He set to work forming a Free French army to fight side by side with the British against Germany and Italy. Caught up for the first few months with organizing his army and the affairs of the French empire, de Gaulle was initially uninterested in

Churchill's plans for the Resistance and a continued struggle within France itself. In fact, de Gaulle forbade Free French sabotage within France for fear that German reprisal against civilians would impact his movement. Instead, the SOE's new "independent French," or F, Section, established in the summer of 1940 and eventually headed by Maurice Buckmaster, began organizing the shadow war in France, much to de Gaulle's disgust.

When the general finally did concede the importance of guerrilla warfare in France, he gave responsibility for it to his own espionage service, eventually called the Bureau Central de Renseignements et d'Action (the BCRA; in English, the Central Office of Information and Action). De Gaulle denied that the SOE's F Section had any right to organize shadow operations in France independently of him. As a concession, in May 1941, the SOE established another department to work in France: RF Section. Through RF, the SOE provided the BCRA with the planes, parachutes, radio communications, and weapons to insert its own agents into France and arm their secret networks.

Buckmaster and Sansom's F Section, however, continued to work in secret from de Gaulle's men. The British did not want their guerrilla warfare hands tied to the interests of a movement that did not necessarily represent all of France. Nor did they believe that the interests of the British and French empires were entirely parallel, common enemies notwithstanding. Furthermore, the British military did not trust that de Gaulle's organization could safely keep its secrets. Besides, duplication of effort would ultimately double the chances of the shadow war's success.

According to the SOE's plan, F Section and RF/BCRA agents each toiled independently toward the same two goals in France. Through sabotage and other carefully pinpointed direct action, they would hinder the German war effort by, for example, stopping production at armament factories. Simultaneously, by recruiting, organizing, training, and arming hundreds of Resistance *réseaux*, or networks, throughout France, they built a clandestine army that would keep itself secret until the coming invasion.

When the Allies finally landed their troops on the French beaches, the secret army would rise up all over France and, like a swarm of bees that incapacitates its enemy with thousands of otherwise negligible stings, the Resistance fighters would block the roads, cut the rails, disrupt German communications, and generally sidetrack the German forces. This would give the men in the Allied landing crafts a chance to crawl up the beaches, reorganize themselves, and launch their attack. That was the theory, anyway. But the SOE's early operations in France did not go off the way its masters had hoped.

In March 1941, the SOE planned its first French sabotage operation: to blow up a bus full of German "pathfinder" pilots who led Luftwaffe bombers to their targets in Britain. The mission, Operation Savanna, fell apart when its five saboteurs arrived in France and discovered that the pilots no longer took the bus. The second mission to France, Josephine B, a sabotage operation that targeted a power station, failed on the first attempt when the plane erroneously dropped the team's equipment, made a U-turn back to England, and crashed, killing or injuring everyone aboard.

Earlier, on November 14, 1940, the first SOE agent destined to begin shadow army organization in France flew all the way across the Channel in his plane and then refused to jump. Next, the very first F Section organizer to reach French soil promptly disappeared without a trace in March 1941. And in May 1941, after the first group of twenty agents finally completed F Section's new, months-long training program, a German air raid killed three of them and injured two. Their feet had never even touched French soil.

Ultimately, in the summer of 1941, twenty or so F Section agent-organizers did actually make it to France, and F Section finally got its foothold, if only a tenuous one. Recruitment of Resistance networks, the agents discovered, was a potentially lethal crapshoot. For every Frenchman bent on resisting the occupation, another fervently collaborated with it. Win a recruit or get betrayed and arrested? The only consolation was that the overwhelming majority of French would sit on the fence, refusing to do an agent a favor but also not doing him harm. The common person in France, neither *résistant* nor collaborator, had adopted the attitude of *attentisme,* or wait and see, toward the occupation.

After all, life in the occupation's first months had not been so unbearable. Adults still went to work. Children attended school. The southeast of France remained completely free of German forces, and the German soldiers who occupied the north and west weren't too bad. *"Ils sont corrects,"* the French said— they behave correctly. Hitler had even left the French World War I hero Marshal Pétain in charge of France's new "government," the État Français, based at Vichy. Things could have been much worse.

German propagandists continually reminded the French that the British had killed nearly thirteen hundred French sailors when they sank the French naval fleet anchored like sitting ducks at Algeria's Mers el-Kébir on July 3, 1940. Never mind that the British acted because they feared that the fleet would fall into German hands and the French had refused to mothball it. The French also remembered bitterly that the British had run home from Dunkirk instead of fighting for France. Who was worse then, the British or the Germans? Certainly, most Frenchmen did not want agents from Britain antagonizing the German occupiers.

Thanks to this French ambivalence, the mistakes of the fledging SOE, and the efficiency of the German counterintelligence services, almost all of F Section's agents in France had been arrested or gone into hiding by the time Maurice Buckmaster took charge in September 1941. More than a year after Churchill had launched the SOE, the shadow war in France had hardly begun.

# CHAPTER THREE
# A SPARK OF REBELLION

At a bridge straddling the frontier between German territory and Russia, the time had come for the morning changing of the guard. From the two sides of the bridge, the newly rested German and Russian soldiers, just coming on duty, approached the middle to greet each other and salute, just as they had at the change of every watch for months. Stalin and Hitler had signed a nonaggression pact, so if the two countries' guards were not friends, at least they were not enemies. As usual, they met in the middle of the bridge, the heels clicked, the Heil Hitlers came, and the Russians greeted their opposite numbers. But this time, instead of returning the friendly gestures, the German guards whipped out their guns and shot the Russians dead.

On June 22, 1941, Hitler began Operation Barbarossa, and that vicious act on the bridge was just a small part of what became one of the most terrible slaughters in the history of warfare. More than three million German troops charged into Russia, ending the Nazi-Soviet nonaggression pact. In the coming series of bloody *Vernichtungsschlachten,* annihilation battles, more men would die on the eastern front of World War II than on all the other fronts combined.

The good news for the Allies, in spite of the terrible suffering, was that Hitler had brought a country of 190 million people into battle against him, forever altering the balance of the war.

At eight in the morning on August 21, 1941, nearly two months to the day after Hitler launched Operation Barbarossa, a young Communist Frenchman quietly climbed aboard a crowded subway carriage at the Barbès-Rochechouart

Métro station in Paris. He drew his revolver, fired three shots, and disappeared into the rush-hour crowd. He left behind a dead German navy officer lying in a pool of blood, his feet sticking out through the subway doors.

Until Hitler's attack on Russia, France's large Communist Party had welcomed the German occupation forces as allies of the Soviet Union. But on the day the murderous Nazi hordes began pouring across Soviet borders, Stalin ordered the French Communist paramilitary organization, the Francs-Tireurs et Partisans (FTP), the French Irregulars and Partisans, to begin attacking Germans. "There must be bands of partisans and saboteurs working underground everywhere," Stalin said within hours of Hitler's abrogation of their treaty.

Within two weeks of the Barbès-Rochechouart Métro killing, another French Communist shot and wounded a German soldier near the Gare de l'Est in Paris. Two weeks later, a German captain fell to the pavement on the city's boulevard de Strasbourg. A month after that, on October 20, a group of young Communists ambushed and killed the local *Feldkommandant* outside the cathedral at Nantes. In Paris, a grenade attack killed two German soldiers at the end of November. The spirit of rebellion was growing, and the Nazis in France reacted harshly.

After the Barbès-Rochechouart killing, the Germans shot three French political prisoners chosen at random from one of the jails. After each of a number of other partisan attacks in the following weeks, the Germans executed more French political prisoners, completely unconnected with the crimes committed, ten at a time. On October 22, the Germans lined up forty-seven more innocents and shot them in revenge for the death of the *Feldkommandant* in Nantes. The next day they shot another fifty in reprisal for the shooting of a Bordeaux military adviser.

The Germans made not even a pretense of connecting the men falling before the firing squads with the "terrorist" acts of the partisans. The numbers executed were in complete disproportion to the Germans killed. Citizens around France were utterly disgusted. "Correct" behavior by the German occupiers had come to a brutal end.

What the Nazis had not counted on was that, rather than suppressing the uprising, their atrocities forced much of the French population off its *attentiste* fence. France had waited, and now it had seen. In the cities, towns, and villages, angry men began to murmur and meet in small groups. By the end of 1941, the French had carried out nearly seventy attacks on German personnel and their installations.

Confirmation of the burgeoning Resistance movement arrived at the shadow chiefs' headquarters on October 20, 1941, when an emissary from France presented himself in London and said that he represented three large Resistance organizations. Jean Moulin, the former *préfet* of the Eure-et-Loire *département* who had refused to cooperate with the Nazis even after torture, had escaped from France over the Pyrenees Mountains and through Spain. Moulin brought the happy news that "tens and even hundreds of thousands" of Frenchmen wanted de Gaulle to lead a united Resistance fight inside France.

This also meant, as far as the spymasters at the SOE were concerned, that there were likely tens or hundreds of thousands of potential French Resistance recruits wanting to fight but not with de Gaulle as their leader. The more muscle the better for the eventual uprising in France. Specifically, the SOE bosses coveted the enlistment in the shadow war of the officers of Vichy France's hundred-thousand-strong Armistice Army, whose disgust with de Gaulle was mutual. The SOE chiefs hoped that F Section agents, in secret from the Free French, might somehow convince the Armistice Army to rise up against the Germans at the beginning of an Allied invasion.

In January 1942, Jean Moulin parachuted back to France as de Gaulle's ambassador to and organizer of the Resistance, and the SOE's RF Section redoubled its work parachuting supplies to those prepared to rise under de Gaulle's flag. Meanwhile, Maurice Buckmaster, behind the backs of de Gaulle and the Free French, enthusiastically renewed F Section's own campaign.

Between September 1941 and the beginning of 1942, he sent twenty-seven new agents to France to organize their networks. The SOE increased the rate of arms and supplies parachuted to the Resistance by over fifteen times, from only 1.5 tons in 1941 to 23 tons in 1942. And late in 1941, two Buckmaster agents reported the excellent news that they had at last opened communications with the Armistice Army. The contact came through a French artist and anti-Gaullist Resistance organizer named André Girard, code-named Carte. The chance to enlist the Armistice Army in the shadow war was potentially F Section's biggest break yet.

Over the coming months, Buckmaster sent several agents to investigate Girard, and exfiltrated one of Girard's lieutenants for questioning. During the process, Girard and his colleagues convinced the SOE spymasters that Girard had both established wide contact with the officer corps of the Armistice Army and assembled a huge network that could muster three hundred thousand men in southeastern France. Given arms and supplies, Girard promised that the Carte network would rise up, join with the Armistice Army, and help liberate France.

The Carte network seemed to be just what Winston Churchill had in mind when he decided to "set Europe ablaze." Its contact with the professional officers of the Armistice Army—as opposed to the simple bakers and farmers of the regular Resistance—evinced particular enthusiasm for the shadow war among conventional military men of the British chiefs of staff. On their insistence, F Section made Carte's already existing secret army its first priority, though it also continued to drop and supply agent-organizers to other parts of France.

In July 1942, Odette Sansom joined F Section as a trainee agent. The housewife and mother of three learned to kill a man with her hands, guide a plane onto a secret landing field, tap Morse code, fight at close range with a machine gun, handle a canoe (for getting to the shore of France from a ship), and trap, kill, and cook a rabbit without removing its skin. In August 1942, Buckmaster sent senior agent Peter Churchill to France as chief liaison between Carte and Baker Street. In October, Odette Sansom, her training complete, climbed out of an SOE launch onto the Côte d'Azur and into France, where she would help Peter Churchill organize Carte's secret army.

But in November 1942, only a month after Odette's arrival, the Allies invaded French North Africa. The Germans used the weak resistance to the invasion by the French troops there as a pretext for breaking its armistice agreement with the Vichy government and occupied the southern zone of France. The Armistice Army, on which the SOE had placed so much hope, did not so much as protest. Hitler dissolved the force and, for all Girard's assurances of its officers' preparedness to fight for the Allies, they locked their weapons in the armories and went quietly back to their homes. Carte's promise had been largely an illusion.

Peter Churchill, Odette, and Adolphe Rabinovich, their radio operator, moved to a hideout in Saint-Jorioz, near Annecy, in the French Alps. Francis Cammaerts, another Buckmaster agent, code-named Roger, parachuted in to help Churchill pick up the pieces of his network in southeastern France.

Despite the crisis, things soon seemed to have settled down, the damage to the Carte network was not as bad as it had seemed, and the British agents got back to organizing their corner of the secret army. At that stage, back at Baker

Street in January 1943, Buckmaster might easily have lulled himself into believing that his worst problem was the inquisitive American OSS men who had begun arriving with the hopes of looking over his shoulder. But it was not.

Back in November, a senior member of the Carte network stupidly lost a briefcase containing a list of Carte's most senior 250 members, complete with addresses and personal details. Since the Germans bided their time, no one realized that it was an agent of the Abwehr who had so easily stolen it.

Four months later, at the end of March 1943, the Germans struck. In southeastern France, where Odette Sansom and Peter Churchill operated, Abwehr squads quietly rounded up and ticked off Resistance members as casually as items on a grocery list. On April 15, 1943, in the middle of the night, while Odette slept in her hotel in Saint-Jorioz, a knock on her door woke her up. When Odette went downstairs and discovered Hugo Bleicher, Luger in hand, supported by a detachment of troops, the last of the Carte network had met its tragic end.

The SOE had lost for good its then greatest hope for the invasion uprising in France. If German counterintelligence continued its successes, the rest of F Section and Free French leadership of the Resistance throughout France would also soon be decimated. Without the leadership of the agent-organizers and the radio operators to call for weapons and receive Allied orders, the mass of Resistance foot soldiers would have no one to coordinate the Allied plan to block roads and derail troop trains when the invasion began. Without these impediments, battle-hardened German soldiers and tanks could rush with crushing speed to any point on France's shoreline.

With just over a year until the cross-Channel invasion, when the Resistance had finally come to life, the Allies were in grave danger of losing the shadow war in France.

When Odette arrived for the second time at the interrogation room at avenue Foche, the Gestapo inquisitor coldly pointed to a chair across the wooden table from him, and Odette sat down. I have nothing to say. I have nothing to say. No introductory meal preceded events today.

"You wasted a great deal of my time yesterday," the inquisitor said. "You will not be permitted to do so again." He glanced at the meager notes spread before him on the table from the previous day's interview. "Where is your wireless operator, Arnaud?" The inquisitor gazed at Odette impatiently.

"I have nothing to say."

"We will see," he said. "It is known that you sent the British officer Roger away to an address in the south of France. What is the address?"

"I have nothing to say."

In her alert state, Odette could virtually smell the inquisitor's waft of irritation.

"Here are the questions again. Where is Arnaud, and where is Roger?" he said with finality. Odette said nothing.

The interrogation room door opened quietly and admitted a Mediterranean-looking man. He carried an iron rod whose tip glowed red-hot. The inquisitor held up his wrist, as though to time a race, and looked at his watch. "I propose to give you one minute to provide the answers," he said, leaving Odette to imagine what would happen with the iron rod after his watch ticked for the sixtieth time. She had nothing to say. She had nothing to say.

The inquisitor looked up from his watch. The minute was over. "I would now like an answer to my questions," he said.

Even at this terrible juncture, the sentence Odette kept echoing inside her head came out of her mouth: "I have nothing to say."

The Mediterranean man rested the red-hot poker on the third vertebra of Odette's back. The sound of sizzling flesh accompanied the pain. Swimming between consciousness and blackout, Odette barely heard a voice.

"Where is Arnaud?" the inquisitor demanded.

He most wanted the radio operator's address, since his capture would mean severing a Resistance group's umbilical cord to London. The Germans also sometimes used captured radios to trick London into parachuting agents straight into their waiting arms. The Germans knew that the Allied spymasters would attempt to shore up the Resistance leadership for the day of the invasion. The Gestapo planned to lie in wait and to eliminate the new operatives as soon as they emerged from the sky. To prepare, the Germans needed to know the locations of dropping grounds and the keys to the radio codes, none of which, Odette resolved, they would get because of her.

"I have nothing to say," she answered again.

The Mediterranean man put down his poker and moved, with a pair of iron pincers, to Odette's feet. He looked up at her with brown eyes that might as well have been blind for the indifference they displayed. He took Odette's left foot in his hand and grasped tight the jaws of his pincers around the nail of her small toe.

"You can bring this ceremony to an end at any time by answering my questions," the inquisitor said.

The Mediterranean man began to slowly pull. A semicircle of blood oozed out of the skin at the base of the nail, and then flooded over it. The man removed the pincers and shook them. The nail fell to the floor.

"Now would you care to tell me Arnaud's address?" Odette could only shake her head. The inquisitor sat on the table swinging his legs like a child. He nodded to the man with the pincers.

Back in London, even before Odette's capture, Buckmaster and his SOE colleagues had begun to worry that the Germans would round up all the Brits' agents before D-Day. What the SOE needed was a gigantic reserve of agents who could jump in and take the captured agents' places to lead the already armed Resistance at the last moment. The SOE planners imagined a scheme where this group of reserves could drop just where they were needed, rush around France, bring German movement to a standstill, and protect the Allied invasion at its most delicate stage.

The scheme was a pipe dream. Already, the main British military had problems finding its supplies, planes, weapons, and people. Where was the SOE and its surreptitious sideshow supposed to get resources for its grand plan? The answer, the SOE chiefs admitted reluctantly, was the pesky Americans. For most of the war, as the Americans had grabbed more and more control of the main military operations, the British had tried to at least maintain control of the shadow war. But they were out of resources.

Back at avenue Foche, from somewhere, Odette heard the inquisitor asking more questions. In a few days, when this was all over, she would stand to attention and laugh as a mock tribunal sentenced her to death. Now, barely conscious and not sure even what they wanted to know, she just shook her head. Another wave of pain rolled in—she realized they were pulling out another nail, and then another. Suddenly the Mediterranean man, for reasons Odette could not quite grasp, stood up. Vaguely, she heard a voice saying something about next time and fingers. All ten of her toenails were gone.

# CHAPTER FOUR
# UNCLE SAM JOINS IN

Back in July 1940, as Hitler's troops swarmed over France and Churchill made plans to "set Europe ablaze," groups of American officials descended on London with the object of snooping around. The Battle of Britain was about to fill the sky with dogfight vapor trails, and on the Continent Hitler amassed troops for Operation Sea Lion, the surge across the Channel to conquer Britain.

Saving the country, Churchill thought, required getting the United States into the war, or at least securing its aid. His government welcomed the teams of nosy officials from across the Atlantic for one purpose: to convince Franklin Roosevelt and his administration that Britain would survive the Nazi onslaught. Providing the United Kingdom with destroyers, aircraft, armaments, munitions, and food would not be a matter of backing a dying horse.

Among the show-and-tell participants was a fifty-seven-year-old Irish American Wall Street lawyer named William "Wild Bill" Donovan. Donovan won the Congressional Medal of Honor for his heroism in World War I. He served as an assistant attorney general in the Coolidge administration, and ran as the Republican nominee for governor of New York in 1933. Some said that if he had not been Catholic, the energetic blue-eyed man would have been president of the United States. On July 14, 1940, he climbed aboard a Pan Am Clipper flying boat and, four days later, showed up in London as an unofficial personal representative of President Roosevelt.

To prove to Donovan their preparedness for war, the Brits showed him their top secret invention of radar, their new high-performance Spitfire aircraft, and a slew of other classified defense capabilities no other American had yet seen. The Brits whisked him to base after base and bragged about how their best-equipped and best-armed troops prepared for a potential airborne operation. During an audience at Buckingham Palace, King George VI himself assured Donovan with regal gravity that there was no possibility of British capitulation.

Prime Minister Winston Churchill lunched with Donovan during one of Donovan's later fact-finding trips in December 1940. For four hours at 10 Downing Street, Churchill expounded to Donovan on his grand strategy: the famous circumference-against-the-center plan. Churchill believed that Britain would founder if it got stuck in a battle of attrition as in World War I. To avoid the horrendous casualties, Churchill proposed draining Hitler's strength by first attacking at his periphery. For this reason, in Allied negotiations, he would push eventually for preliminary invasions of North Africa and Italy, instead of charging directly across the Channel.

Churchill also emphasized the importance of shadow warfare in the fight against the Germans. After Donovan met the heads of the Secret Intelligence Service (SIS) and the SOE and toured their clandestine training installations, his conversion to the secret army concept was complete. He enthusiastically endorsed the use of agents provocateurs to foment Resistance rebellion as a precursor to general attack by the armies and returned to the United States convinced that his country desperately needed a centralized intelligence and subversive warfare outfit of its own.

At that time, the United States had eight separate espionage outfits belonging to the navy, the army air forces, the army, the FBI, the State Department, the Departments of Commerce and Agriculture, and the Board of Economic Warfare. As a result, the U.S. undercover warfare apparatus was dispersed, ineffective, and highly insecure. Donovan wrote, with the assistance of a couple of senior British spies, a plan for the creation of a centralized "Service of Strategic Information." He submitted his plan to President Roosevelt on June 11, 1941.

After the new German battleship *Bismarck* entered the North Atlantic and started chasing the Anglo-American lend-lease convoys on the high seas, Roosevelt declared a state of "unlimited national emergency" on May 27, 1941. To deal with the dangers facing the United States, the president then railroaded through a number of emergency measures, including, on July 11, the establishment of a new government department based on Donovan's plan. The office was called the Coordinator of Information (COI). Roosevelt made Donovan its head.

The Japanese attack on Pearl Harbor came on December 7, 1941, and Germany and Italy joined their Axis ally by declaring war on the United States on December 11. On December 24, the Anglo-American Arcadia Conference convened in Washington to discuss joint strategy. Churchill promoted the secret army idea, and the Allies agreed to jointly maintain "the spirit of revolt in the occupied territories, and the organization of subversive movements." The job of translating the shadow warfare strategy to action remained with the SOE, on the Brits' side, and Wild Bill Donovan's Special Operations branch of the COI, on the Americans'.

In June 1942, Roosevelt moved Donovan's new espionage outfit under the Joint Chiefs of Staff, giving it the respectability and resources of a military establishment. He also changed its name to the Office of Strategic Services (OSS). Donovan now rapidly expanded his intelligence-gathering and subversive warfare operations around the world. The OSS soon employed thirteen thousand people.

To teach its burgeoning staff the espionage game, Donovan relied heavily on the good graces of both the SIS and the SOE. The British spymasters showed the Americans how they trained their agents, what weapons they used, and how their systems of communicating with Resistance fighters and agents worked. In return, Donovan procured for Allied shadow operations American resources and personnel, and promised to keep his organization the junior partner in the undercover racket. In fact, Donovan initially agreed to keep his fledgling organization out of European espionage altogether, signing in June 1942 a pact with Charles Hambro, the SOE's overall chief. The Donovan-Hambro Accord roughly gave charge of Far East espionage skulduggery to the Americans, while leaving Europe mostly in the hands of the SOE.

The British insisted on the accord, for one thing, because SOE chiefs like Maurice Buckmaster did not want inexperienced American amateurs endangering SOE operations and agents. For another, the Brits did not want to train American agents only to find them pushing American policy in Britain's backyard. The British, for example, supported Charles de Gaulle as the leader of the Free French; Roosevelt detested de Gaulle and initially supported his rival, General Henri Giraud. Britain hoped to preserve its colonies through the war; Roosevelt would happily see them independent and open to American business interests.

But perhaps most important, Charles Hambro wanted Donovan out of Europe because the U.S. military disliked Churchill's circumference-against-the-center strategy. The United States pushed for an earlier charge across the Channel. Churchill would not have appreciated having his careful negotiations with the Americans undermined by OSS Special Operations agents running around France making de facto arrangements for an ahead-of-schedule invasion.

By the end of 1942, however, Churchill had prevailed in the strategy debate. The Allies invaded North Africa and plans for the Italian invasion were set. The long-awaited cross-Channel invasion finally loomed on the horizon. Donovan now wanted his own agents in France, organizing their own Resistance networks, to eventually support the American armies. Hambro finally relented.

Donovan's Special Operations people could begin limited operations from London, he agreed, and the SOE would help train them, but only with the proviso that all OSS operations would be under the supervision of the SOE. The OSS could provide American agents, but the SOE would have final say over their work in Europe. OSS staff would also be attached for the purposes of oversight and training to the various sections of the SOE. And so, in January 1943, just as Odette Sansom's Carte network fell apart, a number of fresh-faced Americans arrived at Baker Street like *"jeunes filles en fleur,"* as one British intelligence officer put it, young girls in flower.

One of the Donovan OSS Special Ops envoys arriving in London, thirty-two-year-old Franklin Canfield, had already gotten a taste of wartime Europe three years earlier. Living in Paris with his wife, daughters, and black standard poodle, he represented the New York law firm of Sullivan and Cromwell. In 1939, when Hitler invaded Poland and the war began, family and friends begged the Canfields to come home, but for the sake of Franklin's career they stayed put.

Eventually, though, the bombs fell so close to Paris that the Canfields could hear their thunderous claps. Hitler's May 1940 blitz into France had begun. Suddenly, thousands of blond men, women, and children—ethnic Germans from Alsace-Lorraine who ran from the German tanks—flooded into Paris and turned its parks into refugee campgrounds. The Canfields realized the time to go home had arrived.

They filled their Citroën with what they could, abandoned their home and most of their possessions, and tore southwest to the Atlantic port of Bordeaux. The Canfield family and its poodle crowded aboard the steamship *Washington,* like hundreds of other refugees of all nationalities, just as the Germans entered Paris. Once at sea, Canfield suddenly found himself crammed with his family in a lifeboat, suspended from the gunwale over the ocean's threatening swells. A German U-boat had zeroed in on the *Washington;* it might have torpedoed it at any moment. *"Je ne veux pas me noyer,"* whimpered Canfield's youngest daughter: I don't want to drown.

The *Washington* zigzagged a narrow escape, and once safely back in American territory, Canfield joined the war effort. He first helped to write the Selective Service Act, which brought in the military draft, but soon moved on to the State Department. In May 1941, Canfield flew to North Africa, where he took part in secret negotiations with French colonialists to smooth the way for the coming North African invasion. By early 1942, he was back in Washington, D.C., with the army rank of captain, training to be a spy as a member of the OSS Special Operations branch.

On a cold winter morning at a Montreal airstrip, Franklin Canfield bade farewell to his wife a second time and climbed aboard a British B-17 bomber. It was January 1943, the same month that Charles Hambro finally agreed to let Donovan's Special Operations agents into Europe. When Canfield arrived in London to start running the agents, he wandered blithely into SOE head-quarters at Baker Street along with two similarly inexperienced Donovan envoys, Lieutenant Colonel Paul van der Stricht and Captain John Bross.

In three years of SOE operations, its shadow officers, most of whom had already fought in regular battle, had made themselves professionals at behind-the-lines warfare. The SOE's F Section now controlled, in secret from de Gaulle's Free French, nearly 120 agents in France, in spite of the pending collapse of Carte.

But the war experiences of Canfield, Bross, and van der Stricht—all three of them white-shoe lawyers on leave from Wall Street—did not extend to a single shot, except in training. Even the OSS men's crisp new uniforms trumpeted the fact that their army commissions were only weeks old. To men like Maurice Buckmaster, Canfield's magna cum laude degree from Harvard and Juris Doctor from Columbia qualified him, at best, to sue Hitler. But not, God save everyone, to begin recruiting and sending agents into occupied France.

And Buckmaster and his fellow Hambro underlings, with half their agents dead or captured and the other half on the run and frightened, had little desire to supervise the on-the-job training of Canfield, Bross, and van der Stricht. Instead, the SOE staff connived to keep the Americans away from the secrets of SOE's precious operations by circling them through the various SOE agent-training schools.

Canfield and his colleagues ended up able to pick just about any German lock and code a message in umpteen different ways, which would have been good if they planned to be agents. But after a few wasted weeks they learned little about deploying agents themselves. When John Bross had reason to call on the senior American navy man in London, Admiral Harold Stark, he was announced as a representative of the "O double S." "You don't spell that with an A, do you?" asked the admiral, splitting his sides laughing. Even elements of the American military refused to take Canfield and his Special Operations colleagues seriously.

Meanwhile, the telegrams poured in from Donovan back in Washington. He constantly wanted to know when American agents were going to be dropped, couldn't understand what was taking so long, and insisted that anything the Brits could do, the Americans could do better. By the time SOE's chief of planning, Mike Rowlandson, came to Canfield's office with an invitation to witness an exercise to test an idea for an operation that would replace captured agents in France, the frustrated Canfield had earned his right to bitterness.

Canfield sipped his tea in the comfort of the Control and Dispatch Center, watching SOE officers compose and code messages to their "agents" and move colored pins around on their maps. Poor John Bross, meanwhile, rolled about in the cold, wet mud on the British moors with a group of soldiers, their faces painted black, pretending to be the Resistance. Canfield observed the command-and-control side of the mock SOE operation; Bross watched the operational side. It was March 1943, and this whole setup was part of one huge, elaborate war game.

For over a week, Exercise Spartan, as the game was called, scattered more than one hundred thousand British and Canadian troops over the length and breadth of England. It did not, like every past British military-planning exercise, simulate the defense of the United Kingdom from a German invasion. Instead, Exercise Spartan simulated, for the first time in World War II, the anticipated Allied invasion of the Continent. It was the largest offensive military

exercise ever staged on British soil, and it signaled both the Allies' growing op-
timism and the imminence of the much-awaited cross-Channel invasion. The
big question for Franklin Canfield was why he had been invited to observe it.

Mike Rowlandson had suddenly turned observation of SOE's part in
Spartan into a sort of inter-Allied cloak-and-dagger get-together. He invited
not only Canfield and his colleagues from the OSS Special Ops but also members of de Gaulle's BCRA. Since SOE staff had made it so perfectly clear that
they thought of the American spy chiefs as amateurs and the French as un-
trustworthy, the invitation to Spartan was a suspiciously friendly move.

As the Spartan scenario went, the "Allies," played by the British Second
Army, had gained a "French beachhead," which was actually a barren pasture-
land in the vicinity of Salisbury Plain, about ninety miles southwest of London. They would try to burst out of their "beachhead" and move "inland,"
northeast toward Huntingdon. The "Germans," meanwhile, would try to stop
the "Allies" and drive them back into the "sea."

As this faux battle of the beachhead raged on, several groups of enlisted
men from the Royal Welch Fusiliers ran around behind the "enemy" lines, pretending to be Resistance fighters and generally making a nuisance of themselves to the so-called Germans. "Boykin" agents, playing the part of F and
RF Section agents, led some of the "Resistance" groups, and maintained radio
contact with the SOE's Control and Dispatch Center in "London." To add to
the mix, German "security agents" skulked around trying to catch the Boykins.
The SOE masters hoped to demonstrate to the British high command how
Boykin-led Resistance groups could offer substantial assistance to the main
military effort.

But Rowlandson particularly wanted Canfield and his French and American colleagues to keep their eyes on the Resistance groups who had no Boykin
leadership. Without agent contact with London, these groups lacked not only
trained leaders but also arms, supplies, and strategic direction. Their role
simulated the situation of the decapitated groups in France who had, in the
Odette-type scenario the SOE so much feared, lost their agents and radio operators to German counterintelligence or who, by the invasion on D-Day, had
never established contact with the Allies in the first place. With these groups,
Rowlandson tested his scheme to send new leadership to the secret army in
France at the last moment and to carefully coordinate their fighting with the
D-Day uprising.

Canfield and his American and French colleagues observed while SOE staff officers suddenly dispatched special three-man teams, each composed of a leader, a guide, and a radio operator, to rendezvous with the leaderless fusilier Resistance groups. In the dispatch center, the radio sizzled to life as each of the arriving teams began transmitting their weapons requests on behalf of their Resistance groups. For the purposes of Exercise Spartan, huge trucks rather than airplanes rumbled off carrying the requested booty to the groups. The once-disorganized Resistance was suddenly in action.

As Spartan progressed, the Allies advanced rapidly. The newly contacted Resistance, according to radioed orders received by their new agent-leaders, destroyed bridges and raided German units to waylay their movement toward the front. Spartan umpires painted white x's on killed German backs, and sent the defeated units to their barracks. The simulated invasion overwhelmingly triumphed, and the test of Rowlandson's new scheme was a resounding success. Even better, from Rowlandson's point of view, the test "indoctrinated" Canfield and his OSS Special Ops and BCRA colleagues into the scheme's merits and "imbued them with enthusiasm," to quote SOE records.

Now that Rowlandson had piqued their interest, he explained that this scheme for arming and organizing Resistance at the last minute had originally been intended to assist Operation Sledgehammer, a 1942 Allied plan for the invasion of either the Brittany or Cotentin peninsulas of northern France. The idea had been the brainchild of SOE's eventual head, General Colin Gubbins, but Sledgehammer never took place, and the Resistance scheme had been shelved. But recently, faced with the collapse of Resistance leadership in France, the SOE had dusted off the old idea. It was given the name of a Scottish border town known for hardened fighters who, according to legend, played sports with the heads of defeated Englishmen in the Middle Ages—Jedburgh.

As the revamped plan went, Operation Jedburgh would constitute a strategic reserve of no fewer than seventy highly trained paramilitary teams, in uniform, who would spring into action on D-Day. The bulk of the teams would drop in France, but a small number would be set aside for possible military operations in Holland and Belgium. The team "guide" would always be a citizen of the destination nation. Wherever Resistance fighters needed leadership and contact with the military command, the Jedburgh teams would drop with a load of light arms, establish themselves, organize fresh arms drops to equip as many Resistance fighters as they could, and then harass German movement toward the front with lightning attacks from behind.

Rowlandson's big problem, he now admitted, was assembling the force of some six hundred men, largely officers, who were needed to supply both the agents and the huge operation's support staff. The British had already fished dry their regiments with their "special duty" trawls. Not only that, but since Operation Jedburgh could potentially double the number of agents in France, a new radio station like Station 53 would have to be built and staffed, more planes would be needed to drop supplies, and a new facility to pack the parachuted equipment containers would be required. For all its jealous guarding of special operations in Europe, the SOE finally realized it could not go on alone.

Rowlandson made his pitch to Canfield. If the British offered joint control of Operation Jedburgh, and half the teams were led by Americans, would OSS Special Ops, Rowlandson wondered, like to take part?

Canfield must have been ecstatic. After months of thumb-twiddling, the American guerrilla warfare outfit in London had been invited to take full part in the shadow war. The British had offered equal partnership in this crucial scheme to reinforce the secret army in France with new leadership at the last moment and to carefully coordinate the D-Day uprising. Operation Jedburgh had the potential to be the largest, most aggressive, and most important underground operation yet mounted in France.

With Jedburgh, OSS Special Ops would finally get American agents into France in large numbers. And if the Germans mopped up existing British agents, as the SOE feared, the British, French, and American men of Operation Jedburgh might suddenly become the very backbone of the Resistance in France. Jedburgh might give Canfield and his Special Ops colleagues a central role in the shadow war—effectively making them "shadow chiefs" alongside Maurice Buckmaster and his SOE colleagues—and a chance to make an important contribution to the cross-Channel invasion of France. Canfield enthusiastically agreed that OSS Special Ops should take part. Operation Jedburgh was on.

# PART II
# THE CALL FOR
# HAZARDOUS DUTY

# CHAPTER FIVE
## A SLIM CHANCE

Thirty-six hundred miles across the Atlantic from the United Kingdom, Corporal Lucien "Lou" Lajeunesse, a Connecticut native, balanced a rifle over his shoulder and lazily kicked up clouds of sun-dried dirt as he walked. Wandering past the new radar station, along the hulking, nineteenth-century stone ramparts, and under the imposing muzzles of the sixteen-inch guns, his body followed a prescribed route around Fort Wadsworth on New York's Staten Island. Guard duty bored most boys, but Lajeunesse—always prone to worry—enjoyed leaving his anxieties, at least the work-related ones, to wait for him indoors.

Lajeunesse spent most of the sweltering summer days of 1943 sequestered in a radio room, tapping his Morse key and doing his part to protect the more than five hundred warships and merchant crafts at anchor in New York Harbor. Frighteningly close to American shores, U-boat "wolf packs" had torpedoed hundreds of Allied ships in the open sea. But unsatiated, the Nazi submarine captains hungered for the thousands of sitting ducks in the East Coast's vulnerable ports.

Once, in November 1942, they punctured the defenses of New York Harbor. A U-boat slipped in and out, undetected, leaving behind ten deadly mines. Fortunately, the harbor's minesweepers quickly discovered and defused them. Since then, a new, highly technical network of underwater detectors and remote-controlled mines successfully kept out the Nazis' submarines. But a mistake by Lajeunesse or his cohort could send hundreds of young men to death by burning or drowning.

The possibility, however remote, weighed heavily on the twenty-five-year-old. He felt his judgment had failed him before. In 1940, Hitler's invasion of Poland convinced Lajeunesse and his father that the coming war was inevitable. Let's get in before the draft, Lajeunesse had said to his two brothers, Henry and Leo, while we can still arrange to stay together. Leo, the baby brother, resisted, but Lajeunesse strong-armed him. He signed himself and his two siblings up for the Coastal Artillery, thinking it was a home-based service that would never send them abroad. The day the brothers left for training was the first time Lajeunesse saw his mother cry. Not long after that, Lajeunesse realized he had made the biggest mistake of his life.

Today, at least, marching around this Staten Island fort on guard duty, Lajeunesse thought he had little to worry about. He would eventually arrive at the edge of the sparkling gap of turquoise water that separated Staten Island from Brooklyn. There, he could take the chance to enjoy the sea breeze, watch the ships steam past, and maybe smoke a few cigarettes. But now, two soldiers whom Lajeunesse did not know, neither one from Fort Wadsworth, headed toward him. They had the letters "MP" emblazoned on their armbands.

"We have orders for you to come with us," said one of the military policemen.

Suddenly getting arrested shocked Lajeunesse more than it would less conscientious men. "What am I wanted for?" he stammered.

"Can't tell you."

They threw the bewildered Lajeunesse into a jeep, sped down to the Staten Island Ferry, and steamed across the harbor to Manhattan's Wall Street. Crowds of men in blue, green, brown, and white uniforms of the various services lolled on the corners. These military types inhabited the federal buildings, and it was into one of these that the MPs took Lajeunesse.

At the center of a cavernous, high-ceilinged room stood a huge glass block, the likes of which Lajeunesse had never seen before. It was twice his height, like a solitary, oversize ice cube at the bottom of a giant coffee cup, and it was hollow. Inside it, a lieutenant colonel stood up from a table, beckoning to Lajeunesse. He hesitatingly stepped through a door and in. What have I done? Lajeunesse wanted to ask. What will you do to me? But he held his tongue, even though the colonel volunteered no information other than his name. A manila folder sat on the table. When the colonel closed the transparent door, the sounds of New York disappeared, as if a radio had been unplugged.

"How did you come to speak French?" the colonel asked abruptly.

Like many French Canadians, Lajeunesse's father, Teffy, had migrated to northern Connecticut for the mill work. Over the clanging of the machinery, Teffy's coworkers shouted their jokes and tall tales in French, and he hardly needed to bother with English. He spoke it grudgingly with his children, but forbade it at the dinner table. As a child, when the younger Lajeunesse felt hungry, he learned to ask for *les pommes de terre,* or the bowl of potatoes stayed out of reach.

Lajeunesse explained his language ability to the colonel, but his anxiety only increased. What did his French have to do with this unwanted attention from the military police? Did they think he was involved in some sort of espionage? He finally summoned the courage to ask. "What is this all about?"

The colonel smiled slightly. "How is your accent? Could you pass for a Frenchman in France?"

Lajeunesse suddenly realized that the colonel's folder did not contain a misconduct report; it contained a personnel file. The soundproof room, the nearly anonymous officer, and the questions about French all added up to much more trouble than the mere disciplinary hearing Lajeunesse had feared. The fate of Odette Sansom and countless other agents in France testified to the fact. Though Lajeunesse could not have guessed it, this interview was part of a top secret international recruitment effort for Operation Jedburgh; the unnamed colonel who questioned Lajeunesse belonged to the Office of Strategic Services.

Over in London, the American Franklin Canfield and the Brit Mike Rowlandson had teamed up and pitched their vital plan to the military higher-ups of both countries, pushing for Jedburgh's inclusion in D-Day plans and for permission to assemble the personnel and equipment. While they waited for an answer, meanwhile, Wild Bill Donovan made Operation Jedburgh the OSS's highest priority. He ordered all branches of the OSS to turn over their personnel quotas so that the Jedburgh talent spotters could at least make a start. They had turned up Lajeunesse while fingering their way through military personnel files looking for fluent French speakers.

Lajeunesse's temperament made him an unlikely volunteer for the kind of job the colonel had in mind. He found fighting and killing distasteful. He refused to hunt deer in the Connecticut woods with his friends, and would never even fish with his brother Henry. Besides, keeping the U-boats out of New York Harbor was an important job. On the other hand, since staying home meant that someone else had to ship out, what was more patriotic? Years of Catholic Sunday school had etched into Lajeunesse the practice of penance, and, if only unconsciously, he yearned to pay it to his baby brother Leo.

The colonel, of course, was oblivious to all this. "Tell me about your radio skills," he said.

After Lajeunesse and his brothers completed basic training together, everything went according to plan. But when the three traveled home for their grandfather's funeral, the phone rang with the boys' first assignments while grieving family members crowded the living room. Henry pulled a cook's job in Fort Tilden, New York. Lajeunesse got duty manning the sixteen-inch guns at Fort Wadsworth. But while the older brothers remained safely stateside, the reluctant Leo got orders to ship out with the very first American troops to leave for the European war zone. The news devastated the entire family. Even two years later, with the colonel in the glass room, Lajeunesse needed only to close his eyes to see the betrayed look on Leo's face.

Lajeunesse related none of this in answer to the colonel. He simply explained that after a stint on the big guns at Wadsworth, he had been sent to learn radio operation in Altoona, Pennsylvania. Lajeunesse could now transmit and receive Morse code so fast that he needed a typewriter to transcribe the incoming messages. The colonel seemed pleased.

Many more questions came, and the talking, mostly about background and skills, lulled Lajeunesse. Then, abruptly, the colonel asked: Would you be willing to parachute out of an airplane to save your country and help end the war? The sudden conversational turn shook Lajeunesse for a moment. Strangely, since he had never been higher than the top floor of a four-story building nor even glimpsed the inside of an airplane, he heard himself say that, yes, he would parachute. Whether for penance or patriotism, he did not know, but the argument within him had ended.

Would you be willing to live behind the lines, among the enemy, where no reinforcements could rescue you? Lajeunesse began to shake and sweat, but he said yes. Would you do these things even if I told you there would be only a slim chance of coming out alive? Yes. If I told you that you could not even tell your family, even though you might not see them again? Lajeunesse answered yes one last time.

Suddenly, the colonel stood up and shook Lajeunesse's hand. The interview was over. The same taciturn MPs returned Lajeunesse to the fort, and dumped him at the front gate. The young corporal found himself back at Fort

Wadsworth, preparing for his regular shift on the radio, without having received any explanation for the interview's reasons or consequences. Radio duty
came. Guard duty came. News of the Allied landings on the Italian mainland
came. But from the colonel, secretly immersed in evaluations of other potential radio recruits, no word came. Lajeunesse did not even know whether to
feel disappointed or relieved.

Back in England, on a warm summer day in East Anglia, not too far from the
North Sea coast, twenty-eight-year-old Lieutenant (later Captain) Bernard M. W.
Knox sauntered up and down a train station platform, smoking a cigarette.
The telex machine at the American B-17 bomber base where Knox was stationed had spit out a message calling for volunteers with knowledge of European languages. The message offered no description of the duties, but at that
stage, Knox would have risked anything for a more exciting job.

For the last few months, he had acted as the "defense officer" of his air
base. His job was to prepare for a possible German paratroop invasion, an extremely unlikely proposition. The Germans and Italians had just surrendered
in North Africa; the Allies had invaded Sicily; the Soviets pushed forward on
the eastern front. Hitler would hardly be launching an attack on Britain. Knox
might as well have been preparing for an invasion from Mars. His job was, for
all intents and purposes, obsolete.

He killed time by ticking his way down a list of duties that he thought of as
irrelevant to the war effort. Somehow, he ended up overseeing the work detail
for soldiers who got themselves in trouble and sent to the stockade. Regulations said the prisoners could not lazily while away their hours lying around in
their cells, so Knox had the poor sods moving a pile of rocks from one place to
another and then back again. U.S. Army chickenshit.

Knox jealously watched the B-17 bombers tear down the airstrip and roar
toward Germany. Later, he guiltily counted the bombers as they limped down
through the clouds and home, or didn't. He was bored and frustrated. This was
no way to spend a war. Knox, already a veteran of the Spanish civil war, had an
ideological obsession with fighting fascism. He waited now on the station platform in the anxious hope that he would finally get back into the fray.

By birth, though by neither citizenship nor sentiment, Knox was an
Englishman. His earliest memory was of his nurse carrying him into an under-
ground taxi garage to shelter him from a zeppelin air raid on London during
World War I. Knox's father played piano in one of England's first jazz bands.

The phone in the Knox flat sometimes rang from New York, a voice sang a song while Bernard's father transcribed, and before long, at Murray's River Club, Bernard's father and his band belted out the newest American hit, weeks before anyone else in London played it.

As for the younger Knox, his talents lay not in music but in language. At his London grammar school, he studied French and Latin in class. In his free time, he scoured the secondhand-book stores for textbooks and taught himself Greek, Russian, and Italian. After he got caught doodling omegas, alphas, and epsilons during English class, he got to drop his much-hated chemistry in exchange for accepting private tuition in Greek. It was no surprise that the telex that arrived at the air base calling for language experts had so piqued Knox's interest.

Knox's genius as a polyglot had won him a handsome classics scholarship at St. John's College, Cambridge. That same year, 1933, Adolf Hitler came to power in Germany, partly in response to the Depression, which seemed to have become permanent throughout Europe. In England, unemployment stood at 23 percent, and government assistance amounted to a diet of bread, margarine, and potatoes.

The British political right responded to the economic crisis with the formation, in 1932, of the British Union of Fascists (BUF). Within two years, the BUF's twenty thousand members marched around Britain in their black uniforms and boots, beating up Jewish shopkeepers and smashing their windows. Since the British government, in this period, did little to discourage the BUF and nothing to stop Hitler's expansionism, to young students like Bernard Knox, a fascist Europe seemed a very real and terrible possibility. Knox became a Communist and joined the Cambridge Socialist Club, a fact that might disqualify him from whatever he was about to volunteer for.

Knox's train took him to a London station, and before long he sat in an office with a spur-wearing American cavalry major. While a smartly dressed young female secretary sat quietly, the major began asking Knox questions. Unlike so many new-to-war Americans, Knox had quite a battle experience to relate.

In February 1936, the same year Knox graduated from Cambridge, Spain's Popular Front, a coalition formed by the Spanish Communist Party and the antifascist political parties of the middle class, won a narrow victory at the polls. The following July, a group of right-wing army officers, led by General

Francisco Franco, rose up in a military coup, beginning a three-year civil war that cost half a million lives. Hitler and Mussolini began air-dropping supplies and supplying troops to Franco's Nationalists, while the Soviet Union supported the Republicans and their antifascist volunteers from around the world, known as the International Brigades. The whole mess became a dress rehearsal for World War II.

That September, Knox, who now lived back in London, got a letter from a university friend, the poet John Cornford, asking Knox to join a group of a dozen English lads who wanted to fight in the International Brigades. Knox sold his textbooks for cash, used it to buy equipment, and soon found himself fighting off a Nationalist attack on the outskirts of Madrid.

For six weeks beginning in November 1936, Knox and his chums fought in terrible conditions. Their first guns were literal antiques. The Madrid winter seeped through their bodies no matter how many blankets they wrapped around themselves. Food was so scarce that they killed a donkey and ate it raw; a fire would have made them a bull's-eye for the snipers. Only a few days passed before one of Knox's Cambridge chums was dead.

In December, as Knox's unit attempted to withdraw from a skirmish, he felt a terrible blow and burning pain in his neck. He fell to the ground and blood spurted upward, like a fountain. His carotid artery had been punctured. "I can't do anything about that," the medic said. "God bless you, Bernard," said his friend John, leaving him for dead. The last thing Knox remembered before passing out was the feeling of rage for having to die so young.

Miraculously, he eventually came to. Where once there had been spouting, the blood now only oozed. His wound had quickly clotted, saving his life. In a daze, Knox walked miles to a dressing station, and then rode in an ambulance, screaming agony in symphony with three other wounded soldiers every time it hit a bump. Knox's recovery was slow, and his injury left him with a malfunctioning right arm. The news that his friend John Cornford had been killed convinced him to take his doctor's advice and go home for more expert treatment.

Knox returned to England, got his arm fixed, and reacquainted himself with an American girlfriend he had met at Cambridge. Together, they moved to the United States and, in April 1939, got married. For fifty dollars a month Knox taught Latin at a small private school in Connecticut. Itchingly, he watched from afar the beginnings of World War II. "I've moved heaven and earth to get your visa," his wife said, "and you certainly owe nothing to that government in Britain who collaborated with Hitler." If Knox valued his marriage, he had no chance of getting into the war with the British army.

Then came Pearl Harbor. The United States entered the war at last, and Knox joined the U.S. Army. Though his buddies never let him live down his British background and he could not shake the nickname "Limey," Knox began to think of himself as American. He preferred the "melting pot" aspect of American culture compared to the calcified classifications of British society. His citizenship papers came in 1943 while he worked at his futile job on the East Anglia air base.

Knox itched to get into the fighting. He had stopped calling himself a Communist after the Soviet Union's brutal annexation of the Baltic states and invasion of Finland and the staged show trials of the Bolsheviks, but Knox remained a vehement antifascist. He also had the superstitious idea that he could fight without getting killed—the odds of taking a second bullet seemed small.

He pestered the base adjutant for a more interesting assignment. When the telex came asking for officer volunteers with command of European languages, Knox jumped at the chance. He sent his name in, and he soon received orders to report to an address off Grosvenor Square, London—which was how he now came to be having this conversation with the major.

Knox's battle experience made him particularly interesting to the major. Wild Bill Donovan's OSS cared not a jot if a prospect was a Communist so long as he wanted to fight. There was only one last issue to resolve. Is it true you speak fluent French? the major wanted to know. Of course, Knox told him.

"Miss King, carry on," said the major to the secretary.

"*Bonjour, mon lieutenant,*" said Miss King in an accent that made it clear that hers was a nom de guerre. "*Il paraît que vous parlez couramment le français. Où est-ce que vous l'avez appris?*" Apparently, you speak fluent French. Where did you learn it?

Five minutes of question and answer followed until, at last, "Miss King" turned to the major. "He's OK, Major," she said. And the interview ended as abruptly as Lucien Lajeunesse's.

Shadow warfare recruiters had made a modest start with Lajeunesse, Knox, and others, but nearly four months had passed since Exercise Spartan, and Mike Rowlandson and Franklin Canfield still had not received the approval from the Allied high command to begin preparation in earnest for Operation

Jedburgh. True, Donovan had donated the entire OSS personnel allotment to the scheme, and the recruiters had found a few good prospects, but their efforts were far from sufficient.

Canfield needed, for OSS's part in Jedburgh, fifty speedy radio operators who, like Lucien Lajeunesse, could zap off messages so quickly that a Nazi direction finder would have no time to pinpoint them. Even more difficult, Canfield had to find an equal number of uniquely qualified French-speaking officers of Bernard Knox's caliber: young enough to sprint around the French countryside, experienced enough to command a motley band of rebellious civilians. On top of that, recruiters had to dig up trainers, support staff, and planners for the scheme. "Success of the plan," Canfield wrote to Washington headquarters, "depends exclusively on one thing: qualified personnel to carry it out." For now, he wasn't getting it.

In France, meanwhile, the arrest of Odette Sansom and the destruction of Carte had turned out to be only the beginning of a vicious German bloodbath of the Resistance. In June and July 1943, the Abwehr and Sicherheitsdienst smashed the Paris-based Prosper network, which had taken Carte's place. The Germans massacred as many as fifteen hundred Resistance workers and agents associated with Prosper. If that wasn't bad enough, on June 21, just as de Gaulle's ambassador Jean Moulin had nearly sealed an agreement among the various Resistance factions to accept central direction for their military activity, the Germans arrested him and fourteen other key leaders as they assembled for a meeting at a doctor's house near Lyon.

The work of both the RF and F Sections to organize behind-the-lines forces lay in tatters. The Resistance had become an army with no officers. Reinforcement of the Resistance by the planned Operation Jedburgh was critical.

Without rapid approval from the military higher-ups, however, Canfield and Rowlandson would never get the men they needed. Nor would they get the airplanes, weapons, or construction of the new radio station needed to communicate with the swelling number of radios in France. Without quick movement from the military bureaucracy, Operation Jedburgh would be stillborn, the Americans would never get their agents into France, and the Allies might end up with a bunch of Resistance networks with no agents left to lead them.

Canfield and Rowlandson could only stand by as calendar page after calendar page of crucial agent recruitment time ended up in the trash.

Finally, in July, the senior planner of the D-Day invasion himself, British Lieutenant General Frederick Morgan, the chief of staff to the Supreme

Allied Commander (COSSAC), gave the Jedburgh plan his go-ahead. "I have discussed with SOE their proposal for D-Day," he wrote to the British chiefs of staff. "I have agreed in principle to these proposals and request the transfer to SOE of any personnel necessary." In August, after five precious months, Operation Jedburgh also finally won the enthusiastic endorsement of the commander of the entire American forces in Europe, Lieutenant General Jacob Devers. On September 4, 1943, Franklin Canfield elbowed his way aboard one of the few transatlantic flights and flew to Washington.

Three weeks earlier, on August 11, top military planners had revealed to the senior staff of the SOE and OSS Special Ops that they then planned the invasion for May 1944, only eight months away, and wanted to know exactly how the shadow warriors planned to use their Resistance networks to help. The bolstering of the secret army by Operation Jedburgh had become more crucial than ever. Canfield would have to get his American Jedburghs recruited, tested, cleared for security, trained, and shipped to England by no later than New Year's Day 1944. He had less than four months.

# CHAPTER SIX
# ANYONE HERE SPEAK FRENCH?

At Fort Monmouth in New Jersey, trainee radio operators in the U.S. Signal Corps crowded elbow to elbow at tables that ran the length of the fort's cavernous former airplane hangars. After basic training's weeks of push-ups, rugged marches, and weapons training and infantry exercises, their youthful bodies, in spite of their minds' fears and doubts, ached to fight. Instead, they tapped out practice Morse code messages that meant nothing and went nowhere. To these kids just out of high school, it made as much sense as their parents forcing them to go to preseason football practice and then to take piano lessons when the games finally started.

Now, the hangar door flew open, and a paratroop lieutenant, a stranger to the Monmouth boys, stepped through. "Listen up!" he shouted. The clicking went suddenly quiet. A mass of eager heads turned. None of the fidgety boys needed to be told to take off his headphones. "Any of you guys speak French?" shouted the lieutenant, one of Canfield's recruitment ambassadors. "We're having a meeting you should attend." He turned and went out, followed by a much bigger crowd of curious boys than a survey of language skills might have predicted. Bored men, of course, made good fodder for the secret services.

Private Ted Baumgold, one of the hundred guys who jumped up and ran along, could claim at least a small knowledge of French. He had spent his junior year of college in France, playing his violin and studying music. Now, nearly ten years later, Baumgold was older than most of the other boys traipsing after the lieutenant, and perhaps a little more resolved. Baumgold came from a New York family of Jewish diamond merchants. Because their business cut quartz crystals for the army's radios, he had been exempted from the draft.

He had enlisted voluntarily. Like others, he had his reasons for wanting to fight.

He wandered after the crowd to another of Monmouth's obsolete hangars (they had once housed airplanes used by the Signal Corps to develop aerial photography, among other things, during World War I). A hundred or so boys jostled around the paratroop lieutenant. He had been sent, he told them, to drum up French-speaking volunteers with good radio skills for missions behind the lines in German-occupied territory. "I don't know anything more about the missions," he said, "except that they are extremely dangerous, and you have to be willing to go in by submarine or parachute. Now, go outside, smoke a cigarette, and if you're interested, be back in ten."

Earlier in the war, secret service recruiters like the lieutenant might have found their men more subtly and less publicly, like the way they had come upon Lucien Lajeunesse, by quietly fingering their way through personnel files. Overall, Operation Jedburgh required at least one hundred "pianists," as the secret services called their radio operators—enough to nearly double the Allies' clandestine radio contact with the French Resistance. The D-Day invasion date less than nine months away forced the Jedburgh bosses to accept the security risks of a certain lack of caution.

On military installations on both sides of the Atlantic, from September to November 1943, Jedburgh recruiters plastered bulletin boards with flyers, intoned announcements on camp PA systems, and dispatched letters for officers to read to their troops: "French speaking volunteers needed for immediate overseas assignment." For their officer volunteers, the recruiters looked wherever they might find the gung-ho leaders they wanted, among the paratroopers in the United States, the Commandos in Britain, and the French officer-training schools in North Africa. For radio operator volunteers like Baumgold, the recruiters went wherever the radio trainees concentrated.

One Sunday morning that autumn, for example, in Britain's Yorkshire, gunner-mechanic Norman Smith pulled himself from a tank engine he was repairing. He gathered with his unit around an officer who stood among the parked tanks of the Northamptonshire Yeomanry. "We are looking for men willing to drop into occupied territories to work with the Resistance," the officer said plainly to the crowd. The British Jedburgh recruiters trawled for their radio operators among the men of the Royal Armoured Corps, which trained at least one radioman for every tank.

In Algeria, Sergeant Jean Sassi, a French radio operator who had fought in the Tunisia campaign against Rommel, stood at attention on parade. *"Qui veut rentrer en France aussi vite que possible?"* shouted an officer: Who wants to get back to France as soon as possible? The French Jedburgh recruiters searched for radio operators like Sassi among the Free French divisions in North Africa, which had been idle since the Italians and Germans had surrendered there. Back in the United States, the recruiters fished from the Signal Corps training schools, from Camp Crowder in Missouri to Fort Monmouth in New Jersey, where Baumgold considered the paratroop lieutenant's proposal and smoked his cigarette.

Many of the men the recruiters talked to had lined up outside enlistment offices long before their draft, spurred by news of the horrible losses at Pearl Harbor and, later, after ferocious battles like Guadalcanal. Finding tightly coiled soldiers who wanted to fight was not the challenge. At American camps, forts, and bases, hundreds of boys, like Baumgold and his comrades now inhaling their last drags from their cigarettes outside the hangar, flocked to hear what kind of adventure the secret service recruiters had to offer.

But many men at Monmouth puffed on their cigarettes without giving the paratroop lieutenant's proposal a moment's thought. Few men wanted to volunteer on the basis of recruitment presentations so long on suspense and short on detail. Lest an information leak end with new agents parachuting to waiting platoons of well-armed Germans, the recruiters, if they knew anything about Operation Jedburgh themselves, could reveal little. Speak French? they might as well have said. Lay your life on the line here. Anxiety-provoking phrases like "high expected casualties" and "unusually dangerous" peppered their talks. They emphasized the danger, partly out of moral obligation, partly for lack of other allowable details, and partly to ensure that dropout rates did not skyrocket when volunteers finally discovered exactly what was expected of them.

The men at the paratroop lieutenant's little Monmouth rally were already fated to take part in the biggest amphibious invasion in military history. Most of them thought their present duties would be hazardous enough. They began to drift, one by one, back to their radios to tap out their phantom messages.

Baumgold had more thinking to do. Nearly alone, he drew on his cigarette a little bit longer.

Just as they repelled a large proportion of sane men, the Jedburgh recruiters' presentations also attracted a particularly high number of lunatics. Calls for hazardous duty tended to attract a large proportion of people whose love affairs had gone wrong and who had decided either that life was not worth living or that heroism was the way to win back their sweethearts. These were the types the Jedburgh recruiters tried to avoid.

Instead, they chased down the smattering of men who, like Baumgold, had a special, personal hatred of the Nazis, and the eager warriors whose enthusiasm for regular soldiering had been exhausted on the military treadmill. Men like Corporal Bill Thompson, at Camp Crowder, and Private First Class Jack Poché, at Scott Field, Illinois, both of whom wanted to volunteer for this mysterious "hazardous duty," were among those whom Jedburgh recruiters considered good possibilities.

Thompson, an amateur radio operator in civilian life, had volunteered for the Signal Corps right after Pearl Harbor, intent on delivering his communication skills straight to the front lines. Poché rushed himself into the Army Air Corps, romancing the idea of doing battle in the sky.

But for the gung-ho type, disillusionment with normal military service began with basic training. Men like Poché and Thompson wanted to practice killing the enemy at the rifle range; their sergeants emphasized bed-making, bouncing quarters off their bunks to check that they had tucked in their blankets tightly. Newsreels played in the cinemas of guys clawing up beaches in the Far East; at home, frustrated new interns did fifty push-ups because a fellow squadee left a shirt pocket unbuttoned. The boys stood in circles with their penises hanging out, and milked them like udders while a doctor checked for infectious discharge. They were forced to teach, on orders from their sergeants, backcountry hicks who had not yet learned to piss in a urinal, soap up in the shower, or eat with a knife and fork. Their companies progressed at the rate of the slowest man, and everyone else was kept from the war.

Other men might have been glad of the reprieve, but soldiers of Poché's and Thompson's type were too young and naive to be thankful. Their fathers, if they had been part of the Expeditionary Force in World War I, spared the boys the more grisly stories. The Great War's flying aces and larger-than-life infantrymen had made for compelling adventures in the boys' dime-store novels. Now, noble but romantic notions of heroically defending family and country excited their hopes that the prettiest girls from high school would write to them abroad, and that they would finally prove their manhood to their families. A motley mix of human motivations, flying under the banner of patriotism, propelled the boys to battle, and, ironically, it was too often the army that stood in their way.

As for Bill Thompson, the Signal Corps, in a random shuffle of some junior bureaucrat's papers, suddenly discarded his radio expertise, then bolstered with months of specialist military training, and sent him to train as a stevedore, to load and unload ships. In a parallel twist of typical army irony, the Air Corps turned around and made Poché a radio operator, though his natural aptitude as a flyer had rocketed him through a six-month aviator course in only two. An army quack had noticed a slight curvature in Poché's upper spine, diagnosed "stereololiphosis," and grounded him (years later, Poché would discover that no such medical term existed). Thompson and Poché were furious.

"Never volunteer for anything," the old army adage went. But to a certain brand of talented malcontents, in the absence of information the recruiters withheld, like expected casualty rates of 50 to 75 percent, or Hitler's order to immediately execute any Allied personnel captured behind the lines, the recruiters' scheme might offer the quickest way out of their quagmires. They just had to get themselves selected for it.

Among the volunteers in Britain, tanker Gordon Tack ached for a quick entrance to the fighting. He wanted revenge for the death of his father, whom a German U-boat crew gunned down in his lifeboat after sinking his ship. Glyn Loosemore walked down streets littered with bodies after a German bombing in Swansea, Wales, and thought he would never get a chance to fight back in the Royal Armoured Corps, where the tanks seemed to break down every day.

Jean Sassi, typical of the French volunteers, had been part of the French army bulldozed by Hitler's forces back in 1940. After a childhood filled with stories of the greatness of the French empire, he felt shamed first by the decisive defeat and then by the long German occupation. He waited until the Tunisia campaign to fight the Germans and then found himself idle again, unable to do anything about the Nazis marching up and down the streets of his native Nice. He itched to fight them again, and Jedburgh seemed like the fastest way. Like many of the British and French volunteers, Sassi had more personal axes to grind with the Nazis than most of the American volunteers.

But back in the States, outside the hangar at Fort Monmouth, Ted Baumgold had a personal reason of his own. He stubbed out his finished cigarette, just as the other guys had, but then he stayed put, waiting for the rest of the al-lotted ten minutes to pass. Baumgold knew that letters from the old countries carried awful news. Aunts, uncles, grandmothers, and grandfathers had disappeared from their homes in Poland and Germany and Belgium and France. The few escapees told macabre tales. The American government refused to countenance the stories, and even, in 1939, refused harbor to the SS *St. Louis*, a ship carrying nearly a thousand Jewish refugees from Europe. Baumgold knew the truth.

The ten minutes was over. Baumgold turned and marched back through the door and into the hangar. He had simply realized, in words echoing the saying of the Roman-era rabbi Hillel: "If not me, then who?"

# CHAPTER SEVEN

# WE JUST WANT TO FIGHT

**W**hile some of Canfield's recruiters made their pitches to the enlisted radio operators at the Signal Corps' training camps, others quietly trawled for the American officers needed as Jedburgh team leaders. When the recruiters arrived at Fort Benning, Georgia, the home of the paratroopers, and began fingering through the personnel files, they discovered the promising folder of Second Lieutenant Jack Singlaub. Singlaub, however, spent that September 1943 hundreds of miles away, crashing through the woods, hurdling boulders, and ducking tree branches, ignoring the stutter of gunfire and exploding fountains of dirt. He had been sent on special duty at North Carolina's Camp Mackall.

Singlaub's job required him to trot through the Camp Mackall wilderness alongside company commanders of the 11th Airborne Division during their combat proficiency tests. The commanders and their soldiers wore black face paint and carried weapons; Singlaub wore a white armband and carried a clipboard. When he stopped and scratched his notes, each of the one hundred or so company members watched him anxiously. As a twenty-two-year-old umpire, Singlaub had already earned the power to help decide whether these eager young paratroopers would win their wish to go to war. He had the kind of good looks that could have made these men dislike him, except that his easy smile and protruding ears misleadingly suggested a friendly simplicity or innocence.

Singlaub was exactly the type of officer that Canfield's secret warfare recruiters hoped to sign up. Already, at Fort Polk, Louisiana, they had nabbed

First Lieutenant Aaron Bank, a forty-year-old tactics instructor with long experience in army intelligence, whose frequent requests for transfer were always ignored by superiors who considered him too old for battle. At Fort Riley, Kansas, they netted Second Lieutenant Mason Starring, a gung-ho, polo-playing son of a Wall Street investment banker who joined the cavalry for the horses, but unhappily found himself stuck in a mechanized unit. From military installations across the country, the recruiters seduced the best-trained officers they could, flashing unimpeachable orders Canfield had obtained from the Joint Chiefs of Staff and leaving behind a gaggle of disgruntled COs.

More than any other type of officer, paratroopers like Singlaub from Fort Benning's new Airborne Command would make excellent secret operatives. Paratroopers were accustomed to hazardous duty, trained to a physical peak, and already jump-qualified. Canfield and his colleagues reasoned that paratroopers would be the least likely to balk at the last moment from throwing themselves secretly from black-painted airplanes into the French night. Eagerly, the recruiters made their announcements wherever paratroopers could be found, rifled through personnel files, and held clandestine briefings.

Even if Singlaub had some way of knowing, up in the Camp Mackall forests, that his file numbered among those fingered by Canfield's scouts, he would have been unimpressed. He had slogged hard to win the right, reserved for the parachute-qualified, to blouse his pants into his jump boots. With the rest of the 515th Paratroop Infantry Regiment, he had marched, trained, and sweated his platoon into its current state of battle-readiness. He marked time at Mackall happily, but only because he believed that the day approached when he would, along with thousands of other paratroopers, precipitate on Europe, not skulkingly as Canfield proposed, but proudly, under a storm of mushroomed canopies.

Enticed by an uncle's World War I stories, Singlaub always knew he wanted to be a career officer. But he had been beset by frustrations. Because his father had registered as a Democrat, Singlaub's Republican congressman refused to endorse his application to West Point. After earning top grades studying military science at UCLA, Singlaub lost a promised regular commission when the army canceled the ROTC "honor graduate" program. As an activated reservist, he broke his ankle and got stuck stateside while his regiment shipped out for the invasion of Italy. He could tolerate no more diversions. He would ship to Europe with the 515th, help secure the Continent, shed his reserve status, win, by his actions, his regular army commission, and then come home to marry his girlfriend, Mary Osborne. Joining an outfit like Canfield's played no part in Singlaub's plans.

Singlaub umpired the last of the combat proficiency tests at Camp Mackall, got some unexpected leave, and, before he went back to Benning, excitedly jumped a train to Washington, D.C., for an unplanned rendezvous with Mary. He discovered her there in the company of her old college boyfriend. He was devastated. To make matters worse, when he sulked back to headquarters at Benning, he found that his regiment had been stripped of men to replace the terrible casualties suffered by the 504th in Italy, that his unit had lost its battle-ready status, and that there would be no shipping out to Europe anytime soon. His plans for battle, an army commission, and marriage had all fallen apart.

In Britain, SOE officer recruits, in contrast to the naive young Americans who flocked after Canfield's recruiters in hopes of battlefield excitement, signed up for Operation Jedburgh more out of a dogged sense of duty. One British officer destined for Jedburgh, Captain William Crawshay, had already received a bullet in the thigh in battle against the Italians as a member of the King's African Rifles. Major Adrian Wise had participated in a commando raid on Norway's Nazi-occupied Lofoten Islands. And while the likes of Jack Singlaub yearned to find a way *into* the fighting, twenty-two-year-old Tommy Macpherson, a Scottish officer and future Jedburgh, now schemed to get himself *out of* a German prisoner-of-war camp.

These men typified the fifty or so officers ultimately recruited by SOE to fill the British quota for Operation Jedburgh. Four years of war had already handed them more than enough excitement. Tommy Macpherson, planning his escape, was about to get a little more.

In the prison camp, he carefully studied, through the barbed wire, the rabbit farm kept in the no-man's-land between the camp's two massive fences. If he could dig a tunnel under the first fence, he could attach himself to the prisoners who worked on the rabbit farm and then slip with a prisoner working party through the second fence. Afterward, he could sneak into the woods, toward freedom and away from the tedious inactivity that seemed so far to be the hallmark of his life.

Macpherson had been born a sickly child: a minister christened him at the family home in Inverness-shire, Scotland, within a week of his birth for fear of impending death. A childhood of mollycoddling followed the early illness, and Macpherson's family renewed the stifling when, at age nine, he contracted a near-fatal dose of diphtheria. To top things off, a broken bone in his teens led to a severe case of osteomyelitis. Macpherson spent nearly a year in bed, suffered a doctor repeatedly gouging away his flesh in order to remove infected marrow from his knee and hip, and lost the right to play rugby, his favorite game, when he finally returned to school.

It had taken the war to finally break him away from his cautious family and let him prove himself as capable as all the other boys. Now in Camp Thorn, a transit camp on the Polish-German border, planning his third escape attempt, Macpherson did not intend to waste more of his life in inactivity, waiting out, in a prison camp, the war that had begun for him back on August 28, 1939.

That day, a knock at the door to the Macpherson family home in Scotland revealed a postman with a telegram for Tommy. "Embody," said the one-word message. Macpherson had that summer won the rank of second lieutenant, leading a platoon of local boys in the Territorial Army, the equivalent of the United States' reserves. Orders now mobilized his unit. Four days later, after Hitler invaded Poland, Macpherson sat in his commanding officer's office and listened to Prime Minister Neville Chamberlain announce on the radio that Britain had declared war on Germany.

For the ten months of what would come to be called the Phony War for the lack of fighting, Macpherson's frustration grew as his regiment practiced ceremonial marching and antiquated battle strategies. In June 1940, when all hell broke loose and the Germans chased the British Expeditionary Force home from Dunkirk, Winston Churchill, in addition to forming the SOE, also established a butcher-and-bolt raiding force, known as the Commandos. A call went out for volunteers. Tommy Macpherson, unwilling to follow an idle childhood with an idle war, stepped forward.

After training in the cutthroat techniques of "combined operations," Macpherson started out in the guerrilla fighter's craft during raids on the coasts of Syria, Crete, and North Africa. Finally, in November 1941, he was chosen as an advance scout for the Commandos' famous attempt to kill Hitler's brilliant general Erwin Rommel at his headquarters in North Africa.

Macpherson and three comrades climbed out of a submarine and into canvas canoes, paddled across the Mediterranean to shore, made their reconnaissance for the raid, and the next day paddled out to the rendezvous point where the submarine should have surfaced to pick them up. Macpherson and his comrades spent a day floating on the Mediterranean in ebbing hope that their sub might appear. It didn't. They rowed to shore and decided to try to walk back through enemy territory to the British lines. Fifty or sixty miles later, while ambling along a main road in the pitch-dark night, Macpherson suddenly found himself surrounded by a company of one hundred Italian soldiers on bicycles. Amid a lot of shouting and gun pointing, Macpherson was captured on November 4, 1941, and sent to an "escape-proof" Italian POW camp in a converted medieval castle atop a rocky cliff.

It took nearly two years for Macpherson's first escape opportunity to present itself. In September 1943, he waited at a train station for transfer from Italy to a German prison camp. At the first moment of inattention from his guards, Macpherson sprinted up a mountainside and through a village. Shouts and gunfire followed. Bullets kicked up the dirt at Macpherson's feet, and an old peasant man digging a ditch got shot as Macpherson ran by. Yet Macpherson remained miraculously unwounded. At last, he turned a corner out of view of his guards and ran straight into the arms of a patrol of Germans coming down the hill. Macpherson's freedom had lasted only a matter of seconds.

Within a couple of weeks, at a transit camp in Spittal, Austria, Macpherson and two New Zealand officers inspected the ramshackle battlements and thought, "If we can't get out of here, we can't get out of anywhere." They saved their share of food tins and used them to bribe a couple of French POWs to let them have their work clothes. Macpherson and his two companions strolled out of the camp with a work party, separated from it as soon as they could, and hid in some bushes. They planned to head first for the Italian border, and then down through Italy toward the Allied lines.

Before long, they came to a village that had been garrisoned by Germans and was built into a mountainside so precipitous that the three had no choice but to walk through the village's center. They went one at a time. The first New Zealander made it through the village and out the other side. Macpherson and the second New Zealander's turn came next. They easily made it halfway through, but at 9:02 p.m., as curfew started, the Germans poured out of the pubs and found Macpherson and his buddy standing there. Where are your papers? the Germans shouted. Where are your papers?

The Germans rewarded Macpherson's ingenuity by tossing him and his New Zealand pal into a concrete box—too short to stand up in and too narrow to lie down in—at a Gestapo interrogation camp on the Polish–East Prussian border. After a cursory interrogation, the Gestapo sent them off to Camp Thorn. It was late September 1943, the same month that Franklin Canfield flew to the United States and his recruiters fanned out across American army bases to find prospective Jeds. Macpherson, meanwhile, was due to be sent from Camp Thorn to a secure, closely guarded camp. This was his last chance at escape.

Macpherson's fellow prisoners sold Red Cross cigarettes to the German guards to collect money for his escape attempt. They stole civilian clothes from the prison camp theater for him to hide under his uniform. They negotiated a lift for Macpherson with the Polish trucker who took away Camp Thorn's garbage. Macpherson and his New Zealand escape attempt partner, meanwhile, watched through the fence at the rabbits, impatiently biding their time.

Back in the States, Canfield's scouts had packed up and left Fort Benning happily clutching a sheaf of volunteer forms signed by paratroopers who had now grabbed a place in the war. One promising Jedburgh recruit, Major William Colby, had been stagnating like a benched second-stringer in the officer replacement pool at Camp Mackall. Colby, a Roosevelt Democrat who helped unionize gas station attendants while studying labor law at Columbia, wanted so badly to take his antifascist principles to war that he cheated on his paratroop physical's eye test and got caught (his vision, the doctor nevertheless concluded, was good enough to see the ground rushing toward him from eight hundred feet). Colby would later write that he "wanted to get involved in everything in that eager, urgent way that only a young college student can." His summer spent learning French in the Loire Valley after his junior year meant that Canfield's men would give him that chance.

Another Francophile parachutist raked up by the scouts, First Lieutenant William Dreux, was haunted by his Parisian childhood memories of the *gueules cassées,* the "broken mouths," whose World War I injuries had scarred their faces beyond recognition. Dreux was three and a half when the Great War broke out. He remembered, one Good Friday, when a German Big Bertha shell, fired from seventy-five miles away, massacred the congregation of his neighborhood church. He remembered the thousands of women who always dressed in black. The ghosts of the First World War's more than a million dead Frenchmen urged him to fight. Canfield's operation, he thought, offered the fastest route into the action.

Colby and Dreux awaited their transfer orders, as the desolate Singlaub surveyed the damage to his platoon at Fort Benning. All but the noncommissioned officers had been stripped away, new men had not yet been assigned, and retooling his command to battle-readiness would take at least eight weeks. Singlaub was devastated. Whole divisions had already shipped to Europe. Singlaub would miss the invasion.

He was not in a good state of mind when the regimental adjutant called for him.

"Shut the door," the adjutant told him. He began by warning Singlaub sternly never to repeat the contents of their discussion. Then the adjutant picked up a letter, written by an undisclosed author, and read its few sentences aloud to Singlaub: "We are looking for officers with language ability who want to volunteer for immediate overseas duty of a secret and highly hazardous nature. The work will be similar to commando operations." Singlaub waited for the details, but none were forthcoming. The adjutant put the paper down. "Well?"

It was a coin toss. If Singlaub stayed put, he had no way of knowing if he would ever get to fight. He could end up without battle experience, surplus to the army's requirements when the war finally ended. If he signed up for this operation, he might more quickly get to Europe. But he would be outside the normal chain of command and without a known route to any regular army commission. Singlaub, like Dreux and Colby, was also an idealist who, as President Woodrow Wilson proclaimed in World War I, wanted to help "make the world safe for democracy."

He told the adjutant he would like to join. The adjutant, surprised and irritated at the potential loss of a valued man, dispensed a few more precious details, had Singlaub fill out some forms, and dismissed him. When Canfield's scouts had been at Fort Benning, they had flagged Singlaub's file and left the letter behind for him.

Now Singlaub, like Lajeunesse, Baumgold, Bank, Colby, Dreux, and about a hundred other men, waited for further word. Franklin Canfield, meanwhile, had accomplished his task. The recruits still had the selection and training processes to go through, but if they survived them, Canfield had his men. What he might not have realized was that Operation Jedburgh was now more crucial than ever, for since Odette's arrest, things had only gotten worse for Allied secret operations in France.

Back in September, just as Canfield flew to Washington to start recruiting Jeds, the Sicherheitsdienst (SD) arrested a senior member of the French Resistance, André Grandclément, who worked in the SOE's Scientist network, which stretched from the Pyrenees to Paris and centered on Bordeaux. Scientist had been responsible for blowing up the main radio sender to Admiral Karl Dönitz's Atlantic U-boats and many other important sabotage operations. Grandclément at first refused to talk.

But then the Gestapo arrested his wife and, with a threat to her life as leverage, they convinced Grandclément that Stalin and Communism represented a worse evil than fascism and that the interests of France and Germany in fighting Stalin were the same. Grandclément led the Germans to 132 Resistance arms dumps, nearly 900 canisters of SOE-dropped supplies, and 300 members of the secret army.

In the north, Odette Sansom's captor, Hugo Bleicher, had arrested Roger Bardet, the deputy of the man, André Marsac, whose lost briefcase led to Odette's arrest. Bleicher gave Bardet the same options he had given Odette: cooperate or be turned over to the SD. After a stay in Fresnes, Bardet "escaped" in May 1943, returning to the Resistance as a hero. What they never suspected was that Bardet had been turned and the escape had been staged. Already, thirty-two thousand German agents and informants sniffed in and around Paris for SOE agents and *résistants*.

F Section approached the crucial new year of 1944 and the prospect of the Allied invasion in complete disarray. The betrayals by Grandclément and Bardet made Operation Jedburgh's reinforcement of the secret army in France all the more crucial while at the same time making the mission all the more deadly for the men who took part.

Canfield's recruits, of course, knew nothing of how Odette now languished in a Nazi death camp, nor of the terrible fates of other captured agents. Bill Dreux, the young lieutenant who grew up in World War I Paris, had asked a Canfield recruiter the meaning of the term "maximum casualties." "Don't let those words bother you too much," the recruiter told Dreux. It's "Army jargon."

# CHAPTER EIGHT
# SHRINKS WITH NOTEPADS

Jack Singlaub flipped his cabbie a coin and tugged his duffel bag onto the Constitution Avenue tarmac in Washington, D.C. A few blocks west of the Washington Monument, he stood outside the Munitions Building, a featureless, three-story labyrinth that stretched from Nineteenth Street to Twenty-first and bulged with bureaucrats. He, William Colby, Bill Dreux, Aaron Bank, Mason Starring, and about a hundred other of Canfield's possible Jedburgh recruits had begun arriving in Washington for the assessment and selection process.

Singlaub dragged his gear into the Munitions Building and through the long corridors until he found his way to the office of the army's Adjutant General (AG), where the prospective Jedburghs had been ordered to report. You actually volunteered for the OSS? one of the AG's Washington warriors said to an OSS volunteer named Roger Hall. You don't have a family to support, do you? OSS, the paper pushers seemed to imply, might as well have stood for Officers' Suicide Society.

Singlaub's turn came to have his orders processed in the AG's office, and he stood at attention before a rotund, sleepy, forty-year-old major in a crumpled uniform. Mimeographed orders were piled all over the major's desk. Boxes of personnel files overflowed. Singlaub suddenly worried that some army blunder meant that he had been transferred not to the crack unit he had been promised but to some sort of administrative section—the Office of Stenographic Services, say.

The major stamped Singlaub's papers. Singlaub heaved his duffel bag over his shoulder and lumbered toward the Potomac River. A threatening Great Dane blocked the entrance to Temporary Building Que, where Singlaub had been ordered to report next. The scent of malt hung heavily in the air.

In the OSS's earlier days, its various branches had tucked themselves into the corners of "tempo" buildings belonging to other military services. Decrepit wooden structures, some of the tempos had been intended for demolition since the end of the Civil War, when they had been hastily erected for temporary use. Que Building had been added to this neglected district of Washington when the OSS expansion exceeded its further welcome in other organizations' buildings. It sat on the corner of Twenty-third and Constitution, halfway between a navy mental hospital and a brewery. Singlaub strode quickly past the Great Dane.

He showed the guard his identity card and orders, had his name checked against Canfield's list, and was ushered in. Passing from the monochrome monotony of the conventional military into this inner sanctum of the OSS was like going from black and white to Technicolor. Among the arriving Jedburgh prospects, Bill Dreux, the lieutenant who had been haunted by the French casualties of World War I, was struck by the shades of people in every color of uniform rushing through the halls. They came from the many parts of the world where the OSS operated. Brits sported Sam Browne belts. Scots strode by in kilts. French trotted by in kepis—hats shaped like tin cans with visors. The occasional Far Easterner completed the mix with a turban. Jack Singlaub took a seat with a number of other men in the waiting area of Que's main hall.

An escort shuffled Singlaub from one Que Building room to the next. Every person he met seemed to have another form for him to fill out, and every form seemed to ask who should be notified in case of death.

In the OSS infirmary, Singlaub stuck out his tongue and took four deep breaths. Since the flat-footed and the four-eyed could resort to a hundred different tricks to fool the medic into a passing report, the OSS physical was more a test of initiative than a medical examination. Bill Dreux came in wearing his sunglasses, said he was sensitive to bright light, and read the eye chart perfectly, neglecting to mention that the lenses were corrective. Another guy simply tossed his failed medical in the nearest trash can. At his OSS induction interview, he fumbled for his pockets, felt disingenuously for the medical form, apologized for "losing" it, and recalled that it had been stamped with something like "fit for overseas duty."

Next, an OSS security officer asked Singlaub hard questions about his personal background—the answers would form the basis for a later home-town, door-to-door background check. The security officer tutored Singlaub in the ways of secrecy. You can say you belong to the Office of Strategic Services, but absolutely nothing more, he told Singlaub. You can have your baggage delivered to Que Building, but give out no other information on your whereabouts. Singlaub's family could be told only that he was stationed near the Capitol. Use a post office box as your mailing address.

Aaron Bank, the forty-year-old tactics instructor Canfield's men had dug up at Fort Polk, made the mistake of trying to elicit a hint about his coming assignment during his security indoctrination. "You'll get all that in your briefing," the officer warned Bank. "And whatever you learn about it is to be kept secret."

Finally, for each prospective Jedburgh came the main event of the day: the interview with Franklin Canfield and some of his colleagues from Special Operations' Western European Desk. From the more than one hundred officers Canfield and his recruiters had summoned to Washington, they began the process of paring down the group to around sixty. The largely inexperienced American finalists would have to make up in character and initiative what the British Jedburgh officers already had in experience.

Canfield grabbed Singlaub's file from a pile, and fired his questions. Singlaub breezed through the answers about willingness to parachute behind enemy lines and ability to carry out hazardous duty. As a paratrooper, he had already proved he would perform the unnatural act of throwing himself out of an airplane. He could run six miles in fifty minutes, and was as fit as any man. His only weakness, which he kept to himself, was whether his poor French skills would serve him well enough if he got stuck in occupied France. He cautiously inquired whether he would be working alone—maybe a partner would be a better linguist, he thought to himself. Then one of the interviewing majors took off his glasses, and attacked like a district attorney executing a cross-examination.

"Lieutenant, just what makes you think you are qualified for this kind of duty?"

He caught Singlaub off balance. "Sir, I'm a parachute infantry platoon leader, trained to lead men in small-unit action."

The major frowned. "I have read your file, Lieutenant. That's why you're here. Do you have anything else to say for yourself?"

"I broke my ankle so I volunteered to go to demolition school while my leg was healing. I finished parachute training with more qualifications than most. I guess you could say I have initiative."

The major wrote on a notepad, just far enough away so that Singlaub could not read it. He stared at Singlaub, and pursed his lips. "Report here at 1:00 pm tomorrow," the major finally said, and handed Singlaub the paper with a nearby address. But Singlaub's and the other officers' places in Canfield's secret operation were still far from secure.

A few miles north of the capital in Bethesda, Maryland, the Congressional Country Club's pool had been drained, a city block of tent hutments erected on its tennis courts, and a Douglas C-47 Dakota fuselage dumped on one of its fairways for parachute jump training. The club's stone-and-wood bar, complete with Ping-Pong and pool tables, had become an officers' lounge, the opulent dining room a mess hall, and the members' locker room the showers and latrine. Outside, at all times of day and night, khaki-clad members of the OSS chased over obstacle courses and practiced hand-to-hand combat. The peacetime playground of Washington's rich and powerful, the club had been taken over by the OSS in April 1943, made into a secret training base, and dubbed Area F.

Six months later, on this early October morning, the amplified sounds of reveille echoed through the PA system. Canfield's hundred or so officer recruits sprang out of their cots and quickly threw on their fatigues. In the previous days, the men had arrived at the club after their preliminary interviews at Que Building. They liked what they saw. The hacienda-like clubhouse, with its whitewashed walls and red-tiled roof, was a thousand times better than the sweltering, mosquito-infested mud holes from which they had come.

Gone were the days of swatting flies away before squatting over an outdoor hole in the ground, at least for now. The stringent two-week process of weeding out the weakest of the American Jedburgh candidates was about to begin.

The recruits padded anxiously past the crystal chandeliers, leather club chairs, and gilt-framed paintings toward the club's ballroom. Since they had still never heard the word "Jedburgh," nor had any real idea what the OSS had in mind for them, they looked forward to the briefing scheduled for first thing this morning.

William Colby sat alongside the rest of the exuberant men on folding chairs set amid the ballroom–cum–briefing room's blackboards. Quietly, he surveyed for the first time the motley mix of rough-edged toughs and large characters from the Ivy League—a fertile recruiting ground for the OSS that led to the nickname "Oh So Social." Among the men in the ballroom sat Hod Fuller, a Harvard man who had already sailed around the globe in a small sailboat and fought on Guadalcanal. René Dussaq braved danger on Hollywood sets as a stuntman and now wanted to star in his own real-life war movie. Douglas Bazata made himself famous for his firework displays as a paratroop demolition instructor and had a habit of calling anyone above the rank of colonel "sugar." The boisterous group all shared a lack of inhibition that compelled them to jump into things—like secret hazardous missions—without the faintest idea of what they were getting into.

A hush fell over the group as a colonel stared over his half-framed glasses. "You have been brought here," he said, "to evaluate your suitability for combat duty with Resistance groups in occupied areas." Three thousand miles away from any danger, many of these young officers reacted like boys whose dads had just told them they could go to judo camp. "I'm talking about guerilla warfare, espionage, sabotage," the colonel said. Some in his audience started to grin. "But if we are not completely satisfied with your potential, you will be reassigned to normal duties."

The colonel's stick worried these men at least as much as his carrot excited them. For Aaron Bank, reassignment would mean going back to being a schoolteacher to young conscripts. Colby would be thrown back to the war's sidelines in the officer replacement pool. Dreux would never get the chance to exorcise the French World War I ghosts that haunted him. The competition was on, and none of these men intended to lose.

For the next fourteen days, Colby and the rest stalked around Area F, fulfilling their "missions," evading the "Germans," and trying to notch up whatever kind of points the umpires counted. Each Canfield prospect took turns as leader of small "Resistance" groups, and tried to prove he was a better "guerrilla" than the next guy. Men in tweed jackets—psychologists—shadowed them everywhere and scribbled on clipboards. Ringers from the training staff posed as fellow Jedburgh prospects, joined the Resistance groups, and, as tests of the potential team leaders' characters, surreptitiously tried to derail the missions. Operation Jedburgh's success depended not only on the courage and daring of its warriors but on their ability to keep their cool when their squads of inexperienced European garage mechanics, bakers, and priests in the Resistance screwed up.

"A small bridge is being used by the enemy for a great deal of traffic," said the briefing given to Aaron Bank during his turn as leader. "Move out with your section and destroy the bridge." Bank carefully sneaked his group past the "guards" and painfully crawled toward the bridge when the shrill shouts of children shattered the countryside quiet: "There they are!" The neighborhood kids, eyes sharpened by the promise of candy from Area F's staff, made a game out of spotting the would-be guerrillas. Bank lost his temper. The shrinks frantically scribbled.

What would you do if a Resistance contact who had saved your life turned out to be a Gestapo spy? the shrinks demanded of the Jedburgh candidates. What would you do if you were captured and the Nazis threatened to shoot a schoolchild unless you gave up the location of your Resistance group? What if it were ten schoolchildren? With the Irish Americans, they tried to tease out anti-British patter. "Look," growled Jack Gildee, one of the officers, "I don't give a damn if we fight with them or against them. I just want to get over there and fight."

One at a time, men disappeared and bunks went empty as the selectors culled the group. After two weeks, Colby, Bank, Dreux, Singlaub, and the others who remained had crawled over every square foot of the golf course, "blown up" the caddies' hut a dozen times, and discovered their darkest childhood scenes in a hundred Rorschach inkblots. The driver of the morning milk truck got so accustomed to being ambushed that he delayed his arrival until he got the ready signal from a staff member. The one hundred or so lieutenants, captains, and majors now numbered only fifty-five.

Singlaub climbed the stairs of the old Public Health Service Building, not far from Que, and felt the familiar shortness of breath and tightness in the chest that went with hooking up the parachute static line and facing the open door of an airplane. On the second floor, he walked to the office of General William Donovan. This interview formed the final obstacle of the recruits' stateside selection process.

Singlaub came stiffly to attention before the general's desk. A colonel stood by its side and began to read Singlaub's military qualifications from his personnel file. Donovan nodded to him to desist.

"Lieutenant, you have an excellent training record. And you know how I feel about thorough training." Donovan looked at him with bright blue eyes.

"Yes, sir." Singlaub fixed his own eyes on the rows of ribbons on the general's chest.

"Well, I just want you to know that the combat we'll be in is a lot rougher than training. You do understand that, don't you?"

At Area F, the "explosives" did little more than pop. An overextended chokehold ended with a referee's whistle. The "German" guns fired blanks. None of the Jedburgh candidates had yet heard of Odette's ordeal, of the thousands of Resistance deaths, of the toenail and bathtub tortures, or the gallows that ultimately ended the lives of many captured Allied agents. Singlaub held the general's gaze, believing innocently that he understood the risks of his assignment.

"Yes, sir," Singlaub answered.

# PART III
# MAKING AGENTS

# CHAPTER NINE
# KILLING LESSONS

In the steamy heat of the Signal Corps' Camp Crowder in the Missouri Ozarks, an officer interrupted Private Bob Kehoe's radio practice and put a sealed official envelope into his hands. Like the envelopes that Canfield had dispatched to Lou Lajeunesse, Ted Baumgold, and the sixty-one other radio operators identified by his recruiters, the word RESTRICTED had been stamped in large letters across the seal. According to the instructions of the officer who delivered the envelope to Kehoe, he stuffed it in his pocket unopened, and ran to his barracks to pack his duffel and change into his street clothes. For security reasons, OSS recruits traveled as anonymous civilians.

Fending off nosy questions about his sudden departure from his buddies and superior officers, Kehoe made his way to the train station. Three months earlier, Kehoe had slowly chugged to Camp Crowder from the East Coast aboard a troop train crowded with sweaty young men in new uniforms. Now he settled into a plush, upholstered seat aboard a silver-service Pullman, alongside businessmen in double-breasted suits and beautiful women in expensive hats. He anxiously fingered the still-sealed envelope through his trouser fabric. The luxury and intrigue exhilarated not only Kehoe but all the other radiomen now surreptitiously making their way to the capital at the same time as Singlaub, Colby, Dreux, and the rest of the officers finished their stint at the Congressional Country Club.

In his hometown of New Brunswick, New Jersey, Kehoe had lost his mother after a long illness, eked out fifteen cents an hour picking berries to help his dad pay for her medical bills, and flopped at selling Remington typewriters door-to-door to pay for college science classes he hated. Kehoe had joined the army ahead of the draft, in part to exorcise his feelings of useless-ness. He did not think of himself as brave. In high school, he had washed out in sports and lost every fight. A good time meant hanging out with the debat-ing society or reading a history text. His senior-year yearbook named him most likely to become a lexicographer—Kehoe loved linguistics.

In more affluent times, he might have studied languages at college. Liberal arts degrees even from Ivy League schools, however, had won for his older sib-lings and their friends little but a place in line at the unemployment office. At Rutgers, Kehoe made the "sensible" choice, took science courses to prepare himself for medical school, and watched his motivation and grades nose-dive. Trapped between an academic passion from which he could earn no living and a living from which he could derive no passion, Kehoe felt useless and stuck. Then the Japanese bombed Pearl Harbor.

In the army, nineteen-year-old Kehoe could escape his career dilemma, fulfill his sense of patriotic duty, help rid the world of two terrible enemies, and banish the sense of dust-bowl desperation that he shared with much of his generation. Kehoe's father signed his underage son's enlistment papers, reluc-tantly consigning the last of his three boys to the war in the hope that the Sig-nal Corps would give Bob some skills. Three months after Kehoe shipped to Crowder and God knows how many hours of repetitious radio drills, he began to think he had made a terrible mistake. The old feeling of futility returned.

When Kehoe gave his name to a secretive major who had showed up tout-ing some "hazardous duty," Kehoe's army buddies sat him down at a mess table and told him the scheme sounded crazy. Kehoe worried more about the drudgery he wanted to get himself out of than the danger he might be getting himself into.

Now, a few weeks later, Kehoe's train steamed away from Camp Crowder. In the comfort of his Pullman, he finally tore open his envelope and read his orders: when his train pulled into Washington he was to report to the OSS. He arrived around the same time as Canfield's other bewildered enlisted men, and they all jumped in the back of an olive green truck. They took their turns shouting over the roar of the engine—"Where you from?"—and sized each other up like kids at a new school.

Kehoe met Bill Thompson, Baumgold met Lajeunesse, and the whole crew started talking. After a couple of hours, while the farms, fields, and forests of hilly northern Maryland glided by, the men had figured out that they were all radio operators, had at least two years of college under their belts, spoke some French, and had no real idea what they had volunteered for.

The trucks pulled onto a dirt road and bumped into the wooded hills. Plumes of dust rose behind them. The wheels finally squealed to a stop. Kehoe and the other radiomen jumped out.

When another convoy of trucks from the Congressional Country Club pulled up, Singlaub, Bank, Dreux, and the rest of the officers stepped down and faced Kehoe and the rest of the radio operators for the first time. Just over one hundred men milled about and muttered their self-conscious introductions in the middle of a small complex of log cabins, near Thurmont, Maryland. The Catoctin Mountains towered over them. Visible through the sun-dappled woods, long golden grass in clearings swayed in the wind. A creek bubbled nearby.

The camp was one of a number built by the Civilian Conservation Corps and Works Progress Administration on nine thousand acres acquired in 1935. It had previously been used by mountain farmers, charcoal burners, and timber merchants. In peacetime, the camps were intended for recreational use. After the war started, the OSS appropriated one camp and called it Area B. President Roosevelt appropriated another camp just up the road, called it Shangri-La, and used it for his weekend retreat, entertaining Winston Churchill, among others (President Dwight Eisenhower later renamed the retreat Camp David).

At the center of the complex, the largest of the cabins served as mess hall, classroom, and assembly area. It was here that the men selected by Canfield and his colleagues came together as one group for the first time, still with no clear sense of their operation, its purpose, or its name.

For now, a training instructor took his place in front of the officers. You have been brought to Area B, he told the group, to learn the skills of paramilitary or guerrilla warfare. "A guerrilla," he said, "is cut off from his army and fights in territory that is in the grip of a superior enemy. The guerrilla's main object is to inflict maximum damage to the enemy, and to force him to tie up regular troops who might otherwise be engaged in the main battle."

Guerrilla fighting, unlike conventional warfare, the instructor emphasized, had nothing to do with overwhelming an enemy to win and hold territory. That job belonged to the regular soldier. Instead, paramilitaries banded together in groups of twenty to thirty and engaged in lethal, lightning attacks on much larger troop formations, sometimes numbering in the thousands. The survival of the paramilitary units the recruits would be part of depended not on fighting a good defense—its enemy would always overwhelm it—but on executing a rapid retreat. The guerrilla's success depended on surprise, and his survival depended on stealth. Much of what would save these men's lives in the regular army would get them killed as a paramilitary.

In the coming seven weeks or so, the Area B instructor announced, Singlaub, Dreux, Lajeunesse, Thompson, and the rest would have to unlearn the bad habits of good soldiers and replace them with the animal instincts and survival skills of the guerrilla. For the officers, time for inkblots and questions about childhoods was over. For the radiomen, the nonstop tapping on Morse keys had ended. And for Bob Kehoe, that old feeling of futility was gone.

A five-o'clock reveille jolted Lou Lajeunesse and his exhausted chums out of bed. Each day, before taking a single gulp of coffee, they raced seven miles, competed to trump each other's push-up and pull-up records, and shimmied up ropes, all while wearing weighted backpacks. The gentle-spirited Lajeunesse miraculously found himself sprinting off two-story platforms and somersaulting into sandpits to practice safe landings.

A long, treacherous course of fifty obstacles weaved precariously back and forth across a creek, and the radio operator Dick Franklin regularly watched his comrades get dumped into the water or onto the rocks below. Not until the end of each early-morning exercise misery did the Jeds get a leisurely hour to wolf down an all-you-can-eat breakfast. The good news, at least, was that Area B meals made army chow look like dog food. The bulls got well fed before the slaughter, Bob Kehoe joked.

Next on the morning's schedule, Canfield's posse crowded into the big cabin for the day's lecture. The instructor scrawled on the blackboard; his students scratched notes about surviving among an enemy that outnumbered them many thousands to one. They learned to camouflage their shelters with tree branches, catch trout with their bare hands, and dig cooking fires deep enough in the ground so that the enemy could not spot the flames. They crammed their memories with everything from how to set bone fractures with homemade splints and extract bullets with bayonets to how to read maps and use compasses. After only a couple of hours in the big cabin, they had had enough of the dense bookwork and looked forward to the practical lessons.

Their afternoons outdoors often began at the blasting area, where Jack

Singlaub got appointed assistant instructor. In this pyromaniac's playground, he and the rest of the boys got to play with everything from dynamite to C2 plastic explosive. Under the tutelage of senior demolitions wizard Larry Swank, a paratroop officer who would himself become a Jedburgh, they learned to conjure both the instantaneous, sharp TNT bangs that punctured metal and the slower, sizzling black powder pops that shattered wood. They practiced designing bombs to blow up bridges, roads, railroads, canals, dams, tunnels, water tanks, machine-gun emplacements, and more. When Swank let them loose on old cars and abandoned shacks, they acted like mischievous teenagers with a brick of firecrackers on the Fourth of July. Walk carefully away from a lit fuse—*never* run or you might fall, Swank warned them. Remember not to wire explosives to an electrical blasting circuit during a lightning storm, he said.

Weapons instruction by an eccentric Free French officer, complete with his cake tin–like kepi and interesting accent, took another outdoor slot on the Jeds' Area B syllabus. The Frenchman had the appalling habit of wielding his Thompson submachine gun as an orchestra conductor wielded a baton. With the muzzle dangerously pointed in their direction, the status of the gun's safety catch unknown, and the Frenchman's finger covering the trigger, Dick Franklin and the more jumpy of the future Jeds dove for the ground. "Pairsonally, I dun't geef a dem," the Frenchman replied disdainfully, and the still-standing Jeds laughed in spasms.

With fascination, they absorbed the Frenchman's depth of expertise as he deftly demonstrated the operation, disassembly, cleaning, repair, and reassembly of each of the British, French, and German weapons, from both World War II and World War I, that they might find or steal in Europe. The Frenchman taught them the dull, step-by-step, by-the-book techniques and the more exciting, expedient methods of the swashbuckler.

When a machine gun jammed, radio operator Bill Thompson watched horrified as the crazy Frenchman placed it on a tree stump, bashed it with a sledgehammer, and when it fired, said pridefully that only a French-made weapon could be so easily cleared. Everyone laughed.

After a slug lodged itself in the barrel of a French Lebel 9mm submachine gun, the Frenchman pried a bullet from its brass casing, stuffed a crumpled cigarette in its place, and loaded the "tobacco bullet" into the gun. The recruits backed away, fearing an explosion, and took cover. Dick Franklin again found himself cowering on the ground. Peeking from behind their boulders and tree trunks, they watched the Frenchman nonchalantly pull the trigger, heard a pop, and saw the jammed slug plop out of the barrel. The Frenchman looked around expecting applause or congratulations, but the groups instead looked at him as if he were a lunatic. About that, the Frenchman did not "geef a dem" either.

Another eccentric genius at Area B, a former assistant commissioner from the police force in Shanghai, the reputed home to the world's toughest criminals, taught bare-handed killing and close-quarters weapons combat. Major William Fairbairn, a Brit, habitually wore a collar of needle-sharp spikes to prevent being strangled. The self-defense zealot had developed a system of sixteen lethal maneuvers to silently slay or maim an opponent. His somewhat sadistic bent for demonstrating his system soon had a Jed writhing in pain on the ground. Poor Dick Franklin found Fairbairn's index finger yanking at the corner of his mouth until he thought his lips would tear off. From then on, Franklin kept one eye on whatever Fairbairn was teaching, and another on making sure he never got close to him.

The Jeds learned to poke at the eyes, tear at the face, claw at the ears, and knee in the groin. If you hope to survive, Fairbairn told them, you must discard the boxing rules of gentlemen and take up the nasty scrapping of street fighters. "It is a matter of kill or be killed," he said. If you can't disembowel your enemy, at least smash his windpipe. During a raid, the men understood, there could be no hesitation about throwing an arm around a sentry's neck, driving a knife into his kidneys, and "stirring like hell." If the sentry got off a shot, the enemy's main force would swarm out of its hive, the mission would fail, and the Jedburghs would be slaughtered.

At other Area B pit stops, the prospective Jeds learned to set up a sentry system around their command posts, to move across country under the cover of hedges and ditches, to be the first to fire in a close-quarters gun battle even at the expense of accuracy, to give even more attention to planning retreats than attacks, and, of course, to run like hell. They toiled through long hard days that rarely ended before the autumn sun dropped from the sky, and suffered physical agony and mental exhaustion. They grunted and panted and screamed four-letter gripes. They counted off the last few obstacles on their morning course with a protest in unison—"Forty-eight . . . Forty-nine . . . Fifty . . . SOME SHIT!"

Ambushing an enemy column, sinking a ship, or destroying an air force runway now seemed like a routine part of an exciting life's work. The gung-ho

young warriors came to believe that they would make a meaningful contribution to the war, though this preliminary training here in the United States was
only the beginning. There would be much more to do in England, both for
the prospective Jeds and for their superiors like Franklin Canfield. After all,
Jedburgh's success depended not only on the selection and training of its operatives but on detailed planning and the preparation of a complicated infra-
structure to support the operation.

Over in England, the organization of a training establishment had yet to
be completed for the time when the three-hundred-strong force of American,
British, and French Jedburghs finally assembled. Construction still continued
on the brand-new communications center that would process Jedburgh team
radio transmissions from France. Extra airplanes had to be obtained to drop
the Jeds and their supplies. A new packing station would be required to prepare weapons and ammunition for parachuting to the Resistance with whom
the Jedburghs would work. And, of course, careful liaison with the main
armies had to be established to ensure that the actions of the Jedburghs and
their Resistance groups provided the maximum support to the invasion.

As the liberation of Europe grew closer and closer, there was much work
to be done by Canfield and the rest of the shadow chiefs at the SOE and OSS.
On November 28, 1943, satisfied that he had assembled a group of officers and
enlisted radio operators he could proudly recommend as Jedburghs, Canfield
climbed on an airplane to assist in the massive preparations under way in England, leaving his recruits to their preliminary training at Area B. For them,
reality was about to descend.

## CHAPTER TEN

# GIVE HER A RING
# AND SAY GOOD-BYE

The Catoctin Mountains became a patchwork of golds, reds, and yellows. The season's first frost arrived. The Jeds began stoking their woodstoves. One day, not too long after Canfield left for England, the Jeds assembled in the big cabin, and an officer announced a few days of furlough for the entire group. Cheers went up. Say good-bye to your families, the officer told them; you won't be seeing them for a long time. The cheering quickly died down.

Bob Kehoe caught the train for New Brunswick to see his dad. Now back in the house his father built, Kehoe broke the news that he would soon be shipping overseas. Why so soon? his dad wanted to know.

Kehoe's two older brothers had no travel orders, and they had been in the army twice as long. Kehoe could only shrug. When his father jumped to the conclusion that Kehoe would be stationed at a communications base in England, Kehoe bit his lip and said nothing. He did the kind thing by not frightening his father with talk of a secret assignment, but he felt like a liar and it saddened him to mislead his dad. For the first time since he volunteered at Camp Crowder, Kehoe worried that he might never see his father again.

Up in Connecticut, Lucien Lajeunesse's mother refused to accept his vague answers about his coming departure. She pried and pried, and finally became hysterical when Lou could only refuse her an answer. If that weren't upsetting enough, Lou's plans to propose to his girlfriend had been frustrated by not being able to get a ring in time. It was possible, then, that Lajeunesse might live and die without a girl ever wearing his ring.

Frank Hanson, another radio operator infected by gallows wedding fever, married his girl on his last day of leave but remained, as his fellow Jeds would call him, the "only married virgin living in captivity." Even Jack Singlaub, having determined that Mary's college boyfriend was now just a friend, finally got down on one knee. In a rush and overcome by nerves, he had unconsciously walked Mary into Washington Zoo, summoned his courage, and proposed before an audience of monkeys and apes. In almost the next breath, Singlaub had to tell his new fiancée that he did not know when he would see her again. Back in New Jersey, Bob Kehoe left for the train in a last-minute rush to avoid an emotional farewell with his dad.

Back at Area B, a white blanket of snow covered the mountains. Like Kehoe and Lajeunesse, none of the other Jeds had been able to be honest with their families. They had neither expressed their fears nor had the opportunity to be comforted about them. Now feeling estranged and disconnected from their relatives, the Jeds traipsed through the freezing woods, wearing army footwear that leaked and did little to warm their feet. Several times a day, like a cruel joke, the orderly room loudspeaker blared Bing Crosby singing "I'll Be Home for Christmas." One night, one of the lieutenants broke in and smashed the record. Like the season, the mood at Area B had cooled.

It was mid-December 1943. Italy had long surrendered, and the Allies had chased the Germans up the Italian peninsula from the Salerno beachhead. But the only battle the Jeds had seen was on the cinema newsreels. After all this work, they began to wonder, would they even get into the fight before the war ended? Some of them had detected, too, that certain Area B instructors taught not from experience but straight out of a specially prepared handbook. "This is not the real McCoy," Aaron Bank said to anyone who would listen. Morale plummeted.

Radio operator Lou Goddard, from Fountain City, Tennessee, wrote a couple of disturbing letters home that dwelled on his death. "I thought I would drop you a line and let you know that I am still alive *as yet*," he said in one note. "We were supposed to make our wills, but I didn't have anything to put in one," he said in another.

After chilly mornings in the big cabin and frostbitten afternoons on the firing range, the Jeds began receiving orders to assemble in their dress uniforms for inspection by deskbound generals from the War Department. Washington dignitaries had begun to make sport of dropping by Area B to take a look at Wild Bill Donovan's cutthroats and proclaim their country's pride in them. It did not please the Jeds that, on top of everything else, such chickenshit army routines had begun to reappear.

Last in this series of unwelcome visitors came William Stephenson, a senior British agent with the code name Intrepid. He had been handpicked by Churchill to help bring the United States into the war and had helped Donovan write the memo that resulted in Roosevelt's establishing the OSS. Stephenson's visit was one too many for the Jeds. In the middle of his talk, one of them suddenly initiated their now traditional obstacle course battle cry. "Forty-eight," the Jed shouted. "Forty-nine," called someone else. A last voice cried, "Fifty." Then more than one hundred men shouted in unison, "SOME SHIT!" Stephenson left in disgust.

Lou Goddard's father, meanwhile, had sensed his son's turmoil from his letters. He wrote to his boy, "Let me remind you that there are times when a strong man should not be ashamed to cry."

About ten days before Christmas, the officers suddenly climbed into trucks and motored away. A couple of days later, the radio operators got their own orders to pack their duffels and fall out for one final Area B roll call. They bade farewell to the Maryland hills, and a few hours' train ride landed them in the massive debarkation base at Fort Hamilton, Brooklyn, a straight shot across the Verrazano Narrows from Lou Lajeunesse's former station at Fort Wadsworth.

Along with many thousands of other men waiting for their ships to depart, the Jed radio operators took quarters in one of the row after row of ramshackle barracks. The Transporation Corps' grinding bureaucracy welcomed them with a morning of mind-numbing films: what to expect from life on a troopship, how to climb down its side if it sank, how to contact the post chaplain, and why every soldier should increase his war bond allotment. The radiomen shifted and shuffled on uncomfortable benches, until finally, day passes in hand, they rushed the fort's gate.

Most of them climbed into waiting taxis and, for thirty-five cents, eagerly rode into Manhattan for their first visit to the Broadway lights, but not Dick Franklin, who had lived in Manhattan. Instead Franklin counted about a thousand steps down a Brooklyn street. He rang the doorbell, waited, and, when the door opened, threw himself into the waiting arms of his wife. A year or so earlier, he and Susie had eloped to Hoboken City Hall only hours before he left for the army.

For the next few days, while the Franklins played honeymoon, the rest of the radio operators raised hell. They got thrown out of a Greenwich Village club for trying to drop their lit cigarettes down a large woman's cleavage. One got arrested by MPs after he drunkenly drew his fighting knife in a diner to cut his hamburger in two. During nighttime curfew, a whole group jumped the fort fence, were apprehended in a Brooklyn bar, and brought back to base under guard. The onetime farm boys and academic geeks had become good-natured hooligans.

Finally, after a week's troublemaking, they were restricted to base and told to control their compulsion to jump fences and to keep their duffels packed and zipped on the ends of their bunks.

Under cover of darkness, on the evening of December 23, 1943, the Jed radiomen loaded onto a bus, jumped off at a Manhattan dock, and filed with thousands of others up the gangways of the *Queen Mary,* a British luxury liner converted to troopship. The *Queen Mary* dropped her lines, and on a cold Christmas Eve morning, the New York tugs nudged her out of the harbor.

A winter storm soon blew up and stirred the Atlantic into a fury. To avoid torpedoes, the *Queen Mary* had to make random sharp turns, as often as four times an hour. The stabilizing gyros, which had once made the cruise ship so comfortable for passengers, had been disabled to allow the necessary maneuverability. The result was that the *Queen Mary* rode the huge, wind-driven swells like an oversize Coney Island roller coaster.

Since their orders stipulated that they could be assigned no menial work, the Jed radiomen were given black armbands and made MPs. In a stroke of great luck, Dick Franklin found himself guarding the brig. Down in the bowels of the ship, just above the waterline, it was cool, with a private spic-and-span head and shower and a porthole to bring in fresh air. One cell was occupied by a Brit who had bitten off a nurse's nipple when she refused his advances. Another held a man who had been condemned to death for jumping ship. The third cell was empty.

Franklin retrieved his toothbrush and sleeping bag from the former gift shop and moved in. He left only once to go to the galley. A GI carried a pan of porridge, puked in it, and set it down on Franklin's table, complete with ladle. For the rest of the voyage, Franklin sent his prisoners to purchase turkey sandwiches on the black market from the British sailors.

Bob Kehoe, meanwhile, was spared his MP duties because none of the *Queen Mary* soldiers had the energy to cause any trouble. Instead he acted as a kind of gymnast's spotter, helping to keep a division's worth of men upright as they filed continuously through the galley for two daily meals. Kehoe stationed himself at the end of the mess line, grabbed the belt of the next soldier carrying his tray, and tried to keep him from falling into the disgusting, three-inch-deep throw-up soup at their feet. One out of ten of his charges ended up soaked in the gore, gagging in revulsion.

Meanwhile, around the ship, lookouts in long gray overcoats, struggling for balance, kept a watchful eye through their binoculars. After a couple of days, the Jeds felt the tension go through the crew as the blimp floating overhead, which had been scanning for U-boats, lumbered around in a U-turn and headed for home. Theoretically, the *Queen Mary* forged forward fast enough to avoid the German submarines, and so sailed unescorted and unprotected. But with her load of fifteen thousand men, the Jeds knew, the zealous Nazi U-boat captains would do their best.

On the same day the Jedburgh radio operators first steamed out of New York Harbor, millions of anxious listeners around the world twiddled their radio knobs through the crackling static to tune in to President Roosevelt's Christmas Eve fireside chat. It would be his first radio address since returning from the Allied strategy conference in Tehran, where he had met again with Prime Minister Churchill and, for the first time, with Marshal Stalin. Nothing had been announced yet, but in the cinemas, the newsreel announcers had speculated that the three great leaders had decided the date for the final, gigantic confrontation with Hitler on his own doorstep—the Allied attack on continental Europe.

The time of the broadcast had been carefully chosen to reach concerned citizens of the world everywhere. The second hand ticked to the appointed moment, and Roosevelt took his seat behind the huge radio microphone at his home in Hyde Park, New York. It was afternoon in the United States, evening in Britain, and morning in the Pacific.

"My friends," the president began, "I have just returned from conferring with the leaders of Britain and Russia on plans for stepping up our successful attacks on our enemies." Entire ships' complements, like that of the *Queen Mary,* aboard which the Jed radiomen had begun their journey, went quiet. Christmas Eve parties came to a standstill.

"We agreed on every point concerned with the launching of a gigantic attack upon Germany," the president continued. The Russian army would maintain its "stern offensives" on Germany's eastern front. The Allied armies in Italy and Africa would "bring relentless pressure" from the south. But the era of weakening the Third Reich by wounding it at its extremities had passed, the Allies had finally agreed. The time for the stab at the heart had come at last. "The encirclement will be complete as great American and British forces attack from other points on the compass."

To the hundreds of thousands of Americans who had crowded into Britain through the Glasgow and Liverpool ports, to the American Jed officers in Scotland, and to the radio operators being tossed around by the Atlantic, the words "from other points on the compass" had perfect clarity. They meant from the north, from Britain. The soldiers of the United States, Britain, Canada, and elsewhere would soon pour across the Channel and onto the beaches of France. The invasion was on.

To appoint the leader of this great invasion, Roosevelt, on his way home from the Tehran Conference, had briefly touched down in his plane at Tunis Airport. Waiting to greet him on the tarmac was General Dwight Eisenhower, the kindly faced, bald-headed Kansan who had led the American troops in the victorious Allied invasions in North Africa, Sicily, and Italy. Roosevelt climbed into the back of a staff car with Eisenhower, turned to him, and said simply: "Well, Ike, you are going to command Overlord." Roosevelt announced Eisenhower's appointment as supreme commander near the end of the fireside chat.

To Ike's men who would spearhead the attack, to the nearly four million Americans already serving overseas, and to the rest of the ten million soldiers in the United States' armed services, President Roosevelt added: "In our hearts are prayers for you and all your comrades in arms who fight to rid the world of evil. We ask God's blessing upon you—upon your fathers and mothers, and wives and children—all your loved ones at home."

It was a kind sentiment that must have warmed many mothers' hearts. Soldiers around the world—including the American Jed officers who had just steamed into the port of Glasgow, the radio officers on the *Queen Mary,* and their French and British Jedburgh counterparts—now knew what the next act in this great world drama would be. And still in the dark about their own part, the Jeds—like every other soldier—wondered about only one thing: what will happen to me?

# CHAPTER ELEVEN

# HAPPY NEW YEAR!

P art of the romance of war to a young man is the idea that if he puts himself in extreme circumstances, the hero in him will emerge, along with a transcendent sense of purpose. With the Jeds' inflated sense of themselves, they were perhaps even more disheartened than other soldiers to discover that much of war's suffering was utterly meaningless.

During the *Queen Mary*'s turbulent voyage, radio operator Roger Pierre lost fourteen pounds, most of it in vomit. Another Jed got tossed out of his bunk, slammed into the opposite wall, and broke his nose and teeth. In the "heads," men trying to stand at the thirty-foot urinals fell backward while the fouled water poured over them. Incapacitated, some lay in the filth, spewing waste from both ends of their bodies, and begged for death. The decks on the rest of the ship swilled inches deep with orange vomit after a meal that included boiled apricots. In the face of other men's sickness and despair, Bob Kehoe finally descended into his own loneliness and fear for his future.

Traveling aboard the *Queen Mary*'s sister ship, the *Queen Elizabeth*, experiencing not a whisper of the storm, but overwhelmed by discomforting quietude, Jack Singlaub, bored to death by his magazines, pined for his new fiancée, Mary. "I think I miss her more than I have ever missed anyone," he wrote home to his mother and father. Other Jeds, looking for anything to keep them busy, joined poker games they knew they would lose to fellow Jedburgh and card shark Douglas Bazata.

Idleness among the Jed officers generated a thousand different certain-death scenarios in their minds, and Bill Dreux and his cabinmates began to wonder why the hell they had gotten themselves into this "hazardous duty."

Dreux remembered what a psychiatrist friend had told him. "He was convinced that anyone who volunteered was around the bend," Dreux said to his pals.

"That doesn't get to the bottom of it," one replied. "Maybe we're all glory hunters. Or some guys might have a subconscious death wish."

A third had heard enough. "For Christ's sake, knock it off," he said. They all knew better than to dwell on things. Putting the future out of their minds was the Jedburghs' only defense.

On the day before Christmas Eve, the officers' ship splashed her anchor into the Firth. In the cold drizzle, the Jeds pressed against the rails of the midship, their grim boyish faces balanced atop their orange life preservers, and surveyed the Luftwaffe's destruction of the Glasgow docks. The tugs nudged the *Queen Elizabeth* toward the docks. The Jeds looked out over soot-covered piles of bombed-out rubble, between what warehouses still stood, crumbling over the quays and into the water. The tangled metal of broken cranes hung in the air like the legs of giant dead spiders. Among the detritus milled tens of thousands of soldiers arriving from around the world. Sikhs in turbans, Canadians in black berets, and others, many of whom had already fought in Africa and Italy, poured down the troopship gangways in conveyor-belt fashion.

An OSS training officer, Cyrus Manierre, led the Jedburghs off the ship and to a dockside warehouse converted to a staging area. The training base that had been acquired for Operation Jedburgh had not yet been completed. Manierre had no idea, he admitted, where the Jedburgh officers were supposed to go. "Everything is snafu," the demoralized Jeds shouted at him. Snafu, an army acronym, meant "situation normal all fucked up." Manierre, who would himself become a Jed (and like Odette Sansom end up getting arrested by the Nazis), phoned headquarters in London for instructions and was told the Jeds could just damn well sit still and wait. "Well, boys," he told them when they got ashore and into a temporary barracks, "here we are and here we are going to stay."

What the Jed officers had yet to realize was that in the coming weeks they would be shuffled from SOE training base to training base in a futile effort to keep them busy until their own training area was finally ready. They were stuck in the bureaucracy they thought they had escaped. Instead of being in the fast lane to battle, since the main forces now geared up in earnest for Overlord, they might well have found themselves in the slow one.

One week later, the radio operators also docked in Glasgow and piled off the *Queen Mary*. Whatever the situation with getting into battle, they, at least, were all smiles. Their hellish voyage was over at last. Able to eat for the first time in days, they wolfed down doughnut after doughnut handed to them by Red Cross ladies waiting on the piers. The radiomen jammed themselves into their compartment on a train. As it chugged slowly past backyards crisscrossed with Glasgow's laundry, they smiled tiredly at the open windows crowded with waving and cheering women. When the train arrived at its destination, Operation Jedburgh's American and British radio operators would finally meet.

Three months earlier, in early October 1943, the SOE had installed the fifty or so British wireless operators at a property called Countess Gardens, outside Henley-on-Thames, forty miles west of London. Since then, while Kehoe, Lajeunesse, Franklin, and the rest of the American radio operators trained across the Atlantic at Area B, the British radiomen had heaved themselves out of bed and quick-marched the ten minutes through the early-morning mist to Fawley Court, the stately seventeenth-century home on the banks of the Thames that housed the SOE's Special Training School 54 (STS 54). The British radio operators, largely recruited from the Royal Armoured Corps, had worked their butts off getting their Morse code speeds up to Jedburgh's required fifteen words a minute.

After all the hard work, they thought they deserved, tonight, on New Year's Eve, to be excitedly dressing themselves up for an evening of drunken debauchery with their girlfriends, young women of the First Aid Nursing Yeomanry (FANYs), who were also stationed at Fawley Court. Instead, the crew had pulled hard duty hosting, along with the FANYs, a party for the group of arriving American radiomen—Bob Kehoe and the others.

Translated into real life, this meant they would have to nod and chat politely, sip barely spiked fruit punch from quaint glass cups, and pretend not to notice while a bunch of loudmouthed Yanks tried to steal their girls. The war sometimes seemed to treat young British men worse than it treated Americans.

British radio operator Arthur Brown, for example, had been fourteen on that first day of September 1939, when Hitler roared his panzer tanks into Poland. Like many of his soon-to-be American colleagues, he thought war might be fun. But when the Battle of Britain's dogfights began in the autumn of 1940, Brown sneaked, with his classmates, to the crash site of a German fighter plane. By the side of the crash crater, among the flames and the smoke,

Brown scavenged for mementos and picked up what looked like a pear with the top bitten off. "This Jerry obviously came to stay," Brown joked to his pals, "he's brought his lunch with him." Suddenly Brown realized that he held, not a pear, but a piece of thighbone. A nauseous feeling overwhelmed him. Brown slipped quietly away and prayed while he buried the German pilot's body part. It had taken hardly any time at all for reality to dispel the cartoon image of war the boys of Britain had once entertained.

That September, the Luftwaffe began pounding London and other British cities and carpeting them with flame. In London, radio operator Norman Smith watched helplessly each morning as queues of women and children filed out of the tube stations, where they had gone for shelter, only to find their homes flattened and possessions burned. In Swansea, south Wales, Glyn Loosemore, another British Jed radioman, ran around the burning city frantically trying to help, but sprawling bodies lay dead on the pavements. The terrible smell of burning and the clinking sounds of thousands of people sweeping broken glass from the streets overtook Britain.

Sixty thousand civilians had their lives taken by Hitler's bombs. Innocent children were killed and maimed. Arthur Brown's older brother was captured in the fighting. Jed radio operator Gordon Tack's father was machine-gunned in his lifeboat after his ship was torpedoed. The war killed at random. The world seemed neither rational nor fair. By the time Glyn Loosemore was asked by his SOE interviewers what he planned to do after the war, he answered, "I do not expect that question to arise."

The American radio operators had complained after a rough, one-week sea voyage. By the time they arrived at Henley, their British counterparts had watched their country and families suffer four years of war. Brown and his chums could be excused for pouring out of their huts glumly to make their way to Fawley Court for the so-called party. Mixing different nationalities, cultures, and experiences was one of the dangers of attempting a tripartite operation like Jedburgh.

The American and British radiomen filed into the ballroom and the introductions began. The contrast was stark. The Yanks pranced around in their fancy dress uniforms with the classy lapels, while the Brits slummed it in the coarse woolen battle dress that made them look like coal miners. The Americans smelled all fresh with their newfangled "deodorant." The Brits smelled of body odor because soap had been rationed. The Yanks handed out the high-quality cigarettes the Brits could no longer get hold of, and the FANYs crowded around. The Brits gritted their teeth when their girlfriends laughed a little too hard at the foreigners' jokes.

"You know what they say about British girls' knickers," British soldiers of the time would mutter. "One Yank and they're off."

To be fair, Kehoe, Franklin, Lajeunesse, and the rest of the American boys who made such fast work of chatting up the Brits' girlfriends had grievances of their own. They discovered, in their new digs, plywood bunks that sagged in the middle, straw-filled burlap sacks that pretended to be mattresses, a single coal stove that made a sorry excuse for heating, and an outdoor cold-water pipe sticking out of a wall in, of all things, a stable yard that was supposed to suffice for a shower. A rude introduction to British army rations had come in the form of a greasy stew that was light on meat and heavy on tasteless, over-cooked vegetables like parsnips and turnips. The Americans did not realize that by complaining they rubbed the Brits' noses in conditions they had suf-fered since the war began.

However, though the American radio operators may never have suffered a Luftwaffe attack, the British radio operators had never been shipped three thousand miles from home. When you have hardly been farther than a cousin's house in the next town, arriving in a country where the people drive on the wrong side of the road, speak in an unintelligible brogue, and drink their beer warm comes as a terrible shock. The American radiomen were nervous and disoriented. Unfortunately, they had a way of expressing it that did not endear them to Brown or the rest of his chums.

Still, as the hours passed, the Brits gathered around a piano, began a sing-along, and invited Kehoe and the rest to join in. They taught the Yanks old standards like "The White Cliffs of Dover." The countdown to twelve o'clock began and the group held hands in a circle—boy, girl, boy, girl—a happy bunch of teenagers and early-twenty-year-olds singing "Auld Lang Syne." At the twelfth stroke, a cheer went up, and each girl turned to the boy next to her, whether British or American, pulled him toward her, and kissed him full on the lips.

It was a British custom that brought in the New Year, meant only to last an exhilarating but polite ten or fifteen seconds. As Brown and his friends let go of the girls they embraced, the Yanks, unfamiliar with the tradition, carried on in a vulgar frenzy. The Americans liked the tradition so much that they decided to exercise it with not one but every girl in the room. The party soon broke up. If, as the shadow chiefs believed, the success of Operation Jedburgh depended on how the Brits and the Americans got along, things had not started well.

## CHAPTER TWELVE
# CLOSE TO MUTINY

A few hundred miles north, on the rugged western coast of Scotland, Jack Singlaub and a group of about twenty American Jed officers slogged mile after mile over the hills, dragging along their heavy rucksacks, weapons, and ammunition. The group scrambled with the SOE instructors down a crevice between two rock-strewn ridges. They sank, dispirited and fatigued, ankle deep into the half-frozen bog. Singlaub, whose stomach had been hurting, held his side.

"What a nasty place this would be to be caught in a mortar barrage," one of the Scottish SOE instructors mused mischievously. He pulled a handkerchief from his pocket and waved it in the air as a signal to some unseen colleagues. Suddenly, the dangerous whistling through the air of mortar shells began. The rounds slammed into the hillside above the group. Shards of rock and frozen mud bounced off Singlaub's helmet.

The salvo rained down in loud thumps, moving closer and closer, like a giant's thunderous footsteps. Singlaub and his exhausted friends stood stunned in the shower of pebbles and ice. Hadn't they done enough today? "Well chaps," the instructor shouted, "I shouldn't stooge around here if I were you."

Singlaub dashed up the slope and flopped on his back into the wet heather, taking what cover he could behind a small boulder. Bill Pietsch, a graduate of West Point, threw himself behind another boulder nearby. The pounding explosions moved uncomfortably near.

"Let's get the hell out of here, Jack," Pietsch shouted over the din.

Singlaub rolled over onto his chest to get up. A sudden enormous clang and flash of bright light blinded and deafened him. A mortar had detonated right in the spot where Singlaub had been lying, beside the boulder. He sprinted, terrified, up the hill, stomach pains forgotten. His heart thudded in his ears. Pietsch, though he had been a cross-country champ at West Point, lagged far behind.

This was no Boy Scout camp. It was an SOE paramilitary school that had prepared hundreds of agents already in the occupied territories to engage in and survive lethal encounters with the highly experienced Nazi forces. The training here was deadly serious.

Singlaub and the rest of the American Jed officers had arrived in the Arisaig district of Scotland's West Highlands on Christmas Eve, the same day Roosevelt had announced the impending invasion of Europe, to learn the techniques of the Commando-style "butcher and bolt" raid. The officers had been split into three groups and sent to three of the ten hunting lodges that made up the SOE's paramilitary school.

At Bill Dreux's lodge, the Jeds jolted awake each morning when a bagpiper in full regalia marched up and down the corridors, blowing full blast. A rugged little sergeant major, also in a kilt, then escorted Dreux's group through the predawn darkness on a two-mile run up and down the mountain roads. "Come along now, gentlemen, a little faster if you please. Righto!" After all, the Jeds would have to count on their well-developed endurance and ability to keep their heads while being shot at. There would be plenty of running and live rounds to dodge in France, especially once the merciless German anti-Resistance squads began to hunt them.

You choose the location of your ambush for the ease of the getaway, the Commando instructors taught the Jeds. You study it with binoculars. You sketch the retreats your men are to follow. You take position, blow up the lead vehicle in the German convoy, shower the rest with bullets as they screech to a halt, toot a whistle to signal cease fire, and run like hell. Assign two men to lag behind with a machine gun to make pursuit unattractive to any Nazi zealots.

The Jeds practiced this scenario over and over as they crawled through Scotland's waterlogged heather, climbed ropes up cliffs, and hid in rain-filled ditches. The snap of a sniper's all-too-real bullet and the explosion of splinters off a nearby rock warned the Jeds if they moved too visibly. "Snoop and poop" the SOE instructors called the sniper-fire exercise. The bullet would ricochet away from the Jeds, if all went according to theory, but they learned quickly to stay hidden or, at least, to stay cool under fire.

"Bloody poor show, that," an instructor said if a practice raid ended badly. "You would have caught a packet from the Jerries on that one."

An ambush should be over in less than ten minutes. The top priorities are the survival of the squad and the preservation of its weapons and equipment. The planning should be careful. The heroics should be minimal. Surprise gives the guerrilla his only advantage. The moment an encounter becomes a pitched battle with the Germans' much larger, much better trained and armed forces, the advantage has been lost. In other words, bat for singles, a metaphor that worked equally well in baseball and in cricket.

At Arisaig, the Jeds made their first acquaintance with the most important weapons of the Resistance. The British Sten submachine gun, stamped in mass production from a metal mold at a cost of only thirty shillings (about $7.20) each, had already been parachuted by the tens of thousands into France. Easily dismantled and hidden, able to use captured German 9mm ammunition, the Sten would be the most common weapon used by the Jed's Resistance foot soldiers.

Heavier firepower came in the form of the Bren light machine gun. Carried by one man in each better-armed Resistance squad, and also used by the British and Canadian infantry, it was capable of firing five hundred rounds per minute. Since, in addition to their other Resistance roles, the Jeds would act as weapons instructors and repairmen, they practiced until they could load, fire, clean, dismantle, and reassemble the Brens while blindfolded, as though in a pitch-black night in a forest—as they one day would be.

The Jeds learned to swim with a limpet mine and affix it to a ship's hull, to mold plastic explosive to make it look like a lump of coal that could be tossed into a locomotive tender, and to prepare pressure switches that would detonate when a train wheel rolled over them. They learned to use an igniter that could be clamped on a bomb fuse and then struck like a match. They met the time-pencil detonator, a contraption containing acid at one end which, when released, ate through a wire and triggered a tiny, spring-loaded plunger. Shove it in a fistful of plastic explosive, pinch one end to release the acid, wait for the allotted time, and—kaboom!—no more bridge.

"Now we're getting the real McCoy," Aaron Bank said happily to the others. The SOE had a more sophisticated training setup because it had been involved in guerrilla action throughout the war. The instructors didn't need the manuals like at Area B; the teachers had all seen action behind the lines, either on Commando raids or as agents in Yugoslavia, Greece, or France. One of them, a concert pianist before the war, had had his hand blown off and wore a prosthesis covered by a black leather glove. And yet these seasoned warriors made it all seem like one big game, albeit a deadly serious one.

New Year's Eve arrived, and while, down in Henley, the British and American radio operators began their sulky introductions, the American Jed officers happily downed whiskeys with their Scottish Commando hosts. They sang and danced and caroused. The bagpiper got so drunk he could no longer play. The Americans yelled "Wahoo!" like cowboys and banged their heels and jumped around as though at some kind of a music-less barn dance. In a fair exchange of culture, the Commandos shushed their students and taught them their last lesson: a traditionally vulgar British rugby and fighting song about a wedding celebration, called "The Ball of Kirriemuir."

Hungover and dreary, the Jed officers bid their farewells to the paramilitary instructors in Scotland. They jumped off their train a day later in Hampshire, in southwestern England, and made their way to Stodham Park, a country estate near Liss where the SOE had established its Special Training School 3 (STS 3). There, Military Testing Officers (MTOs) attached themselves to each Jed like pilot fish and began jotting down their observations. Bill Dreux quickly felt like a tiny bacillus squirming on a microscope slide.

"You will be here for four days," announced STS 3's commanding officer, Major Sinclair. "You will be tested by psychologists, interrogated by psychiatrists, called on to solve all sorts of individual and group problems under the whiplash of the MTOs, and then finally interviewed by me. This is what we call 'assessment.' "

"What if we flunk out?" one of the Jeds asked.

"Well, of course, that would be a pity, now wouldn't it?"

Dreux and the American Jed officers grumbled angrily. They had been promised a shortcut into the action, yet they had already spent four months in school, however rough. Were there now more hurdles? Why, while regular troops ran around Britain practicing invasion scenarios, were the American Jed officers wasting time in yet another "booby hatch," answering ridiculous questions about when they stopped wetting the bed?

Bill Dreux impatiently scratched out answers to coding and radio aptitude tests that determined whether he could take over if his radio operator was killed. He concocted a paragraph of drivel on each of three meaningless Rorschach ink blobs. He filled out a form that asked about the characters of the five other guys in his group—commonly known as a "fuck your buddy test"—and graded the men on their qualities of tact and leadership.

On the following days, the American officers traipsed into the woods, following an MTO until they arrived at each of eleven testing stations. The Jed teams crossed a river with a hundred-pound box of "delicate radio equipment," traversed a "minefield," moved over a pool of "sulfuric acid," escaped a "Gestapo raid," proved they could keep secrets under "interrogation," detected "Resistance double-crossers," and bravely jumped from a fifty-foot-high platform to a rope suspended six feet away. The MTOs, meanwhile, scratched their notes.

Dreux, Singlaub, Bank, Colby, and, indeed, the rest of the American Jed officers matched or exceeded the performance on these tests of their already battle-hardened British counterparts who, like the French, were also required to complete this assessment process. But then came the interviews with the psychiatrists and either the school commander, Major Sinclair, or his second in command, Major "Bing" Crosby, who would later become a Jedburgh himself.

In a word-association test, one Jed automatically answered "girls," "girls," "girls" to every cue. Another had studied abnormal psychology in college and made a lark out of giving answers that would imply he was a psychotic maniac. A third said flippantly that he had volunteered "for the danger pay." The American Jeds were like "a horde of cowboys hitting town after a rodeo," as a later OSS psychological study would conclude. Their culture and that of the British assessors utterly clashed.

The British expected to be convinced that all Jedburgh candidates wanted to serve their country and take an active part in the war, which was, in fact, true. To say as much, however, the Americans thought, would be boastful. Instead, Singlaub, Dreux, and the rest found the interviews embarrassing and coped by making jokes. The Brits, after four years of fighting and bombs falling on their cities, weren't laughing. The Student Assessment Board rejected eighteen out of sixty-one, nearly one-third, from the ranks of Franklin Canfield's officer recruits.

The remaining Americans were already furious when they found themselves thrown in with the British and French officer recruits at yet another training school. National resentments quickly surfaced. The Americans thought the Brits were stuck up and they also despised the French for opposing the Allied invasion of North Africa. The French fumed over the British sinking of the

French fleet at Mers el-Kébir, to ensure that it did not fall into German hands. Everyone thought the Americans were an undisciplined menagerie who had entered the war far too late.

The feuding international group found itself shifting together from one SOE training base to the next, like orphans with no home, because the main Jedburgh training area was still not complete. The Jeds' new commander, a stiff-backed British colonel named Spooner, won no points when he decided to fill the idle time of his now highly qualified men on foot drills and roll calls. Then the paratroopers among the American Jed officers suddenly discovered that a promise not to stop their hundred-dollar-a-month danger pay had been broken.

To top it all off, the Jeds still knew almost nothing about their prospective operation. Many had first been recruited in October, and four months was a long time to know you are destined for hazardous duty without knowing the where, the when, or the how. Some felt like animals slated for slaughter. Some couldn't sleep. The imminent danger gnawed at them. They all shared the same anxiety. Everyone was sick of being kept in the dark. It didn't help that visitors from London headquarters managed to start the preposterous half-truths that the Jeds would be expected to "attack Panzer divisions" and "neutralize the Luftwaffe." What were they being trained for?

As tensions boiled over, an American Jedburgh officer, Conrad Dillow, got drunk one night and spent the evening, as an official complaint against him recalled, "violently insulting and abusing the British people, their army and their part in our mutual war effort." Jeds of all three nationalities made sport out of kicking Spooner's dog, a chow named Mr. Wu. One unknown person used his newly acquired demolition skills to booby-trap Spooner's toilet, which exploded when the colonel pulled the chain. Spooner responded by restricting them all to base and canceling their leave.

"Never has so little been done by so many," Bill Pietsch wrote in big letters on a blackboard. Some Jeds began to consider requesting reassignment to their units in the hopes of taking part in the big show. With all the shenanigans, they had begun to think that the "secret" in secret operation might mean nonexistent.

It took a month after the Americans' arrival in Britain before the Jeds finally arrived at their permanent training home in February 1944: a vast wooded estate located outside Peterborough, about ninety miles north of London, called Milton Hall. Disgruntled with their treatment so far and appalled to find themselves still under the command of Colonel Spooner, an angry group of American Jeds followed Douglas Bazata into the mess hall, where Bazata jumped on a chair.

"Boys, let's give a cheer," he shouted. "Forty-eight," the Jeds roared. "Forty-nine," they screamed. "Fifty," they belted. "SOME SHIT!"

Oblivious to the problems, the shadow chiefs in London furiously marked their maps and made their plans for the Jedburghs' role in Eisenhower's coming invasion, which was less than six months away. They did not yet realize how close to falling apart the operation—and all the potential help it could give to the Allied military forces—had come.

# CHAPTER THIRTEEN
# EISENHOWER'S PLAN

**D**wight Eisenhower had begun setting up the Supreme Headquarters of the Allied Expeditionary Force (SHAEF) in London on January 15, 1944. Planning for Overlord was already in full swing, and on January 21, Eisenhower presided over the first top secret meeting at SHAEF's Norfolk House of the coming invasion's senior commanders. He invited his British ground commander, General Sir Bernard "Monty" Montgomery, to take the floor. With careful precision, Monty began to unveil to his fellow commanders the most important Allied secrets of the war in Europe—the details of the plan for the largest amphibious invasion in history.

Operation Overlord's 175,000 men, Monty explained, would scramble up five beaches on the English Channel, not those closest to Britain in Pas-de-Calais, where Hitler expected the invasion, but farther west in Normandy. With the crucial element of surprise in their favor, the invasion forces would overwhelm the Nazi battlements and secure the landing areas. The navy would tow in specially constructed artificial harbors, known as Mulberries. During the days and weeks after D-Day, in what would come to be known as the Battle of the Buildup, Ike's first wave would push inland. They would keep the German tanks away from the vulnerable landing areas on the beaches, and Allied ships would ferry troops and equipment into the Mulberries, preparing for the final breakout from the coastal landing area into the high plains of northern France.

As the scenario went, Ike's planners hoped for a speedy sweep west to conquer northwestern France's deepwater harbors, first in Cherbourg and later on the Brittany peninsula. Into these ports, Ike intended to pour the six to

seven hundred tons of daily supplies needed by each division to nourish his attack. His well-fed men and gassed-up tanks could then turn east and chase the
German forces the long distance across northern France to the border.

Meanwhile, in another prong of Ike's invasion plan, a second Allied force
would swarm over the southern Mediterranean beaches of Provence to chase
the Germans north—Operation Anvil. This second invasion would have the
effects of first dividing Hitler's forces between north and south, and later providing a much-needed second supply route from the Mediterranean ports for
the Overlord forces. Ultimately, the forces of Overlord and Anvil would together push relentlessly toward France's northeastern corner, closing the jaws
of Eisenhower's strategic vise and trapping the desperately fleeing men and
equipment of Hitler's French occupation force. From there, Ike would regroup
and launch his final attack on the Third Reich's fatherland.

That, simply put, was the entire plan for the invasion of France. In the
coming weeks and months, scores of logisticians would work ceaselessly to organize the Overlord armada of 5,333 ships and flights of nearly 11,000 aircraft
that would first bombard Hitler's coastal defenses and then land the infantrymen. But it was not the landing or its massive scale that most concerned Eisenhower and his commanders. They believed the element of surprise would be
enough to get their forces ashore and past the initial crust of German artillery
and infantry defenses. Instead, what worried Eisenhower most was the first
few weeks between the initial invasion and the breakout—the Battle of the
Buildup.

Hitler had dotted his panzer tank divisions, the most fanatical and effective forces of World War II, along the vulnerable coasts of France and northern
Europe, concentrating them particularly at Pas-de-Calais, where he expected
the Allied invasion to come. He also kept reserves of tanks and motorized infantry behind all the coasts of France to rush in and reinforce his troops wherever the invasion began.

When the Allied forces hit Normandy, Hitler would consider moving men
from Brittany, Pas-de-Calais, the Atlantic coast of France, the Mediterranean
coast, and northern Europe and Germany. The Battle of the Buildup would
amount to a full-speed race to Normandy between the Allied forces arriving by
ship and the ferocious German panzer tank divisions and crack infantry
forces, which would charge from Hitler's strategic positions around France
and northern Europe.

"The crux of the operation," wrote British Lieutenant General Frederick

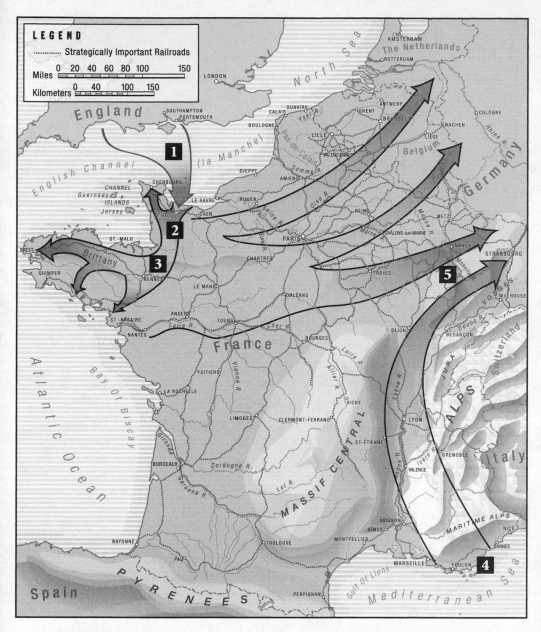

## IKE'S INVASION STRATEGY

1. Landing: The 175,000 men of Operation Overlord would scramble up the Normandy beaches.
2. Battle of the Buildup: The Navy would tow in Mulberry harbors into which would pour Ike's troops and supplies. His landing forces would push inland to keep the Germans at bay.
3. Deepwater harbors: A quick westward sweep into the peninsulas of Cherbourg and Brittany would win important docking areas for supply and troop ships.
4. Southern invasion: The threat of Operation Anvil would keep German forces tied down in the south and away from Normandy.
5. Breakout: Overlord and Anvil forces would together rush to the northeast corner of France, where Ike would regroup for his final attack on Germany.

Morgan, the chief architect of the Overlord plan, "is likely to be our ability to drive off the German reserves rather than the initial breaking of the coastal crust." In fact, Morgan estimated that the invasion would fail if Hitler could move more than twelve of his reserve divisions to Normandy before the break-out began.

Winning the Battle of the Buildup, in other words, was crucial to Overlord's success. Quickly establishing and maintaining superior forces over the enemy was a difficult task, however, when your tanks had to essentially swim out of the sea while the enemy's just had to drive down the road. If the Allies hoped to beat Hitler in the buildup, they first had to ensure that Hitler's fighter-bombers could not interfere with the invasion ships landing men and equipment on the beaches. Second, the Allies had to render unusable the roads and railways along which the Germans would try to flood to Normandy. The two preconditions for victory in France, Ike and his planners had resolved, were air superiority over the Channel and the delay of German ground reinforcements to the beachhead.

The Allies had devised three ways to keep the Germans at bay. First, the Mediterranean invasion, Anvil, would pin down German forces based in the south. Second, the deception scheme code-named Fortitude would persuade Hitler that the Normandy invasion was only a diversion from the "real" invasion to come at Pas-de-Calais, where he should leave his panzer divisions. Third, Eisenhower's Transportation Plan called for using air force bombers and Resistance saboteurs to make the roads, railways, and bridges that would otherwise lead the sixty German divisions in France to the Normandy battlefield impassable.

Overlord's planners studied their maps and carefully scratched bull's-eyes over points where German movement to the battlegrounds could be bottlenecked. Ike invested huge importance in the Transportation Plan's cutting off German access to his invasion area, and insisted on overall control of the air forces in order to implement it. At first, Winston Churchill resisted giving Ike command of the Allied bombers. Ike threatened to quit. Without control of the planes, Ike would "simply have to go home." Ike got his bombers.

As for the role of the French Resistance in the Transportation Plan, Overlord's early military planners had been skeptical of how a bunch of farmers, students, and bakers could help, and refused to write the SOE and its Resistance armies into the Overlord scheme. The planners instead considered any potential Resistance action a "bonus." But Eisenhower, it turned out, desperately

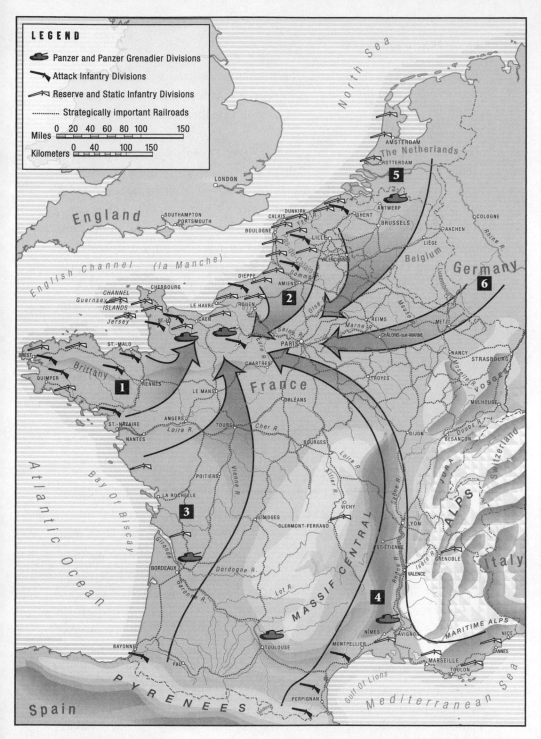

## BATTLE OF THE BUILDUP

When the Normandy invasion started, Hitler would consider moving his forces from (1) Brittany, (2) Pas-de-Calais, (3) the Atlantic coast, (4) the Mediterranean coast, (5) northern Europe, and (6) Germany. Eisenhower considered slowing this movement fundamental to Allied success.

wanted that bonus maximized. The Resistance fighters' lightning raids and well-placed pieces of *plastique*, as the French called the explosive, would sever rail lines, collapse bridges, and, hand in hand with the air force bombing raids, Ike hoped, keep Hitler away from his men in Normandy.

"We are going to need very badly," Eisenhower wrote in an ultra-secret memo to President Roosevelt, "the support of the Resistance groups in France." From early 1944, SHAEF gave the shadow chiefs increased air support and weaponry for the four hundred thousand behind-the-lines Resistance fighters. SOE and OSS Special Operations in London put an end to their turf war and combined into a single organization, which soon came to be known as Special Forces Headquarters (SFHQ). Ike's SHAEF staff took direct control of the SFHQ, and ordered the shadow bosses to ensure that all Resistance action fell in line with Ike's grand scheme for the invasion and was coordinated with his military commanders. The Jedburghs, though they still had not been informed of the fact, now trained and prepared to carry the last-minute requirements of the military commanders to the Resistance.

With the Jeds still in training, the SFHQ quickly dispatched 187 other agents by parachute into France, Belgium, and Holland in the first quarter of 1944 to begin preparations for the invasion. Lieutenant General Frederick Morgan had first revealed the kernel of the Overlord plan to the shadow bosses back in August. Ever since, planning chiefs Franklin Canfield and Mike Rowlandson had feverishly developed their two-phase Resistance plan to help with the invasion.

In the first few months of 1944, the SFHQ's new agents in northern Europe ran around executing the first pre-D-Day phase of the Resistance plan. They sent oil refineries up in towers of flame, dried canals that carried German war supplies, and reduced to a trickle the production of airplane parts at certain factories. In January and February alone, agent-led Resistance forces wrecked 671 locomotives that would otherwise pull trainloads of German troops and equipment to battle. In line with SHAEF's orders, this first phase of the SFHQ's Resistance plan aimed to assist the air force bombers in reducing Hitler's war strength and ensuring that he couldn't get his planes off the ground to shoot up Ike's invasion in June.

Meanwhile, in London, Canfield and Rowlandson turned their SFHQ planning staff toward their Resistance plan's second phase—the one involving the Jedburghs. SHAEF had ordered the SFHQ, in the last few days before D-Day and the weeks that followed it, to use their Resistance forces to obstruct

German reinforcements pouring toward Normandy and, in certain areas, to tie up German forces by engaging in so much guerrilla activity that the Germans could not leave. Though each attack by a Resistance group would be small, their cumulative effect, as a division moved across France, would be to delay its movement and lower the morale of its German troops when they arrived at the battle zone. Canfield and Rowlandson's teams based their Resistance plans on what they knew of how a German division was called into action.

First, individual German units would be alerted by telephone from divisional headquarters. Sirens or school bells would be used to call the troops from their billets. When possible, German troops far from the landing areas would load their men and equipment onto trains. When troops were forced to move by road, petrol kept in two-hundred-liter drums at army headquarters would be distributed in twenty-liter cans in open trucks to divisions. The German warriors would then lumber down the road in their trucks at a sluggish twelve to eighteen miles an hour with a distance of thirty yards between vehicles.

Guerrilla squads, the SFHQ planners reasoned, could harass German movement at any stage of this mobilization. Resistance could attack the headquarters responsible for the transmission of the alerts, sever the telecommunications, interfere with electricity supplies that rang the bells and sirens, shoot the men emerging from their billets, and blow up the petrol supplies. Once a German division was on the move, Resistance forces could tear down or turn around traffic signs, lay mines, throw grenades, attack the vehicles, litter roads with tire bursters, fell trees, snipe at troops awaiting transport, cause train derailments, and cut the tracks.

On this basis, the SFHQ developed the "colored" plans for Resistance action. Plans Vert, Tortue, and Violet, for example, identified crucial railway targets, important points for roadblocks, and key telecommunications line cuts that would most hurt German movement. Huge maps stuck with different-colored pins went up in the SFHQ "war room" showing the position of targets and the nearby concentrations of Resistance fighters and agents who could attack them.

In the coming months, the shadow chiefs would secretly communicate the thousands of targets to their agents already in France. The agents, in turn, distributed their stores of *plastique* to Resistance operatives. When the BBC, during its middle-of-the-night *messages personnels,* transmitted the designated "action phrases," the Resistance would plant its bombs and, hopefully, Hitler's tanks would not be able to move a mile before encountering a felled tree or a

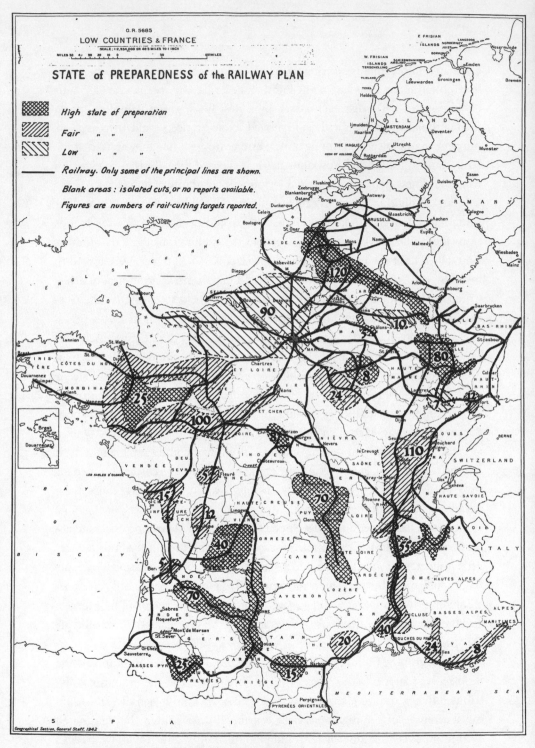

## SPECIAL FORCES HEADQUARTERS RAILWAY PLAN

This facsimile of an original SFHQ planning map shows the important railway lines targeted for sabotage, the number of potential places to cut the rails in each region, and the preparedness of the nearby Resistance fighters to make the cuts.

blown bridge. Three years of behind-the-lines organization would begin to pay off in the very few days before D-Day.

The big worry for the shadow chiefs was the need for continuous last-minute coordination with the Resistance fighters. That was a problem. Already in the spring and summer of 1943, when Odette was arrested, the Nazis had successfully severed some lines of communication between the shadow armies and the Allied command and decimated the leadership of the French Resistance. Night after night, Gestapo agents continued to raid the houses of Resistance leaders, dragging them off to the torture chambers.

How would Hitler respond to the Allied landing? What behind-the-lines actions would most assist the military commanders as the battle developed? It was impossible to tell ahead of time. Perhaps a mass Resistance uprising in one area or another might be needed to create confusion. Maybe partisans could take custody of and protect facilities of importance to Allied progress, such as ports or bridges. But such requirements could be communicated to the Resistance only at the last moment, when the need arose. Everything would fall apart if the Germans managed to arrest the Resistance leaders and agents on the eve of the invasion. When the Allied military commanders' coded orders squawked from the radio receivers that had been so carefully infiltrated into France, there would be no one left to hear them.

By the beginning of 1944, the shadow bosses had also realized that there were about fifty thousand potential new fighters who had no agent-leaders and with whom the Allied shadow chiefs had never established communications. These young men were not part of the traditional Resistance. Instead, they had fled to the mountains and forests to avoid being sent to Germany and enrolled in Hitler's forced labor program. The maquis, as they were called, after the scrubby Mediterranean vegetation in which some of them lived, were, at first, the sort of adopted children of the secret army, who offered little but needed food and protection. They were untrained and ill equipped. But with weapons and radio links to the supreme commander through SFHQ, the passage of time made clear, they could render huge assistance to the Allies.

All the last-minute developments, like the growth of the maquis, the arrests of agents and leaders, and changes in military instructions for the Resistance, were the raison d'être for the Jedburghs and the plan to drop them into France at the last moment. Organizing and training maquis would be another task for the Jeds when they finally dropped. As events unfolded, Churchill's entire secret army scheme and the help it could give Ike might ultimately rest with the strategic reserve of agents provided by Operation Jedburgh.

And as far as the London shadow warriors knew, their Jedburgh plan shaped up nicely. Final selection of the British, French, and American Jedburghs was complete. They had installed themselves at Milton Hall, their main training base. The Jeds now rotated through a specialist parachute-jump school, where even American paratroopers grappled with the unconventional through-a-hole-in-the-floor techniques of the black-painted SFHQ bombers. Everything seemed on course. Until, that is, Lieutenants Dreux and Bank arrived from Milton Hall and climbed up the steps to the London headquarters to warn Franklin Canfield that the American Jedburghs were close to mutiny.

Enough was enough: the Jeds hated their British food, couldn't get along with the Brits and French, were tired of repetitive training, disliked being restricted to base, raged about the loss of their jump pay, felt sick of being kept in the dark about their mission, worried that they would never get into the battle, and thought that their OSS handlers were amateurs. "There seems to be a general impression that the plan is already a failure," wrote Major Henry Coxe, the American SFHQ officer who now, along with a British officer named Lieutenant Colonel Carlton-Smith, shared overall command of the Jedburghs.

To make matters worse, in January and February 1944, the Germans scored a whole new round of arrests and executions of top Resistance leadership in France, substantially weakening the existing secret army structure. Two senior members of de Gaulle's shadow warfare outfit, the BCRA, returned from a surreptitious visit across the Channel very concerned that many more of the Resistance leaders would be captured by D-Day.

"I am frankly worried about the present situation concerning the Jedburgh plan," Major Coxe wrote urgently to his SFHQ superiors. With the German counterintelligence successes, there was a good chance that the Jedburghs would have to be, as Coxe wrote, "the backbone of the Resistance movement" by the time the invasion began. Yet after Dreux and Bank's visit, it was clear that Jedburgh morale had fallen to such an all-time low that the operation's survival, and the prospect of the Resistance's crucial contribution to Ike's Transportation Plan, was in grave danger.

# CHAPTER FOURTEEN
## SOME SHIT

Bernard Knox stepped up to what looked like the window of a railway ticket office at the SOE's secret parachute school at Ringway, near Manchester in northern England. From the other side of the counter, a beautiful young FANY smiled seductively. Across the counter she passed a canvas sack with shoulder straps, and Knox took it with the same enthusiasm he might have had for a poisonous snake. He had never parachuted before. He was not looking forward to it. "Please, sir," the FANY said, "if for any reason you find you are unable to use it, please be sure to return it to me personally, won't you?"

She smiled at him again and batted her eyes. Who of the men would want to humiliate himself by refusing to jump and then have to explain the fact when returning his chute to this natural beauty?

In the dressing room, Knox reluctantly pulled on the straps, buckled them, and had them checked by an instructor. With the exception of those who had been in the paratroops, many of the Jeds had never even been in an airplane before. "Hell, I've never been higher than the top of a stepladder," Lou Lajeunesse liked to say. Knox marched past a line of waiting men who nervously danced in place. The prospect of jumping six hundred feet to the ground made a good contribution to their forgetting, at least temporarily, the morale problems they had been having with Colonel Spooner back at Milton Hall.

On the airfield, way above the Jedburghs' heads, barely visible through the fog, floated a big, helium-filled balloon. It looked a lot like the ordinary barrage balloons that hovered over convoys at sea and over all British cities as protection against enemy aircraft, except that this one had a big wicker basket suspended beneath it. Every few seconds, a man flew through a hole in the basket's bottom, his chute blossomed open, and he descended to earth, most often peacefully—sometimes not.

British Jedburgh Oliver Brown watched horrified as one parachute developed into nothing more than a long, white flame, a "Roman candle." The would-be agent was, in the Ringway parlance, "squashed." Another trainee-agent had swung back and forth in ever increasing arcs until he flew over his chute, fell down into it, and plummeted to the ground. "There was nothing to do but tie up the ends for burial," a Ringway instructor said. The Jeds themselves, on one inauspicious day, suffered two or three broken legs and one broken spine. Knox and his Jedburgh friends did not know it, but according to SOE estimates, one in nine hundred jumps ended in death.

A chugging diesel-powered winch pulled the balloon down by heavy cable. Four men climbed into the basket and the balloon floated back up. When Bob Kehoe awaited his turn, he noticed big wet stains appearing in the pant crotches of a couple of colleagues as their queue inched slowly forward. Bravery did not mean a lack of fear. It meant overcoming it by force of will.

Every one of the French, British, and American Jeds had to complete this terrifying three-day initiation ritual at Ringway, even those already qualified as paratroops. American parachutists customarily heaved themselves out of the doors of slow-moving transport planes called C-47s, or Dakotas. The British leapt from faster four-engined bombers, such as Lancasters or B-24s. They exited through a hole in the floor of the fuselage called the "Joe hole," named for the agents whom the SOE called "Joes." The trick of the Joe hole was to drop cleanly through it without losing your teeth on its front edge or knocking yourself unconscious on its back. "Careful not to ring the bell, now, sir," the British instructors were fond of saying. "Go out straight, like a guardsman."

Knox climbed with three others into the gondola and felt his heart begin to pound as he slowly floated upward. Teeth marks gouged the side of the hole, made by men who had not kept their heads straight. Knox and his colleagues pushed themselves into the corners, as far from the hole as they could. The instructor had tethered himself to the gondola. A panicking student had once grabbed hold of an instructor's leg on his way out of the hole and pulled his parachute-less victim with him. For his pains, the student got a desperate bear hug all the way down and a good hard punch on the nose when he hit the ground.

"You first, sir, on my signal," an instructor said to one of the Jeds. The ground was barely visible through the fog. The gondola swayed gently in the wind. Mason Starring got on his belly and forced himself to crawl to the hole.

"That's not the way we do it, sir," the instructor said.

"It's the goddamned way I do it," snapped Starring.

He dove headfirst through the hole. The static line, attached to the gondola at one end and to the chute at the other, suddenly went taut as Starring reached its length and then slack when he broke away. René Dussaq, the Jed who had been a Hollywood stuntman, said to hell with the hole and swandived over the edge. Knox simply went out feetfirst, boring and conventional though it may have seemed. The ground rushed toward him.

"One one thousand," Knox said to himself. He had been taught the count by his paratrooper buddies and told that by three one thousand you should feel the hard jerk of the parachute opening.

"Two one thousand."

"Three one thousand."

"Four one thousand."

When the chute had not opened at the same stage for Jack Singlaub, he had begun desperately clawing at the place where the rip cord for his reserve chute should have been, but the British did not supply reserve chutes. "Would it break His Majesty's government to spring for two parachutes?" one of the Americans had wisecracked. Patiently, an instructor explained that during an agent's low-altitude jump, by the time you realized your chute was not opening, "You've had it, chum." Knox reached five one thousand and the ground still rushed toward him. "Jesus Christ!" he shouted loudly.

Suddenly, the jerk came, the rustling of silk began, and the parachute blossomed open. Less than fifteen seconds after he left the gondola, Knox hit the ground with about the same landing shock as jumping off a fourteen-foot wall. "Land like a sack of you know what, sir," his instructors had told him.

Back on the ground, an instructor explained to a group of shaken Jedburghs that parachutes took longer to open when jumping from a balloon than from a plane because there is no airspeed to take up the static line. That was why the counts got to five one thousand before the chutes opened. American John Gildee grabbed the instructor roughly by the shirt: "Why didn't you tell us that before, you son of a bitch!" By the time the Jeds had all floated down to Mother Earth after two jumps from airplanes, they knew how to move in a five- or six-man group, or "stick," up the fuselage and out of a hole, in day or night, all while flying at 125 miles an hour.

Back at Milton Hall, the Jeds discovered, happily, that the rigid, by-the-book Spooner had been replaced by a pleasant, friendly man named Colonel Musgrave, much more to the Jeds' liking. Excellent mess cooks and top rations had been brought in, and three-day passes to London would be issued every ten days. The Jedburgh officers got "bat-men," soldiers in the British army whose job was to bring officers tea, clean their equipment, and help them get dressed every morning. The American paratroopers even found that their parachute pay had been restored.

"Every effort should be made to show the students that their interests are being looked after," Jedburgh co-commander Henry Coxe had written to the shadow bosses after Dreux and Bank reported the crisis of morale. The shadow chiefs also made the radio operators happy. An officer passed through the radiomen's quarters at Milton Hall handing out stripes. "Sew these on," he said. "You've all been made sergeants."

The nearly three hundred Americans, British, and French, both officers and radio operators, who had since arriving in England been broken into groups, had finally now come face-to-face in the Elizabethan Milton Hall with its oak-beamed living rooms and traditional armor-lined corridors. Happier with the new conditions, the British radiomen forgave the theft of their girls by the Americans, especially after the French wireless operators, in turn, stole them from the Yanks. The international groups began good-natured competition in sports matches. The French even adapted the American Jeds' war cry: "*quarante-neuf, cinquante . . . merde!*"

The shadow chiefs in London could breathe a sigh of relief. Things were largely back in order with the Jedburgh scheme. The chiefs had only to address the Jeds' one last complaint: that they had no idea what the nature of their final mission would be.

On February 24, 1944, a buzz went through the corridors of Milton Hall. One of the chiefs from London headquarters, Brigadier E. F. Mockler-Ferryman, the head of the London group of SOE and co-commander of SFHQ, along with the London OSS Special Operations chief, Colonel Joe Haskell, was to make a speech in the main ballroom. The Jeds were finally going to get their briefing.

The ballroom was full before the brigadier arrived. Around three hundred Jeds, composed of about a hundred each of Frenchmen, Brits, and Americans, along with a smattering of Belgians and Dutchmen, sat in the audience. When Mockler-Ferryman finally strolled to the front of the room and began to speak, not even the more loudmouthed of the Americans had to be told to quiet down.

As you can all see, Mockler-Ferryman said, a number of nations are represented here. Your unit, known as Operation Jedburgh, has been comprised of an international group of officers and radio operators because you will be operating behind the lines in enemy-occupied territories, where language skills and familiarity with the country are important. The overwhelming majority of you will be parachuting into France, but some of you will be infiltrated into Holland or Belgium.

In each of these countries of northern Europe, Mockler-Ferryman went on to explain, many thousands of men have run away from the cities, towns, and villages to escape the Germans. These groups, known collectively as the maquis, are made up of both committed members of the Resistance and men who simply hoped to avoid the German labor draft. Since it is likely that the Germans will intern male citizens in the towns and villages or at least restrict civilian movement on the advent of the Allied invasion, most of you will probably be dropped to such maquis, who have already taken to the forests and the mountains.

In some cases, the Jeds would be dropped to a parachute-reception committee organized by the Resistance; in others, they would be dropped "blind" and then find their way to their Resistance group, who might not even be expecting them. In such cases, the Jeds would prove their bona fides with a general order, personally signed by Eisenhower himself. "The bearer of this document is a regular member of the Allied Forces," the order would say. "It is required that you should give such members of the Allied Forces any assistance which they may require and which may lie within your power, including freedom of movement, provision of information, provision of transport where possible and provision of food and shelter."

Once with their maquis or Resistance group, the Jeds, Mockler-Ferryman went on to explain, would form a link between Resistance forces in their district and the Allied command, integrating Resistance action with the plans of the regular armies. In the headquarters of SHAEF and each of the armies, the

SFHQ had installed groups of specially trained officers, the "Special Force Detachments." Their job was to advise the military commanders of what could reasonably be expected of the shadow armies, and then to relay the requirements of the commanders through the SFHQ to the Resistance.

If no radio link exists with the Resistance group to carry out the orders, continued Mockler-Ferryman, either because there never has been one or because of the arrest or death of existing agents, a Jedburgh team may be dispatched both to relay the orders and to establish ongoing communications with us here in London. Similarly, if SFHQ receives information of an as-yet uncoordinated maquis group that might in the future prove useful or one that has grown too large to be led by existing operatives, a Jedburgh team might be sent.

In the coming weeks, you will form teams of three, Mockler-Ferryman told the Jeds, consisting of one British or American officer, one officer of your destination country, and a radio operator. Since your job is to operate with the Resistance groups of whatever country you drop into, the French, Belgian, and Dutch officers will be of particular importance. They will carry the chief responsibility of linking up the Jedburgh team with a district's various Resistance groups. Each team's British or American officer, meanwhile, will call for drops of arms and supplies, instruct his maquisards in the use of their weapons, and then lead them in the action assigned to them against the Germans.

That assigned action might include anything from destroying a bridge before the enemy could use it to protecting a tunnel for the advancing Allies. The Jeds and their maquis might just as likely be ordered to harass the movement of a particular German division on its way to the battlefield or to provide liaison between Resistance and British Special Air Service (SAS) or OSS Operational Groups (OGs) dropped behind the lines. The SAS and OGs were highly trained uniformed soldiers whose job was to drop in groups of thirty and attack targets too technically difficult or too well protected for the relatively untrained Resistance.

Mockler-Ferryman spoke on: When a Jed team completes its initial task, it will remain with its Resistance group and continue to cause maximum harm to the enemy. You should expect to remain in enemy territory for a matter of months. Should the Germans break up your Resistance group or capture your radio, or should conditions become too dangerous for your continued operation, you may attempt to contact other groups for assistance, to take cover at one of the Resistance "hides" until you are overrun by regular forces, or with-draw from France by a clandestine escape route across the Alps and into Switzerland or over the Pyrenees and into Spain.

Mockler-Ferryman had only one other surprise in line for the Jeds in the Milton Hall ballroom. Unlike the many clandestine agents already operating in France in civilian clothes to maintain their cover, he said, you will be dropped and expected to operate in full uniform. The Jeds' uniforms entitled them to POW protection under the Geneva convention, the shadow bosses reasoned. The appearance of uniformed officers among the maquis, furthermore, would give them a tremendous uplift in morale and help convince them to make the transition from secretive mischief making to open attacks on the Germans. The uniforms would also lend the Jedburghs the authority of the supreme commander and help convince the maquis to follow orders.

Though you will most definitely parachute in uniform, you can change into civilian clothes if you feel the need. You should feel pleased that your uni-forms may also provide you with a measure of protection and better treatment if you are captured, Mockler-Ferryman added. But then again, they might also make your capture more likely. With this last not-so-heartening tidbit, the briefing was over.

"Any questions?" Mockler-Ferryman asked.

"Yes, sir," one of the Jeds piped up. "How many Germans are there in France?"

"Not many over half a million," came the weary answer.

A tense silence followed. "Oh, that's all?" shouted one of the brash Ameri-cans at the back, and all of the Jeds, even the most austere of the French, laughed hilariously.

## CHAPTER FIFTEEN
# IN CASE OF DEATH

Now that the Jeds had at last an inkling of what they were in for, their skills training—the weapons work, the hand-to-hand combat, the map reading—came to an end. The time had come to form their teams and begin to prepare for the mission proper, the "operational training." In this second and final phase of their preparation, the Jeds would work in their teams to practice leading "Resistance" fighters—groups of British civilians—in the war against the "Germans," who would be played by the British Home Guard.

Around this time, at the end of February 1944, the last of a group of new American officers, recruited from American bases around England to replace those rejected by the Student Assessment Board, arrived at Milton Hall. Among them was Lieutenant Stewart Alsop, a well-to-do burgeoning journalist whose mother was a first cousin of Eleanor Roosevelt's. Alsop had joined the King's Royal Rifle Corps after all three American services had turned him down because of his asthma and high blood pressure. Having fought with the KRRC in Italy, the thirty-year-old returned to London to pursue his hopes of both a wedding to an eighteen-year-old English girl with whom he had fallen in love and a transfer to the American army. The girl's parents initially nixed the marriage, but the Jedburgh recruiters obliged with the transfer. Now Alsop joined the Milton Hall "animals," as the training staff called the Jeds.

At dinner one night around the time of Alsop's arrival, the new Milton Hall commandant Colonel Musgrave stood up and announced that neither he nor the London shadow bosses would pair the officers for the three-man teams. "You chaps go ahead and make your own 'marriages,' " Musgrave said, and then, together, the partners chose their radio operators. Since every team destined for France had to have one French officer, it was the American and British officers who did the wooing and courting, and over the next few days, the Jed officers began to form tentative pairings, which they called getting "engaged."

Bernard Knox chose an ugly, scar-faced captain named Paul Grall. Bill Dreux joined ranks with Major Carbuccia. William Colby "proposed" to Lieutenant Camille Lelong. Jack Singlaub paired up with Lieutenant Jacques de Penguilly. The "fiancés" then together chose their radio operators. Bob Kehoe was tagged by the former British Commando Major Adrian Wise, the Frenchman Jean Sassi by the American Lieutenant Henry McIntosh, Dick Franklin by Stewart Alsop. Arthur Brown, the radio operator who had been upset when he found a German's thighbone at a crash site in 1939, became part of a team with Major Tommy Macpherson, the Scottish Commando who had been captured in North Africa.

Macpherson and his New Zealand partner had successfully escaped from Camp Thorn, sneaked up the gangway of a Swedish ship, and eventually landed in Britain. Macpherson arrived at his family home in Scotland on November 4, 1943, exactly two years after his capture. After his ordeal, he imagined being awarded a desk and some sort of staff job for the rest of the war. When a telegram ordered him to report to London, he guessed it was to discuss such a possibility.

Instead, he found himself standing before Colonel Carlton-Smith, the co-commander of the Jeds. After a short interview, Carlton-Smith said, "Well, Macpherson, I'm so glad you have decided to volunteer for special operations." Macpherson had no idea what the colonel was talking about, but because he was a senior officer the major said "yes sir" and marched out. Next thing Macpherson knew, he got orders to report to Milton Hall.

Macpherson's team was code-named Quinine; Knox's, Giles; and Aaron Bank's, Packard. The team names, presumably assigned at random, were men's first names (Brian, Basil), types of medicine (Novocaine, Chloroform), or cars (Packard, Chrysler).

Formed and dubbed, the teams now trained on the German weapons they might have to capture to arm their maquis, learned to choose a "drop zone" on which to receive parachuted supplies, and listened to the tales told by returning agents. One agent had demolished a large bridge in Greece. Another had shot his Gestapo captor in the back of the head. "A man's second best friend over there is his gun," the agent said, and his first best friend was "his luck, touch wood." These men who had been in the field did not look forward to going back. Tired and irritable, they reeked of doom.

France was not a country where you could run around expecting everyone but the Germans to be your friend, the veteran agents told the Jeds. For one thing, not all the Resistance groups got along, and they had been known to ambush one another at parachute drops in order to get weapons for their own men.

De Gaulle had declared that all Resistance fighters were now united under his umbrella organization, the Forces Français de l'Intérieur (French Forces of the Interior, or FFI), but declaring something to be so does not necessarily make it a reality. Some groups of the French Irregulars and Partisans, for example, who took their orders from Russia, were more interested in stockpiling weapons for a postwar revolution to win France over to Communism. Also, the Vichy government had formed a secret police organization that hunted the Resistance. The Milice attracted fanatical fascists who supported Hitler's goals for Europe and hoped France might take its place as the Third Reich's right hand. As vicious as any Gestapo agent, undercover officers of the Milice were much more dangerous because they could more easily infiltrate Resistance groups.

Weeks passed. The rambunctious Jeds, supposedly living off the land while participating in field exercises, fed themselves by terrorizing farmers and raiding their henhouses while discharging their weapons and shouting in false German accents. To avoid nights spent outdoors and "capture," they rang the bell clappers of the stately homes of the landed gentry, and explained that they were members of a special Allied unit, in the hope of being invited to stay. They got back to Milton Hall and to their beds by telling railway signal men that they had to search the coming train for Germans and then hopping aboard. Off duty, in the villages, they schmoozed with the girls and got into fights with both British and American units.

Meanwhile, the military traffic heading south by both rail and road from the northern ports got denser and denser. More than a million and a half Americans had shipped out to Britain. Southern England had become one huge enclave of army tents, ammunitions dumps, and vehicle parks. Then, in mid-April, all the Jeds were sent on "embarkation leave" and were told to "get their affairs in order." In the beginning of May, twenty-five Jed teams, including those of Tommy Macpherson, Arthur Brown, and Aaron Bank, climbed aboard the SS *Capetown Castle* and sailed to Algeria, from where a parachute drop into France's southern regions would be easier.

For the Jeds who stayed in England, travel became so restricted that movement around London in a uniform was not possible without a pass. Tension suddenly filled Milton Hall. Mealtimes became more muted. Despite their daytime bonhomie, the Jeds brooded when alone in bed at night. What did it feel like to get shot? What did it feel like to shoot someone else?

Loving their mothers, getting good grades in school, everything they had ever been told was important to their futures, in fact, was not. They might live. They might not. Death would come capriciously. Lou Lajeunesse went to a church to talk to a priest. If killing was wrong, he wanted to know, would he be damned for going to war? Killing to save lives, the priest reassured him, is not a sin. The moral ambiguities of war are much easier to shake off for those who will never face them.

In the beginning of June, Bernard Knox parachuted with his team into the countryside of southern Scotland. The idea of this exercise was to practice receiving drops of supplies, and Team Giles had to find a good drop ground and radio back its coordinates. While passing through a salmon fishing village, Knox stopped in a hotel to get a scotch.

"You aren't by chance Captain Knox, are you?" the bartender asked.

"I am."

"We have a message for you. You and your team are to return to base as soon as possible, by rail or whatever means you can find."

American officer Paul Cyr, radio operator Bob Kehoe, and his British colleague Jesse Gardner got similar messages, and they all ended up back at an empty Milton Hall, where they were told to draw their weapons and pack.

After a couple of hours' drive, they arrived at a safe house in London, and the shadow bosses told the small group of Jeds to write their final letters home. Printed forms they filled out asked who should be notified in case of death and to whom personal effects should be sent. Bill Dreux felt like a terminally ill patient told by his doctor that the time to write a will had come. Some excused themselves from the safe house to find a church and make confession. A few hours later, they found themselves in a dressing hut at a secret airfield; a black-painted plane waited nearby. Their parachutes would be buckled on one last time.

Across the Channel, meanwhile, on the Brittany peninsula, a teacher silently crawled through the dusty rafters of his attic to his hiding place. Four hundred miles southeast, in the Auvergne, a garage mechanic quietly shifted aside the rusty car parts that concealed his own secret cache. And like them, hundreds of other Resistance leaders, from the fishing villages on France's Riviera to the hamlets of its Vosges Mountains, sneaked away to their hideouts. They dusted off their secreted radios and, by the weak yellow light of their dials, tuned into the French-language broadcast of the BBC.

Four nights earlier, on June 1, the BBC had transmitted a long list of seemingly nonsensical phrases that were really coded messages, alerting the leaders to pay special attention to the broadcasts of the coming few days. Each evening since then, the Resistance men and women had fidgeted nervously in the dark over their hidden receivers, only to feel tremendously let down when the transmissions contained nothing unusual. But tonight was the night of June 5.

At 9:15 p.m., just as darkness settled over the rain-soaked countryside of France, the Resistance leaders listened as the BBC announcer completed his newscast. Their radios emitted the first few bars of the theme song that announced the segment they were waiting for. *"Et voici maintenant quelques messages personnels"*—and here are some personal messages—the announcer intoned. Suddenly, the long-awaited orders to action began.

The first part of each seemingly nonsensical sentence, known as the reference phrase, acted like a postal address, indicating that the coming message was intended for a particular agent or Resistance leader. The second part of the sentence contained a coded instruction, telling him or her what to do. "The tomatoes must be picked," for example, exhorted leaders to execute their pre-arranged plans for rail sabotage. The advantage of the system was that, while the Germans knew the BBC messages contained orders for the Resistance, they had no way of knowing exactly what the messages meant.

Each evening's personal messages usually lasted about six minutes, containing about twenty coded sentences. They gave notice of parachute drops or other routine events in the lives of secret agents and Resistance workers. But tonight began, as the British Commonwealth's military chief, Field Marshal Sir Alan Brooke, scribbled in his diary, what "might be the most ghastly disaster of the war." Winston Churchill had gone to bed telling his wife that twenty thousand men might be dead by the time they woke up. And the BBC announcer read hundreds of *messages personnels* during a broadcast that went on for many times its usual duration.

The announcer completed his script. Over the past few months, the shadow bosses had delivered to the Resistance a wish list of hundreds of rail targets for Ike's Transportation Plan. The agents and leaders had studied their maps, surreptitiously visited the targets, planned their groups' attacks, and confirmed their arrangements with London. Now, all over France, Resistance squads went into action. They checked their clips for ammo, tucked their pistols into their belts, threw their rifles over their shoulders, grabbed their sacks of explosives and detonators, and went out into the night.

At Milton Hall, just a few hours after the BBC announcer had completed his script, Jed radio operator Dick Franklin slept under a tree beside his hut. He had taken to spending the pleasant early summer nights outside in his sleeping bag.

Tonight, in the dark hours of the morning, he suddenly bolted awake. The air was filled with a terrible noise. He opened his eyes and, as the roar grew louder and louder, saw that the entire pitch-black sky, in every direction, was filled with the lights of aircraft.

Later that morning, Jack Singlaub, lying in a hospital bed where he recovered from having his appendix removed, listened to Eisenhower on the ward radio: "People of western Europe. A landing was made today on the coast of France. . . ." The invasion had begun.

# PART IV
# INITIAL TARGETS

# CHAPTER SIXTEEN
# SUICIDE PILLS

On the Normandy beaches, the light of a gray dawn pierced for a moment the fog that, beneath billowing rain clouds, blanketed the storm-tossed Channel. To the Germans peering through binoculars from their bunkers on the beaches, the armada of five thousand gray ships filling the horizon was momentarily revealed. Two purple flares suddenly flew a thousand feet into the air. The ships raised their cannons. In deafening concert with hundreds of U.S. Flying Fortresses and British Liberators flying overhead, they let fire a tremendous bombardment that spread an inferno of red flame over a hundred miles of coastline.

The entire cacophony, from the roar of bombers to the thousands of tons of pounding shells, was executed with one purpose in mind: to make safer the tens of thousands of boys and young men who would soon claw their way up the beaches against Hitler's artillery and machine-gun fire. As the plan went, British and American airborne units who had dropped during the night would act as gatekeepers on the local roads, preventing nearby German panzers from roaring onto the beachhead and ensuring that the Allied troops could hustle off the landing craft to safety. The aerial and naval bombardments would mangle the machine-gun nests, pulverize the bunkers, and detonate the minefields already in place on Hitler's "Atlantic Wall." If all went well with these preliminary actions, D-Day might end with far fewer deaths than Churchill had despondently prophesied to his wife the night before.

But all did not go well.

Besides the hundreds of airborne troops who were blown apart by flak or riddled by machine-gun bullets before they hit the ground, many other paratroopers landed in swamps and drowned under the weight of their equipment. Others touched down in the middle of German positions and were immediately mowed down. Over half of the 82nd Airborne's troop-transporting gliders careened into trees and hedgerows. The crunch of snapping wood mingled with shouts and moans. By midmorning, the division could not account for four thousand of its men and 60 percent of its equipment.

Meanwhile, though the air force and navy had ceased their bombardment not one moment earlier than scheduled, the men aboard the hundreds of landing craft battling the high seas ran crucially late. Seasick soldiers used their helmets to help bail out a vile stew of salt water and vomit from their boats. Onshore, the German officers, taking advantage of the unexpected respite from the firestorm, shouted their men out of the rubble of their bunkers and into new defensive positions from which to blast the Allied troops who desperately charged from the shoreline at Gold, Juno, Sword, and Utah beaches.

At Omaha beach, unknown to the Allies, the crack troops of the German 352nd Division, battle-hardened by their experience on the Russian front, had recently dug themselves into the steep hundred-foot-cliffs that overlooked the vulnerable waterline. Here, the Allied bombardment, marked by insufficient naval fire and inaccurate aerial attack, had the undesirable effect of putting the Germans on alert while leaving many of their cliff-top machine-gun nests and bunkers intact.

The ramps of the boats destined for Omaha beach flipped open. The German machine gunners, safely ensconced in their pillboxes, opened fire. Row after row of American boys stumbled dead into the surf. Troops on assault boats hit by heavy German artillery simply vaporized. In their landing craft, the V Corps of the First American Army drifted into a slaughterhouse. Without firing a single shot, the first company of the V Corps to go ashore lost 96 percent of its men.

Those who made it off the boats alive struggled for breath while machine-gun and mortar fire boiled the neck-deep water around them. Only a little more than a third of the first wave of attackers ever reached dry land. Land mines littered the only paths inland and the passages between the cliffs, trapping them on the beach. Forty percent of the army engineers who tried to clear the routes were dead within half an hour. The survivors huddled helplessly behind the dunes, having lost their heavy weapons in the surf. Below them, injured men bled on the beach, unable to escape the rising tide. The surf rolled in. The moans and cries of the wounded went silent.

Annihilation of V Corps might have been complete except that, at about three o'clock that morning, two tiny teams of three British soldiers each, along with hundreds of exploding dummies, had parachuted near Isigny on the southeast corner of the Cotentin peninsula. Armed with flare guns and phonographic recordings of soldier talk and gunfire, the teams, along with a few lost stragglers from the American paratroop divisions, managed to take on the appearance of an entire airborne invasion. A regiment of Germans based near Omaha had climbed into trucks and rumbled after them. The six men kept the couple of thousand enemy troops busy for half a day, by which time their return to the beachhead could not dislodge the Allied attack. By nightfall, thirty-four thousand Americans had inched their way forward and up the bluffs. Omaha's coastal villages were in Allied hands.

By the end of D-Day plus one, as the strategists called it, more than 155,000 of Ike's men had made their way ashore. None of the other D-Day objectives, however, had been achieved.

The four adjacent bridgeheads had not been joined to form a consolidated front; they all faced the danger of being surrounded and obliterated. At Omaha, the Americans had only a tenuous hold on a slender strip of shorefront; the German big guns had not been pushed back and, as Ike would later write, "sustained a most annoying artillery fire against our beaches and landing ships." The British had failed to take Caen, which meant the ground south of the city had not been secured, as planned, to set up airstrips. And the heavy winds and high seas threatened to continue delaying the buildup of men and supplies. Eisenhower and his commanders had gained only a precarious toehold on the beach.

The good news was that back in England they still had many hundreds of thousands of men ready to flood into France. The bad news was that Hitler also had plenty of men and equipment ready to reinforce his defenses. The two warrior chiefs, in other words, now locked themselves in the exact race whose prospect had so frightened Eisenhower in the planning stage. In the opening gambit of a huge and lethal chess game, each hoped desperately to be the player who most quickly moved his pieces into position for the final attack. Everything depended on who moved fastest.

For their part, Resistance forces, ever since the transmission of the BBC messages, had begun cutting the rails and performing other sabotage to slow the Germans' progress. The secret armies, and the bomber pilots of the air forces, were now frontline warriors in the Battle of the Buildup. Ike desperately wanted to squeeze from the Resistance its entire strategic "bonus" for his Transportation Plan, but the SFHQ had still not made contact with the Resistance in large swaths of France through which the German reinforcements would march. Some of the Jeds had been urgently called off the Scotland training scheme to establish that contact. In the four days following D-Day, the SFHQ sent its first seven Jed teams into France.

Roaring down a runway at a secret air base outside London, a black-painted Stirling bomber bounced two or three times before slipping into the night and banking toward France. Bob Kehoe sat on the floor, behind the bomb bay, with his knees cramped to his chest and his parachute bunched up on his back. The full moon hung close to the horizon. The checkerboard of English farm fields slid past in the ivory glow below. The light oil and tinny smell of military aircraft filled the cabin. Kehoe felt suddenly nauseous.

At eight thousand feet, the jumpmaster's dim lamp threw yellowed light and sharp shadows across the face of Major Adrian Wise, who faced Kehoe from the other side of the bomb bay. Wise, a graduate of the British military academy at Sandhurst and a former Commando, was Team Frederick's leader. Crowded against Wise's back sat Team Frederick's second officer. Lieutenant Paul Aguirec, as Wise and Kehoe knew him, had taken a nom de guerre, like all the French Jedburghs, to protect his family in France from Nazi retaliation. His real name, Kehoe would not learn until later, was Paul Bloch-Auroch.

The rumbling engines made talk impossible, so Kehoe could only try to construe from their faces his teammates' thoughts. Stretching into the recesses of the airplane's cabin, both in front and back of Kehoe's team, was a group of about fifteen other parachutists, wild men from the French battalion of the British Special Air Service (SAS). Suddenly, from toward the cockpit, Kehoe heard one of them hollering.

"What's the matter with him?" Kehoe asked the SAS man behind him.

"Drunk," came the answer. The SAS men had been confined to base for several days with nothing to do but sip from their hip flasks.

The inebriate settled down, and the silence rolled in again. Kehoe thought mostly about the uniform he wore and how he would stay alive while wearing it in what the briefing officer had said would be one of the highest concentrations of German soldiers in France.

Back at Milton Hall, when Kehoe, Knox, Cyr, Gardner, and their teams had been alerted, they went to the supply hut to draw their weapons, equipment, and ammunition. Bernard Knox took out a pen to sign for them. Throughout Knox's career in the U.S. military, he had signed for every compass, every jeep, every item, in fact, that the army owned and expected to get back. "You don't have to sign, sir," the supply sergeant at Milton Hall said casually. There followed an unpleasant moment of realization. The army did not expect to get this equipment back. It did not expect to ever see these Jeds again.

Kehoe's plane flew past the white sand beaches of Brighton and out of British airspace. The jumpmaster switched off his meager light and closed the blackout curtains over the bomber's tiny windows. Complete darkness prevailed. When the jumpmaster moved about through the tangle of legs and webbing straps to hand out sandwiches, whiskey, and kindness to his serious-looking passengers, he used what the British called a torch, a flashlight. The Stirling droned on through the night and across the English Channel.

Team Frederick, their briefing officers had told them, would be dropped in the Côtes-du-Nord department of northern Brittany, along with this detachment of SAS. Together, the two groups would set up a command post, Samwest, from which the Jeds would begin organizing Resistance groups to undertake sabotage missions while the SAS burst immediately into action, attacking targets and cutting rail lines of greatest importance to Eisenhower's armies just over one hundred miles away. A second SAS detachment and Jed team, Paul Cyr's Team George, would establish a similar base, Dingson, in Morbihan, in the south of the Breton peninsula.

Brittany had particular strategic importance both because of its deep-water ports, which Eisenhower hoped to eventually conquer, and because of the three German paratroop and two other mobile divisions stationed there. At any moment, these German fighters might rush with crushing speed the couple of hundred miles to the Normandy beaches. The first mission for the Jed teams and SAS men at Samwest and Dingson was to cut off the German forces in Brittany from the mainland of France. That would leave sixty thousand fewer German cutthroats for Ike to worry about.

At a later stage, Jed Teams Frederick and George would turn their energies to quietly organizing, arming, and training the Breton Resistance. This, in fact, was the way most Jed teams would typically be used. They would jump in with a specific urgent task and then, while undertaking ongoing sabotage, turn their energies to quietly creating a huge underground force. Across France, each of the various Jed teams surreptitiously assembled forces to rise up in mass rebellion when it best suited the Allied cause. Until that call to action came, the

Jeds would carefully avoid German attention in order to ensure their mission's survival.

With all this pressing on his mind as he flew over the Channel, Bob Kehoe pretended to be as calm as everyone else pretended to be. To worry would simply make things more difficult.

At the air base after the briefing, a team of dressers had helped them strap on their equipment: a carbine across the chest, a bag filled with emergency rations, a first-aid kit, extra clips of ammo, a water canteen, a .45 pistol, a commando knife, and binoculars. Under all this was fastened a bulging money belt filled with several hundred thousand francs, counterfeited in London, to pay for requisition supplies and bribes. By the time Kehoe donned his parachute, he could barely hobble to the plane.

As Bernard Knox lumbered up to the aircraft ladder, a British officer approached him. "Good luck, old man," he said. "Here are your pills." He handed Knox a glass tube containing three large tablets. "This one is a knockout pill to drop in Jerry's coffee. The middle one is Benzedrine when you need to make it through a few nights with no sleep. The last one's a cyanide pill if things get too rough after capture. There you go. Good luck."

Jedburgh officer Oliver Brown kept his suicide pill in a gap in his teeth throughout his entire mission in France. Lou Lajeunesse kept his glued to the indentation behind his collarbone with chewing gum. Knox simply could not remember which end of the tube held the suicide pill and which held the knockout pill. "*Merde,*" Knox's French teammate said. "If I get wounded and left behind I'm going to shoot myself like a soldier." They threw the pills out the window over the Channel.

Over Brittany, the pilot of Kehoe's plane throttled back and shed altitude. "The Lord is my shepherd, I shall not want," Kehoe heard himself saying, though he had not been to church in nearly five years. The plane banked and turned.

Since Eisenhower's forces back in Normandy so desperately needed whatever Resistance action would stymie the German reinforcement of Normandy, the shadow chiefs urgently dispatched not just Teams Frederick and George, but five other Jed teams in the four days that followed D-Day. Bernard Knox's plane had to turn back when it couldn't find the drop zone. But of the rest, George and Frederick helped cut off Brittany, and Tommy Macpherson's Team Quinine and Jacob Berlin's Team Ammonia would do their best in the southwest to forestall the northward movement of two similarly huge panzer divisions at Toulouse and Bordeaux.

Team Harry parachuted into the Morvan Mountains to cut communications there. Team Hugh, led by William Crawshay, dropped in central France and would help cut all lines leading north and west to Normandy. Like Teams Frederick and George, these teams, with their initial tasks complete, would all later turn to quietly organizing, training, and arming in preparation for the "paramilitary" phase of the shadow war.

Meanwhile, on the same night Kehoe flew to France, at about the same time, another radio operator, Jesse Gardner, flew with his team in a black-painted bomber over the Drôme region of France, a few hundred miles away in the southeast. Team Veganin was dropping to help delay movement of the 164 tanks and fifteen thousand men of a panzer division in Avignon.

Gardner, a former tank operator, had been on leave eight months earlier when the SOE came around asking for volunteers. A friend put Gardner's name down. "I'm not doing that," Gardner said when he got back, but he had gone along, all the same, to be with his pal. He had even falsified his Morse speed, and then worked his butt off to make reality match the lie. Now, like Kehoe, he prepared to jump the six hundred feet into occupied France.

Over Brittany, Kehoe's jumpmaster, following an order in his headset from the pilot, opened the bomb-bay doors and exposed the Joe hole. Next to it was an unilluminated green light. "Running in! Action station, number one!" the jumpmaster shouted. He raised his right hand above his head, and the first of the SAS men maneuvered into position with his legs dangling out of the bomb bay. Cold air rushed through the plane. The green light flashed on. The jumpmaster brought down his arm: "Go!" The SAS man disappeared into the darkness.

Kehoe wiggled himself forward. "He makes me lie down in green pastures; he leadeth me beside still waters; he restoreth my soul." Kehoe dangled his legs out the Joe hole. "Go!" shouted the jumpmaster. "He leads me in right paths for his name's sake."

When Jesse Gardner, over the Drôme, launched himself out of the hole, he must, like the other Jeds, have felt the slap of prop wash against his face. What Gardner did not feel was the hard jerk on his shoulder straps.

Kehoe looked up to see his canopy unfolding into the moonlight. Gardner didn't. In Brittany, Kehoe heard the bomber engines droning away, and a dog

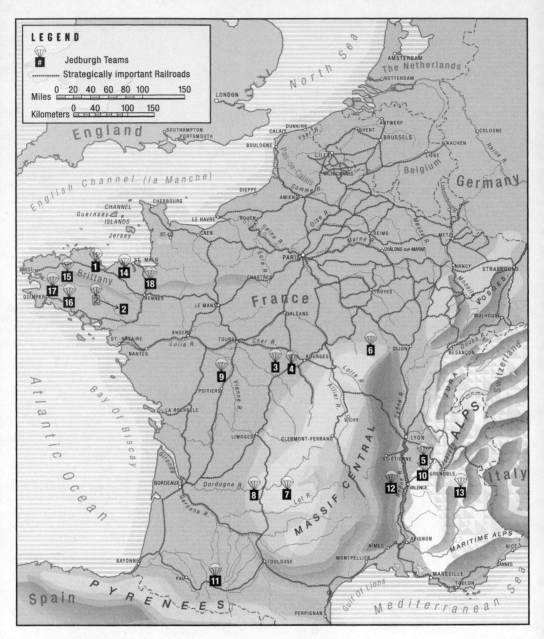

## FIRST JEDBURGH TEAMS DROPPED INTO FRANCE—D-DAY TO JULY 14

(Note proximity to important railroads.)

1. Bob Kehoe's Team Frederick
2. Paul Cyr's Team George
3. William Crawshay's Team Hugh
4. Bob Anstett's Team Hamish
5. Jesse Gardner's Team Veganin
6. Team Harry
7. Tommy Macpherson's Team Quinine
8. Jacob Berlin's Team Ammonia
9. Team Ian

10. Cy Manierre's Team Dodge
11. Hod Fuller's Team Bugatti
12. Team Willys
13. Jean Sassi's Team Chloroform
14. Team Felix
15. Bernard Knox's Team Giles
16. Team Francis
17. Team Gilbert
18. Bill Dreux's Team Gavin/Guy

barking in a farmyard. In Drôme, Jesse Gardner's body lay in a broken heap on the ground. His parachute had failed to open.

When the surviving Jeds heard about their first casualty, they would be furious. All their complaining, all their troublemaking had been a resistance against essentially one thing: futility. They could accept their deaths as long as their lives were not wasted. But Gardner had lost his life before exchanging his password with the Resistance.

Back in Brittany, Kehoe, still floating in the black sky, saw figures running in a field below. He strained to see if they were German or French. A futile fate like Gardner's was what Kehoe now feared. He heard a sound like pistol fire— Pop! Pop! Pop! Kehoe wondered if Team Frederick might be killed in battle before they even hit the ground.

## CHAPTER SEVENTEEN
# FORGET ABOUT VENGEANCE

In a field in southern Brittany's Morbihan, the three signal fires set by the maquis to guide the airplanes leapt up seven feet, and the snapping shower of orange sparks flew even higher. Dancing brightly in the darkness, the conflagrations announced the drop zone not only to the pilots of the black-painted bombers but to any German in sight.

When he hit the ground, Paul Cyr struggled desperately to reach the .45 on his hip, but the shroud lines and canopy of his chute tangled tightly around his arms and legs. From one hundred feet in the air, Cyr had watched fifteen men running to the spot where he was destined to land. "It was a very uncomfortable feeling," he would later report. He had no way of knowing who they were. Now on the ground, the mass of hands grabbing at him through his parachute silk might easily belong to Frenchmen working for the Germans.

"Hey, Joe, is that you?" Cyr heard someone shout in French from far away. Jesus, how could they be so noisy? Their voices must carry for miles.

At about the same time, some 250 miles to the south in Dordogne, Jacob Berlin, radio operator for Team Ammonia, lay in another dark field, dazed with pain. He had landed on a rock. One leg felt as if it had been ripped off. Berlin's team leader, Captain Benton McD. "Mac" Austin, might have run to his rescue, except that Austin still dangled precariously from the branches of the tree he had landed in. Berlin tried not to moan. Someone quietly approached, silhouetted against the moonlight, and Berlin recognized the unmistakable form of a German helmet. He grabbed his pistol from its holster, released the safety catch, and took aim.

*"Bienvenu, mon bonhomme"*—welcome, my good man—cried the squeaky

voice of a happy adolescent. The careless boy had killed a German the day before and had proudly worn the helmet as a trophy for his new friends, the
parachuted soldiers. "Are you crazy?" Berlin whispered hoarsely to the crest-
fallen boy. "I was just about to blow your head off."

About fifty miles to the south and east, in Cantal, bordering on Lot,
Arthur Brown and Team Quinine landed in a tangle of scrubby brush. The Resistance men receiving the parachute drop ran haphazardly, crashing through
the dark in all directions. Procedure required Brown to offer a password, and
he tried, over and over. "*Connaissez-vous Monsieur Chênier?*" Do you know
Mr. Chênier? No one bothered to listen, let alone give the correct reply. In the
sky, the engines of Team Quinine's plane strained as they turned and came
back to drop the long cylindrical containers that carried the radios, guns,
boots, uniforms, ammunition, explosives, and detonators.

"*J'ai un Français ici,*" Brown heard a Resistance man shout jubilantly from
across the field—I've got a Frenchman here. The loudmouth had stumbled on
Brown's teammates, Michel de Bourbon and Tommy Macpherson, coming
through the brush with their balled-up parachutes in their arms. Though
some Resistance groups had been alerted to expect the Jeds as well as their
parachuted supplies, this one had not. The appearance of three uniformed
soldiers on the dropping ground came as an exciting surprise. Regarding
Macpherson's kilt, the man who found him and Bourbon shouted again, "*Il est
venu avec son épouse!*" He has brought his wife! Brown felt shock. Was this
some kind of joke? These Frenchmen acted as if receiving agents and weapons
were some sort of a game.

Brown and the rest of the Jeds arriving in France were not laughing. In
northern Brittany, the muted sound of pops Bob Kehoe and Team Frederick
had heard as they parachuted through the darkness convinced them that they
had descended into a battle. In the Drôme, Jesse Gardner's Veganin teammates
realized something had gone terribly wrong as they nervously scanned the
moonlit sky for his chute. Nothing was the way it was supposed to be at the
landing sites.

Back in England, Cyr, Kehoe, Brown, and the others had been trained to
build small signal fires dug into the ground that could be seen only from
above. They were taught to receive a parachute drop in stealth and silence, as
though the Germans skulked around every corner, to speak only in a whisper,
to take care never to bang the parachuted equipment containers together. The
maquis who received the Jeds gave a damn for none of these precautions. The

troops had only just hit the beaches to the north, said the BBC news over France's hidden radios; these Resistance, already sloppy when it came to security, now behaved as though the war were won.

*Silence, s'il vous plaît!* Paul Cyr hissed when he finally untangled himself from his chute in Morbihan. *Silence!*

Instead, when the peasants surrounding him saw his uniform and realized he was American, they began to whoop and shout. *Vous êtes la garde anticipée pour une invasion complète?* You are the advance guard for a full-scale invasion? They hugged and kissed him. *Les américains, ils viendront ici pour finir les fichus allemands?* The Americans, they will come here to finish the damn Germans? The maquis lifted Cyr onto their shoulders. "It was like a regular circus," Cyr would later report.

*S'il vous plaît,* he pleaded. *S'il vous plaît.*

"*Ça ne risque rien,*" came the answer. This risks nothing. It was a favorite cry of the security-lax Resistance, and they seemed to say it the most right before a terrible disaster. Tonight was no exception.

"Don't worry. The Germans are far away," someone told Cyr.

"How far?" he asked.

"About a mile."

Cyr, who had been well briefed on German viciousness, was not exactly reassured.

In May, for example, in a small town in the district of Lot-et-Garonne, a shot aimed at members of the 4th SS Panzer Grenadier Regiment rang out but missed. German soldiers burst into the house from which the shot had come and hanged from the rafters the thirty-year-old woman who lived there for refusing to identify the shooter. When, in a different incident in the same town, the Germans caught a woman who shot at them, they hanged her in the main street from a lamppost. An officer then ordered all men between the ages of eighteen and sixty to assemble. He had every fifth man shot, and the remainder sent to Germany as slave labor.

In Cantal, Arthur Brown gathered up his chute and walked apprehensively toward the fire where everyone seemed to be gathering—another crazy idea. The Jeds had been taught to stay away from landing ground fires. The bright flames illuminated targets for any Germans sneaking through the woods. The intense heat could create a lethal explosion if a parachuted detonator or

Odette Sansom, one of a series of Special Operations Executive (SOE) agents whose capture by the Germans in 1943 made it clear that SOE would need a reserve of replacements to drop into France at the last moment if it hoped to direct Resistance efforts when the cross-Channel invasion finally began.

General William "Wild Bill" Donovan *(left)*, director of the United States' wartime spy service, the Office of Strategic Services (OSS), was eager to get American agents into France and jumped at the chance to become SOE's partner in building the "strategic reserve" of agents known collectively as Operation Jedburgh.

Operation Jedburgh's first hurdle was finding two hundred officers and one hundred enlisted radio operators willing to parachute behind enemy lines. OSS recruiters began their search for American recruits at U.S. bases in England, where they turned up Bernard Knox, a veteran of the Spanish civil war who had become disenchanted with regular army service.

OSS recruiters also returned to the United States, where Lou Lajeunesse, a bewildered radioman, found himself being interrogated in a soundproof glass room as part of the Jedburgh selection process.

While Americans recruited for Operation Jedburgh yearned to find a way *into* the fighting, twenty-two-year-old Tommy Macpherson, a Scottish officer and future Jedburgh, still schemed to get himself *out of* a German prisoner-of-war camp.

In the United States, officer candidates for Operation Jedburgh converged on the Congressional Country Club, which had been taken over by OSS and designated Area F. The selection process there included a battery of initiative and psychological tests.

OSS had several training areas in the woods of northern Virginia and Maryland like this one known as Area C. For two months, the Jed officers and radio operators trained at a nearby sister camp, Area B, which would eventually become part of the famous presidential retreat, Camp David.

The explosives and hand-to-hand combat training at Area B was pure fun for the American Jedburgh radio operators, who here look barely old enough to smoke. The American recruits did not realize as fully as their British and French colleagues that war was not a game. Roger Coté *(third from left)* and Lou Goddard *(second from right)* would not survive their stint as Jedburghs.

In early December 1943, the American Jeds were sent home for a final visit with their families before shipping out. This was the last time Roger Coté ever saw his dog or his family.

The Jedburgh radio operators' rude introduction to the misery of war came during a rough transatlantic crossing aboard the *Queen Mary,* a luxury liner converted into a troopship. Dick Franklin lucked out when he was assigned guard duty belowdecks in the ship's comfortable brig.

While the American Jed officers trained in paramilitary techniques
in Scotland, the American radiomen joined their British counterparts
at SOE's training base at Henley-on-Thames, where this picture was
taken. The Brits at first thought the irreverent Americans were a
bunch of undisciplined hooligans.

In February 1944, after circling endlessly around a number of SOE training schools, the entire international group of Jed officers and radiomen arrived at last at their permanent training base at Milton Hall. Colonel F. V. Spooner, their first commanding officer, contributed to their dangerously low morale with his parade-ground drills and army "chickenshit," which the Jeds thought they had long left behind.

Parachute training distracted the Jeds from their gripes. By the time they had finished at Ringway, the SOE parachute school near Manchester, they had completed one jump from a balloon gondola and two from airplanes. They had learned how to move in a "stick" of five or six men up the aircraft fuselage and out the "Joe hole."

"I am frankly worried about the present situation concerning the Jedburgh plan," Major Henry Coxe (left) wrote urgently to his SFHQ overlords. With the German counterintelligence successes, there was a good chance that the Jedburghs would have to be, as Coxe wrote, "the backbone of the Resistance movement" by the time the invasion began. He is pictured with Lieutenant Colonel D. L. G. Carlton-Smith, his British counterpart at SFHQ and co-commander of the Jeds.

When the Jeds returned to Milton Hall from Ringway, they were overjoyed to find that Spooner had been replaced by Colonel G. R. Musgrave, pictured here, and that living conditions were much improved. Morale rose and Operation Jedburgh was back on track.

Since the Germans controlled the roads in France, the Jeds would need to haul their weapons and equipment through the woods. Therefore, physical fitness training was vital.

Because the Jeds would train the maquis in weapons use and maintenance, they had to become firearms and munitions experts.

Like Stewart Alsop *(right)*, all the officers took radio training in case their radiomen were killed.

One night, Colonel Musgrave stood up and announced that neither he nor the London shadow bosses would choose the officers for the three-man teams. "You chaps go ahead and make your own 'marriages,'" Musgrave said. Radio operator Bob Kehoe *(center)* is pictured with the Team Frederick leader, British Major Adrian Wise *(right)*, and his French second in command, Lieutenant Paul Bloch-Auroch.

When the first Jeds were alerted for their drops into France in June 1944, they went to the supply room to get their equipment. "You don't have to sign, sir," the supply sergeant at Milton Hall said casually to Bernard Knox. There followed an unpleasant moment of realization for Knox. The army did not expect to get this equipment back. It did not expect ever to see these Jeds again.

At the air base, a team of dressers helped the Jeds strap on their equipment: a carbine across the chest, a bag filled with emergency rations, a first-aid kit, extra clips of ammo, a water canteen, a .45 pistol, a commando knife, and binoculars. Jack Singlaub poses wearing his gear.

"Running in! Action station, number one!" the jumpmaster shouted when the Jeds' planes approached their drop zones. As Bob Kehoe wiggled toward the Joe hole in his plane over Brittany, he found himself reciting the Twenty-third Psalm.

As Bernard Knox lumbered up to a black-painted bomber like this one, a British officer approached him. "Good luck, old man," he said. "Here are your pills." He handed Knox a glass tube containing three large tablets. "This one is a knockout pill to drop in Jerry's coffee. The middle one is Benzedrine when you need to make it through a few nights with no sleep. The last one's a cyanide pill if things get too rough after capture. There you go. Good luck."

When Bob Kehoe, floating in the black sky like the practice jumper pictured here, jumped into northern Brittany, he saw figures running in a field below. He strained to see if they were German or French. He heard a sound like pistol fire—*Pop! Pop! Pop!* Kehoe wondered if Team Frederick might be killed in battle before they even hit the ground.

When Paul Cyr hit the ground in southern Brittany, he struggled desperately to reach the .45 on his hip, but the shroud lines and canopy of his chute tangled tightly around his arms and legs. From one hundred feet in the air, Cyr had watched fifteen men running to the spot where he was destined to land. "It was a very uncomfortable feeling," he would later report.

To slow the German advance on Normandy, French children dropped lumps of sugar in the Germans' gas tanks and clogged their engines. Villagers stretched wires across roads to behead German motorcycle outriders. Farmers removed road signs at crossroads, causing wrong turns and traffic pileups that wasted precious time for the Germans, as captured POWs would later confirm. Trees and telephone poles strewn across the roads forced entire convoys to come to a halt.

ammunition container fell in it. But some Resistance had grown weary of being constantly careful. Looking over one's shoulder got tiring after so many years of living among the enemy. Sadly, the graves were full of Frenchman who had died by German hands because they refused to live like mice.

On Team Quinine's landing ground, the maquis shouted out orders and used flaming branches from the fire to light their cigarettes. Brown was appalled. They had a military mission that could not be accomplished by dead men, no matter how proudly they had flouted the German threat. Brown suddenly saw on the side of the field the animated faces of the wives and children the Resistance men had brought to watch the drop-zone spectacle. "It was," he later wrote, "like Blackheath fair," where London crowds bustled every year to watch a traveling circus and its freak shows.

But whatever the danger, the Jeds had urgent work to do. Uppermost was finding their parachuted containers of supplies, carrying them to a hideout, and beginning immediate operations to slow the Nazi migration toward Normandy. They also had to get away from these crowded, fire-illuminated drop zones before the Germans showed up.

Tommy Macpherson, who did not intend to be captured for a fourth time, grabbed a man with gray hair and a long face who appeared to be in charge. "Who the hell are you?" Macpherson shouted in French. The man, who was tall and looked about forty, explained calmly that he was the mayor of the local village, the proprietor of the local garage, and, since 1942, the administrator for the secret services of this drop zone. His name was Bernard Cournil. He pointed into the darkness.

"See that farmer there with his two pair of oxen?" Cournil asked Macpherson. "My men will collect all the containers and load them on his cart." Cournil noticed, perhaps, a skeptical look in Macpherson's eye. "It will be safe," he said. All Macpherson had to do, like the rest of the Jeds landing in France, was trust his safety to strangers who hardly gave a care for their own.

In Brittany, Bob Kehoe fidgeted by the fire for an hour while the maquis searched for containers, their shouts echoing through the woods. Kehoe's team leader, Adrian Wise, conversed in serious tones with the Resistance men. Kehoe could follow only snippets of the rapid-fire French. Occasionally, someone jutted his chin out toward the boyish-looking Kehoe and asked Wise in French, "Who is the kid?" Kindly men and women handed Kehoe cup after cup of bitter Breton cider. He chewed on chunks of country bread deliciously smeared with butter and cheese and tried to smile his thanks. An intense feeling of disorientation washed over him.

How the hell did I get here? Only a few short months ago, he wasted humdrum days wearing a white lab coat in a New Jersey chemical plant during time off from Rutgers to figure out what he really wanted to do with his life. Living in the woods in a foreign country surrounded by an enemy whose goal was to kill him had not topped his list. What if Hitler pushed Ike's invasion back into the sea? The surviving troops would rush to the ships and sail for home. The Jeds, on the other hand, had parachuted into France. They could not parachute out.

"Is it true," a child asked an agent ten minutes after he had landed, "that in England they have machines that milk the cows?" Such innocence just made the situation seem all the more surreal.

Kehoe's gloomy reverie came to an abrupt end when a man ran breathlessly out of the darkness. *On a trouvé un corps.* We found a body. It turned out to be the drunken SAS man who had caused the commotion during the flight over the Channel. He had apparently primed some explosives before parachuting, thinking he would run straight off and perform his sabotage. The popping noises Team Frederick had heard had not been a battle at all, but this poor man being blown apart in the air by his own bombs.

The other body discovered that night was Jesse Gardner's. His French teammate in the Rhône Valley stumbled across him while looking for containers. Gardner's chute remained folded perfectly in its bag. Apparently, he had forgotten to clip his static line to the plane, and his jumpmaster had forgotten to check it. Another pointless death.

*Allons!* someone at the Team Frederick drop zone in northern Brittany shouted at last. Let's go. The fires had died down. The containers had been found. The Jeds wound their way along paths through the woods. Some of the Resistance men who guided them had great bulges of cloth under their shirts. Others draped the silk parachute canopies around their necks. The Jeds had planned to bury their parachutes using specially supplied shovels they dropped with so the Germans would find no evidence of agent activity.

"Are you crazy? You can't buy that stuff here," one agent was told. Whole families could be dressed in underwear made from a single chute. Whole families might also be slaughtered by the Germans if the silk was discovered, the Jeds and non-uniformed agents knew. Resistance men dismissed their concerns. *Ça ne risque rien.* The Jeds would get along with the French, they had been taught, by giving them cigarettes, by staying away from their women, and, so they now learned, by shutting up about the parachutes.

In northern Brittany, Bob Kehoe's march through the woods came to a halt about a mile from the drop zone. He and his team leaned their weapons on trees and boulders, then happily pulled off their backpacks and dropped them on the leafy top of a steep hillside in the Forêt de Doualt. In Cantal, Team Quinine laid out their sleeping bags in a camp area sheltered by camouflaged parachute cloth in the middle of a wood of walnut trees said to be so large that a man who had hanged himself in it was not discovered for ten years. Jacob Berlin sat in a farmhouse where an old woman sautéed omelets in a big black pan over an open fire. Paul Cyr and his Team George found themselves ensconced at the Farm de la Nouée.

It took some negotiating by the Jeds to get the Resistance to assign men to guard the perimeters, but finally it was done. Now, the celebrations started. Women, children, and old men laughed and cried with joy. Young girls kissed the Jeds and gave them flowers and wine and cognac. Then came the Frenchmen's long tributes to America and Britain.

When they were done, the Frenchmen waited, expecting each American and Brit to make their own toasts. The Jeds, some of them self-conscious about their pidgin French, simply stood up and sputtered, *"À la France,"* sufficient to cause enthusiastic applause and more kissing from the girls. The Jeds gave away what chocolate they had, the whiskey the air crews had given them, and the requisite cigarettes. The SAS teams, meanwhile, had already moved out to begin cutting rails.

In the middle of the night, as the festivities calmed, the Jeds and agents got on with the job of explaining their roles. The Jeds patiently explained to their enthusiastic recruits the importance of coordinating guerrilla action with the needs of the military commanders at the beachhead. Yes, yes, yes, the maquis leaders answered, we have been waiting to kill the bastard *boches.* The maquisards wanted to go immediately to the villages and shoot the Germans in the cafés while they sipped their coffees or to the farms and houses they had commandeered from the maquis' parents, grandparents, siblings, and friends.

Not yet, the Jeds said to the maquis. For now, it is imperative that you forget about vengeance raids on local garrisons. There must be no prideful, foolhardy attempts to liberate towns from the Germans. That kind of fighting would only end in mangled bodies, the loss of precious weapons and ammunition, and the possible failure of the mission. Halting the German march to Normandy, the Jeds told the Resistance fighters, must remain the main objective.

Most maquis agreed to operate along these lines, but not altogether happily. The Germans had killed their relatives, raided their farms, taken their food, and tortured their friends. In their hearts, most maquisards had less interest in whatever small good they could do for Allied strategy than in killing some bastard Germans before it was too late. Still, as a gesture of trust, in the dark night, the arriving Jeds handed out what weapons they had brought.

Not until the sky began to lighten did the Resistance let the small campfires die down. Paul Cyr settled himself in a hayloft and found that his uniform had effects the shadow bosses had not necessarily predicted. A beautiful young Frenchwoman lay beside him. A few miles to the north, Bob Kehoe crawled into his sleeping bag on the forest floor. He did not have Paul Cyr's good luck. Next to him lay a snoring maquis, unshaven and in dirty clothes, smelling of body odor and garlic.

On such men the lives of Allied soldiers in Normandy depended. They lacked discipline, training, and military experience. They had only their hatred of the Germans, hatred that the Jeds told them they must for now keep in check. Keep yourselves in line, the Jeds promised, and a manna of weapons will arrive. Eventually, an end will come to the clandestine part of the shadow war, said the Jeds, and the Allies will ask the Resistance to rise up en masse to liberate France. That will be the time for vengeance.

# CHAPTER EIGHTEEN
# BOYS VS. PANZERS

On June 9, Tommy Macpherson, not even twelve hours after his landing, bumped his way anxiously in a two-ton truck toward the moment when this quiet, largely unused country lane would spit him out onto a highway frequently trafficked by Germans. A Wehrmacht motorcycle with a machine-gun-armed sidecar, or a truckload full of edgy occupation troops, might then roar out of the darkness at any moment. Macpherson had proudly sewn onto his uniform the shoulder flashes of the Commandos, whom, after their raid on Dieppe in 1942, Hitler had ordered shot on sight. If this symbol, or Macpherson's kilt, did not throw a German patrol into a rage, his bundle of primed time bombs would. Macpherson was on his way, with teammate Michel de Bourbon and some new Resistance colleagues, to blow a bridge.

At the back of their rusty old truck, a vertical cast-iron cylinder, like a furnace, belched smoke from a stovepipe and provided their propulsion. The French had responded to the German theft of nearly all of Europe's gasoline by bolting such jerry-rigs, known as gasogenes, to their vehicles. Chop up some wood, throw in a match, occasionally clean out the ashes, and the contraption pumped out combustible fumes that could drive a gas engine.

Macpherson glanced nervously at his driver, Joseph, a big clumsy man with a slight stutter. This gasogene engine rattled, Macpherson thought, like a regiment of tanks. It did not inspire confidence. Team Quinine needed, luckily, only to cross the main road, not to drive along it. Still, gasogenes had a terrible habit of conking out at the worst moments and always moved far too sluggishly to outrun a German vehicle in pursuit.

What troubled Macpherson more was that he had not inspected the bridge with binoculars to check for armed guards. Nor had he tested the route they now drove. He had not even sketched out a retreat. Instead, he trusted his fate to a map, a rough drawing of the bridge, and a long conversation with Bernard Cournil, whom he had known for a grand total of twenty-four hours. Now Macpherson and Bourbon's lives rested in the hands of another stranger, Cournil's brother Joseph, the truck driver, who could just as easily be headed for the nearest German garrison as for the bridge.

Macpherson's instincts rebelled. He had learned bitter lessons on trust from the submarine commander who had abandoned him to the Germans in the Mediterranean and his subsequent two years as a prisoner of war. But Macpherson came from a brand of British boarding-school boys who had been taught an unflagging loyalty to king and country. His mission, he had decided, not his self-preservation, must come first. For that reason, back in England, he had studiously avoided involvement with women. He wanted no attachment that would cause him to cling to life if survival conflicted with fulfilling his duty. The war, he believed, would ultimately kill him anyway.

Perhaps, too, after being kept prisoner for so many years, first by his childhood illness and then by the Germans, he shared with many Resistance workers a measure of the reckless and almost suicidal desire for vengeance. For now, his first duty was to form and arm the maquis as quickly as possible, and to do that, he urgently needed to start with a bang, literally.

The Resistance in Cantal did not have the strength Cyr and Kehoe had discovered in Brittany. There, a crowd of Breton men, aged twelve to seventy-five, had wanted to grab Cyr's weapons and attack the nearby German garrison the very night he arrived. Macpherson's little Cantal group treated the weapons containers more like barrels of snakes. The little cell of farmers and fugitives from the labor draft seemed content with running the drop zone and making ripples rather than waves in the liberation of France. "We have not come here to enjoy ourselves," Macpherson lectured them. "We expect action from you."

It was to prove his point and to attract visits from nearby maquis groups that he rumbled noisily to the bridge chosen by Cournil. As dangerous as this action might be, for the sake of his mission, Macpherson desperately needed to stimulate Resistance activity.

He and his group rumbled in their gasogene across the main road without incident and came to a stop in the darkness. Macpherson could feel excitement sizzle through his Resistance men as they handled their still unfamiliar Sten submachine guns. His plan was already working. He imagined them rushing back to their wives. The wives in turn would tell their friends and before long the whole area would know that a British major in a kilt had weapons for anyone who would follow him in the fight against the dirty Germans.

Cournil's little group now gathered around Macpherson in the dark. You two, Macpherson ordered. You will hide here in the bushes and fire on any German patrol that threatens to cross the bridge and discover us. Then he pointed to two others. You will go to the far side of the bridge and do the same. When I whistle, you will run back to this side and we will get in the truck and get the hell out of here. The Resistance would stand guard. Team Quinine would attach the bombs.

It took Macpherson and Bourbon about ten minutes to place the charges and squeeze the tips off the five-minute time pencils. Macpherson whistled, everyone withdrew, they climbed in the truck, and the terrific rattle of its engine began again. They had crossed safely back over the main road by the time they heard the massive boom. A great cheer went up in the truck. "The Cantal Resistance," Macpherson said years later, "was now in business."

A former French army officer, complete with waxed mustache and dusted-off uniform, marched pompously into Team Quinine's camp proclaiming that he led a nearby group who wanted to help liberate France. Minutes later, two boys, who were also leaders of a nearby maquis, tore in on a motorized bicycle, looking to fight. Macpherson's bridge-blowing strategy had worked.

To Team George's camp in Brittany, men in clogs and overalls walked as far as fifty miles. The arrival of the uniformed Jeds drew new Resistance fighters out of the woods exactly as the shadow chiefs had hoped. Meanwhile, the leaders of France's existing Resistance groups, whose memberships numbered from the tens to the thousands, also poured into the command posts set up by the seven newly arrived Jedburgh teams and the other French, British, and American agents already in France.

Over and over, as each group of maquis leaders arrived, the Jeds reiterated their mission. The point is not just to kill Germans. The point is to do whatever it takes to help the Allied armies. Each maquis leader got the same speech and gave the same retort: We have been waiting so long for our chance for revenge. It was hard to imagine that the maquis would be able to keep themselves focused on the tasks the Jeds and agents would assign them—trouble was bound to come. But the job desperately needed to be done.

In Normandy, Ike needed the Resistance "bonus" even more than he had anticipated. On the eastern end of his beachhead, the British under Montgomery had still failed to take their D-Day objective: the strategically crucial city of Caen, whose roads led straight to Paris. Across the Caen region's flat landscape, Hitler had easily roared up with his panzer corps and, using the villages as defensive obstacles, maintained a punishing checkerboard defense. Montgomery tried again to take Caen on June 7 and one more time on June 13. Both times he failed.

On the western beaches, after the terrible slog at Omaha, the Americans had barely moved inland when they found themselves bogged down in a maze of thousands of shrub- and tree-topped earthen walls—the hedgerows that crisscrossed northern France. Norman farmers had built the walls nearly two millennia earlier, in Roman times, to mark the borders between their pastures and contain their cows. Yet American intelligence had entirely failed both to take note of them and to bring them to the attention of the military planners.

With no forewarning, therefore, the tired, frightened American infantrymen on the ground faced the hedgerows that towered, one every hundred yards, like twenty-foot-high, ten-foot-thick fortress battlements. An average of fourteen hedgerows per kilometer knotted the Normandy landscape and into each one seemed to be dug yet another German machine-gun nest. The Americans had loaded hundreds of ships with Sherman tanks and risked thousands of lives bringing them ashore, but they now discovered that in this terrain the tanks were virtually useless.

The French called the countryside of western Normandy the *bocage*, meaning the land of the groves, for the thousands of them contained by the hedgerows. The Battle of the Bocage, as it would come to be called, was a fight not of the air force or the tank corps, but of the riflemen. It was a slug by slug, climb over your dead buddy, one farm field at a time battle. Clear across the seventy-mile front line, thousands of little skirmishes were fought, and thousands of men on both sides died over territory the size of football fields. It was a far cry from the easy advance the Allies had envisioned, and things fell even further behind schedule.

Eisenhower's strategists had hoped to take the deepwater harbor at Cherbourg by June 16; it was June 18 before the attack on Cherbourg was even ready to begin. They planned to push their troops quickly inland by thirty-five miles, to a line between Granville and Falaise, by June 23. As things stood, it had taken nearly an entire week, until June 12, a third of the allotted time, for the Allies to move barely five miles inland. That wasn't the worst.

Since the Granville-Falaise line made the planned launching point for the breakout into Brittany and the massive eastward sweep to chase the Germans home, the second phase of Overlord was way behind schedule before it had even started. This left Hitler with plenty of time to organize his second line of defense and to bring in forces from a distance.

On June 8, the 2nd SS Panzer Division began snaking its way up the backbone of France from Toulouse. On June 12, Hitler ordered an entire SS panzer corps of thirty-five thousand men and two SS armored divisions to move to Normandy from the Russian front. Panzer and infantry divisions began trudging to the battlefield from Brittany, the Netherlands, Bordeaux, Poland, Hungary, Denmark, and Norway. To drive Eisenhower back into the sea, all the Germans in Normandy needed to do was hold out until these tens of thousands of reinforcements arrived.

In London, on June 7, Eisenhower, acknowledging his need for Resistance help, gave General Pierre Koenig, commander of the French Forces of the Interior (FFI), de Gaulle's umbrella organization for the Resistance, a position on the SHAEF staff. Eisenhower hoped this would bolster the morale of the Resistance and spur them to further action. Koenig took charge of the Jeds and agents in France, began integrating his own French officers into the F and RF structure of SFHQ, and named his headquarters the État Major, Forces Français de l'Intérieur (EMFFI). Even more than Ike ever imagined, thanks to Overlord's poor start, he needed the air forces and the French Resistance to defuse the pressure on his troops and slow down the German advance.

In their command posts in the forests of France, the Jed teams spread out their maps, circled sections of train tracks that had not yet been cut, gave the maquis leaders sacks of bombs, and urged them on their way. First, a group in Brittany assigned to the track between Rennes and Dol, say, might mangle a fifty-yard length of rail near Rennes. While the Germans repaired that, the maquis teams would blow, or even remove with sledgehammers and shovels, another length near Dol. When the overworked German repair crews turned their attention to the new cut, the group attacked a length right in the middle. This would make rail lines impassable for the Germans moving to Normandy.

In the southwest, meanwhile, a column of the 2nd SS Panzer Division, ordered to move from Toulouse, had already been forced to resort to the roads. A couple of days after Macpherson had blown his bridge, the 2nd SS Panzer began to wind along the roads of Team Quinine's area. Since cutting rails would do nothing, Macpherson had to find another way to slow them down with his newly invigorated Resistance.

With five or six maquisards, he sneaked through the woods with as much plastic explosive as they could carry. They crawled along a winding path to the road and saw, through the failing evening light, that the trucks, cars, and tanks of the division had pulled over for the night. The German troops set up camps in groups of about four hundred with an interval of a mile between each. The convoy extended as far as the eye could see.

Darkness fell. The echoes of the German voices went quiet. Macpherson and his recruits moved gingerly up the road. In deadly silence, lest they alert the German lookouts, they ringed four tree trunks, two on each side of the road, with primed explosives. They prepared the fuses, but did not yet light them. They dug a hole through the thin tarmac and planted a mine. It would be hidden by the fallen trees. By the time the morning sky began to change from black to violet, Macpherson and his crew had stealthily prepared to fell not one but three booby-trapped barricades across the road.

The sun rose. A German voice shouted orders. The first of the convoy's engines roared to life. A loud series of bangs echoed warningly through the woods. The convoy rolled cautiously forward, around a corner, and discovered a messy interlocking barrier of tree branches and leaves. The Germans squealed to a stop.

Suddenly, the rattling automatic fire of a single Sten gun sounded from the woods. In the back of a soft-topped troop transport, several German soldiers shouted out in pain. Others slumped over dead. The shooting ceased as suddenly as it started. A Resistance man crashed ecstatically through the woods with his emptied Sten gun, laughing as he went. Macpherson watched the action from his hiding place two hundred yards away in the brush.

On the road, an armored car drove up the German column and tried to push the trees out of the way. They were too heavy. The Germans sent for a tank with a bulldozer blade. It took an hour for all the trucks and cars to move off the road to let it pass. Up came the tank, and quickly it shoved the trees aside. It turned around, mission accomplished, and hit the hidden mine. One of the tank's tracks lay on the road like a piece of ripped clothing. The disabling of the tank had made the roadblock even worse.

A second tank roared up the column to tow the first away. This time, it took only half an hour since the support vehicles had already been moved off the road. Finally, all the engines of the column came to life, roaring together like a pride of lions, and began to move. But—*Achtung!*—just up the road they ran into the second barrier. *Halt!* The Germans squealed to another stop. Again, a man with a Sten gun opened fire and again a few Germans slumped dead in their trucks.

This time the Nazis sent up some engineers to examine the barrier for mines, but there were none. Instead, Macpherson's group had suspended grenades in the branches by their pins, which they had greased. An engineer unknowingly bumped one, the grenade slipped off its pin and exploded, and the engineer lay in a bloody heap. Farther up the road, at the third and last group of felled trees, Macpherson had not laid a booby trap at all. The funny part was that the Germans wasted an hour looking for mines and grenades that were not there.

By the time they cleared Macpherson's little ambush, the troops of the panzer division had wasted over six hours. Ten to twenty men had been killed. Macpherson and his men climbed into the back of the gasogene truck at the prearranged rendezvous point. They laughed and slapped one another's backs and told their stories. True, a six-hour delay was only an inconvenience. But even the Germans recognized that if it were repeated, say, every ten miles over the length of a five-hundred-mile journey, the delay would be crucial. And the Germans did not plan on losing a battle because of some "terrorists."

# CHAPTER NINETEEN
## *"ALLES KAPUTT"*

In the week after D-Day, the Resistance made 950 cuts in the French rail lines. In Indre, where Jedburgh Team Hugh operated, the maquis added further cuts in the line arriving at Châteauroux from Toulouse, permanently frustrating the rail movement of the 2nd SS Panzer Division that Team Quinine had attacked in Cantal. In the Rhône Valley, every train leaving Marseille for Lyon after June 6 was derailed at least once. "Railway movement in area now nil," radioed Arthur Brown of Team Quinine.

By the time the Resistance and Allied air forces were done, Ike's intelligence officers reported, hardly a train could move in France. Hitler's frustrated reinforcements had no choice but to hop off the trains and forge a slow slog to Normandy by road, where nuisances of all kinds could slow them down.

French children dropped lumps of sugar in German gas tanks and clogged their engines. Villagers stretched wires across roads to behead German motorcycle outriders. Farmers removed road signs at crossroads, causing wrong turns and traffic pileups that captured POWs would later confirm wasted precious time for the Germans. Trees and telephone poles strewn across the roads forced entire convoys to come to a halt.

Near Jasseron, in Ain, not far from the Swiss border, a maquis group felled every tree for a mile and a half and laid them across the Germans' path. The Nazis took the local mayor hostage and threatened to shoot him if the road was not cleared in twelve hours. The population pushed the trees to the side of the road. A message then came from the maquis: if the trees were not replaced in three hours, *they* would shoot the mayor. The citizens put their aching backs again to work, replaced the trees, and the mayor, thinking he would be safer, ran off to fight with the maquis.

Such seemingly trivial interferences in the movement of troops and equipment by road, repeated over the length and breadth of France, caused Hitler massive confusion and delay. The Germans crawled toward Normandy at a snail's pace at best. With each small victory against the Germans, the French became even bolder, more men disappeared into woods to join the Resistance fight, and the effort grew.

But with increased boldness came decreased discipline, and despite Jedburgh and agent exhortations of caution, vengeance attacks began. Near the Breton town of Lamballe, two soldiers casually strolling to the store for butter were assassinated. In Morbihan, Breton guerrilla fighters, armed by Paul Cyr's groups, burst into cafés, sprayed coffee-sipping Germans with bullets, and then hijacked their trucks and motorcycles.

In Bob Kehoe's neck of the woods, on June 11, two German officers stopped in their staff car at a farm on the edge of the forest where Kehoe's team had set up its command post. As chance would have it, a group of Resistance men, armed by the SAS before Team Frederick had a chance to warn them against trigger-happy vengeance, had gathered in the farmhouse. One of the German officers knocked politely and, in his best French, asked if he might please have directions to the town of Carhaix. "The answer received," as Kehoe's team leader Adrian Wise wrote in his report, "was about five slugs in the belly."

To the German high command, the increased and emboldened activity of the "terrorist movement," as it called the French Resistance, already represented an unacceptable security risk to its defense against the invasion. Hitler ordered his commanders in France to take all necessary steps against the undercover fighters.

Just as the Allied shadow chiefs had feared, the Germans launched extensive operations to neutralize the Resistance threat. The SS hunted down all known Resistance leaders. Thirty-five "generals" and eighty-five "colonels" of the Armée Secrète were arrested, endangering the Resistance effort to assist Ike's Transportation Plan just as the shadow bosses had anticipated when they first instituted the Jedburgh scheme.

The German soldiers began to think of the Resistance fighters as murderous bandits who bore no resemblance to a properly uniformed, "honorable" battlefield adversary. The Germans would viciously carry out Hitler's orders to root out the Resistance. Since the "terrorists" did not abide by the rules of war, they would not be protected by them. The Resistance would find no refuge in the Geneva convention's dictates regarding the treatment of prisoners.

The 2nd SS Panzer Division, the target of Tommy Macpherson's Team Quinine and many other Resistance groups, issued a special order for battling the maquis. "Houses from which shots have been fired, together with their neighboring houses, will be burnt to the ground," the orders said. For every German soldier wounded, three maquis will be killed. For every German killed, execute ten.

Within less than a week after D-Day, momentum in the German fight against the maquis and Resistance miscreants who caused so many nuisances reached a sudden climax. The Jeds, agents, and Resistance fighters had gotten off to a good start, but the Germans were not about to lose the war because of a bunch of farmers, bakers, and students. The Resistance element of Ike's Transportation Plan, now so important because of the delays in Normandy, was in grave danger. The Germans launched a massive purge to extinguish the Resistance interference with their migration to Normandy. If they were successful, they would be one step closer to pushing Eisenhower off the beaches.

In Côtes-du-Nord, on the afternoon of the killing of the two German officers who stopped at the farmhouse to ask directions, Bob Kehoe and Team Frederick leader Adrian Wise heard the tat tat tat of sporadic gunfire coming from the east side of their hiding place in the Forêt de Doualt. The Resistance sentries must have exchanged fire with a German patrol, Kehoe and Wise thought, and worried no more.

But as the day progressed, the sporadic gunfire became more regular. The shooting spread to the west side of the forest, and before long, the battle sounds popped continuously from all directions. That was when Kehoe and Wise finally realized that the 2nd Parachute Division had launched a huge attack.

"What are we going to do?" Kehoe asked Wise, now that he finally understood his predicament.

"Stay here," Wise said.

Kehoe worried that the gung-ho SAS would want Team Frederick to join them in fighting a pitched battle, the one thing the Jeds had been taught never to do. How could a motley crew of Resistance fighters ever be expected to beat a much larger, more experienced, and better equipped German force?

Kehoe whispered to Wise, "If we stay here, we'll just end up in the grave."

"But if we move out, then what are we going to do?" To abandon their post, Wise thought, would mean the end of their mission and an end to the important task of stopping German movement from Brittany.

A messenger suddenly came crashing through the woods. The Germans have surrounded the forest with a force of about four hundred troops, he said. Team Frederick, the SAS, and the entire base would soon be trapped. Wise told Kehoe to hide the radios, which were too heavy to carry on the run. The SAS commander had ordered a general withdrawal.

In the best tradition of Jedburgh training, Kehoe, Wise, and Bloch-Auroch sprinted away through the woods as fast as they could. They flung themselves over the Breton hedgerows from one cow pasture into the next. Desperately, they increased the distance between themselves and the gunfire and by sheer good luck found their way through a gap in the German cordon. Darkness fell, and Team Frederick hid itself in a farm field's ditch.

Separated from their radio, Team Frederick was useless to Eisenhower and the Allies, but they would, at least for now, survive the Germans' vicious purge of French Resistance. Eight hundred desperate civilians in Cantal and five hundred Resistance fighters in Morbihan would not. The German attempt to annihilate the maquis assistance to Eisenhower's forces had begun.

On June 9, two days before the attack on Team Frederick in the Forêt de Doualt, two companies of the now notorious 2nd SS Panzer Division roared into the small Corrèze town of Tulle, about fifty miles north of where Macpherson and Team Quinine had been dropped. The Germans, arriving in Tulle, had lashed live Frenchmen to the front of their vehicles as a deterrent against Resistance snipers who would not wish to kill their countrymen. The next day, 120 men of the same panzer division swooped down on the village of Oradour-sur-Glane, sixty miles away, north of Limoges. And on June 18, the crack warriors of a German paratroop division attacked Paul Cyr's Team George and the SAS's Base Dingson, where about five thousand maquisards had now gathered.

The descent on Dingson came after a huge equipment drop by a flight of thirty planes, which aroused German suspicion. The Germans arrived at

Oradour because they mistakenly believed a rumor that the peaceful town harbored a maquis group who had captured a German official and intended to publicly execute and burn him. They went to Tulle because, for a day, the town had been occupied by a fierce group of maquisards, who had briefly defeated the small garrison. Forty of its troops had been "murdered," and the maquisards, the Germans claimed, had cut off their victims' testicles and stuffed them in their mouths. The arriving detachments of the 2nd SS Panzer Division, in both Tulle and Oradour, would wreak the German revenge.

In Oradour, SS troopers assembled in the village square the entire citizenry of about 650, including the children who attended the school from out of town. They cried for their absent mothers. In the courtyard of Tulle's armaments factory, the troopers gathered only its three thousand men. Up in Morbihan, the loud march of German paratroop boots on asphalt announced their placement of heavy mortars and machine-gun nests around the five to nine hundred barely armed civilians, most of whom, with the exception of the SAS and Jeds mingling among them, had never even learned how to aim. The German Resistance purge was in full swing.

In the Oradour village square, a German officer demanded that the mayor name hostages, for use in negotiation, presumably, with the nonexistent maquis. "I name myself," the mayor said, "and if that is not sufficient, I name all the members of my family." It wasn't sufficient. The Germans ordered all the women to go to the church. Mothers with babies, grandmothers, and children shuffled down the hill. More than four hundred had crowded under the spired house of worship when the doors slammed closed.

In Tulle, the Germans decided, three maquisards would pay with their lives for each of the forty Germans killed there, a total, as the terrible arithmetic went, of 120. A call for volunteer hangmen went out. One German enlisted man walked away in tears—he said he could not do it—but sufficient others stepped forward. By afternoon, the Germans had been able to identify only two genuine maquis among the three thousand townsmen, but that stopped nothing. "Why are your shoes so dirty?" a German officer shouted at one man. "If you were a decent citizen, they would be clean. You must be a maquisard." A bicycle factory worker, a teacher, a barber, because the officer deemed them dirty or unshaved, stood to one side of the courtyard. The selection of men like them went on until 120 had been chosen.

The men of Oradour were marched out of the village square and distributed between a coach house and five garages and barns, where they huddled away from their weapons-toting captors at the doors. In Morbihan, German tracer bullets had quickly started a forest fire. The sadly inexperienced Resistance could barely see. Some waited before pulling the trigger to confirm that a figure in the smoke was an enemy and not a friend. Many waited too long. The battle-hardened German paratroopers entertained no such qualms. As many as four thousand maquis from all over the Breton district, more fodder for the German bullets, began moving in to help.

The soldiers in Tulle led the first ten of the selected men out onto the street. The Nazi commander allowed the local priest to bless them. An SS officer read the order for their execution, as though this formality could make such things legitimate. Some of the condemned cried. Others stood stoically and said nothing. One or two still grasped loaves of bread they had earlier brought with them in case they got hungry. Two Algerians began to shriek. "We good Frenchman. We good Algerians."

"Make an act of contrition for all your sins," the priest said to the men about to be hanged in Tulle, "and I will give you absolution." The whole group did as they were told. But, after the day's horrendous events unfolded, the Germans who surrounded them would be in far more desperate need of God's forgiveness.

In Morbihan, all the professional soldiers, nearly every SAS officer, were now dead. Paul Cyr, who had been fighting all day, walked past an impromptu first-aid station that could not handle a tenth of the wounded. Hundreds of men, many of them either barely teenagers or longtime grandfathers, lay around the farmyard dead or dying. Some screamed; some said nothing. Everything was utter confusion. Defeat had been admitted, every man for himself had been declared, and the wounded men argued over who should stay behind, winning honor and certain death, to blow the weapons cache. "Don't be foolish," one man said to another who wished to be the hero. "You're only shot through the arms and legs and I'm shot through the chest."

In Tulle, when the condemned men got up from their knees, the troopers escorted them to the first lamppost, from which a noose already dangled and against which two ladders leaned. The victim climbed up one ladder, the hangman up the other. It was a simple matter of slipping the noose around the victim's neck, pushing him off his rung, and proceeding to the next lamppost. When the lampposts were filled, the Germans began hanging nooses from the balconies of houses. Some victims died instantly. Others twitched and convulsed until an irritated German delivered a coup de grâce.

When the Germans opened fired with their machine guns on the Oradour men boxed in the garages, many of them screamed for their mothers or wives or children. When the firing and the screaming stopped, the soldiers callously stomped over the tangles of arms and legs and finished off with their pistols anyone who moved or moaned. Then they hauled in straw and hay, tossed matches on it, closed the doors, and left.

In the church where the women and children were, a group of soldiers lugged in a heavy box, put it in the nave, lit a fuse that came out of the box, and left. Thick black smoke began to pour out. When the women and children began to scream, the soldiers shut them up with rifle fire and grenades. Some straw, a few matches, and the entire building was ablaze. The roof timbers soon crackled and collapsed.

The total number of men, women, and children killed in Oradour was 642. In Morbihan, Paul Cyr had seen six hundred Resistance boys die in just one hour of fighting. In Tulle, the Germans, after they had hanged ninety-nine men, ran out of rope. The only way to carry on would have been to cut corpses down and reuse their nooses. The Germans looked at their handiwork hanging along the length of the street, eyed the twenty-one men still left to hang, and gave them clemency. Enough, the Germans decided, is enough.

When the children did not return to their homes in the hills at the end of their school day in Oradour, it still took twelve hours for their parents to summon the courage to venture to the village themselves. A couple of hundred miles north in Brittany, however, it took only hours after the battle at Base Dingson for the Germans to tack posters on the trees and telephone poles about parachuted agents like Paul Cyr and Bob Kehoe. "All persons of the male sex," the notice said, "who should aid directly or indirectly the crews or personnel of enemy airplanes dropped by parachute will be shot on the spot. Women who are guilty of a similar offense will be sent to concentration camps in Germany." Nearby in Carhaix, the Germans, not yet sated, hanged four maquis in the streets with a sign that read: "This happens to any man who kills a German soldier."

Paul Cyr and his Team George had found a way to break through the German lines and escape. That night, about two o'clock in the morning, a huge explosion from several miles away knocked them off their feet. The wounded men back at the farm had settled their argument, it seemed. Bob Kehoe, still hiding out in Brittany, saw the sign about assisting the paratroopers. "You don't say," he said sarcastically. The German operation had managed to scatter the Breton Resistance and completely sever their crucial contact with the SFHQ, the planes that brought them arms, and the Allied commanders they were supposed to help.

Down south, meanwhile, the first parent to summon the nerve finally came down from the hills and approached a German sentry on the edge of Oradour. "Where are the children?" he asked. The sentry looked at him. *"Alles kaputt,"* he said. *"Alles kaputt."*

# CHAPTER TWENTY
# BLOWING TRAINS TO BITS

Beginning on D-Day plus thirteen, June 19, the worst storm in forty years whipped up a raging gale over the English Channel. It drove eight-foot waves against the Normandy beaches and flooded ships' engines and smashed their hulls. In only three days, the storm grounded eight hundred Allied vessels above the high-water mark and disabled five hundred more. Over the entire Normandy campaign, not even all the German guns, mines, and bombs would destroy so many.

With the navy unable to make deliveries, the buildup of men and supplies slowed to a trickle. By June 22, only 57 percent of Operation Overlord's targeted supplies and 78 percent of its planned personnel had made it to the beach. The six hundred thousand troops ashore were desperately short of supplies, reinforcements, and ammunition. The ferocious winds also grounded Allied planes, which meant nearby Germans could move freely toward the battle zone without fear of bombing or strafing. Things for Eisenhower's Overlord had gone from bad to worse.

Still bogged down in the hedgerows, meanwhile, thousands of men fought and died in the ongoing Battle of the Bocage. Far behind schedule, the armies still had taken neither the strategically important gateway to northern France at Caen nor the much-needed deepwater harbor at Cherbourg. Nowhere had the Allies pushed more than twenty-five miles inland, and in most places they had moved five or less. The lack of elbow room had plagued the buildup effort with traffic jams and holdups, a largely academic problem now, since the artificial harbor at Omaha had been savaged by the storm.

In those hopeless last weeks of June, high-ranking visitors to Eisenhower's headquarters gloomily began to discuss the possibility of defeat. They thought, Eisenhower would write, "that we were stalemated and that those who had prophesied a gloomy fate for Overlord were being proved correct." Eisenhower more than ever needed the shadow armies' "bonus"—at just the time of the Germans' attempt to purge the Resistance in France.

Fortunately, although the Germans had managed to sever Allied contact with the Jeds and maquis in Brittany, their attack on the Resistance in the rest of France had been far more vicious than successful. There was still a possibility that the stiffened Resistance efforts could do to the Germans what the storm had done to the Allies—slow them down—and even the score while the Allied armies recovered.

On the same night the wind and rain began to wash away the Allied military commanders' advantage in the Battle of the Buildup, Michel de Bourbon, Team Quinine's second in command, snipped the phone lines that ran from a railway stationmaster's hut outside a little town between Cahors and Souillac. It was after midnight and pitch dark. SHAEF had ordered the SFHQ to redouble efforts to keep Germans from Normandy, and the Jeds, agents, and Resistance all over France blew bridges, cut rails, and attacked troop columns.

For his part, Bourbon planned to derail a German troop train tonight. Slipping with two Sten-toting maquis into the station hut, Bourbon noisily pulled some of the rail switches and waited for a response. He needed the stationmaster's help to ensure that he did not mistakenly bomb a passenger train and its hundreds of innocent civilians. Before long, an old man in a nightgown came stumbling down the stairs.

"What are you doing!" the stationmaster demanded.

Before he answered, Bourbon listened carefully for the footsteps of anyone hiding upstairs. His comrades pointed their guns at the stationmaster. All was quiet. "We are Free French," Bourbon finally said. "We are going to cut the line and we want to know when the next military train is coming. Are you with us or against us?"

The next train, the stationmaster said, would be coming in about an hour. "But it would be best to phone to make sure."

"The phones no longer work," Bourbon told him, referring to the wires he had snipped outside the hut. Go upstairs and get dressed, he told the stationmaster. When too much time passed, Bourbon became suspicious and climbed the stairs himself. The stationmaster had the phone in his hand.

"I . . . I was trying to confirm the time of the train."

"I told you the phone does not work," Bourbon growled.

"It does," the stationmaster said, tapping frantically on the phone cradle.

Bourbon went to the wall and ripped out the phone line. "That proves the phone won't work!" he said. "Now if you're coming with us, get your things. Or you can wait here to be shot by the Germans."

Bourbon, the stationmaster, and the maquis followed the moonlit glint of the rails to where they gently curved into the countryside. With duct tape, Bourbon carefully affixed explosives in two places, about three yards apart, on the outside of the curve. Back in England, the shadow warfare boffins had manufactured the bombs to fit perfectly in the indentation in the rails. A pressure switch placed just up the track would detonate them when the train's front wheel rolled over it.

If all went according to Bourbon's Milton Hall training, the locomotives, with no rail to guide them around the curve, would keep going straight, piling down the embankment. And the Nazis would have to send not just a team to mend the rail, but a crane to move the train cars off the tracks.

Bourbon and his crew slipped off into the night, safe from any angry Germans who might survive the wreck.

"Have blown rail near station. Repair effectively hindered," signaled Bourbon through Team Quinine's radio operator, Arthur Brown. "Have blown railway four places south Maurs," Brown radioed again within hours. Team Quinine, along with the seven Jed teams dropped into France, kept frantically busy, and in mid-June, the SFHQ dropped two more Jed teams into France to join the fray.

After parachuting into central France on June 20, Team Ian quickly disabled the Bordeaux-Paris rail line and destroyed a factory that made charcoal for German gasogene trucks. "Have been playing games with Boche patrols," radioed the other newcomer Jed team, Team Hamish, who had been dropped in the same region a week earlier. "It's fun."

Jeds, agents, and Resistance furiously continued to fell trees on roads, halt German vehicles with tire-bursters, uproot road signs, and radio convoy positions to London for action by the air forces. The lethal combination of the bombing from the air and the sabotage on the ground meant that the German reinforcements moved to Normandy at a sluggish pace of only forty-five miles a day, a quarter of their average in normal conditions.

In the north of France, for example, the first elements of the German 265th Infantry Division left Quimper in Brittany on June 6. The last arrived at the Normandy front on June 13; it took them seven days to travel two hundred miles. Resistance tire-bursters flattened so many of the 265th's tires that they ran out of repair kits. From Vannes, in Brittany, the 275th Infantry Division took six days to move sixty-seven miles to the beachhead. A division of tanks, the Panzer Lehr, could not manage a mere 150 miles in less than five days.

From farther afield, a panzer division raced from Russia to the Rhine in a week, then slogged for three weeks to get only four hundred miles across France to Caen. The 271st Infantry Division, stationed on the Mediterranean coast, required twenty days to traverse a distance that should have taken three. The 277th Infantry Division needed twenty-two days to make its way from southern France. Because of the threat of a complete Resistance takeover there, many of Hitler's best troops could not be moved north at all.

On June 17, for example, three thousand German troops that might have otherwise been sent to Normandy had to attack a maquis concentration in Corrèze. The containment of another huge maquis uprising on the Vercors plateau, in the southeast, distracted thousands of other Nazi troops.

The ferocious 2nd SS Panzer Division, "Das Reich," which had perpetrated the terrible atrocities at Tulle and Oradour, had been massively delayed by Tommy Macpherson's booby-trapped trees, hundreds of other Resistance actions along the length of France, and the air force bombings of the bridges over the Loire. Das Reich left Toulouse on D-Day and arrived, weakened and demoralized, at Normandy's Saint-Lô seventeen days later.

The delay of Das Reich in particular, military analysts would later report, was crucial to the Allies. Had the division's thousands of hardened warriors arrived with their hundreds of tanks before the storm was over, they might have pushed Operation Overlord back into the sea. But as it was, while Das Reich and the rest of the German stragglers slowly humped their way across France, Ike's storm-washed forces had the chance to rehabilitate themselves.

"The combined action of resistance groups and Allied air forces have achieved success beyond expectation in restricting German troop movement by rail," said an Allied 21st Army Group intelligence summary dated June 23, the same day the last dregs of Das Reich staggered into Normandy. "The terrorist movement crippled certain parts of France," said the diary of the German forces in France. "Cases became numerous where whole formations of troops were surrounded for many days and, in isolated locations, simply killed off," wrote Field Marshal Gerd von Rundstedt, the overall commander of German defenses in France.

Far beyond the hoped-for "bonus," what Eisenhower got, according to the official historian of the SOE's work, "was of a size and importance comparable to the Air Forces." On June 20, Prime Minister Winston Churchill wrote to his minister of economic warfare: "Every effort must be made to supply the Maquis at once with rifles, Bren guns, Piat guns, mortars and bazookas and whatever else is needful to prevent the collapse of the Movement and extend it."

At four in the morning on June 25, five days after Churchill wrote his memo, 180 B-17s took off with fighter escorts and flew toward France. Flak downed one bomber, a German fighter another, and two more planes ran into engine trouble and turned back. The rest, in what was called Operation Zebra, dropped more than two thousand containers of Brens, Stens, ammunition, and other supplies to the Resistance in France.

Up in Normandy, the Channel gale finally blew itself out, and the Allied logisticians quickly resumed the supply chain and troop buildup. By the last week of June, 13,500 and 7,000 tons of daily supplies crowded the landing areas at Omaha and Utah beaches, respectively.

On June 22, the Allies at last began their assault on Cherbourg. By June 27, they had won it. As June came to a close, Ike's forces had finally achieved the first critical objective of the Normandy campaign—permanently securing the beachhead and installing adequate avenues of supply.

For the first time since D-Day, Ike and his military commanders began looking forward to the second phase of Overlord—the breakout from the bubble of German forces surrounding the beachhead and into the countryside of northern France. What the Allied forces had to do first, however, was advance to the position from which the breakout attack could be effectively launched.

The plan called for the First U.S. and the Second British armies to shove shoulder to shoulder as a vast human bulldozer, pushing back the encirclement of German defenders to a distance of thirty-five miles from the beach—the starting position for the breakout attempt. As the troops crawled over the hedgerows toward this inland line, fleet after fleet of Allied vessels would meanwhile wash in waves over the Channel, depositing more than a million men and 177,000 vehicles on the beaches in anticipation of the "second D-Day."

The idea was that when this preparatory stage was complete, the Americans to the west would find themselves in possession of the marvelous rolling high-lands as far south as Granville that, free of hedgerows, made beautiful fighting ground in which their Sherman tanks could at last roar eastward toward Germany and westward into Brittany. To the east, the British would have not only triumphed in Caen but conquered farther to Falaise, opening up much-coveted flatlands, both for their armored fighting machines and for building new runways and air bases from which shorter-range Allied fighter-bombers could support the ensuing battle.

With these advantageous inland positions, and with the necessary men and supplies then deposited on the beaches, Ike's strategists envisioned a deci-sive all-out attack. If successful, the Allies would break through the German encirclement and finally be in a position to conquer the peninsula of Brittany and its valuable deepwater ports, begin the eastward chase toward the German border, and land the southern invasion forces of Operation Anvil on the Mediterranean beaches.

But the success of these next phases of Overlord, like that of the landing it-self, depended on ensuring that no more than a trickle of German reinforce-ments arrived in the area, either while the Normandy troops slogged through the *bocage* toward the breakout starting line or later during the breakout attempt itself. Efforts to delay German migration to Normandy had to be renewed.

Looking slightly beyond the breakout to the expansion into the Brittany peninsula, Allied commanders dreaded the prospect of facing still more earthen obstacles in the hedgerow-crisscrossed Breton landscape. Tacticians looked for ways to dislodge German defenders who might lethally entrench themselves in Breton hedgerows the way they had in the Normandy *bocage*. The Resistance, the planners hoped, offered the possibility of sweeping aside German machine gunners in the Brittany hedgerows by rising up from behind and, in essence, shooting them in the back.

In mid-June, therefore, Eisenhower's headquarters ordered the EMFFI and SFHQ shadow chiefs to continue both to "prevent or delay movement of enemy formations into the battle area" and to prepare, "at a later date, to ren-der maximum assistance to the allied advance into the Brittany Peninsula." In early July, SHAEF added to this a directive to stop southern German forces from heading north by compelling "the enemy to maintain large forces in the southern zone for the purposes of containing Resistance."

In much of France, as events unfolded, the Resistance would spend July as it had spent June: stalling German troops who might otherwise charge to Normandy. In the north and northeast of France, for example, the idea was to maintain sabotage along the enemy's supply routes and carry out attacks sufficient to tie down German forces coming from the east. In the center of France, where Team Hugh worked, the shadow chiefs hoped the Resistance might take complete control, forcing German troops moving through the area to fight every inch of the way.

But in southern France, the SFHQ hoped to arm and train seventy-seven thousand Resistance fighters by the end of July, in time for Operation Anvil. That mass of guerrillas would create a military diversion of such magnitude that Hitler could neither afford to move forces north to defend against Overlord nor effectively defend against the southern invasion when it came. And in Brittany, the plan was to quietly arm 30,500 men by the beginning of August in order to attack the Germans from behind when Overlord's expansion into the peninsula was hoped to begin.

The problem with the new shadow army plan for Brittany was that the German attacks on the Samwest and Dingson bases in mid-June had left Jed Teams Frederick and George on the run and the shadow chiefs out of contact with whatever was left of the Breton Resistance. Unless that contact could be reestablished, there would be no one to send the arms containers to, no one to train the Breton Resistance, and no one to help the Allied troops get past the Germans in the hedgerows when the expansion into Brittany finally began.

## CHAPTER TWENTY-ONE
# BACK IN ACTION

Large dark shadows passed over Bob Kehoe and his Team Frederick team-mates as they slept in the bottom of a farm field ditch in Brittany. The grass rustled. A hornlike bellow sounded. Kehoe bolted awake. The ebullient, "nothing will happen to me," Milton Hall attitude had been completely dispelled; fresh perspiration ran from Kehoe's armpits. He snapped his head around. What was that sound?

It was the day after Team Frederick had abandoned its radio and barely escaped the German raid on the Forêt de Doualt. Predawn brewed a steely gray light in the overcast sky. Stalks of grass stuck to Kehoe's troubled face, and patches of olive uniform, shredded by branches and briars during his frantic escape from the Forêt de Doualt, wilted from his prostrate body. Mud and manure caked him. He stank of yesterday's sweat.

The image of a German motorcycle with a machine-gun-mounted sidecar racing toward him the day before still haunted Kehoe. He and Team Frederick had arrived at the empty road that bordered the forest, thinking they only had to get across the tarmac to make their final getaway. They climbed onto the road, temporarily trapping themselves between the hedgerows on either side. Suddenly, the blare of a motorcycle engine echoed toward them.

Team Frederick threw themselves against the roadside earthen mound and tried to scramble away, but they were too slow. The machine gunner in the sidecar took aim. The Jed team was done for. Then, at the last moment, a Royal Air Force Beaufighter buzzed out of the sky and let loose its guns on Team Frederick's two-wheeled pursuer. Bob Kehoe and his colleagues had barely gotten away. By the time the team stumbled, terrified, to the bottom of this gully in the farm field, darkness completely submerged them. Nervously nibbling on crusts of bread from their pockets, they could not see a thing. They were too exhausted to care anymore.

Now Kehoe woke up to this strange sound of the bellowing and the rustling in the grass above. What was it? Pressing his body to the ground, he crawled up the side of the ditch. Carefully, he peeked over the edge. Team Frederick, Kehoe discovered, was surrounded—by Breton cows. He breathed a sigh of relief. But that did not mean Team Frederick was safe.

Together, Kehoe and his teammates silently took stock of their surroundings, keeping close to the ground, spying through the weeds. A farmhouse loomed over them, only fifty yards away. German troops or French collaborators might be billeted within, they knew. Kehoe and his companions quietly watched. Now what?

Team Frederick had no food or water. They had lost all contact with the maquisards they had met in the forest, and they had buried their two heavy radios in order to make a quick getaway. Without the radios, Team Frederick could get no guidance from London and give no help to the Allies. Alone in enemy-occupied France, they had no way of telling who could be trusted, no knowledge of the area, no clothes other than their uniforms, no ammunition, and no supplies. Without help, they could not possibly survive, let alone complete their mission.

They would have to take their chances with whoever lived in the farmhouse. Lieutenant Paul Bloch-Auroch, the team's native French speaker, heaved himself out of the ditch and strolled out of sight.

In central France, when Team Hugh similarly decided to call on the help of strangers, leader William Crawshay threw himself through the front door while his second in command burst in the back, both of them with their weapons at their shoulders, safety catches off. It took Crawshay and his team half an hour to convince the shrieking farmer and his family that they were not Germans. Bloch-Auroch took a more diplomatic approach in Brittany: he knocked on the farmhouse's front door.

Half an hour after his polite tap, he was ensconced again in the ditch, along with the twenty-two-year-old granddaughter of the farmhouse owner. The young woman, Simone Le Göeffic, dished out potatoes in gravy and bread to the famished men. She told Team Frederick that she was one of the Resistance's battalion of female bicycle couriers. She taught at a local school, which entitled her to travel on her bike around Brittany. In secret from the occupiers who examined her pass at checkpoints, she carried hastily scribbled messages in her bike's hollow handlebars or seat stem.

Or so she said. So far, Team Frederick had learned nothing that could reassure them that she was not, in fact, a Milice spy. "The area is crawling with enemy patrols," Simone said in French. "You must wait for me here until after dark." Tonight, she said, she would take Team Frederick to the leaders of Brittany's Resistance. Or, if she was lying, into the hands of the Gestapo. To Kehoe's teammates, Simone's story sounded almost too good to be true.

In wartime France, the Jeds and agents had quickly learned that deciding how to deal with strangers often meant a simple choice between trusting them and killing them. In the district of Saône-et-Loire, for example, two potential Resistance recruits presented themselves to a maquis leader. "They did not appear to be on the level," an American agent later reported matter-of-factly, "so he took them for a walk and shot them through the head."

Danger stimulates a sort of feral second sense in men. Err on the side of caution, and you might later find that you killed a fifteen-year-old boy who had done no wrong. Show mercy or trust, and you could end up in a Gestapo torture chamber. This was Team Frederick's dilemma. They decided not to shoot Simone. She departed, and the three spent an anxious day lying in the ditch, dozing on and off, and waiting for Simone's promised return. They prayed that they would not find out what it meant if she had lied.

The sun set, darkness descended, and Simone returned—alone. Team Frederick relaxed just a little. *Suivez-moi,* Simone whispered, follow me. The three walked cautiously with her along dark roads, through blacked-out towns, and along a winding path outside the Côtes-du-Nord village of Peumerit-Quintin. They came to a decrepit old farmhouse, thatched and made of stone, that its owner used for cows and hay. Making one more decision to trust, Team Frederick opened the door and walked through. Inside, a group of dirty, unshaven men crowded around. They were the leaders of all of the area's Resistance.

As the introductions began, one of them noticed the baby-faced looks of Bob Kehoe. "You must have forged your enlistment papers," the Resistance man said. Do the Americans send their children to fight their war? joked someone else. Kehoe blushed, everyone laughed, and the shaking of hands and clapping of backs continued. Simone Le Göeffic, as Bob Kehoe would write many years later, "was indeed the team's savior."

Almost immediately, the group began hatching plans for arming and training thousands of men throughout the Breton peninsula. Wise and Bloch-Auroch stabbed at a map, showing the leaders what rail lines had to be cut. The Resistance leaders marked farm fields that would make good drop grounds for weapons and supplies.

Team Frederick was back in business but for one huge problem: they still had no radio. Without it, there would be no manna of arms from the sky, no Allied authority to command the maquis, no reception of more Jed teams, and no assisting the Allied military commanders with the coming assault on Brittany. At least one member of Team Frederick would have to brave a return visit to the scene of the German attack on the Forêt de Doualt. And no one could be sure that the Germans, after the battle, had not planted mines or stationed snipers to lie in wait against such a return.

In pitch darkness, Kehoe and two maquis teenagers pulled out to the main road with the car's headlights turned off. They flew a terrifying fifteen miles through the blacked-out villages. They roared along German-controlled roads and through German-garrisoned towns. Headlights or not, Kehoe, in his American uniform, felt as bright as Times Square. But even civilian clothes would have done him no good if he got caught in a contraband automobile, after curfew, and had to explain himself in his high-school French.

Back at the farmhouse, a Resistance man had led Kehoe, Wise, and Bloch-Auroch to a shed and thrown open the doors. Inside, jacked up on timbers with its wheels removed, sat the automobile Kehoe was now riding in. The occupiers had appropriated nearly every vehicle in the area, but the Resistance man had deliberately made this one look worthless. He had smuggled home gallons of strictly rationed gasoline, one cup at a time, from the factory where he worked, and now he grandly offered to donate it to the Allied cause. *Pour vous!* he said. For you!

The Jeds and the Resistance men got to work. They retrieved the hidden wheels, bolted them in place, applied their muscle to the crank handle, and cheered as the engine rattled to life. The two teenage boys, members of the Resistance who knew the roads, had jumped in the front seats. Kehoe, before his teammates had a chance to think, jumped in the back. A determined look warned his colleagues not to tell him to get out.

Ever since Kehoe's arrival, the maquis had made a point of mentioning his young looks. Kehoe planned to take this chance to prove himself.

*Pas vous,* not you, one of the Frenchmen said. The errand in the forest was too important for this young kid. Not only would he have to get the radio, but he would have to make absolutely sure the Germans did not realize that Allied parachutists had arrived in the area. If Kehoe screwed up and got caught, the Germans would begin a widespread manhunt for his colleagues in northern Brittany. The suffering would be as awful as it had been during the Germans' search for Team George and their SAS colleagues in the peninsula's south.

There, the Germans, in their search, had nailed a five-year-old boy to a farmhouse door and bayoneted him in the stomach, leaving him moaning for hours before he finally died. They caught a Resistance liaison girl, lashed one end of a rope under her armpits, the other end to the saddle of a horse, and dragged her to her death. Discovering a farm that had been Team George's onetime hiding place, the Germans wrenched the live farmer's head off his neck, and then stabbed his wife and children.

The Germans would be equally ruthless in northern Brittany if they realized Team Frederick existed. The lives of many depended on Kehoe's making it back to the forest without getting caught. Still, Kehoe's teammates stood behind his decision to go, and now Kehoe flew with the two boys along the Breton roads. Finally, at the edge of the Forêt de Doualt, the car skidded to a stop.

While the French boys stayed with the vehicle, Kehoe anxiously marched down a path to Team Frederick's old command post. No matter how gingerly he stepped, twigs snapped under his feet. Tiptoeing would be no help at all if the Germans had planted land mines. Kehoe's heart beat wildly. An hour later, he arrived at the boulder behind which he had cached his first radio. German footprints blanketed the area. Kehoe's heart sank. The radio was gone.

Kehoe trudged forward to where he had hidden the second radio. When he buried it, he had written himself directions—so many paces from this rock and so many from that tree—like a pirate's treasure map. But the rocks and trees all around him looked the same. Kehoe ran about wildly. He picked up one rock, looked under it, replaced it, picked up another, then went back to the first. He checked under the same boulders again and again. Why did I have to insist on coming here alone? he wondered. To prove myself? That was just stupid.

Team Frederick would be nothing without the radio. The mission would be a failure.

In a frenzy, Kehoe rolled over rocks. The sky lightened. The morning sun threatened to tip over the horizon. He could not continue his futile search without threatening both himself and his Resistance colleagues waiting at the car. Dejectedly, he lifted one last boulder. There, incredibly, he found the radio. In a moment of ecstasy, he bent over to pick it up. Then he froze.

What if it's booby-trapped? he suddenly thought.

To hell with it, he decided.

He grabbed the forty-pound radio and sprinted through the woods to the car. Kehoe and the two Resistance boys raced back to the hideout where Wise and Bloch-Auroch paced anxiously. A wide grin covered Kehoe's face as he entered. I may look young, his expression said triumphantly to anyone who watched, but I'm the one who found the radio.

Back in England, a month after D-Day, Bill Dreux and the rest of the Milton Hall–based Jeds still crawled on their stomachs through muddy sheep pastures, playing what seemed like ridiculous war games and bitching every step of the way. At the Jedburgh base in Algeria, Aaron Bank, Bill Thompson, and the rest of about twenty-five Jed teams who had shipped to North Africa for drops into southern France wasted their time climbing up and down the Atlas Mountains. Poor Jack Singlaub, still recovering from his appendectomy at Milton Hall, scrambled to get medical permission to return to active duty before the battle for France had finished.

The Jeds scanned the U.S. Army newspaper *Stars and Stripes* and grimaced at headlines trumpeting the daring exploits of their former units who now fought in France or Italy. The Milton Hall mavericks had thought they would beat their buddies to France. They had thought of themselves as top-ranking schoolboys who had budged to the front of the line. Now they felt like class clowns who had been sent to the back.

By June 25, the SFHQ had dropped only nine Jed teams. The slow progress of the armies at Normandy meant there were no new orders to carry to the Resistance, and the anticipated German purge of the Resistance had not been as successful as the shadow chiefs had feared. More Jed teams had not yet been needed.

But now the main military forces prepared for the breakout, SHAEF had ordered renewed efforts to delay German reinforcements and the bolstering of the Resistance in Brittany and the southeast, and a radio message had been received at last from Bob Kehoe's Team Frederick. "Boche communications in chaos," Kehoe tapped out on his Morse key the morning he recovered his radio from the forest. "Our morale terrific."

In the last week of June and the coming month of July, fifteen more Jed teams—eleven from England, four from North Africa—would buckle on their parachutes and float through the night sky into France to assist with the next stage of Overlord. The total number of Jedburgh teams in France would then stand at twenty-four. Of these more than seventy men, two of them arriving in July, would break limbs on landing, and two others would barely live to see August.

# CHAPTER TWENTY-TWO
# NAPOLEON'S HAT

In the dead of night, hoping desperately to avoid German patrols, Bill Dreux followed a Resistance worker down the main street of the small German-occupied town of Courcité. It was his first full night in Pays de la Loire, the region east of Brittany and south of Normandy. Lumbering under the weight of the Sten guns, radio, and ammunition he parachuted with, Dreux could not stop imagining the effect the sight of this equipment, along with the six-by-four-inch American flag sewn on his shoulder, would have on a squad of German soldiers. Dreux's Team Gavin might die very stupidly, he thought, their adventure ending just as it began.

Dreux and his team had the mission of organizing the maquis in the north of Ille-et-Vilaine, a department at the base of Brittany, the closest to Normandy and the first into which the Allied breakout would eventually pour.

In the weeks from the end of June to mid-July, the Allied shadow chiefs now under Koenig's command packed ten Jed teams all over the Brittany peninsula. Their job was to drop to Resistance groups contacted by Bob Kehoe's reinvigorated Team Frederick, arm and train their shadow fighters, and then wait quietly to rise up when the Allies finally advanced into Brittany.

No Resistance in Ille-et-Vilaine could be contacted, however, so Dreux and his team dropped to the nearest known reception committee, seventy-five miles to the southeast. Until a way of transporting Team Gavin to its area of operations could be found, the Resistance there planned to stash Dreux and his colleagues in a safe house, which was why they now tiptoed through Courcité's main square.

A large church with a high steeple, gray in the dim moonlight, loomed ahead, and the Resistance man led Team Gavin toward it. Just how "safe" could any safe house be, right in the center of a German-occupied village? Dreux wondered.

Taking care that no one saw their approach, the group sneaked to a door at the side of the church rectory. The Resistance man knocked lightly. The door opened, and a sturdy, gray-haired priest quietly led them in, smiled, and shook their hands. When Dreux and his colleagues dumped their pile of guns and ammunition on the floor, the smile fell from the curé's lined face.

"I wasn't expecting anything like this," he said nervously to the Resistance man. "I thought I would be getting three agents in civilian clothes. Instead I get three paratroopers in full uniform with pistols, carbines, Sten guns, knives and the Good Lord knows what else."

The priest turned to Dreux's team leader, Major Carbuccia. "You know there are a good many Germans around here."

"Yes, Father, we know that."

"You aren't planning on turning my rectory into a battle station, are you?"

"No, Father."

The next day, Team Gavin radioed headquarters in London from the rectory attic. Five minutes later, a German direction-finding van drove into the main square, apparently having latched on to their signal. As the terribly suspenseful minutes passed, the frightened priest prayed fervently but silently while counseling parishioners. One old lady rattled on about her grandson and how big he was for his age. "Oh, my God help us," the priest said out loud. "God please help us." The old lady left in a huff.


A few hundred miles to the southeast, in the opposite corner of France, Henry McIntosh and his French teammates, Jean Sassi and Jacques Martin, climbed aboard an old truck, complete with a machine gun mounted over the cab. Team Chloroform was one of four Jed teams dropped in the south of France at the end of June both to assist with the effort to keep the Germans in the south from traveling north and to help train the hoped-for seventy-seven thousand Resistance fighters who would eventually rise up en masse.

Chloroform dropped in Drôme, on the outskirts of the Vercors plateau. Jean Sassi, the radio operator, parachuted from too high an altitude, drifted away from the drop zone, landed in a tree, and was nearly killed by a Resistance leader's booby trap. After all that, the team discovered that its assigned mission, to cut the north-south railroad from Valence to Gap and organize the local maquis, had already been accomplished.

So many maquis and parachutists had massed on the Vercors plateau, in fact, that work for Team Chloroform could hardly be found. Frustrated, McIntosh, Sassi, and Martin decided to travel forty miles east with a Resistance leader code-named Hermine. They planned to develop maquis squads for attack on the German north-south routes in the Hautes-Alpes, near the city of Gap. First, like Dreux and Team Gavin in the north, they had to risk moving through thick concentrations of Germans.

Bumping downhill in their truck from the Vercors with a group of maquis, Sassi and McIntosh twisted along the mountain roads, proudly displaying their Allied uniforms from the back of their truck, hoping to boost the morale of the populace. Instead, citizens who saw them threw themselves off the roads and hid in the ditches. One group of brave villagers accused Team Chloroform of working for the Germans, the only people they had yet seen in uniforms.

"We are French patriots," Sassi objected.

"All the same," they said, "get the hell out of here before the Germans come and burn our village."

In Brittany, Bill Dreux and his team began their seventy-five-mile journey on foot. After two nights and only thirty miles, blisters crippled Team Gavin's radioman, and Dreux searched for bicycles, but they had all been taken by the Germans. Finally, Dreux met a farmer who, for ten thousand francs counterfeited in London, sold him an old black Citroën and two tins of petrol. The car had a dead battery and a passenger door that did not open, and needed a push to get started. The roads, only a hundred miles or so south of the Normandy battle zone, were thick with Germans. But it was drive or give up on the mission, just as it was for Team Chloroform, now motoring their way through German-torched villages and towns.

Everywhere Sassi and McIntosh looked, roofs had caved in and walls were charred black. In one village Sassi and McIntosh drove through, twenty human bodies lay on one side of the road, and the bloated carcasses of cows and horses lay in the fields on the other.

Team Chloroform pulled down a winding road and into a valley filled with all colors of wildflowers. The scenery might have made a pleasant respite from the horror, except that just then, bullets started tearing into the truck from farther up the road, where it curved around the other side of the valley. Sassi and McIntosh spotted German officers standing on the back of transports, looking straight at them through binoculars.

"Turn around," the Resistance leader Hermine shouted to the driver. The firing suddenly stopped, but four German outriders on motorcycles with machine-gun sidecars raced toward them. The gears of Chloroform's truck ground as the driver desperately tried to maneuver it away. One of the young maquis, frightened for his life, suddenly jumped off and ran away up the road.

The German motorcyclists, with their guns drawn, now screeched to a stop, only ten yards away. Sassi and McIntosh stood by the machine gun on the truck's cab. "Shoot!" McIntosh said.

"No, don't move," Sassi shouted, countermanding his superior officer's order.

Sassi saw the fear in the German outriders' eyes. There were only four of them, and Sassi and McIntosh had ten other men. The Germans knew they could not survive a firefight. If Team Chloroform started shooting, they would kill the outriders, but then the German trucks across the valley would again let loose. This was a showdown where either everyone goes home or everyone dies.

Bill Dreux faced a similar dilemma in Pays de la Loire. Dreux, bent down in his new Citroën, was studying his map with a flashlight when, just as his team rolled out into the road to begin their trip, a German truck came flying around the bend. It slammed on its brakes just in time to avoid hitting them. Before Dreux could reach for his gun, a German jumped off the truck, ran to the Citroën, and poked his Schmeisser submachine gun in Dreux's chest.

"*Was ist los?*" the German screamed. "*Was ist los?*"

Good God almighty, Dreux thought to himself, this is how it ends.

Three more Germans with their Schmeissers now rushed to Dreux's car. "*Was ist los? Was ist los?*" the first one shouted again. Dreux was pinned.

Never freeze, he learned at Milton Hall. Do something. It may be the wrong thing, but do it. The shouting German had a square face with a jagged scar through his lips, and he was big. Dreux forced himself to look at him. "OK, take it easy," Dreux said in English.

The German's tone changed. He seemed confused. He stared at Dreux and shook his head. "*Was ist los?*" he asked again more quietly.

I've got him puzzled, Dreux thought. "Your truck is in our way. Get it off to the side, you dumb bastard." Dreux spoke in English and tried to make it sound like an order. Miraculously, instead of killing Dreux on the spot, the Germans walked back to their truck to confer. They did not shoot.

Very calmly, Dreux got out of his car and walked the twenty-five yards into a farm field, waving his radio operator to follow him away from the Germans. He took cover in the field and, gratefully, heard the Germans start their motor and rumble away. So close to Normandy, they had better things to do than to chase after Dreux and his stragglers. The farmer who had sold Dreux the car watched from a distance. He ran up. *"Bon Dieu de bon Dieu,"* he said.

Dreux got back in his car to continue his journey to Ille-et-Vilaine. He forced himself past one set of German sentries and four German convoys while the spluttering engine of his Citroën threatened to peter out at any moment. "Son of a bitch," he mumbled out loud. "Son of a bitch."

In the south, the German motorcyclists Team Chloroform had encountered also had not fired. Instead, they wrestled their motorcycles around and roared back to their convoy. Team Chloroform rapidly did a U-turn of their own and rushed out of the valley in the direction they had come. They quickly came across the Resistance man who had run away and picked him up. He sobbed. He wanted to kill himself with shame. Later, in battle, he would insist on standing up to fire to prove his bravery, and Sassi would constantly have to pull him down to save them all.

The next day, Sassi and Team Chloroform turned around again and braved the valley where they had encountered the motorcyclists. Finally, they made it safely to their intended area of operations in Hautes-Alpes. Dreux's Team Gavin arrived safely in Ille-et-Vilaine. And in the same period, the other thirteen Jed teams also settled into their areas of operation.

In Brittany, with its dense population of German paratroopers, the newly arrived Jeds moved cautiously from their countryside landing zones to their assigned positions in more densely populated areas. Bernard Knox and his Team Giles dropped into Finistère in Brittany, then climbed in the back of a truck with a maquis group of their own. "The three of us were not a little worried, especially by the truck, which made as much noise as a Sherman tank," Knox later wrote in his report.

Team Horace, hidden in wine barrels, traveled in the back of a truck to the outskirts of Brest. Team Gilbert tucked itself under a filthy cargo of charcoal and made it to the outskirts of Quimper. Even Paul Cyr's Team George, who had so narrowly survived the attack on Base Dingson in mid-June, got itself to

the strategically important position at the southern base of the Breton peninsula in Loire Inférieure, by traveling in a livestock transport full of pigs.

But for now, for Jed Teams Giles, Gavin, Chloroform, and twenty-one
others who arrived in France by mid-July, the ordeal had only just started, because the Resistance now entered the second and most tricky phase of its work.
In the first phase, they had identified and attacked sabotage targets—cut railways, blocked roads, destroyed telecommunication systems—which would
cause delays for the Germans. In the third stage, the Resistance would rise up
en masse and attack the Germans in every direction.

In this second phase, however, under the direction of the Jeds and agents,
the Resistance had to keep its first-phase sabotage targets out of action while
at the same time arming themselves and training for the mass uprising in the
third stage. The difficulty was in maintaining the careful balance between too
little action, which would allow the Germans to advance to Normandy, and
too much action, which would force them to retaliate and wipe out the Resistance groups before the third phase began.

In Brittany, the arrival of the third phase and the general Resistance explosion would start when, on the *messages personnels,* the BBC announcer intoned
the code phrase *"Le chapeau de Napoléon, est-il encore à Perros-Guirec?"* It was
a seemingly nonsensical question that asked whether a natural rock formation
known as Napoleon's hat was still where it always had been—on the coast of
Brittany at the village of Perros-Guirec. Other code phrases were given to the
Jeds and agents in other parts of France.

The hard part would be surviving this period of preparation until the Allied breakout began and the code phrases were finally transmitted.

# PART V
# PREPARING THE FIGHTERS

# CHAPTER TWENTY-THREE
# MANNA OF WEAPONS

By the side of a clearing in central Finistère, near the tip of Brittany, shadowed from the moonlight under the trees, a group of maquis leaders huddled around Bernard Knox. Already, he had dispatched a detail to guard the drop zone so the rest of his men could keep their minds on their work. The horses that would later pull the wagonloads of parachuted supplies had been taken a distance away so the roaring planes did not panic them. At three points in a line along the length of the field, piles of firewood had been arranged, along with jars of kerosene and matches to ignite them as signals in a hurry. Knox's men had chosen the field itself for its distance from German garrisons, church steeples, radio towers and other tall obstacles that could be dangerous for Allied aircraft.

This was the beginning of a typical night for a Jed or an Allied agent in France in July 1944. It was only under the cover of darkness that their hardest work could be done. Bernard Knox and Team Giles, for their part, concentrated on quietly arming and training Resistance groups in Finistère, who would hide in the woods and then rise up behind the Germans on the BBC announcer's signal, when the Allies finally pushed into Brittany.

*Comprenez-vous?* Knox asked the leaders who had listened to his explanation of how he had chosen the drop ground. Do you understand? They were here to learn to supervise a "reception committee," so that weapons and perhaps even Jed teams could be parachuted to the leaders' groups at grounds in their own locations.

After tonight, Knox's radio operator, Gordon Tack, would transmit to London the coordinates of the grounds the leaders chose along with a code phrase that referred to them. Each night, the maquis groups would listen to the BBC French broadcast and the *messages personnels*. "*La lune brille sur le dolmen*," for example, alerted the maquis whose ground had been dubbed *le dolmen* that the planes would make a delivery that night. By this method, in preparation for eventual, all-out guerrilla warfare, Jeds like Knox could avoid ferrying weapons through Nazi-infested territory and instead arm groups throughout France directly by airdrop.

Knox sat down on the ground. *Maintenant, nous attendons.* Now we wait. To pass the time someone handed around chunks of country bread and a jug of strong cider. Waiting was the part of reception committee work maquis hated even more than lugging the heavy containers when they landed, agents and Jeds around France would report. Sitting in the dark at a drop zone was boring and dangerous.

Eventually, the sound of engines rumbled in the distance, just as they did at the same time at drop zones in many other parts of Brittany and France. To prepare the Resistance for their role in the coming breakout attempt, Allied flight squadrons parachuted seventy planeloads of weapons into the various Brittany drop zones every July night, along with what they delivered to the rest of France.

Now that the planes approached, someone ran onto the field, poured the kerosene onto the piles of wood, threw matches on top, and watched the three towers of flame rise in a whoosh to greet the four-engine bombers. Knox pointed a flashlight at the lead aircraft and clicked on and off in the pattern of a prearranged letter in Morse code, alerting the pilot that he was in the right place. While Knox's maquis leaders took cover in the woods to protect themselves from the heavy containers that would fall from the sky, the bombers banked in a circle and swept in.

Parachutes snapped open in the moonlit sky, and the shadow warriors' black-painted planes lumbered around for one more pass over the drop zone before flying back toward the Channel and home. Weapons containers, under their canopies, came crashing through the tree branches. On one night earlier in July, three hundred German paratroops charged into the drop zone area only five minutes after Bernard Knox and Team Giles had left. Tonight, bushwhacking haphazardly through the darkened forest to find their falling supplies, Knox and his maquis rushed to round up the containers and lug them to their wagons and trucks. They wanted no more close calls.

———

As the July nights ended, the yellow sliver of moon that guided the planes dipped under the horizon. The sky grew thick with the predawn darkness. The time for sleep had arrived at last.

Down south, Tommy Macpherson once found himself knocking on the door of a convent, asking for refuge, and bedding down. In the Hautes-Alpes, Jean Sassi of Team Chloroform often tucked himself with his boots and equipment into a *bergerie,* a shepherd's earthen hovel dug into the mountainside. Bob Kehoe, in Côtes-du-Nord, lay on the dirt floor of the abandoned stone cottage Team Frederick made its headquarters. Or, when the sky kept the rain to itself, the Jeds around France often sprawled themselves on ground sheets and slept out of doors, under the fading stars.

Bernard Knox, at his command post in Finistère, collapsed to his knees, exhausted, near an old stone barn with a thatched roof. He refused to sleep inside, though, with only one, easily blocked door through which to escape. Instead, soaked with sweat and sore from the night's exertion, Knox tugged handfuls of straw from the base of a haystack and burrowed a meager shelter for himself. Any chance of a few hours' rest before daytime depended on the hope that the soldiers of the German 2nd Parachute Division did not stumble over his hiding place in the night or, worse, launch a full-scale planned attack.

Twenty or so of the maquis, part of the hundred-strong group Team Giles had adopted as headquarters staff, bodyguard, and parachute drop reception committee, prepared to take their turn at guard duty. From over Knox's shoulder came the click click click as the maquis shoved home their ammunition clips into their Sten guns. Around France, maquis on sentry duty threw their weapons over their shoulders and walked into the darkness, down the paths and trails that made the approaches to their Jed or agent command posts. These villagers and city men, in charge of protecting the perimeters of Jed compounds, were dangerously out of place in this behind-the-lines war against the highly trained Germans.

Knox tucked himself inside his musty haystack cocoon. Around him, the Frenchmen also rustled themselves into straw beds, the more cavalier into the warmth of the barn, the more cautious into little shelters of hay like Knox. Knox unrolled his sleeping bag and climbed in. In the southeast, Jean Sassi carefully wrapped his arms around his gun the way a newlywed groom sleeps with his wife. Everything was quiet.

What sentries were supposed to do, in case of danger, was stealthily warn the Jeds and their maquis so that they could fade away without confrontation.

In Bill Dreux's experience, nonetheless, frightened guards sometimes fired blindly at suspicious shadows that turned out to be cows, threw the sleeping men of the command post into sudden chaos, and alerted Germans for miles around. One night in central France, after the report of a Sten gun awoke a Jed team, they discovered that a young sentry had tragically wasted his life by falling asleep with his chin resting on its barrel.

But if the night was uneventful, the Frenchmen in camp, seemingly ignorant of the constant danger, began to snore. They were able to sleep. The Jeds and agents, however, often did not.

The flutter of a bird disturbed from its nest, the snap of a twig, a cough in the distance: any of these or a hundred other sounds might signal that a squad of Germans had sneaked silently past the sentries. Even if a Jed had no other bedtime worries, there was always the possibility that the Germans were gathering in a large semicircle around the command post. Over and over through the night, the Jeds bolted awake and listened for trouble.

Knox and the other Jed officers knew that Hitler's forces always executed their Resistance raids in exactly the same way. They formed a cordon of roadblocks and search squads around an area ten miles in diameter. Then, usually at dawn, they began to tighten their noose, pushing sector by sector through the woods, ticking off their searches farm by farm, and questioning civilians one by one.

This German emphasis on routine and procedure meant the Jeds, with just an hour or two's warning, could escape the "surprise" attack before the tightening of the cordon. In Lot, Tommy Macpherson got his advance warnings from the French telephone operators who worked on the German switchboards. In southwest Finistère, Team Gilbert got its tips from the gendarmes. In central Finistère, Knox had, in addition to the sentries around Team Giles's command post, runners stationed at all the major road junctions to monitor German movements for miles around.

One day, the mayor of the nearby village of Laz arrived breathlessly at Knox's command post to warn that a restaurateur had looked over the shoulder of a German patron and seen that he had a map with Team Giles's position circled in red, a clear sign of a coming attack. Another day, a captured Milicien escaped, presumably taking the Jeds' exact position straight to the Germans. The result was that by dawn of nearly every day since Knox had arrived, he had marched ten to fifteen miles to escape an attack. He and his men were exhausted.

And yet, around 3:30 each morning, Knox dragged himself out of his sleeping bag to take the runners' reports. At some Jed command posts, the incoming runners quietly whistled the subdued melodies of "Sur le Pont d'Avignon" or "It's a Long Way to Tipperary," announcing themselves with an unofficial musical password that would, hopefully, comfort the trigger-happy guards and keep the runners from getting shot. They brought news of German early-morning movement from the posts at the area's important crossroads. If they brought bad news of another sweep, it would be even worse for the region's civilians.

At one farm Team Giles had abandoned in advance of a search, Knox had given chocolate to the farmer's children. On another occasion, at another farm, a maquis fighter had carelessly left behind a single ammunition cartridge by the side of the haystack he slept in. The German paratroopers had found both the cartridge and the chocolate's silver wrapping paper. They shot the farmers and their families.

Is there any movement on the roads? Knox would ask the runners.

No, nothing. Not tonight, they would answer, if it was to be an easy night.

In their own way, the Jeds and agents working in France had it harder than the frontline troops in Normandy. Ultimately, the Jeds would experience the same rate of casualties. But there was never another unit to cover their backs. In the whole summer of Overlord, no one would ever be sent forward to relieve them. No matter how terrible things became, they never got a pass to go back to headquarters. There was no R&R. But at least on a night like tonight, if the runners brought the news that the Germans planned no major attack, for perhaps the two hours before sunrise, Bernard Knox and the rest of the Jeds could finally get some sleep.

## CHAPTER TWENTY-FOUR
# WHAT WOULD DAD THINK?

Shadowy figures moved through the command post darkness, knelt to the ground, and gently nudged the shoulders of the Jedburgh officers. *Mon capitaine*, they whispered, *mon capitaine*. The soldiers' hands tightened for a moment on their weapons before their flickering eyes snapped open. Seeing a friend, their faces relaxed. In the dark purple beginnings of day, bundled in their sleeping bags, if they still had them, or wrapped in the generous folds of a silk parachute, if they had lost their bags in the chase like Bob Kehoe, they propped themselves on their elbows. Groggily, the Jeds accepted the bowls of steaming liquid held out to them.

*Merci.*

*De rien.*

The Jeds cupped their hot drinks in both hands and blew cooling ripples across the surface. They watched through half-closed lids the silhouetted Frenchmen tiptoe back across the camp, like gray ghosts in the retreating darkness, to poke, in dancing circles of light, at small cooking fires. This was the typical day's beginning for Allied officers with the French maquis as July marched forward.

In western Normandy, there had been no letup for the Allied troops who battled to advance one tiny field at a time in the hedgerows. The American 30th Division alone lost three thousand killed and wounded in the second two weeks of July; the 9th lost twenty-five hundred in a similar period. At the eastern end of the beachhead, the British and Canadians faced a seemingly impenetrable wall of Hitler's panzers. On July 9, Montgomery had unleashed yet another attack against Caen. After two days of desperate fighting, he won only half the city and lost nearly 25 percent of his men.

"It was," Eisenhower would write later, "dogged doughboy fighting at its worst." Ike would consider the fighting at the Normandy front that July to be "some of the fiercest and most sanguinary of the war." Even by the end of July, at D plus fifty, the Allies would only have pushed the Germans back to a line they had hoped to win within a week of the invasion.

As for the Jeds, some of whom had suffered life in the woods of France for nearly a month and a half, the memory of hot baths and soft beds grew distant. Now, even this predawn fake coffee with its washed-out taste—the real stuff could no longer be found—gave comfort. In the south, Team Ammonia's Jacob Berlin drank a brew made from roasted acorns. American agent Bill Morgan, in Creuse, sipped an infusion made from chicory. Other agents swallowed a concoction made from toasted wheat.

No one noticed anymore the dried, dark stains on the rims of the unwashed bowls and the smudged impressions of other men's lips, Bill Morgan would report. The agents barely even troubled to scoop from their drinks a drowned gnat or hornet.

This was the safest time of day. The hazards of nighttime operations and the risk of the German daybreak attack had passed. As long as the maquis did nothing especially stupid, no major attack would come and no one would die for twelve more hours. Bob Kehoe, Bernard Knox, Tommy Macpherson, Jean Sassi, and all the other Jeds in France savored, with the curtains of sleep still only half opened, these private moments of repose. Only they ended almost as soon as they began.

Men began to rouse themselves. The camp cook stoked the fire, and the scent of breakfast, if there was food to be had that day, wafted in the air. The rising sun, when it shone, cast dawn's long shadows, and the facts of the Jeds' behind-the-lines life began to press against them. Last night's parachuted containers had to be emptied and the weapons distributed. Men had to be trained, radio messages from London read and answered, maquis leaders met, the following night's sabotage and reception operations assigned, prisoners interrogated, and traitors tried. This was July's daily routine.

Lifting himself out of his mountainside *bergerie* in Drôme, Jean Sassi always grabbed for his carbine. "Imagine yourself behind some tree," the SOE instructors had told him in England, "dropping your shorts to take care of your needs. If you've left your weapon in camp, the German who finds you will laugh his head off." In Finistère, where Bernard Knox and Team Giles operated, in fact, it had been two maquis who enjoyed such a giggle. They hid in the bushes while an unarmed German did his business, then knocked him over the head as he fastened his belt. The result was a nice new pair of boots for the maquis, and two bullets in the head for the German sergeant major—but only after he had been forced to dig his own grave.

Bernard Knox dug out of his backpack his double-edged razor and shaving soap. A bath, even a cold one, was too much to ask. Once a week, if Knox was lucky, he both encountered a stream and had the time to enjoy it. Bill Dreux never bathed without a comrade to stand guard with his Sten or carbine while the clear rushing water carried away the sweat and grime. Then Dreux took his turn as lookout while his comrade waded in.

In Lot, Arthur Brown punched holes in the bottom of a biscuit tin, heated water over the fire, and occasionally enjoyed something resembling a shower. The maquis laughed at Brown. Most Jeds contented themselves with a bowlful of cold water to splash in. They quickly learned to itch and stink.

"There are no officers and men here," one British agent, George Millar, code-named Emile, said to his maquis.

"What are there then?" they asked.

"Leaders and men," he answered.

If the Jeds and Allied agents hoped that these motley crews of Frenchmen would voluntarily follow their orders, they had to gain their trust. The smartest Jeds never slipped off to the nearby farmhouse or château. They took no special privileges and made no servants. If the maquis couldn't do it, the Jeds wouldn't either. They had to live alongside their men, eat the same food, drink the same drinks, sleep in the same dirt, get infested with the same lice.

This is why Team Chloroform's Jean Sassi, in Drôme, sent no one else to fill his washbowl; he traipsed around camp looking for water himself. Leadership by example: respect could only be earned in the maquis; it could not be sewn onto a uniform in stripes, as in the army.

By now, outdoor living had left Team Giles's Bernard Knox with only his paratroop boots and khaki pants to distinguish him as a member of the commissioned military. The rest of his uniform was lost or destroyed. Extra uniform shirts were dropped, but the maquis often spirited away such things before the Jeds even knew they had arrived.

In Côtes-du-Nord, Bob Kehoe was lucky enough to have clean under-wear—of a sort. Headquarters mistakenly parachuted a container full of women's knickers. As for Knox, he found himself a woolen British jacket and a black beret to which he pinned his captain's bars. He looked these days like most Resistance fighters, which is why every morning he lathered up in his washbowl and dragged his razor across his face. With so little left to dig-nify him, being clean shaven, at least, would visually differentiate him among his men.

At breakfast, the Jeds tucked their legs under a makeshift dining table, if there was one: a plank or two, perhaps, nailed between two tree stumps. Jed-burgh Roger Pierre ate breakfast while a condemned cow, tied to a stake and intended for dinner, swished flies away with its tail.

Maquisards came to the table, grunted their hellos, and rolled their morn-ing cigarettes. Tobacco was one of the few luxuries available in the woods, but at a high cost. More maquis were killed, some agents complained, *"en braquant les bureaux de tabac,"* holding up tobacco stores to get cigarettes, than in fire-fights with Germans. Messengers ran into camp, saluted, clicked their heels, and excitedly reported rumors of German movements in the area. Reconnais-sance patrols marched out to take a look.

Someone thumped down, occasionally, a bundle of personal letters from home that London had sent in the parachute drop. Bob Kehoe fingered en-velopes with his father's handwriting sprawled strangely across them. To see something so familiar made everything in the campsite feel so suddenly alien. Selling typewriters door-to-door, worrying about what to study at Rutgers—after only a month in France, all that felt like an entirely different life. Excite-ment, loneliness, and fear flooded Kehoe all at once as he took the bundle of letters and held it in his hands. Then breakfast arrived.

In Creuse, for the morning meal, American agent William Morgan got a chunk of jaw-straining cured pork, piping hot brewed chicory with no milk, and a cup of wine. In Côtes-du-Nord, Team Frederick got big wedges of peas-ant bread and steaming milk, but, even at dinner, no wine. In Finistère, Bernard Knox got eggs for breakfast, eggs for lunch, eggs for dinner, and lots of Breton cider. The Jeds fed only on whatever their region had in plenty.

When radio operator Lou Lajeunesse finally arrived in eastern France, he discovered that something resembling bread would often be baked in a hole in the ground, filled with huge globs of dough and covered for three hours with a wood-burning campfire. Carve away the three-inch crust, along with the dirt and pebbles, and out came a loaf the size of two basketballs.

In Dordogne, Team Ammonia's Jacob Berlin spent afternoons picking off rabbits with a farmer's borrowed shotgun. Some groups, with the help of their loaded Stens, persuaded farmers and victualers to grudgingly accept IOUs, payable after the war, in exchange for food. Other groups didn't even bother with a promise to pay. Bernard Knox paid the Breton dairy farmers in airlifted—and fake—francs.

One Breton farmer feeding Knox's maquis cut his farm's rich, tasty butter in slabs like cheese and slathered it on bread. He handed a serving to Knox and shoved another, more than Knox thought could fit, into his own mouth. He chewed noisily and grotesquely, as though mastication required an audience.

"I like your butter very much," Knox said politely.

"The Germans love butter, too," the farmer said, bits of food falling out of his mouth as he spoke, "but *they* eat like *pigs*."

When a letter arrived in Côtes-du-Nord, Kehoe took himself off a little way to carefully tear open the delicate blue airmail paper in privacy and savor the reports from home. His father still drove back and forth to his job at Johnson and Johnson. The girlfriend he met at the chemical plant still worked there. Arthur Brown, reading a letter of his own in Lot, silently celebrated news of his sister's marriage.

While the Jeds read their correspondence and pined for their old work and family routines, the maquis would sit around the fire, talking with bravado about killing some Germans. *Boches* or *schleuhs* or *stols, shlocks,* or Fritz, the maquis around France called their Teutonic enemy. *Mort à les boches!* Death to the *boches!* they sometimes shouted.

What would my father think? Kehoe wondered. What would my girlfriend think? Kehoe had made a home in the mud. Dirt covered his fingernails, his body, and his hair. Around him, thousands of teenagers and boys in their early twenties ran lawlessly through the forests. Given the chance, they would shoot the nearest German in the head, steal his watch, wedding ring, and boots, and celebrate the gruesome death the same way they would a school soccer match—with neither remorse nor reflection.

In honorable warfare, Kehoe imagined, a captured POW was treated as a fellow soldier. This shadow war was a blood feud in which once-placid French boys became thugs who laughed when an enemy's brains exploded; Germans the same age would slice off a Frenchman's testicles to get him to talk. Things could be no different in a world where the rules of war were not applied, and Kehoe almost grew used to it. That is, until letters from home triggered his old, college-kid perspective. How ethereal it all seemed. How bloody. How utterly irreversible.

"We've been lucky until now," Kehoe suddenly realized, "but how long is it going to last?" The real battle, the final general uprising, had not even begun. A desperate desire to go home washed over him. He stood up, dusted himself off, and put his letters somewhere safe. Reading them gave him an uncomfortable way of looking at things that did little to boost his morale. He could take only so much. Besides, by seven o'clock in the morning it was time to get to work.

# CHAPTER TWENTY-FIVE

# INSUBORDINATION

Jean Sassi kicked through the layers of pine needles that covered the woodland floor and realized that the mountainside forest was conspicuously empty of men's voices. Breakfast had finished, and Sassi approached a secret rendezvous in the woods where he was supposed to meet one of Team Chloroform's groups of maquis. Jeds and agents often traveled to distant forest clearings to train maquis in weapons and guerrilla tactics in order to avoid attracting attention to their command posts.

Sassi emerged from the trees and into the bleached brightness of the clearing. Only the eerie creaking of swaying branches greeted him. No one was here. Sassi was not pleased. Nor was he surprised.

Team Chloroform's officers had repeatedly warned this group to follow orders and show up on time. They never listened. Their swaggering leader dismissed Team Chloroform's chastisement with arrogant shrugs. This show of rebelliousness was calculated to win the admiration of the district's maquis. The Jeds found some French leaders to be far more concerned with individual prestige and power than with assisting the Allied cause.

Left unchecked, such defiance by maquis leaders could metastasize through a region, eating away at the Jeds' and agents' authority. An urgent message had to be sent. Success of the secret armies' assistance to the Overlord forces depended on the ability of the maquis to follow orders. Discipline was not optional. The cancer of insubordination could not be left untreated.

"It was a matter of extreme urgency to inculcate into the maquis a sense of discipline," reported Captain Vuchot of Team Veganin. "We insisted on discipline," wrote Lieutenant Bob Anstett of Team Hamish. This was why, the night before Jean Sassi found himself alone in a clearing waiting for the tardy maquis group, Team Chloroform officers Jacques Martin and Henry McIntosh had manhandled their unsubmissive leader into a car and roared off into the darkness. One way or another, they had "relieved him of duty."

Now Sassi breathed the sharp alpine air and listened intently for the snapping of branches underfoot. He made an easy target. There was, after all, a chance that by removing their leader Team Chloroform had made this group of fifty men angry enough to want to kill Sassi.

A couple of hundred miles west, Tommy Macpherson had been ambushed twice at a rendezvous, once by the Germans and once by a renegade Frenchman he had been waiting to meet. The first time, he escaped because the rumbling of too many engines alerted him and he made a dash for it. The second time, fate drove him inexplicably out a café's back door while machine-gun bullets downed comrades who left through the front.

Still, Sassi waited. On another day, his patience might give the impression of weakness; today, it suggested bravery. When these potential rebels finally arrived in the clearing, things would either change for the better or get terribly worse.

All over France, Jeds like Sassi used the morning hours to organize and train their various groups for the uprising and assign them to the coming night's sabotage and parachute reception operations.

Team Quinine's Tommy Macpherson tore around Lot and Cantal in a stolen black Citroën, searching out leaders he could work with and keeping away from those he couldn't. Teams Felix and Francis diplomatically persuaded larger maquis congregations in Brittany to break up into companies of one hundred, so they could more easily hide, and smaller smatterings to merge, so they could fight more effectively. In preparation for when the battle started in earnest, Knox's Team Giles organized doctors and nurses to care for the wounded. Team Veganin assembled makeshift spy networks to report on German plans and movements.

Some of the Jed-organized groups were static, attacking only targets in their own districts. Others, the *sédentaires,* were armed and trained and then sent back to their homes to live their civilian lives, only to join the maquis when the all-out uprising finally began. Still others were made mobile, and consisted of the best men, handpicked by the Jeds, to charge in trucks and cars to wherever a battle flared up and they were most needed. It was for one of the mobile groups or "commandos," as Team Chloroform called them, that Sassi now waited.

In his clearing in the pines, Sassi finally heard the snap of branches in the distance as footsteps trampled through the woods. Gruff voices drifted through the forest as the fifty men approached. There was no joking.

"Where is our chief?" one of the men asked Sassi accusingly.

Sassi wore an Allied uniform and carried his laissez-passer signed both by Eisenhower and by Koenig, the leader of the French Forces of the Interior. Sassi had his moral authority as a representative of the high command, a .45 on his hip, and a carbine on his shoulder. He raised himself up and faced the angry Frenchmen. "You won't see your chief anymore," he said.

"Why not?"

"Because he does not know how to obey," Sassi answered.

It was not that the maquis around France stubbornly resisted all that the Jeds asked. When one American agent, William Morgan, made a target of an upended parachute container, the maquis in Creuse gladly submitted to his mandatory weapons training and blasted away with their newly supplied Colt .45s. After the right-handed Morgan displayed his own marksmanship by left-handedly planting six out of six shots in the container's "belly," the French boys cheered and affectionately christened him *"le Chicago gangster,"* a nickname that stuck throughout the summer. Near Châteauroux, the guerrillas-in-training extended the same camaraderie to René Dussaq when his lesson plan included sneaking over a hill and blowing up a German armored car. They dubbed him "Captain Bazooka."

Even Jean Sassi's commandos in the Alps bubbled over with adolescent enthusiasm when it came to playing cowboy in the woods. They got to tote guns, look tough, and congratulate themselves for being the saviors of France without ever leaving the safety of their hiding places. The problems came when the Jeds began to press the swaggering boys with soldierly obligations that required discipline, hard work, or facing an enemy who might actually fire back.

We are tired, Bernard Knox's maquis whined the first time he roused them in the middle of the night and quick-marched them out of a German encirclement. Surely, we've come far enough, *mon capitaine,* they complained after crossing only the first couple of miles of Finistère farmland. We could leave this equipment behind, no? It is too heavy. Knox arrived, ten miles later, at the farm that made his new command post with very few of his fifty men. The rest had hidden themselves in sleeping places in the hedgerows and straggled into camp the next morning.

Over and over, the Jeds around France repeated their lectures on weapons safety while maquis fighters yawned with indifference. Sten guns' cocking knobs easily slipped from too shallow safety slots, causing spontaneous discharge. So leave your guns uncocked, the Jeds commanded. Rust and grime filled the maquis' gun barrels, despite exhortations to strip and clean them. Don't you understand that you could die if your gun jams? The Jeds hoped to boost behind-the-lines success through the precautionary tenets of military discipline. The maquis preferred a laissez-faire attitude that suggested that if the weapon had not yet jammed, it was obviously not dirty. "Why should we obey you?" maquis boys had said defiantly to Sassi.

In Loir-et-Cher, a maquisard who intended to slit the throats of two injured Germans instead knocked a grenade from his own belt and blew himself up. In central France, a group of maquis boys, too lazy to wrestle along a route through the forest undergrowth, ignored American agent John Alsop's orders to stay off a road, and were mowed down by Germans. The clowning in this life-and-death circus act had to end, which is why Jean Sassi's Team Chloroform officers had settled on kidnapping their commando group's leader to get their message across.

Jeds faced similar confrontations all over France as they tried to force an alien discipline and obedience on boys and men who had never actually volunteered to be Resistance fighters; most maquis had been forced into the ill-fitting role by the terrible turns of history. Skinny-legged students, overweight wine merchants, taciturn farmers, and supercilious Parisian law clerks were the manner of men Sassi and the rest of the Jeds tried to shape into a force that could effectively harass the Germans. Many had ended up in the woods merely because there was no other way to escape the German labor draft, or because their homes had been burned or their families killed.

In Brittany, the entire male population of the village of Peumerit-Quintin had joined the Resistance after one of their wives took in three badly injured SAS soldiers from the battle in the Forêt de Doualt. The village's men decided they would rather die in the woods than wait for the Germans to discover the convalescing "terrorists." Grand and heroic and vulgar and selfish motives propelled men into the maquis, but very few had the ambition of assisting the armies in Normandy. Often, maquis crowded not to the leaders with the greatest reputations for killing Germans, but to those who provided the best food.

"We don't want to be soldiers," Sassi's group protested one day. "Why are we waiting to attack?" they asked when the next day brought a different frame of mind. So much stirred inside these Frenchmen trapped by history: fear and pride and bravado and adventurism and grief and hunger and anxiety and lust and hatred and violence and extremely low morale.

Very few believed they could have any influence on the war's outcome. Some hoped to hide in the woods until the war ended. Others burned with a desperate need for vengeance and saw little use in the reasoned calculation of the Jeds' military plans and tactics. They simply wanted to make other men scared, the way they felt scared; to hear other men scream, the way they screamed; to make German mothers sob, the way French mothers sobbed.

In Finistère, a young maquis whose brother had been killed the previous day climbed into a Citroën with its doors removed, drove alongside a German column of armored cars, and fired at the soldiers who were drinking tea on break. He got five cars down the column before the Germans fired back and killed him. His suicide mission may have avenged his brother, but exchanging his life for a few injured or killed German foot soldiers made not one iota of difference to the Allied cause. Half the men wanted to fight too little; the other half wanted to fight too much.

It did not help Jeds like Jean Sassi that the leaders to whom the maquis gravitated all had agendas and allegiances of their own. In the woods of France, the Jeds discovered tiny groups of men identified by the acronyms of the big organizations to which their leaders had attached them. Tommy Macpherson called these groups the "Alphabetical Resistance,"

The largest organizations of the maquis were the Gaullist Armée Secrète (AS) and the French Communist Francs-Tireurs et Partisans (FTP), both of which operated throughout France. Some of the newer groups centered on small gatherings of former comrades of now-dissolved French army regiments. The *naphtalines,* or mothballs, the inveterate Resistance fighters called them, because of the smell of the uniforms they had kept hidden away for so long.

Since all the groups had supposedly united under the banner of de Gaulle's Forces Français de l'Intérieur (FFI), the Jeds theoretically should have been able to flash their orders signed by FFI commander Koenig, and the maquis leaders would leap into action behind them. But the maquis leaders had loyalty to many things other than de Gaulle and France.

The *naphtalines,* it seemed to Tommy Macpherson, planned to hide in the woods until liberation, don their gold braid and big hats, and march in the streets to take the credit. Some FTP groups around France cared most about stockpiling weapons in order to rise up and win postwar France for Communism. Other maquis groups plotted a return to the monarchy. There were even Spanish Communists, holdovers from the Spanish civil war, who planned eventually to go back into Spain to liquidate Franco.

Convincing the leaders of these groups to align their men with the aims of the Allied high command required tact, persuasion, and sometimes force. The Jeds attended one diplomatic dinner after the next, drank toasts, kissed leaders' daughters, and sang all the national anthems in order to establish a friendly atmosphere for their eventual negotiations. We'll give you these weapons if you do as we ask, the Jeds said. When you prove your word is good, we might give you more.

In Lot, the regional commander of a large network of FTP groups immediately fell in with Tommy Macpherson and ordered his men to establish ambushes on every road that might be used by the Germans to travel to Normandy. In line with Allied strategy for the Resistance in Brittany, Finistère leaders of the FTP agreed to keep their groups quiet until the code phrase for all-out guerrilla warfare was broadcast over the BBC. "We are in agreement with the strategy of the Allied High Command," they told Bernard Knox grandly. In Saône-et-Loire, however, an FTP group ambushed Team Anthony's landing zones and made off with the weapons. In Nièvre, Team Harry contended with a group led by a paranoiac who apprehended, for weeks at a time, liaison agents and even a radio operator heading through their area on the pretext of security.

Meanwhile, in Normandy, American forces in mid-July desperately fought for the town of Saint-Lô. Even after that battle was over, the U.S. First Army would face more of the hedgerows and small woods that had plagued them since D-Day.

After all these long weeks stuck in the *bocage,* the commander of the American ground forces, General Omar Bradley, had begun to think that he could not waste more time grinding toward Granville. He began to look for alternatives. There was talk of landing a second invasion in Brittany; there was talk of a modified breakout attempt from the Périers-Saint-Lô line, when the

Allies finally reached it. Either way, the day when the military commanders called for the concentrated attacks behind the lines in France quickly approached, and maquis tomfoolery could not be allowed to put Allied plans for the secret armies at risk.

In Creuse, when a maquis member refused an order, American agent Bill Morgan pulled his Colt .45, primed it, and pointed it at the insubordinate's chest. "If you do not obey, I'll shoot you," he said.

"We decided we would get rid of 'Napoleons,' even executing them if necessary," Paul Cyr of Brittany's Team George reported. In Indre, Team Hamish shot a maquis who had been accused of rape. In Isère, Team Veganin's group surrounded a house containing four renegade maquis members who had been on a looting rampage. A shoot-out ended with two of the outlaws dead. Veganin's group took the other two prisoners and executed them. In Hautes-Alpes, McIntosh and Martin had made off with the leader of the group Sassi now faced.

"You will choose a new chief," Sassi told them. "You will choose one like us who obeys."

Was their leader killed, was he kidnapped, or did he just agree to leave? Perhaps the maquis would never know, and perhaps that was best. If they imagined that the Jeds were capable of the final sanction, it would improve discipline. If they knew for sure, they might think them brutal. Word of what had happened quickly spread, and discipline improved remarkably in all of Team Chloroform's maquis, just as it did for Team Veganin after the renegades were executed, and for Team Hamish after the rapist was shot.

In the clearing in the Alps, Sassi's men backed down, quit their grumbling, and got on with practicing their scouting patrols, infantry formation, and the loading and firing of their Brens. Like many of the Jeds across France, Sassi spent the morning instructing his men; when afternoon came, it was time to assign missions, plan reception committees, and interrogate recently captured traitors and spies.

In Côtes-du-Nord, Bob Kehoe followed a rush of maquis voyeurs up a hill to where two suspected informants had been detained. He found himself in a dimly lit clearing with long shadows cast by small campfires. A man lay with his hands and feet tied to stakes in the ground. A woman with a scarf over her head sat next to him, sobbing.

In the Alps to the south, Jean Sassi watched six so-called jurors gather under a tent to try a French interpreter who had been captured in a nearby village for doing his job with the Germans too eagerly. The maquis dragged the skinny little twenty-year-old with a long, wispy beard and wire-rimmed glasses to the tent where the tribunal convened. When the boy saw Jean Sassi's uniform, he threw himself to his knees.

"I'm innocent," he cried. "I'm innocent."

"I don't know you," Sassi told him. "It's your own people who are going to judge you."

All over France, these interrogations and bush trials—of German POWs, of German spies claiming to be Allied pilots shot down over France, of French collaborators—became a daily part of the Jeds' and agents' work. Team Hamish had to set aside a part of every afternoon for attending interrogations. "We stayed completely out of all trials of traitors," reported Team Hamish's Bob Anstett. "It was not for us, but for the French to handle all these questions." But the Jeds and agents attended interrogations as observers in case information emerged that was important to their mission.

In Vosges, British agent George Millar followed a maquis chief named Paincheau along a wagon track through a field to a two-acre wood where they saw a tall man with a small mouth and a thin mustache and a voluptuous, dark-haired woman wearing purple lipstick. The pair, captured by Paincheau's men, sat on an earthen bank and smoked. Their personal possessions lay on a log nearby.

Paincheau emptied the man's wallet and the woman's handbag. He shuffled through their papers. As the male prisoner fidgeted incessantly with the buttons of his coat, his eyes darted around the clearing, from one captor to the next. The woman looked only at Paincheau. She smiled at him when he looked back, making an appeal of her good looks. Millar noted with distaste that she subtly moved away from her companion, denying the man she admitted had been her lover. He might die, she seemed to think, but not me.

In their papers, Paincheau found Vichy passes for "special police duties." They also had lists of "criminals" suspected of listening to the BBC or keeping secret stashes of British and Swiss money. The man's wallet contained pictures of his comrades in their Gestapo-like uniforms. The woman's held a signed picture of Joseph Darnand, the head of the Vichy militia.

"Miliciens!" Paincheau spat. "Stand up."

The interrogation began.

———

In Yonne, maquis working with an American agent, René Défourneaux, got the answers they wanted by dragging one suspected female collaborator through the woods by her hair for miles before shooting her point-blank in the head. They extracted a hasty confession from another woman by tying her to a tree, shaving her head, and then burning plastic explosives between her toes and legs. They let her suffer until maggots gathered and gnawed at her black, charred wounds before finally putting her out of her misery with a shot.

In the campfire-lit clearing in Côtes-du-Nord, Bob Kehoe stood by silently horrified while the maquis took turns spitting on and kicking and punching the captive they had strapped to the ground. His features disappeared into a purple mess.

"How do you know he is guilty?" Kehoe asked the maquis, when he could contain himself no more.

"We know!" one of them answered.

For "interrogations," these proceedings in the woods of France were often conspicuously absent of questions.

British agent Henry Peulevé, working near Bordeaux, suspected a man who claimed to be an escaped RAF pilot of actually being a German agent who would later betray everyone who had risked their lives to help him. The suspect refused to answer questions. A maquisard tied him to a tree, affixed a live detonator between his legs, and lit a match. "I am a German officer," the suspect admitted at last. For the snotty whimperings and pleadings of such stool pigeons and death-mongers almost no one felt pity.

In the Alps, a perhaps more sympathetic type of turncoat, the skinny translator whose tribunal Sassi witnessed, said, "The Germans would have killed my family if I didn't work for them." In peacetime the translator's kind of moral weakness might have caused the sort of poor choices that ended in bankruptcy, divorce, or, at worst, public shame and ridicule. In France, war gave no second chances, not for him and not for the young maquis whose eyes the Germans removed with forks and whose testicles they shoved in their mouths. Whatever the traitors' excuses, they met the same fate.

In Aube, a tribunal of thirteen men convened by James La Rosee, an American agent, condemned a man who sold downed aviators to the Germans for fifty thousand francs. The thirteen put their names in a hat, and a man named Williams pulled his out. He would be the executioner. The vendor of aviators' lives refused to go into the woods to face his sentence, so Williams shot him where he stood and blood splattered over everyone. In the Alps, a young student, not even old enough to have a career, loaded his rifle and prepared to lead the whimpering translator's firing squad. "I was just doing my job like a mailman delivering letters," the translator cried. "Like a mailman delivering letters."

All over France, traitors led Germans to command posts and drop grounds. These dangerous turncoats had to be stopped, yet in the Alps, at the trial of the young translator, Jean Sassi felt disgust. He had once wanted to be a priest. This was not a real tribunal, he thought. It was a sham. In Brittany, Bob Kehoe said nothing about the man's vicious beatings in the clearing. Team Frederick must not appear weak. In Yonne, agent Défourneaux kept quiet about the woman's torture by fire. He might receive the same punishment. Sassi made no comment about the farce of a tribunal. You do not fight with your friends, he decided, to save an enemy.

No one feels brave when a man is killed with his hands tied behind his back. Some members of a firing squad would miss on purpose. Some would enjoy it. Some would throw up.

For all the Jeds' stateside enthusiasm, it turned out they could do no good in war without also doing bad. Going around a circle the wrong way still got you to the right place, they hoped. The soldier risked his life, yes, but far more devastating in his memory, if he lived, would be that he had also risked his soul. There was no such thing as an unstained hero. In the woods of Côtes-du-Nord, the traitor strapped to the ground had death coming to him, but for the rest of Bob Kehoe's life, he would regret not stopping the torture.

In Vosges, Paincheau handed the pretty woman and the man two spades and a pick, and ordered them to dig. As they worked, the woman occasionally heaved a dry sob. She scratched barely a dimple into the hard-packed, root-tangled ground. Her perfume hung in the air. A maquisard picked up a pick and loosened the earth for her. She had no reason to thank him.

The Milicien man stood looking down into the hole he had finished digging for his own body. Suddenly he shuddered as though electricity ran through him, and he tried to make a run for it. He got fifteen paces before five shots echoed through the forest and his body suddenly crumpled to the ground. The maquisard who shot him lowered his Sten. Two men dragged the body back to where the woman still stood knee deep in her hole with her spade. They threw his body in his grave.

Now the woman climbed out of her hole and pleaded for her life. "I have tried for a long time to leave the militia," she said. "I hated them and their brutality. I wanted to be on your side. Take me in the maquis. I will cook or fight or spy or anything."

By now she was on her knees in front of Paincheau with her hands clasped together in prayer.

"Get up from your knees," he told her. There was no expression in his face. She rose up, grabbing at his clothes.

"Please, Monsieur Jacques, please," she said. She did not notice that he had stretched his arms behind and away from her as though she were poison.

Paincheau jerked his head at a man behind her and reached around the woman's body to make a gesture. The man approached, raised his pistol, and while the woman still clutched at Paincheau, he blew off the back of her head.

## CHAPTER TWENTY-SIX
# THE BREAKOUT APPROACHES

With their wire antennae draped over tree branches or farmhouse rafters and some poor maquis boy cranking the radio's generator handle to make electricity, Jedburgh radio operators like Arthur Brown sent home messages of their teams' successes and failures, as well as requests for supplies. Messages arrived in London hourly calling for all manner of necessities, and the black-painted bombers flew constantly into the night sky and across the Channel.

As demands grew, packing the correct items for the correct groups and then navigating them to the right landing ground over a blacked-out France through storms and German antiaircraft fire became a logistical nightmare. It didn't help that General Koenig, commanding the EMFFI, confused matters further by installing his inexperienced French officers, who had trouble communicating in English, in crucial positions at London headquarters. "Do not send messages in French," radioed Team Horace from Brittany. "Send in English. Embarrassing when I have a collaborator translate your French for me."

Team Andy, whose drop into central France from too low an altitude ended up crippling both officers with broken legs, got no reply at all to their emergency transmissions. They convalesced like sitting ducks in a Resistance farmhouse, unable to run away if the Germans arrived. "Very surprised no instructions received," they radioed frantically. "Cable immediately what you want to do with us." Meanwhile, some Jeds and agents got all the weapons they wanted. Others got little or nothing. "We had one constant occupation which was becoming a real nightmare: arms, arms, arms," Paul Cyr would write in his

Team George report. "We could never understand why the planes never arrived."

One American agent, after calling for sleeping bags, instead got twelve lamp shades and a few cans of corned beef. In a more amusing sort of snafu, one container, dropped to one of British agent George Millar's groups in Vosges, contained a letter from the Scottish woman who had packed it saying that she would love to meet a maquis boy, dark-haired preferred. She supplied her name and address.

Despite the problems, the ranks of the armed Resistance swelled. On July 14, France's Bastille Day, the shadow chiefs celebrated with the largest-ever single American Army Air Force drop of supplies to the French Resistance. The massive dump totaled 3,791 containers, under red, blue, and white parachutes, the colors of the French flag, floating down from 320 planes flying over central and southeastern France. On a more routine basis, the British and American bombers dropped a monthly total of approximately 2,100 tons of weapons and supplies.

Team Ian, working in central France, reported distributing Sten and Bren guns to six thousand men; in Brittany, Team Felix armed three thousand; Team Hugh, another six thousand. Reports of such numbers, armed and trained by Jeds and Allied agents, repeated themselves all over France. Hundreds of thousands of Resistance fighters desperately awaited the breakout and the transmission of the Napoleon's-hat-type BBC code phrase that at last ordered their region to rise up en masse. In the meantime, between trainings and lectures, they enthusiastically maintained the sabotage program that helped keep more Germans from joining the Battle of the Bocage.

"Sabotaged 46 locomotives at the Capdenac depot," read Tommy Macpherson's Team Quinine radio message on July 5. "Coordinated attack upon all long distance high tension lines," went his transmission after he felled, amid showers of sparks and groans of metal girders, the pylons throughout the district, stopping electricity to the armaments factory in Clermont-Ferrand. He radioed on July 20, "360 rail cuts." His messages read like a catalog of subterfuge techniques. "Gestapo placed price of one million francs on 'an English major with a skirt,' " the kilt-wearing Scot radioed headquarters, gleefully offering evidence of his effect on the Germans. "Consider your head undervalued," headquarters radioed back.

Farther south, near the Spanish border, American Major Hod Fuller's

Team Bugatti forced the Germans to permanently abandon the Tarbes-to-Toulouse railway, an important line that they had used to move their forces back and forth between the Atlantic and Mediterranean coasts. From central France, on July 5, Team Hamish radioed, "Sabotage blown 3 bridges." In the southeast on July 28, the Team Dodge radio operator tapped out, "12 wagons on petrol train at Veugris burned." Many Jed teams and agents also helped spirit downed Allied aircrews out of France and back to England.

To let off steam, and for the purposes of training, Bernard Knox occasionally allowed his maquisards to ambush German vehicles and garrisons, in spite of London's orders to lay low. His men raided one German post just to steal their cigarettes. In central France, an American agent sent his maquisards to assassinate members of the Milice, letting them practice their new guerrilla warfare skills without fear of reprisal—the Germans did not bother to retaliate after attacks on French collaborators.

In the department of Indre, Bob Anstett of Team Hamish ambushed a German truck carrying fifteen tons of butter and distributed it throughout the country. "We had never seen so much butter before," Anstett reported. These little operations, trivial though they seemed, had the vastly important effect of bolstering the morale of the maquis and convincing them that, when the time for the final uprising came, they could actually beat the Germans. But the sabotage program took first priority.

Bridges fell into rivers and ravines, telephone poles tumbled down, and trucks blew up and blocked roads. Not a night went by without tens of rail cuts on the crucial northerly routes. Throughout July, Jeds, agents, and maquis in France jabbed at the Germans on an overwhelming scale. As a result, new German units arrived at Normandy in little more than drips.

The German 271st Infantry Division took nearly the first three weeks of July to get to the battle zone from Sète-Montpellier, a journey that should have taken three days. By July 20, the 11th Panzer Division, mired in anti-Resistance operations, had not even departed from Dordogne, near where Teams Ammonia and Quinine operated. As late as July 27, elements from the 9th Panzer and 338th Infantry divisions still expended their energy trying to swat the maquis buzzing in the Rhône Valley, the working area of Teams Chloroform, Dodge, and Veganin.

Finally, in late July, a gathering of six thousand Resistance in the uplands of Vercors, southwest of the city of Grenoble, so threatened communications along the Rhône Valley that it attracted German forces in unprecedented proportions—thirteen infantry battalions, a parachute battalion, a tank battalion, and artillery. Eleven thousand German troops were thus kept from the fighting in Normandy. General Johannes Blaskowitz, commanding German forces in the south of France, reported that the FFI "no longer constituted a mere terrorist movement in southern France, but had evolved into an organized army at his rear."

Meanwhile, at Milton Hall and at the Jed base in Algiers, undeployed Jedburghs still waited around for their chance to go to France. They played poker for increasingly reckless stakes. They drank the local pub dry. Jack Singlaub charged around American bases looking for a doctor who would sign orders returning him to jump status. The battle for France would end before they even joined it, the Jeds worried. The war would leave them behind.

Of the ninety-three Jed teams who would eventually drop into France, sixty-nine still rotted in their training bases and had not been given firm departure dates. They felt deceived and neglected. Their mood was mutinous. When the next tired assurance of their imminent departure came, the Jeds laughed derisively. They blew raspberries. "Forty-eight," someone called. "Forty-nine . . . Fifty . . . Some shit!"

If the shadow chiefs had been slow in dropping the Jeds, it was partly because Omar Bradley's American forces in Normandy had by July 20 still only reached the Périers-Saint-Lô road, about ten miles inland. The Allies now held a line running roughly from Caen to Saint-Lô, a position they had hoped to hold within five days of D-Day. After only six weeks in France, in other words, Eisenhower's forces were already five weeks behind schedule.

As for the future, the U.S. First Army faced more of the hedgerows and small woods that had plagued them. The commanders bitterly coveted the terrain beyond those hedgerows that rose to the more open, rolling plateau of dry ground and pastoral hillsides and better roads, the land beyond the Granville-Falaise line where the breakout had been planned to begin. They were still over thirty miles short of that goal.

The Americans had quietly discovered a way for their tanks, so long incapacitated by the hedgerows of the *bocage,* to cut through them. In secret from the Germans, the Americans welded huge, jagged steel teeth to the snouts of about 60 percent of their VII Corps tanks. These "Rhinos," as the men dubbed the adapted tanks, sliced through the hedgerows. Bradley, Montgomery, and

Eisenhower planned to use their new secret weapon to spearhead an all-out attack. To hell with clawing their way yard by yard to the Granville-Falaise line.

What they would do instead, according to an audacious new plan code-named Cobra, was bomb and blast to smithereens the Germans defending the south side of a narrow, seven-thousand-yard stretch of the Périers-Saint-Lô road. On the ground, with the thunderous conflagration complete, three American infantry divisions would charge forward, side by side, to punch a hole in what remained of Hitler's defensive crust. As the foot soldiers held the hole open, two tank divisions and one motorized infantry division would then pound south, make a right turn, charge west behind the enemy to the coastal town of Coutances, and encircle a slew of German defenders.

Most important, by the end of Operation Cobra, the Allies would no longer be mired in the checkerboard obstacle course of the *bocage*. They would, after weeks of frustrating near-stalemate, at last hold the southern Normandy flat grounds across which their modern, mechanized army could rapidly charge. From there, the Allies would regroup and, eventually, begin both their attack into Brittany and the massive leftward wheel across northern France toward the German border.

The plan was a gamble. The daring thrust could win in a matter of days twice the territory the Allies had taken in six weeks or leave a number of valuable American divisions dangling without support in German-held territory. Happily for the Jeds still in Milton Hall, however, if all went well, soon after Cobra would come the breakout, the invasion of Brittany, the southern invasion, and the charge across northern France—for all of which the shadow chiefs planned massive Resistance support. The Jeds would come pouring down from the sky.

All the American forces needed to begin Cobra was a clear day so the bomber pilots could see their targets. But there was a problem: the Germans could no longer tolerate the threat of the Resistance at their rear and had launched another nationwide purge. The question was whether the shadow armies would survive as a fighting force until Cobra's blue skies arrived.

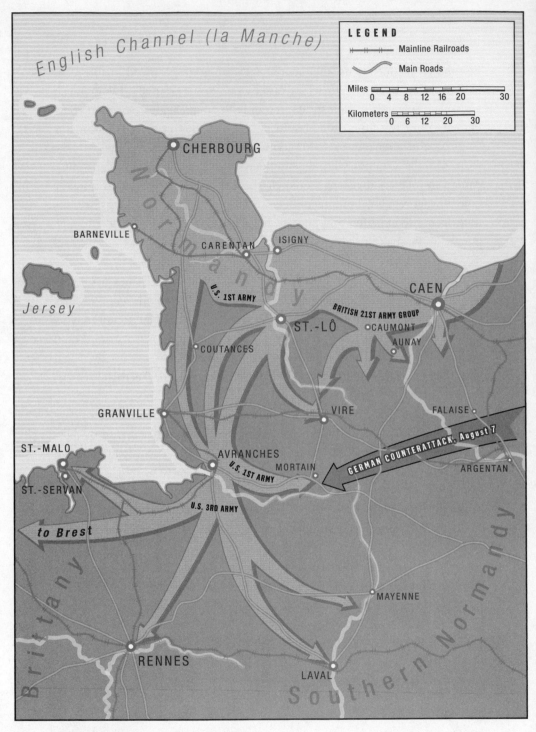

**OPERATION COBRA—JULY 25 TO AUGUST 6**

After the success of Operation Cobra, the Jeds and Resistance would assist Patton's VIII Corps in its westward rush to Brest in Brittany and protect the southern flank of the rest of his Third Army as it charged into southern Normandy and turned east toward Germany.

# CHAPTER TWENTY-SEVEN
## "IN GRAVE DANGER"

**B**ob Kehoe pressed a headphone to his ear and listened. It was a mid-July night and, ninety miles to his east, the American infantry still slogged toward Saint-Lô. Kehoe, working by the dim yellow glow of his flashlight, sat with his radio receiver at the ramshackle table where Team Frederick now did all its coding, decoding, eating, drinking, debating, and planning. On July 9, Team Frederick had relocated themselves to this one-room stone cottage in Côtes-du-Nord tucked away in an overgrown, unused farm field. The tiny village of Canihuel sat just down the hill; it was an hour's walk to the larger town of Saint-Nicolas-du-Pélem.

Kehoe twiddled the radio dial. Through the crackle came the voice of the BBC's French service. Outside, everything was quiet. Approach should have been impossible without exchanging passwords with the sentries. Inside the cottage, six or seven different snores droned out of time. The sleepers lay at Kehoe's feet, all lined up, males on one side, females on the other.

The cottage had holes in the walls where there once had been windows; the dirt floor made a lumpy, filthy bed for the members of the command post. Still, it had a fireplace to cook on and a thatched roof that kept out nearly all the rain. On the wall, Major Adrian Wise and Lieutenant Paul Bloch-Auroch had posted a map of all the local maquis groups and their corresponding drop zones. It was a sign of their overconfidence.

Kehoe waited for the BBC's *messages personnels* and their coded news of arms drops and other operations. He watched the snorers. He listened to the crickets. Then, without warning from the sentinels, came a knock at the door.

The sleepers awoke instantly. The metallic clicks of weapons being cocked and loaded filled the cabin. When the door opened, a heavy-set, round-faced blond woman named Aïde filled the threshold. She was sweating and out of breath. Team Frederick lowered their weapons. Aïde was a Resistance courier whom Kehoe had never before seen frightened. Tonight, her entire body trembled. Team Frederick had sent her on her bicycle to a drop, twenty miles to the east, to retrieve any messages or news. She had turned around almost as soon as she arrived and pedaled frantically back through the darkness.

I had gone out to the barn, she stammered. The drop zone reception committee was finishing their supper in the farmhouse. Aïde could hear their muffled voices drifting toward her through the night. Then came the unexpected rumble of military vehicles, the crunch of rolling tires, the squeal of brakes. From the pitch darkness of the barn, Aïde heard the farmhouse door bang open, the immediate rattle of machine-gun fire, and, ominously, not a single shout. Aïde stayed hidden. Before long, a yellow light danced into the barn, cast by flames. The Germans had set the farmhouse on fire. Finally, their trucks growled away and Aïde summoned the courage to try to help her comrades.

They were all dead, she cried now at Team Frederick's command post. Only after she had told the whole story did Aïde begin to cry. Sit down, someone said. Drink some wine. Stay here. But Aïde, having delivered the tragic news, wanted to warn others that a traitor might be giving away the locations of Resistance workers. She flew out the door, into the darkness and onto her bike.

On the morning of July 20, a few days after the raid on Aïde's reception committee, a Team Frederick lookout spotted a German direction-finding van crawling slowly down a nearby road. The area's farmers observed unusual German movements. Maquis reported soldiers searching the woods. Bob Kehoe felt very nervous tapping on his Morse key outside of the cottage, but Team Frederick had already supplied weapons to twenty-two hundred out of the forty-two hundred men they would eventually arm. Officers Wise and Bloch-Auroch had been seduced into complacency by their own success.

What they had not considered was that the raid on Aïde's reception committee had not been the work of a solitary traitor, but was part of a well-planned program intended to defang the Resistance. The Nazis had realized they could no longer afford to allow their movement and communications to be interfered with, and, on July 7, the German high command had ordered troops in France to stomp out behind-the-lines annoyances once and for all.

On July 21, for example, the occupiers finally launched their eleven-thousand-man operation in Vercors, where 630 maquis would die. In Vienne, Jedburgh Team Ian experienced the Germans' new resolve when an entire eight-hundred-strong regiment on anti-Resistance duty suddenly entrenched themselves in a barbed wire–surrounded base camp. They prepared to wipe out Team Ian's maquis who had so successfully harassed German move-ment on the important north-south rails and roads leading up the French west coast and into Angoulême. The Germans mounted similar operations all over France.

But nothing had alerted Bob Kehoe's Team Frederick to the growing German fury and the fact that the attack on Aïde's reception committee was not an isolated incident. They strutted about in their uniforms. They stayed on the radio too long, ignoring the fact that the Germans might latch onto their signal. They left their transmitter's antenna up for all who passed to see. "We have information that the enemy is preparing large-scale action against the maquis," radioed Bernard Knox to headquarters from only thirty miles away. Team Frederick knew nothing.

The machine guns opened up from only a couple of hundred yards away. Bul-lets landed everywhere. Globs of dirt exploded into the air. Coming up the trails and across the fields, more than six hundred soldiers closed a cordon around the Team Frederick command post.

Kehoe snatched the crystals from his radio. He stuffed his codebooks into his pockets and ran. Beside him, Wise and Bloch-Auroch burst out of the cot-tage, each with a carbine and a bundle of hand grenades. Kehoe had only the Colt .45 on his hip. Cavalry on horses galloped up one side of the hill; Kehoe, Wise, and Bloch-Auroch sprinted desperately down the other. In a stroke of luck, the horsemen stopped to examine the command post cottage—they had apparently not seen Team Frederick sprinting away.

Kehoe and his colleagues threw themselves into a briar patch and quickly crawled on their hands and knees into its tangled center. They prayed that the Germans had no bloodhounds. Shots rang out in all directions. Cornered maquisards were mowed down by machine-gun fire.

Patrols of Germans walked through the field where Team Frederick hid.

They discharged their weapons randomly into the clumps of bushes, trying to flush out their quarry. Bob Kehoe, lying on his stomach, watched the German boots marching past on the trail over the trembling muzzle of his .45. If the Germans began shooting in their direction, Team Frederick decided, they would return fire and try to run. It would, essentially, be suicide. Kehoe, Wise, and Bloch-Auroch had made a pact: they would not allow themselves to be taken prisoner.

In their frustration, the Germans had notched up their Resistance sweep into a frenzied massacre, not just in Côtes-du-Nord but all over Brittany and in other parts of France. In Finistère, where Team Giles and Team Francis operated, the German 2nd Parachute Division burned farms and shot farmers anywhere near the suspected hiding places of maquis or Jeds. The soldiers tortured and killed any maquis they captured by tearing out their eyes, and then, for a sidesplitting joke, putting potatoes in the bloody sockets.

They used clubs to break legs, rings of iron spikes to crush heads, and chains to suspend men by their feet. In Team Ian's area of operations in Vienne, the anti-Resistance regiment burned and pillaged the town of Ambernac and then executed the civilians. Around Brittany, the Allies would later find trenches filled with the decomposed bodies of those the Germans had massacred.

"In grave danger," Bernard Knox radioed London. "Boche concentrating all around us." Knox's maquisards furiously insisted that the time had come to attack the Germans, with or without the signal from the BBC. Knox knew that this was just what the Germans hoped for. They wanted to enrage the maquis, flush them out into the open, and then slaughter them with superior forces and equipment. Knox struggled to avoid premature confrontations between his maquis and the Germans, but skirmishes broke out. "The FTP are reaching boiling point and explosion may occur if Boche continues to hunt them," Knox warned.

"You must avoid in any circumstances to enter into action until operations start," the shadow bosses bounced back.

Knox was furious. He now commanded about two thousand armed men. Where was he supposed to hide them? And if he could not hide them, how could he possibly convince them not to fight back?

"We repeat in words of one syllable," Knox radioed again. "If Boche attacks maquis in this area, no power on earth can prevent general explosion."

But Knox's maquis did not explode, because they were not the Germans' next target.

At 9:10 p.m. on July 29, German trucks squealed to a stop at Team Francis's command post at a farm in southwest Finistère. The chatter of gunfire began.

A soldier ran into the farmhouse and stabbed his bayonet through the back of the harmless seventy-one-year-old farmer. A shot tore through the stomach of Team Francis's British leader, Major Colin Ogden-Smith. A grenade wounded an SAS man who threw himself to the ground and fired at the Germans while his colleagues ran. Ogden-Smith managed to crawl to the edge of the woods. Behind him, the life of the SAS man would last exactly as long as it took him to expend his four clips of ammo.

In Vienne, the anti-Resistance battalion launched its purge and marched with heavy machine guns and mortars toward Team Ian's maquis positions. Team Ian, making its getaway in a car, charged through the town of Pleuville and straight into a column of four hundred Germans. Captain Desfarges, Team Ian's French officer, maneuvered the car in a U-turn, while Americans Major John Gildee and Sergeant Lucien Bourgoin blasted away at the German swarm. Three machine guns chattered and mortars poured down a barrage upon them. The car's engine expired.

Team Ian scrambled into the streets of Pleuville. It was each man for himself. Bourgoin ran in one direction, and the two officers in another. They chased through the alleys and houses, pursued by Germans and continuous fire. The Germans ransacked the houses in Pleuville and set fire to eighteen buildings. Gildee and Desfarges hid in the woods. Later, with a group of maquis, they tried to search for Bourgoin, but the Germans were too plentiful. After nearly twenty-four hours, with amazing luck, Gildee and Desfarges managed to sneak past the outposts to safety.

Back in Côtes-du-Nord, a group of ten Germans stopped by Team Frederick's bushes within three yards of their heads. If the Germans stopped talking, Kehoe thought, they would hear us breathing. The soldiers moved away and things finally went quiet.

After several hours of full-bladder agony, Kehoe finally turned on his side, unzipped his fly, and began to pee. Wise scowled at him, but a few minutes later it was his turn to relieve himself while Bloch-Auroch grimaced. When Bloch-Auroch finally relented and emptied his bladder, too, Team Frederick allowed themselves a smile. They spotted a young farm boy bringing his cows home and spoke to him. He had seen no patrols for half an hour. Team Frederick crawled out of the bushes and the boy guided them to a farm where some maquis had hidden. By the end of the evening, Bob Kehoe happily dined on boiled potatoes.

Teams Ian and Frederick had both escaped the frenzied German attacks, but in Finistère, the SAS man who protected the injured Major Colin Ogden-Smith finally ran out of ammunition. "You need not be afraid," he shouted to the Germans. "I have no more ammunition."

"Put your hands up," they shouted back, and he did.

They shot him first with a burst from a submachine gun. Then they finished him off with a shot through the temple. Bleeding profusely from his stomach wound, Ogden-Smith watched from nearby. It would be only a matter of moments before the Germans found him, too. When their work was finished, according to maquisards watching from hiding places in the woods, the Germans torched the farm and watched it burn, collected jewelry and money from the corpses, and laughed and joked.

Back at Bernard Knox's command post, Captain Leborgne, Ogden-Smith's French officer, suddenly arrived, shaken and scared. During their Milton Hall days, Knox and Ogden-Smith had been best friends. Now, Knox listened to Leborgne's story. When Leborgne was finished, Knox sadly coded a message to headquarters: "Major Ogden-Smith killed."

After the Germans had killed the SAS man, they dispatched the injured Ogden-Smith with a shot to the head. In Vienne, John Gildee of Team Ian coded a sad message of his own. He had found Sergeant Bourgoin in a field with three bullets in his body. Jeds number two and three, of the nineteen who would die in France that summer, had been killed just as the Allies readied themselves to break out of the beachhead and the shadow army, or what was left of them, prepared to erupt.

# PART VI

# FRANCE EXPLODES

## CHAPTER TWENTY-EIGHT
# COBRA STRIKE

After days of torrential rain, the clouds cleared over Normandy and the rising sun's bright rays shone through the crisp blue sky the Allies had been waiting for. To the German soldiers hiding in their bunkers and foxholes on the southern side of the Périers-Saint-Lô road, the morning seemed to bring more than improved weather. As they warily peeked over their sandbags, the Americans packed up and withdrew. "Looks as if they've got cold feet," the operations officer of the Panzer Lehr Division said cheerfully.

The keenest of the Germans sprinted across the road and made themselves at home in the abandoned American dugouts, thinking they had reclaimed a few easy yards for Germany. At 9:30 that morning, when the deafening roar of 550 American Mustangs and other fighter-bombers suddenly filled the western Normandy sky, the Germans realized their mistake. The Americans had not retreated at all; they had been ordered to scramble back twelve hundred yards to avoid being vaporized in an impending storm of fire. It was July 25, the Allied "second D-Day."

The Mustangs swarmed down in precise, deadly arcs and dropped their bombs on German machine guns, mortar nests, and foxholes. Their cannons rattled bullets at the enemy soldiers making a run for it. "Bombing attacks by endless waves of aircraft," the terrified Germans radioed their divisional headquarters. But the conflagration had only just begun. When the first onslaught of Allied fighter-bombers expended the last of their ammunition, turned tail, and flew home, the Allied cannons began to boom. Over a thousand now pounded the Germans with artillery fire.

To the Germans' horror, high above them, 1,880 medium and four-engine heavy bombers droned slowly over the horizon. Omar Bradley, in his plans for Cobra, had departed from military dogma, which said that the big bombers were too inaccurate to support ground battles. He assigned to them the job of pulverizing, from altitudes of many thousands of feet, the twenty-five hundred yards behind the German front. With 140,000 artillery shells and over eight million pounds of bombs, the idea was to reduce Nazi defenses to irrelevance.

German trucks exploded and flipped upside down. Bright white flashes left thirty-foot craters. Everything burned. Young German soldiers, faced with their melting flesh and the desperate screams of their companions, blew their own brains out. Ordered by the German high command to hold his position, the leader of the Panzer Lehr Division replied, "My grenadiers and the pioneers, my anti-tank gunners, they're holding. None of them have left their positions, none. They're lying in their holes, still and mute, because they are dead. Dead. Do you understand?"

For an hour and a half, the Germans took the awful punishment that left nearly one thousand of them dead. The American infantrymen, meanwhile, ensconced across the Périers-Saint-Lô road, covered their ears and watched from a distance. Then, it slowly dawned on the Americans that the blasting had begun inching toward them.

The Allied bombers had quickly obliterated the landmarks that oriented them. The bombardiers in their flying machines, high in the sky, had little to aim at besides the huge carpet of smoke made by the previous bombs. They did not realize that, thanks to a nice, gentle breeze, the smoke now drifted toward the American infantrymen. "We stood tensed in muscle and frozen in intellect," wrote Ernie Pyle, an American newspaper columnist huddled with a group of American infantry, "watching each flight approach and pass over us, feeling trapped and completely helpless."

Some Americans dove under trucks. Others desperately dug foxholes. Many cowered behind garden walls and hid in ramshackle barns. As the deafening bangs sounded around them, the terrified soldiers covered their ears, screamed, cried, and prayed. For two hours, the bombardment lasted. When it ended, some American infantrymen had gone crazy and had to be forcibly carried to the rear, 111 had been killed, and 490 were maimed and lay screaming for aid.

"The attack goes ahead as scheduled," ordered one American general, as reports of the friendly-fire decimation poured in. "Even if you only have two or three men, the attack is made." The Americans still had surprise on their side, whatever their tragic losses, and they had to make use of it. Slowly, three American infantry divisions, under VII Corps commander General J. Lawton Collins, pulled themselves together and moved forward through the destruction, attempting to punch the planned hole in the German defensive crust.

The German side of the front was devastated: trees were uprooted, rifle positions and machine-gun nests buried, tanks overturned, whole roads destroyed. The bad news for the shell-shocked American attackers was that many of the well-armed defenders had survived. German artillery began blaring while snipers and riflemen fired furiously from atop the hedgerows. American vehicles got stuck in the bomb craters, making sitting ducks of their passengers. Firefights as vicious as any of the Battle of the Bocage broke out everywhere. This was a far cry from stepping over dead German bodies, as had been planned.

Twelve hours after the carpet bombing, as the sun set, no one could be sure that Collins's infantry had punctured the German bubble. The day's hoped-for decisive breakout had not arrived. Allied generals began talking about the lessons that had to be learned. "It's always slow going in the early phases of such an attack," Bradley told them all. Things, he said, would be different the next day.

On the morning of July 26, General Collins gambled that his VII Corps infantry had, in fact, forged a path through the German defenders and launched the second stage of his attack: the southward thrust by the tanks. Two armored divisions roared forward. Happily, the stiff German resistance, fractured by the previous day's onslaught, now lay shattered in pieces across the entire front.

Collins's tanks raced through the countryside. A hedgerow delayed the Rhinos for no more than an average of two and a half minutes. Easily plowing passages through each earthen mound, the Rhinos made way for whole columns of armor that then went charging through. Momentum built. Pockets of German resistance took minutes for the American infantry to tear apart. Two days after the attack began, the VII Corps contended not with the German defense, but with the chaos of their fleeing men and vehicles looking for an escape route. They no longer presented any real danger to the success of Operation Cobra.

Meanwhile, the American VIII Corps, under Major General Troy H. Middleton, launched a second attack down the western coast of the Cotentin peninsula. Together, the tanks and troops of Collins and Middleton pushed relentlessly forward. Crowds of celebrating townspeople, out from under the Nazi jackboot at last, cheered the exhilarated American troops and clung to the sides of their tanks as they lumbered through the streets. Truckloads of American GIs waved frantically to the ecstatic French people. On July 28, the Americans at last reached Cobra's objective—the town of Coutances.

When Omar Bradley originally conceived of Operation Cobra, he had intended it merely as a means to climb out of the hedgerow country and onto the high flatlands where he could regroup and launch the breakout proper. But the unexpected disintegration of the German defense in western Normandy resulting from Cobra presented Bradley with incredible opportunities. Now was not the time, he realized, to stop.

He ordered his army to continue south. "We shall continue attacking, never give him a chance to rest, never give him a chance to dig in," he wrote in his diary. On July 29, four armored divisions slashed their way down Normandy's western coast south of Coutances toward the base of the Brittany peninsula. On July 31, Bradley's forces arrived at Avranches, a gateway to both Brittany to the west and southern Normandy to the east.

The next day, on August 1, Bradley activated the new Third Army to take advantage of the Avranches gateway and charge into Hitler's rear. Bradley gave command of the Third Army and its audacious onward attack to the one man he thought could ensure its success: Lieutenant General George S. Patton, the United States' most talented and idiosyncratic leader of mobile warfare.

A horseman who came up through the cavalry, Patton was unashamedly romanced by war and fancied himself the reincarnation of Hannibal, the Carthaginian general of the second century BC. Patton had problems with authority, took little interest in the trivialities of military planning, and lusted after battlefield glory.

A year earlier, as Seventh Army commander during the Sicily campaign, Patton twice flew into a rage when he discovered men in field hospitals suffering from "shell shock," a term that to him simply meant cowardice. Patton slapped one of these men and threatened to shoot the other. He drew his pistol, called the man "a yellow son of a bitch," said "I ought to shoot you myself right now, God damn you," thought better of it, and punched him twice in the head.

That incident cost Patton command of the Seventh Army, and he would have been sent home, except that Eisenhower considered him too important to lose. Patton's character flaws also made him a brilliantly imaginative, unpredictable military commander. The Germans feared him more than any other Allied battlefield commander, which was why, at this crucial stage of the breakout, Bradley brought him to Normandy and back into the war.

With the four corps of his Third Army, Patton wanted to charge through the breach at Avranches, "murder those lousy Hun bastards by the bushel," and chase the survivors east past Paris to Germany. But both Eisenhower and Bradley worried that come October the winter storms would destroy the artificial harbors in Normandy, stranding their troops with neither reinforcements nor supplies. They still considered critical to victory the capture of Brest and the southern Brittany coastline at Quiberon Bay, where they planned to build a well-sheltered port facility.

As the compromise plan went, the American First Army would hold back the Germans and keep open the bottleneck at Avranches while the tanks and infantry of the Third Army's VIII, XII, XV, and XX Corps immediately began pouring through. Patton could gallop into southern Normandy with three of his corps, but his VIII Corps, Bradley insisted, would have to conquer Brittany.

Patton detested the idea of attacking westward—"winning the war the wrong way." He despised, also, the SHAEF planners' time-consuming idea of slogging across Brittany on a broad front, field by field. Patton determined that the battle would not last a single unnecessary moment, and he opted for an unrelenting armored charge straight for the ports.

Patton shook British Field Marshal Bernard Law Montgomery by the hand, bet him five pounds that VIII Corps would be at the western tip of Brittany in five days, and launched his attack. The 6th Armored Division under Major General Robert Grow, Patton decided, would spearhead the VIII Corps advance. Patton grabbed Grow by the shoulder and said simply, "Take Brest." He seemed to think it was the next town instead of a fortified citadel 150 miles deep in enemy territory.

Bill Dreux's sopping shirt stuck to his back, and sweat, running down his face, stung his eyes. Here at the base of the Brittany peninsula on this second day of August, Dreux and his team leader, Major Carbuccia, dispensed with the normal cross-country trudge. They walked openly on the main highway toward the town of Combourg, only twenty-five miles or so from the Allied break-through at Avranches. Their weapons hung over their shoulders, and their packs dangled heavily from their backs. At Combourg, Team Gavin hoped at last to make contact with the area's Resistance leaders.

Since first landing and hiding in the Courcité rectory, Dreux and his colleagues had precariously pushed the seventy-five miles toward the department of Ille-et-Vilaine through a whirlpool of German troops trying to organize themselves against the Cobra attack. As the German convoys raced toward Avranches, Dreux and Carbuccia darted between them. Frustrated and exhausted, Team Gavin had reached their intended area of operations only three days earlier. The rumble of distant Allied artillery and bombing echoed like an approaching thunderstorm, but Team Gavin had yet to blow a bridge.

Now, as Dreux and Carbuccia walked toward Combourg, the growl of powerful engines and the tinkle of metal treads reached them from the distance. Carbuccia glanced at Dreux with a sardonic smile. "Soon you'll get to greet your compatriots," he said, knowing that Dreux wanted nothing less. Suddenly, from around a bend in the road, a huge olive-green Sherman tank with a big white star on its chest raced toward and past them, followed by a dozen other American tanks of General Grow's 6th Armored Division. The first tanks of Patton's advance had arrived.

At the other end of Brittany, 140 miles to Dreux's west, messengers tore into Bernard Knox's command post near the village of Plessis. Maquis chiefs throughout Finistère had dispatched them with urgent news. *Les boches partent!* they shouted excitedly. The Germans are leaving! What trucks the Germans had not already sent to Normandy, they now piled high with ammunition and supplies. They led the horses from the stables and harnessed them to wooden carts. They commandeered bicycles from civilians. They stoked locomotive engines with coal. They filled their canteens, heaved on their packs, and prepared to march.

In the early hours of August 1, Hitler himself had given Field Marshal Günther von Kluge, the new commander of Germany's western forces, permission to abandon some of Brittany's coastal defenses to meet the Allied advance. Kluge, in turn, ordered the 2nd Parachute Division, the vicious hooligans who had so terrorized Brittany, to pour out of Brest and its outlying garrisons and move east. They, and the four other German divisions in Brittany, planned to bring to an end Patton's unconventional assault.

What shall we tell our chiefs to do? each of the maquis messengers who arrived at Knox's headquarters asked anxiously.

The Allied attack on Brittany had at last begun, and the maquis believed their part in the war had come. The time for vengeance the maquis had been waiting for, they thought, had finally arrived.

*Attendez,* Knox said. Wait.

Wait? Wait for what? The German paratroopers had torched Breton farms, bayoneted schoolchildren, pillaged jewelry from French corpses. Were the maquis now supposed to let their commandeered horse carts clip-clop safely past and the German foot soldiers stroll by as though they were on a country walk? Our homes have been burnt. Our families are dead, the maquis said to Bernard Knox. Surely you don't expect us to let the bastards just pick up and leave!

Knox and the rest of the Jeds around Brittany sympathized with the maquis. Headquarters clearly did not understand the situation. The Jedburgh radio operators furiously tapped out messages demanding to know why the "Napoleon's hat" action message had not yet been transmitted. In Morbihan, Captain S. J. Knerly, the American commander of Team Gerald, decided that London's swivel-chair men could go to hell. He ignored their orders and told the maquis to start attacking the German convoys. Bernard Knox and the other Jeds wavered on the verge of doing the same, but as though reading their minds, London sent a new directive.

"Allied forces advancing into Brittany," the headquarters directive to the Jeds in Brittany said. "Most important prevent general flare up until you get order."

*Merde!* said the maquis chiefs when they received Knox's relayed messages. *Putain!*

That same day, at the base of the Brittany peninsula, Dreux and his teammates had followed Patton's tank column past Combourg's castle and into the town. Celebrating citizens filled the streets. Both the French Tricolor and the American Stars and Stripes hung everywhere. Frenchmen climbed onto the tanks and women and children crowded around the military police, who, in their glossy helmets and shiny boots, already directed the flow of vehicles. Traffic cops now became heroes, Bill Dreux noted bitterly, while after all the

Jeds' training and willingness to risk their lives behind the lines, his team were just stragglers walking unnoticed down a side street.

"*Le chapeau de Napoléon, est-il encore à Perros-Guirec?*" Dreux's team leader Carbuccia said sourly. "*Merde.*"

Like Knox's maquis in Finistère, Dreux and his teammates felt they had been reduced to insignificance by Patton's Sherman tanks. They did not realize that the appearance of the tanks and the movement of Hitler's 2nd Parachute Division to meet them meant not the end of the battle for Brittany for the Jeds and the Resistance, but only the beginning.

# CHAPTER TWENTY-NINE
# "A MESSAGE OF THE HIGHEST IMPORTANCE"

In planning his audacious Brittany campaign, George Patton focused not on the maze of Breton hedgerows that so frightened the SHAEF planners but on the two good, wide roads to Brest and the disorganization of the German army caused by the sudden Allied breakout. Patton had no interest in winning inland Breton territory, and he gave not a moment's thought to the planners' slogging, checkers-game vision of the Brittany campaign. Patton wanted only Brittany's coast, especially its ports, and he wanted it fast. As for the Germans, he planned to rip out their "Goddamned guts and use them to grease the treads of our tanks." Then he could turn his VIII Corps around and send them chasing across France to Germany with the rest of the Third Army.

By August 2, the VIII Corps' 6th Armored Division poured into Brittany, passing Bill Dreux and Team Gavin at Combourg and moving toward one of the two good roads that so enamored Patton. The 6th Armored's intended route ran straight along the spine of Brittany, from the city of Rennes at the peninsula's base to the town of Châteaulin at its tip. Its charge would be the deepest behind enemy lines of the entire war. Patton chose this inland route where the Germans were most sparse for General Grow's 6th Armored. He wanted Grow's tanks to get straight to the job of conquering Brest without engaging in any distracting skirmishes along the way.

Meanwhile, to a second armored column, known as Task Force A, Patton gave the job of deliberately confronting the heaviest concentrations of Germans. Task Force A would traverse a road along the northern shore from Avranches through Saint-Brieuc to Brest, past every major German coastal installation in between. The northern road ran parallel to a long railway from

Brest that would be crucial to transporting Allied military supplies to Normandy and beyond. As the plan went, Task Force A would secure the coastal road and railway, take the northern port of Saint-Malo, and entrap the Germans in the other coastal forts until they were conquered.

In the final element of Patton's Brittany plan, a third column of VIII Corps tanks, the 4th Armored Division, would fling itself south from Avranches past Rennes to the southern coast, cutting Brittany off at its base and trapping Hitler's Breton forces within. The 4th Armored would capture the towns of Vannes and Lorient and win the important coastline of Quiberon Bay, where the Allies planned to build a sheltered port facility. Hitler's Breton troops would then be removed from the war, and, through the ports, Patton would have won for the Allies a vast new means of supply. The Brittany campaign would be complete.

To conservative military thinkers, the plan was crazy. For starters, VIII Corps armor would, at least initially, lack infantry flank guards to stop its tanks from getting sideswiped. And if they did run into trouble, the tanks would be submerged too far in German territory for easy military reinforcement. On top of these drawbacks, only a minor delaying action by the Germans would win them time to destroy the Brest port facilities, wreck the rail bridges that led away from them, and empty Patton's prospective victory of significance.

The VIII Corps, as one of its officers said, was like a bunch of "stagecoaches making a run through Indian territory." As for reliable intelligence of the enemy's strongpoints, "We had nothing but a map of Brittany and the knowledge that enemy resistance was where you found it," General Grow wrote. Meanwhile, Bernard Knox of Jedburgh Team Giles had reported by radio that the hardened warriors of Hitler's 2nd Parachute Division already rushed eastward along both the inland and the coastal roads to block the VIII Corps' advance.

Patton's tank commanders needed reliable intelligence and knowledgeable guides to lead them around the enemy strongpoints. The commanders needed a way to prevent the destruction of the Brest port facilities and the rail bridges until they got there. And at least until the slower-going infantry could catch up with them, they needed flank guards to protect them from German sideswipes and cutoffs. This, the SFHQ suggested to Patton, was where Brittany's rabble of thirty thousand Jedburgh-organized Resistance fighters could come in.

On August 1, Colonel Robert "Rip" Powell, the SFHQ's chief liaison with the Third Army, unrolled a map, stabbed his finger at point after point, and showed Patton's staff where hundreds of companies of Breton Resistance lay in hiding. Powell told the Third Army chiefs how the groups had been armed and trained by Jeds and other Allied agents and how he also had at his disposal Special Air Service and OSS Operational Groups who could parachute in at a moment's notice for the most difficult behind-the-lines jobs.

Powell explained that the maquis could harass and slow an enemy counter-attack, protect Patton's flanks, provide intelligence, protect the crucial rail bridges until Task Force A arrived, and mop up German positions as the military roared past. Powell even had messages from Jed Team Horace saying that their two thousand men in Brest might be able to delay German destruction of its harbor installations—*if* they got sufficient weapons.

Patton immediately requested and received overall command of the Breton Resistance. He was exactly the type of unconventional leader to see more opportunity than risk in giving such unprecedented battlefield responsibility to a crew of hardly shod, barely armed, poorly trained behind-the-lines Frenchmen. Rip Powell, meanwhile, flew to London to brief the SFHQ shadow chiefs and finalize plans. The next day, Jedburgh radio operators around Brittany found themselves decoding the first of their exciting new orders.

"Advancing Allied troops lay great stress on military intelligence," the first of the radioed orders to the Jeds said. "Please arrange for maximum of 30 of your men who know the district well to move towards the Allied front line by different routes." The runners would collect information on the positions of German troop concentrations and heavy gun emplacements and headquarters. They would infiltrate the German front lines toward Patton's approaching tanks, and then guide the troops past the danger points.

Next, the Jeds and agents throughout Brittany got orders to prepare to carry out guerrilla activity in line with newly assigned missions. In the north, the maquis groups of Teams Frederick, Felix, and Hilary would blast away at Germans who emerged from the coastal installations and attempted to blow up the three large rail bridges at Saint-Brieuc and the two near Morlaix or to attack Task Force A on the coast road.

In central Finistère, along the Châteaulin to Rennes road, Bernard Knox's Team Giles would pour fire on the 2nd Parachute Division's attempt to block Patton's 6th Armored Division. Farther south, Teams Gilbert and Francis would assist the 4th Armored Division's drive to the coast by harassing

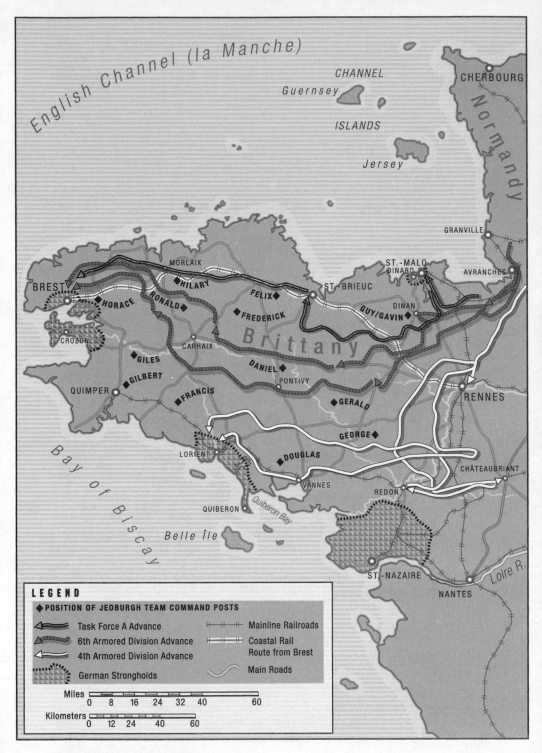

**THE LIBERATION OF BRITTANY**

The Jedburgh teams and their maquis groups moved into position along the important roads in order to forestall German counterattacks against Patton's advance into Brittany.

German movement from the end of the peninsula along the southern coastal road toward Lorient.

And in the northwest, Team Horace's three thousand men in Brest would give hell to demolition teams attempting to wreck the docks and harbor installations as well as a nearby coastal railway bridge. So dangerous was the area that the air force refused to brave the coastal antiaircraft guns to drop sufficient arms. By radio, Team Horace begged headquarters one more time for the weapons they needed. "My opinion, if this show still on, arming Brest area important enough to risk planes," radioed Team Horace's leader.

Meanwhile, around Brittany, runners sprinted out of the Jed command posts to give the maquis leaders their new orders. Thousands of men moved stealthily through the countryside toward their assigned positions and, in groups of thirty or forty, waited in the woods and on farms while their leaders chose their ambush spots. Messengers knocked quietly on the front doors of nearby farmers and villagers, and warned them to move away or face German reprisals.

Just as they had been taught by the Jeds and Allied agents, the riflemen in the ambush groups methodically field-stripped and cleaned their weapons before the action started. Machine gunners loaded their ammunition belts with bullets. Grenadiers carefully constructed "gammon grenades," devices packed with plastic explosive and shards of steel and nails that would detonate on impact with a German vehicle.

Muscles tightened. Necks ached. Tempers frayed. And thirty thousand maquis of the Breton Resistance kept an ear tuned to the BBC and listened for "Napoleon's hat."

Back in Normandy, while VIII Corps drove into Brittany, the rest of Patton's Third Army charged southeast through the Avranches bottleneck into the barely defended rear of Hitler's Normandy force. The Allies had at last begun their crushing leftward turn; the borders of Germany itself waited on the horizon; Patton intended to race there.

A thousand miles farther south, meanwhile, in the Mediterranean theater, U.S. General Alexander Patch prepared to storm a forty-five-mile stretch of the south coast of France with the three divisions of the Seventh U.S. Army and the seven divisions of the First French Army—Operation Anvil, now renamed Dragoon for security reasons. The dangers for the troops of Operation Dragoon would be much the same as for the troops of Operation Overlord.

First, if the Germans arrived at the invasion zone in force, they might blast the Dragoon forces back into the sea. Second, when the Dragoon forces clawed their way off the coast and began their scramble north, they faced possible sideswipes from Germans in both the southwest of France and across the Alps in northern Italy. The flank danger was one that would be similarly faced by Patton's Third Army as it raced east across northern France.

"Let the other son of a bitch worry about flanks," Patton said when someone pointed out that his planned charge would be vulnerable to the German forces still based on the far side of the Loire River in the south of France. Patton gave the shadow armies the job of keeping the Germans in the south from crossing the Loire and sideswiping him. Patch gave them the similar job of protecting his eastern and western flanks, along with stopping German movement to his beachhead.

The "other son of a bitch," it turned out, meant the air forces, the Resistance, and the Jeds and agents who worked with them. For all the Jeds' impatience over waiting to drop into France, the shadow chiefs had always intended them as a "strategic reserve" for emergency use as military events unfolded. That time had now come.

In those first days of August, the shadow chiefs, both in England and in Algiers, prepared a slew of Jed teams, as well as other agents and commando-like groups, to drop into France. Each afternoon at Milton Hall, Jeds summoned to Colonel Musgrave's office came back down the stairs looking serious, saying nothing, and trying not to seem frightened. Rolled-up mattresses now gathered dust in the bunks where more and more Jeds once slept. A new anxiety pervaded the Milton Hall atmosphere.

Radioman Roger Coté, from Manchester, New Hampshire, sat down at a table with a pen and paper. As he wrote his last letter home, he fondly remembered things like his mother's fury after he drew wax lines on the living room window to make it looked cracked as a practical joke. He remembered his father's piano sing-alongs and skating on the frozen pond with his four brothers and sisters. He remembered his whole family sobbing as they stood at the train station, waving good-bye to him.

"This evening I am sitting here trying to put my thoughts into words," he began his letter. "I have a lot to say but I cannot say everything, as you know.

"I would like to ask all of you to pray for me so that I will have the courage to do the work I was trained for," Coté wrote. "I need your prayers. Please do not forget me. Please excuse me for this letter. I can't help my feelings. Don't worry too much. Everything will be alright. I ask God to stay with you, protect you and give you good health." Coté signed his letter, "Your son who loves you very, very much."

The father of another radio operator, Lewis Frelan "Lou" Goddard, had written to him when he was back at Area B in Maryland "that there are times when a strong man should not be ashamed to cry." Now Goddard had recurring dreams of home. He wrote to his mother after he woke from one of them: "It was sure good while it lasted."

Even the gung-ho Jack Singlaub found himself writing a last letter home. "Even if you don't hear from me for a long time, don't worry," he wrote.

In all of June and July, an average of only three Jed teams a week had dropped. Now Aaron Bank's Team Packard, Ted Baumgold's Team Collodion, and Bill Thompson's Team Novocaine all donned their chutes and prepared to jump into the south of France. In the first two weeks of August alone, twenty-four Jed teams floated through the night.

"And now a message of the highest importance," a female announcer on the BBC's French service said. "I repeat, a message of the highest importance."

It was August 2 at 6:00 p.m., 1800 hours in military parlance. Across Brittany, thousands of maquisards crowded around their radios. Fingers dirty from months or years of living in the woods hastily reached for the knob and turned up the volume. "*Le chapeau de Napoléon,*" intoned the announcer, "*est-il encore à Perros-Guirec?*" Napoleon's hat, is it still at Perros-Guirec?

To an innocent ear, the question remained ridiculous, just as intended. How could a natural rock formation weighing so many tons be anywhere but where it had always been? But to the thirty thousand listeners in the know, the question meant everything.

The demolition crews snatched up their sacks of explosives. The ambush gangs threw their guns over their shoulders. From fields and villages and farms and woodlands, the long-suffering civilians-turned-soldiers, still with no uniforms, finally came out into the open. "I have only one thing to say to you," one Finistère leader working with Team Gilbert said to his men. "They're the rabbits now and we're going to hunt them."

On farms, in fields, and in the woods, maquis leaders, Jeds, and Allied agents handed out ammunition to the ambush squads and gave their last-minute instructions: Two clips is all you get. That way you won't stay too long. The groups sneaked behind the hedgerows toward the ambush sites.

Remember, the Jeds and agents reminded them, do not fire at the motorcycle outriders, or the main convoy will be prepared to fight us. Upon arrival at carefully chosen spots that looked down on the road and offered plenty of cover, the thirty-man teams broke up into units of three or four. No heroics! When you hear the whistle, run like hell and meet at the rendezvous!

Silently, the units moved out and nervously took their places in positions overlooking the roads. Boys who had barely reached their teens clicked the safety catches of their Sten guns on and off. Grandfathers, usually too old for military service, kissed their crosses. Some stole last-minute glimpses of photos of their girlfriends or wives. Others drank stiff gulps of brandy.

"How can the Germans hit you when they don't know where you are?" the Jeds and agents urgently whispered to try to reassure them. And then, from the distance, came the guttural sound of the first German voices and the rumblings of the first German trucks.

## CHAPTER THIRTY
# FLYING BODY PARTS

To ambush a German convoy the way the Jeds had trained them, a maquis squad's rifle and machine-gun teams spread themselves atop a quarter of a mile of hedgerow or ledge, making a sort of tunnel of vengeance out of the road below. At the tunnel end farthest from the direction the Germans would come sat a bazooka, gammon grenade, or demolition team. As a convoy's outriders roared past on their motorcycles, the maquis riflemen crouched behind boulders or trees, watched over their rifle sights, and restrained themselves. Shooting the motorcyclists would just alert the body of the convoy a couple of hundred yards behind.

Next came a pause that seemed to last forever. The wind rustled the shrubs. The sound of the engines grew louder.

Finally, the first of the wood-sided troop transports approached, but, almost ludicrously, because of the tactics of the ambush, these first Germans were allowed to rumble by. Over the tailgate at the back of the truck, the maquis might glimpse thirty or forty uniformed German soldiers nodding side by side on their benches with the butts of their rifles on the floor and the barrels pointing toward the sky.

Bastards! the maquis muttered.

As the mechanics of the surprise attack went, the lead truck had to reach the bazooka or demolition team at the far end of the ambush, and the main body of the convoy had to enter the tunnel, before the firing finally began. The idea was to blast apart the lead truck and make a blockade out of it, so the trucks behind would have no choice but to come to a screeching halt. Once the Germans were trapped and couldn't simply accelerate away, that's when the shooting would start.

Two or three more trucks roared past.

A maquisard on his first ambush might think to hell with command and tactics; he just wanted to shoot the first German bastard who came along. If all went well, a fourth, fifth, and even sixth truck might roar past, kicking more dust into the cloud hanging over the road. And still, no signal for attack.

By now, the same maquisard who seconds earlier couldn't wait to shoot had had time to realize the seriousness of what he had gotten himself into. A desperate urge to turn around and run away descended. Some, after all, were only fourteen or fifteen years old. Many had never done anything more adult than milk their fathers' cows or help them run their shops. Often, because there weren't enough Sten guns to go around, these young boys carried nothing more lethal than wood-stocked, single-shot rifles from World War I.

In the trucks rumbling past on the Breton roads, on the other hand, traveled the professional soldiers of Hitler's 2nd Parachute Division. They had fought on the Russian front where even Generalissimo Stalin's cossacks could not crush them. These were among the toughest, most hardened warriors of the war in Europe. What had they to fear from a bunch of young cowherds? Even a fully trained Allied solider might have hoped that the ambush leader had decided to let this caravan get away. That it was too big. Too small. Too anything. But then . . . Kaboom!

In Morbihan, the blast that began Team Gerald's first ambush felled a huge tree that landed on top of the convoy's lead truck, stopped it, and killed several Germans inside before the first shot was fired. A cloud of white smoke drifted upward.

In Finistère, orange flames leapt from the side of a convoy lead truck after a Team Giles bazooka shell slammed into it. Dull thuds punctuated the shower of pebbles and rubble: the sound of body parts hitting the ground. "Bits and pieces of people flew all over the place," Knox later said. A lonesome, torn-away arm or the purple slop of a man's insides sometimes littered the road.

Truck brakes squealed and gravel crunched under sliding wheels. A caravan of 2nd Parachute Division vehicles that stretched over, say, three hundred yards now skidded into a haphazard zigzag. Two or three seconds ticked quietly by. Nothing happened. Jeds, agents, or leaders who earlier wondered if their maquisards would fire too early now had a moment to worry if they would fire at all.

Down on the roads, doors of the truck cabs swung open. German soldiers began to climb out. Dark, wet patches suddenly bloomed on their chests, and their bodies fell to the ground. Cack, cack, cack! Furious gunfire had erupted at last. "Concentrate first on the drivers and officers in the cabs and then on the troops in the back," the Jeds told the maquis.

On top of the hedgerows, the arms of prostrate maquisard machine gunners rattled with recoil; their assistants anchored the Bren gun bipods to the ground. Maquis riflemen squeezed off their shots, threw back their gun bolts, reloaded, and fired again. Short experience as soldiers quickly taught them to care less for accuracy than for sheer volume of fire.

Truck windshields exploded and shattered. Dead men slumped over their steering wheels. Little bursts of dust puffed from where the bullets hit the back of the trucks. Loud grunts and shouts came from within.

When the first panicked soldiers poured out of the trucks, maquisard grenadiers would lob six-pound lumps of plastic explosive, packed with nails and nuts and bolts to tear through their flesh. A popping sound, then most of the soldiers collapsed. The one or two survivors tried to run away. The maquis riflemen swung their barrels after them and fired. Some Germans fell; others found shelter.

Those who managed to clamber away from their trucks gathered in small groups plastered to the sides of the hedgerows for cover. Unable to see the hidden maquis, they shot blindly into the woods and shrubs. Their tracer bullets streaked white through the air. Mortars flew out of their tubes with a hollow pop, hiss, and boom. Stay down when they fire, the Jeds warned the maquis during training. Do not draw fire to yourself by flying up like pheasants at a pheasant shoot.

It was almost unfair. The Germans could find no targets; the maquis shot fish in a barrel. In ambushes in the Alps, Team Chloroform's Jean Sassi knocked over maquisards who stood up and deliberately exposed themselves to give their enemy a chance, as if bound by the honor of the duel.

Eventually came the shouts of a German trying to organize his men for a counterattack. These paratroopers were incredible soldiers, Jeds wrote in their reports. Even under such oppressive fire, the Germans did not give up. "Though their trucks might be shot up and stopped cold in the middle of the road under heavy fire from all sides," Phil Chadbourne, leader of Jed Team Hilary, wrote in his report, "they would continue to fire back until they were all dead."

But if they weren't all dead, a group of them would try to gain purchase on the hedgerows and begin climbing. If they got to the top and managed to out-flank the maquis, the ambush would turn into a pitched battle, in which the Germans, with their superior training and equipment, had the advantage. It would soon be time to call an end to the ambush.

"He who fights and runs away," the Jeds liked to joke, "lives to fight another day." The most important outcome of a successful ambush was living long enough to launch the next one. Unlike in regular battle, no reserves waited in the rear to take the maquisards' places when they were killed, and no arms depot would send forward new weapons if theirs were captured.

This was why, after two or five or twelve minutes, the maquis now heard the sharp toot of their leader's whistle. Time to withdraw.

The maquis rifle teams laid down a volley of covering fire to protect the bazooka men, grenadiers, and machine gunners who made a run for it. The riflemen themselves then vacated the ambush starting at the middle, just the way they had practiced during training. The men at either end, meanwhile, continued firing to discourage German flankers from giving chase. Finally, the last of the maquis ran away as fast as they could. The report of the German guns faded behind them.

At the agreed-upon rendezvous, usually at a farmhouse a couple of miles away, men passed around cider bottles. The first ambush was over. The maquis drank and shook hands and slapped backs and kissed cheeks. They sang the Marseillaise and congratulated each other, but no one really ever talked about what happened. It was too much to comprehend.

On the road behind them lay the twisted bodies of dozens of dead German soldiers in their gray uniforms. Their eyes were still open in their greenish white faces, and their hands still clutched their rifles.

Now that it was over, some maquis couldn't wait to fight more. Others felt terrible disappointment that revenge did nothing to dissipate their grief. Some wanted to cry. After the ignominy of four years of Hitler's occupation, no one had reckoned on such a reaction to killing German soldiers. All pretended to feel gratified, or at least pretended that they weren't disturbed.

When the war was over, these men—even if they were the types to admit their infidelities—often refused to tell their wives about these battles. They said nothing about how the bodies bloated in the August sun, nothing about how some of the dead Germans looked like friends or relatives, nothing about how a bullet to the head forces brains to sprout out of a corpse's nose. The maquisards wouldn't tell their wives, they wouldn't tell their children, and, now, they didn't bring it up with their comrades.

In Ille-et-Vilaine, a group working with Bill Dreux ambushed a lone German cyclist—an older man—and then brought him back to the command post where he bled to death. "The shooting of the German brought me no satisfaction," Dreux wrote.

The Breton maquisards' first ambushes were over, but certainly not their war. These thousands of Bretons were no longer farmers or villagers with grievances to settle. They were soldiers now, who may already have seen more than they wanted to see. Most now realized that they would never brag about how many Germans they had killed. Instead, they threw their weapons over their shoulders and hoped that Patton's tanks would arrive soon.

Germans in their tens of thousands tried to claw their way toward Patton's Allied spearhead, and the maquis did their damnedest to stop them everywhere. In Finistère, where the 2nd Parachute Division poured out of Brest, thousands of maquis working with Jed Teams Hilary and Horace frustrated German attempts both to blow the railway viaducts and to block Task Force A's advance along the coast road.

Farther east, in Côtes-du-Nord, the Resistance throngs, under the leadership of Jed Teams Frederick and Felix, set up their ambushes on the roads leading from the German coastal installations and inland garrisons, pouring fire upon columns attempting to sideswipe Task Force A. On the southern coastal road, Teams Gilbert, Ronald, and Francis harassed Germans trying to attack the 4th Armored Division as it roared toward Lorient.

In central Finistère, where the Germans marched east from Châteaulin to block General Grow's crucial 6th Armored rush to Brest, maquis working with Bernard Knox and Team Giles blew a bridge near Carhaix, stopping cold a German column of thousands. Following the guidance of Jed Team Gerald, which was positioned farther east, General Grow's advance then made a right turn just before Carhaix, avoiding the Germans stranded by Team Giles's demolition, while Knox's maquis mounted a huge ambush that sent the traffic jam of Germans running into the countryside.

All over Brittany, the bombs blew, the trees fell, the bullets flew, and just when the Germans poured out of their trucks and began to return fire, the whistle came and the maquis disappeared again into the woods. At the end of each ambush, the German survivors poured petrol over their disabled vehicles and equipment to deny their use to the French shadow fighters. The Germans desolately collected themselves and continued their move until they faced the next trap, perhaps only a quarter of a mile away. Later, the Germans would force French villagers to return to the ambush spots to collect the dead soldiers.

Plumes of black smoke rose in columns from all directions over Brittany. Shots rang out constantly. It was a turkey shoot. Some Germans did not even move by truck but by horse cart, foot, and bicycle. The first unlucky members of the 2nd Parachute Division to encounter Phil Chadbourne's Team Hilary ambush in northern Finistère were ten men on bicycles. "Bren gun and rifle fire finished them off with no trouble," Chadbourne wrote in his team report.

Some German officers tried to save their troops by ordering the roundup of innocent villagers to act as human shields. At the village of Cléder, after a Resistance sniper picked off a German sergeant, the Germans executed five French hostages who had connections to neither the sniper nor the village where the sergeant was shot. Frustrated by a Team Felix ambush at Merdrignac, the Germans shot six innocent bystanders; at Moncontour, thirteen. The twisted bodies of the hostages littered the roads of Brittany along with those of the German soldiers, their horses, and the burned-out carcasses of vehicles.

As the awful spell of German invincibility began to lift, pride returned to the maquis fighters, who found new confidence as soldiers. In the heat of battle, the younger among them became men, almost overnight, like pottery rapidly dried in a kiln instead of slow-baked in the sun. They no longer wanted to cry or stifle their screams. When an FFI detachment advanced between Brest and Le Conquet with a company of American soldiers, the American commander asked the FFI leader if he wanted to go ahead or follow behind the Americans. "Ahead," he replied. "It's our duty."

By August 4, the 4th Armored Division, driving south across the base of the Breton peninsula, already approached Quiberon Bay, its objective on the south coast. Task Force A, on the northern coast road, battled under the ramparts of the fortified port of Saint-Malo. General Grow's 6th Armored Division pushed over a stunning one hundred miles along the center of Brittany, to only about sixty miles short of Brest. "In view of rapid Allied advance," the SFHQ radioed the Jeds already in Brittany, "orders for Resistance are for maximum activity.

All isolated detachments should be attacked and all measures taken to demoralize the enemy."

This was exactly the part of the battle the Breton maquis had been waiting for: the chance to wreak unrestrained vengeance on the Germans, to take back possession of the town and city halls, to force the occupiers out of French homes as they fled for their lives into the countryside. Bob Kehoe's Team Frederick quickly reported the occupation by the maquis of the towns of Guingamp, Saint-Brieuc, and Lannion along Brittany's northern coast. Team Francis, in southern Finistère, reported the liberation of Quimperlé, Bannalec, Scaër, Bouin, and Le Faou. The list went on and on.

All over Brittany, house shutters slammed open, French flags suddenly flew out windows, and parties began in the streets. The maquis in the towns and on the roads had reversed roles with the Germans, who in many areas now hid in the woods. But the merrymaking, in other areas, was tragically premature, for the Germans had realized by now that they had lost the battle for Brittany, and Hitler's 2nd Parachute Division had retreated in chaos.

The roads suddenly filled with Germans marching out of the little towns and toward the coast. Hitler had ordered not just his parachutists but all of his Brittany troops to converge on the fortress ports of Brest, Saint-Nazaire, and Lorient and to defend them "to the last man, the last cartridge." He hoped to deny the ports to the Allies and to keep their forces tied up in battles there while he reorganized his own armies farther east. "Elements of German forces . . . have turned back and are heading west," Knox radioed on August 5. "We are attacking them all along the road."

The German troops in Brittany were trapped and desperate. As they struggled past ambushes at the same sites they had earlier fought out of, they became furiously violent. In the Finistère village of Lesneven, they killed everyone they saw. In Châteauneuf, fifty massacred civilians lay dead. The Germans shot farmers in their fields for no apparent reason. They charged into towns in the midst of the liberation festivities and machine-gunned the celebrants. "People being tortured and killed and houses being burned to the ground," radioed Team Hilary's American leader, Phil Chadbourne.

In return, the maquis began executing the German prisoners they captured. Having been the object of German atrocities for so long, their interpretation of the rules of war and the Geneva convention differed widely from that of regular troops. "Even if we had wished to prevent this shooting, we would have been powerless," Bernard Knox wrote in his report. "These men had burned farms and killed farmers with their wives and children all the way along the road."

Everything became a vicious circle of violence for violence, where terror avenged terror. In the Morbihan village of Kerhoaden, the Germans hammered the flesh of a captured maquis into rags on an anvil. At Vannes, Wehrmacht soldiers castrated the patriots they captured. The death and pain escalated. Pity and mercy had disappeared from Brittany, just as it would, in only a matter of days, from the rest of France.

## CHAPTER THIRTY-ONE
# ARRESTED

The hollow footfall of military boots against wooden railway ties suddenly echoed through the gully under a bridge in southeastern France, and the American Jedburgh Cy Manierre froze. Without warning from Manierre's lookout, a patrol of six German soldiers had arrived. Rifles hanging by leather straps from their shoulders, they sauntered across this crucial railway bridge below which Manierre had been planting explosives.

The heavy scent of ripening grapes and baked summer earth swirled around. Stay still, Manierre told himself. Don't move. Stay still.

For now, the six soldiers, working their way along the tracks and between the vineyards, sweated in the sun and gossiped quietly. In that tense beginning of August, the Germans had taken to patrolling the most important railways and bridges in France, like the one under which Manierre now hid. Near the town of Serves-sur-Rhône, about halfway between the coast and Lyon, this bridge was part of the railway that ran up the east side of the Rhône, a critical German escape route if things got any worse for them in southern France.

It was August 4. Patton's VIII Corps raced to Brest while the rest of his Third Army poured through the bottleneck at Avranches and south toward the Loire. As if that weren't enough for the Germans to worry about, their spies had determined that a second Allied invasion of the Continent would soon come, though they weren't sure whether it would come from northwest Italy or the south of France. Some of Hitler's commanders had already suggested negotiating for peace, but he had refused.

Instead, Hitler ordered his forces in southern France and northwest Italy to stiffen themselves for the possible second invasion. He commanded soldiers in northern France to prepare for a massive counterattack. Hitler intended to throw every available piece of armor toward Avranches to try to cut off the Allied breakthrough. If the attack failed, tens of thousands of Hitler's northern troops would be vulnerable to encirclement by the Allies. The German troops in southern France might be trapped and left to the mercy of the French "terrorists," who already hobbled movement of the German forces.

German soldiers in France feared for their survival. The patrol on the Rhône River railway bridge would not be kind if they discovered Team Dodge's Cy Manierre concealed beneath it.

Manierre quieted his breath. He wore the dirty, sweaty clothes of a peasant. His uniform made him too conspicuous along this well-guarded and often patrolled rail and road route up the east side of the Rhône. Pedaling his rusty old bike down a dirt road or sipping espresso in a café, flashing his forged identity documents, Manierre could pass for an innocent French farmer. But not here. Not underneath a crucial Rhône Valley railway bridge. Not with a bunch of peach baskets filled with more than 150 pounds of explosives.

A few days earlier, Manierre, bored with constant training and organizing, joined forces with a Frenchman who had taken the nom de guerre "Captain Martin." The fifty-year-old had flown planes in World War I and now led a maquis of former French army cadets. Manierre and Martin decided that together they would halt all German rail traffic on the east side of the Rhône.

Near Serves-sur-Rhône, the two had discovered this bridge, with its excellent hiding places in the crags of rock above it for both riflemen and grenadiers that made it the perfect spot for a railway ambush. News had come from a railway worker that a troop train would clank over this bridge around midnight of July 5, carrying five hundred soldiers of the 9th Panzer Division, along with their tanks and equipment, to reinforce the German counterattack in Normandy. Manierre and Martin planned to blow the bridge just as the troop train crossed it.

This was why Cy Manierre now crouched under the bridge with his peach baskets full of explosives while his potential captors lollygagged twenty feet above him.

Manierre looked around. Fifty yards away, in one of the vineyards, stood Captain Martin, Manierre's supposed lookout. The "captain" should have warned Manierre of the patrol's approach. He didn't. Instead, he tried to save himself by furiously wrapping grapevines around their poles, tying them in knots, and trying to look like a vineyard worker. It wasn't exactly the methodology of a man who put Allied interests first.

If the Germans captured Manierre, they would look in his pockets. They would find his dog tags. They would handcuff him, drag him away, and beat him with belt buckles. It would not take them long to realize that he was the one who had blown the roof off the electricity plant at Beaumont-Monteux and coordinated a deadly attack on a troop train near Saint-Vallier.

Before the Germans killed Manierre, they would want to know his codes, the location of his radio operator, the names of his colleagues. They would want to know the location of his maquis groups and how to stop the devastation in the Rhône Valley. To find out such things, they routinely broke noses, burst kidneys, burned flesh. Even the more humane among the German forces had adopted the ruthlessness of the nearly doomed.

The footsteps above Manierre moved away. This was his chance. He glanced regretfully at the peach baskets and the very last of his explosives; he had no choice but to leave them behind.

Summoning all of his self-control, he strolled leisurely out from under the bridge, playing the part of a vineyard worker who had nothing on his mind but growing grapes. The Germans paid him no attention. He got a hundred feet away and had nearly escaped when nerves overcame him. He threw himself to his stomach and looked back. What a fool, he realized. I've made myself look suspicious. He jumped up, walked to the nearest vine and made himself look busy.

*Alt!* one of the Germans suddenly shouted. *Alt!*

The Germans began to talk loudly among themselves and point. Manierre furiously trimmed vines and tied them into knots around the poles the way Martin had. The Germans began to shoulder their weapons. Manierre bolted.

Shots rang out. Manierre sprinted across the vineyard, kicking up stones and tufts of grass. Now into a field. More shots. Finally, Manierre disappeared into the woods, where he found Martin, and together they melted away. The Germans knew better than to follow into the woods where a maquis group might be waiting for them.

Back at the command post, sweat poured off Manierre and Martin, and their pulses pounded. They had made their escape. But they had lost the last of their explosives. *Putain de putain!*

Manierre and Martin got control of their breath. Their plan had been to blow the bridge as the locomotive arrived, sending it plummeting into the ravine below. Resistance bazookas, fired from the precipice above, would then tear into the boxcars and tank carriers, mangling metal and bodies alike. As the surviving troops swarmed onto the tracks, Bren machine-gun fire and gammon grenades would rain down upon them. Hundreds of Hitler's troops would be wounded or killed. Tanks would be destroyed. The rail would be useless.

The timing was crucial. The Allied position in Normandy remained delicate. Though Hitler's counterattack was vulnerable, so was the long Allied column Patton had thrust into southern Normandy. In the south, General Patch's American and French infantrymen would soon face the terrible dangers of a beach invasion against an entrenched enemy. Hitler's Rhône River artery had to be severed.

More important than ever were the groups, including some of Manierre's, who already bombed, sniped, and ambushed the Rhône Valley roads and rails that Hitler so badly needed for both northward and southward movement. As for Manierre, if he wanted to keep to his plan to blow up the soldiers of the 9th Panzer Division, he had twenty-four hours to find more explosives.

In England, the day after Manierre's near capture and the day before Hitler launched his counterattack, Lewis Goddard, the American radio operator who had seen his home for the last time in his dreams, climbed the steps to the bombers that would drop him into France. Goddard's Team Ivor was the first of three new teams dispatched to central France to help protect Patton's southern underbelly. The other two teams, Alec and Julian, would drop in the following few days.

With the exception of VIII Corps in Brittany, Patton's Third Army now stood shoulder to shoulder along a sixty-mile north-south front from Angers to Mayenne in southern Normandy. They began to cross the Mayenne River to push eastward along a course that paralleled the Loire River toward Germany. Without assistance, the Third Army's long right flank—from Nantes on the southern coast of Brittany to the city of Orléans, south of Paris—was dangerously vulnerable to attack from the German forces in the south.

Already, Paul Cyr's Team George in Loire Inférieure organized groups on the north of the Loire to blow bridges, block crossings, and keep the Germans from forging north. At the same time, Teams Ian and Harold, just across the Loire from Cyr, along with William Crawshay's Team Hugh and Bob Anstett's Team Hamish, in the Cher and Indre areas of France, helped organize the

Resistance to protect Patton's exposed right flank from the south side of the river. Meanwhile, the SFHQ dispatched three new Jed teams that included Ivor to assist Teams Hugh and Hamish, as part of the flood of Jeds now dropping into France.

Lou Goddard, along with Captain John Cox, the Brit who commanded Team Ivor, and their French teammate, Lieutenant Colin, sat nervously in their aircraft's dark fuselage as it rumbled down the runway.

Goddard, the radio operator whose father had written to him that it was OK to cry, was a cheerful hard worker who was especially popular among the Jeds. He had been an outdoorsman long before joining the army, and his high-school hiking club elected him its first president. The Knoxville newspapers made a hero of him when he saved the life of a fellow Boy Scout who had been trapped under a rock slide while exploring a cave. Now, in the plane, Goddard listened to the rumble of the engines as the wind tossed Team Ivor about, first over the Channel and then over Normandy.

Below him, Hitler's forces prepared for the Mortain attack and Patton's Third Army marched along the Loire. Just south of Saint-Amand, in Cher, Goddard's airplane began to slow, its engines sang a few notes lower, and it lopped over and banked in a wide circle.

The jumpmaster shoved out the weapons and equipment containers, which always went first so that they did not come crashing down on top of the parachutists. This time, however, unknown to the Jeds or the jumpmaster, the chute and static line of one of the containers did not detach from the plane and, beneath its belly, the heavy canister whipped dangerously back and forth, like a flag snapping in the wind.

Inside, a light suddenly shone red on the jumpmaster's control board. "Action stations," he shouted. Lou Goddard took his place on the side of the Joe hole, his legs dangling beneath. In the cockpit, the pilot hit a switch. The red light disappeared and the green light flashed on. The jumpmaster shouted: "Go!" Lou Goddard jumped. Just at that moment, the tangled canister detached itself and went flying toward the back of the plane and straight into Goddard. Cox jumped next, then Colin.

On the ground, Captain Cox's jump boots dug into the edge of a hole as he landed, twisting his ankle. Colin also landed in a ditch and, in the fall, his loaded revolver discharged and the bullet passed into his leg. The pilot had mistakenly dropped them in an abandoned gravel pit. At first, Cox and Colin were too busy worrying about their own injuries to realize that Goddard was dead. One of the maquis soon brought them the news. They found Goddard's crumpled body on the ground, the folds of his deflated parachute gently wafting in the wind.

On the morning of August 7, they buried Lewis Frelan Goddard, with an honor guard of maquis standing by, in a little village churchyard. Two hundred townspeople attended the service. It would be two weeks before Goddard's kind, reassuring father received the letter from the War Department's adjutant general. Because of Operation Jedburgh's highly secret nature, it contained no details of Goddard's death. It said simply, "It is with regret that I inform you of the death of your son."

On August 6, the same day Goddard and Team Ivor took off in their bomber, in southeastern France, Cy Manierre and two maquisards climbed into the cab of an old farm truck with the intention of finishing the job on the Serves-sur-Rhône bridge. With the Mortain counterattack about to launch, the necessity of preventing German reinforcement and protecting Patton's flank made stopping the 9th Panzer Division's troop train more important than ever.

Manierre and the maquisards, with a crop of peaches in the truck bed behind them, rattled along the roads through German-infested territory toward the maquis group with whom Manierre's Team Veganin colleague Captain Vuchot now worked. Manierre hoped to get more explosives from Vuchot. Along the way, a man jumped out and waved his arms excitedly. The truck squealed to a stop. Manierre knew this Frenchman to be working for an American agent.

The Germans are surrounding the maquis in this area, the agent warned Manierre. There are patrols on the roads.

Manierre thought for a moment. The Germans always hunted down the maquis along the Rhône Valley railway. Hitler's forces needed to keep the route open as badly as the Allies needed to keep it closed.

I'm going ahead anyway, Manierre said. I'll tell them I'm on my way to the fruit market.

Manierre's truck now wound a course straight into a sector about to be raided by the Germans. By the time Manierre arrived at Vuchot's command post, men ran in all directions, packing equipment, rolling up maps, shouldering weapons. This group planned to make a run for it. The safest thing for you to do, Captain Vuchot told Manierre, is to stay with me and forget about that troop train. Manierre would not listen. He retrieved Vuchot's stash of explosives from its hiding place in a cave.

With the explosives nestled under a basket of peaches, Manierre rattled in his truck up the hill and along the valley back toward where he had started. Around a bend, and suddenly up ahead, a number of Frenchmen standing in the middle of the road behind two felled trees motioned the truck to stop. *Merde!*

From the FFI armbands, Manierre surmised this group fought for de Gaulle. They had probably hoped to hijack the truck for their work. Manierre could explain who he was and probably dissuade them, but it would take precious time. As he rolled to a standstill, Manierre saw perhaps thirty men lying in the grass by the sides of the road, covering the truck with their Stens and Brens.

Manierre's driver hopped out to do the talking. He strolled with the leader of this group out of Manierre's view to the back of the truck. Suddenly, angry words drifted forward. Manierre jumped out and rushed toward the shouting. The barrel of a Sten jabbed violently into his stomach. A pair of handcuffs clicked over his wrists. Now hands searched through Manierre's pockets until, tragically, the dog tags that identified him as an American soldier were dangled portentously before his eyes.

"You Yankees must understand that there is only one chief in France," someone said in French, "and he is Marshal Pétain."

Someone else manhandled Manierre into the back of a truck. The engine started. He heard a click as a pistol was cocked, and felt its hard barrel shoved sharply into his head behind his ear. These Miliciens had dressed as FFI—it was a trap.

Manierre would soon find himself on a hard stone floor at Gestapo headquarters in Lyon. Well-coiffed female secretaries would impassively type memos while polished black boots kicked his face and groin. You will be tried and sentenced to death as a spy, he would be told. With no uniform, you are not entitled to recognition as regular military.

For now, however, Manierre bumped along in the back of the truck at the mercy of these French traitors. The man holding the gun to Manierre's ear taunted him. Say, "Down with Roosevelt, down with Jews." Say, "Long live Pétain." Say it or I'll shoot.

Manierre said nothing. The man raised his gun to Manierre's forehead so he could see the finger squeezing the trigger. Click. No bullet filled the first chamber, but that did not mean that the next one would be empty.

Say it!

Click.

Say it!

Click.

Say it!

Click. Click. Click.

# CHAPTER THIRTY-TWO
# JEDS RAIN DOWN

On August 6, the day Manierre got arrested, Bernard Knox marched through the woods with his maquis patrol and heard shots where he did not expect them. The unmistakable report of a German heavy machine gun chattered in two or three last spurts, then stopped.

Knox and his men moved in to investigate, stepping out of the woods and onto the road. The first members of the 6th Armored Division had arrived at the end of the Brittany peninsula, but they had been surprised by some Germans. Their dead bodies littered the road and their jeep was in flames.

As Knox examined the scene, a woman rushed out of the nearest house and pulled him inside by the sleeve. On her parlor floor lay an unconscious American soldier. A pool of blood expanded beneath him. His breathing was labored, and there was a hole in his chest. This boy and his dead colleagues outside were advance scouts for Patton's charging column of tanks.

Knox bent down and looked at the soldier's dog tags. They said he was a Roman Catholic. The boy looked scared. "It's all right soldier," Knox said to him. "You're among friends."

The soldier's finger went to his chest, he felt the hole, and his face filled with panic. "I'll send for a priest," Knox said.

The soldier grabbed Knox's jacket with both hands, raised his head, and said furiously, "I don't want a goddamn priest, I want a doctor."

Knox's maquis stripped off the soldier's uniform. They smuggled him into the hospital of one of the towns still garrisoned by the Germans, where in his delirium he kept waking up and shouting that he wanted his PX rations of candy and cigarettes. Lying next to injured members of the 2nd Parachute

Division who would just as soon kill him, the soldier could not be made to understand that he ought to shut up.

To the Jed-organized Resistance, Patton had assigned the liberation of the small towns and villages throughout Brittany, like the one where the soldier now recovered. Until that job was done, the doctors in the hospital kept the soldier quiet by pumping him full of morphine. He would not have to stay that way for long.

It was August 7. Thanks, in part, to the flank protection and guidance of the Resistance, the 6th Armored Division had already driven more than two hundred miles down the center of the peninsula. Sweeping into Brittany, Patton's troops had found, as the official SOE history would say, "that their way had been made clear for them." Six days after the Brittany campaign had begun, Patton's tanks pulled up to the outskirts of Brest, penning thirty thousand Germans within. Patton had lost his bet with Montgomery by one day.

A couple of days later, in a safe house in southern England, Jack Singlaub and the rest of Team James listened intently while a French lieutenant explained their mission. Events were unfolding so quickly that new Jed teams were dropping into France every night. Team James would drop into the southern department of Corrèze, the French lieutenant told them, in the wooded foothills of the Massif Central, just north of the area where Tommy Macpherson and Team Quinine now worked.

Eight thousand maquisards, organized into one-hundred-strong companies, already waited in the area for the radioed order to burst into action. The French lieutenant punctuated Singlaub's briefing with jabs of his index finger at a map on an easel.

Two days earlier, on August 7, the day Patton's VIII Corps began the battle for Brest, Hitler's northern France forces had launched their counterattack at Mortain, attempting to plug up the Allied breakthrough at Avranches and cut off Patton's troops in Brittany and southern Normandy. To execute the attack, hundreds of Hitler's tanks had to abandon important defensive positions and move forward into a dangerous nether region that was already surrounded by the Allies on the northern, western, and southern sides. It was a desperate and foolhardy move for Hitler. And a marvelous opportunity for the Allies.

From the Normandy coast, Field Marshal Montgomery sent the Canadian First Army thrusting south toward Falaise. From southern Normandy, Patton, whose XII, XX, and XV Corps already raced side by side along the Loire, turned XV Corps north toward Argentan. The result would be a massive encirclement that might capture many tens of thousands of Germans.

Back in London, meanwhile, in the war room at SFHQ and EMFFI headquarters, things had become more hectic than ever. Radio messages poured in. Colored pins were stuck into maps marked with the positions of new Jed teams. Demands for weapons arrived. The black-painted bombers were constantly in flight, carrying personnel and supplies to be parachuted into France.

Resistance fighters battled in Brittany to assist the VIII Corps' capture of the fortified ports, harassed the Germans south of the Loire to protect Patton's right flank, and prepared for the coming Operation Dragoon in southern France. The stable, single-front days of the Normandy campaign had come to an end. The Allied armies now battled across the breadth of northern France and would soon do so in the south. The Resistance assisted everywhere.

The Allies knew the Falaise encirclement was the beginning of the end for the Germans. Even while Hitler poured his tanks into the ill-fated Mortain counterattack, he also built a new defensive line down the east side of France, a home base to which his broken forces could later escape. He was making preparations to withdraw. The last thing Eisenhower wanted was to have beaten half a million German soldiers in Operations Overlord and Dragoon, only to fight the same soldiers again after they escaped from France. On top of everything else, therefore, the Allied shadow chiefs prepared the Resistance to help stop Hitler's troops from getting out of France.

Jack Singlaub was now being briefed to take part in harassing the German withdrawal. Team James and two other teams were to drop in a north-south line along the west side of the mountains of the Massif Central. American Captain Charlie Brown's Team Lee would drop into Haute-Vienne, Dick Franklin and Stewart Alsop's Team Alexander into Dordogne, and Singlaub's Team James into Corrèze.

Their job was to block the various eastward routes from the Atlantic coast into the Massif Central, preventing the Germans in the southwest from disappearing into the mountainous terrain where the fighter-bombers of the Allied air forces could not reach them. The Allies wanted to force them to travel north along the Atlantic coast and then east along the Loire, where the Allied planes could blast them to pieces. The German withdrawal would not start, however, until sometime after the southern invasion.

At the map in the London safe house, Singlaub's briefing officer now traced with his finger a major highway, Route Nationale 89, which ran from

Bordeaux, northeast through Corrèze, through Clermont-Ferrand, and on to Lyons, on the other side of France.

"This is the main German escape route from southwestern France," the briefing officer said.

Team James's job would be to help coordinate Resistance attacks to shut down the main rail and road through the Corrèze Valley, denying that route through the mountain range. Already, Tommy Macpherson's Team Quinine and their maquis were blowing bridges over the Lot River to prevent German entrance into the Massif Central from the south. Team Lee would do similar work farther north.

The French lieutenant briefing Jack Singlaub tapped the map three times, at the towns of Brive, Tulle, and Egletons. In these towns, the Germans had concentrated nearly eighteen hundred troops, whose job was to protect the German escape route from maquis attacks. The Resistance in Corrèze now waited for the southern equivalent of the "Napoleon's hat" message, which would signal the go-ahead to attack these garrisons. Team James would assist in these attacks and help close the route.

The next day, Team James crossed the airfield and climbed the steps to their plane. Fifteen hundred miles to their south, at the Italian ports of Naples and Salerno, the infantrymen of the American Seventh Army filed up the gangways and boarded the gray-painted ships to southern France.

On August 10, the first of Operation Dragoon troop transports, along with their battleships, dropped their mooring lines, hauled up their anchors, and steamed out to sea. At about the same time, across the Mediterranean, in the port of Oran in North Africa, tugboats nudged away from their docks the vessels carrying the tanks and men of the French 1st Armored Division. Hundreds of other Allied ships slid out into the open water at Brindisi and Taranto in southern Italy.

Undercover Nazi agents, keeping their eyes on the docks and quaysides of the Mediterranean ports, scribbled in their notebooks. They watched the black smokestack clouds disappear over the horizon, coded their messages, rushed to their transmitters, and sent their intelligence to the German high command. Since July, Hitler's commanders had expected a second Allied invasion somewhere in the Mediterranean, either on the northwest coast of Italy or on the southern coast of France. Now, they knew it was coming, but they still weren't sure where. General Alexander Patch, the American commander of the U.S. Seventh and First French Armies, hoped to keep it that way.

Each of his convoys churned their white wakes along carefully chosen, circuitous routes that would not give away their destination. Only at the last moment would they merge at meticulously scheduled and closely guarded rendezvous, finally flowing together into one great armada and beginning the attack on August 15.

Until then, Operation Dragoon was at its most vulnerable. The five days it would take the one hundred thousand troops of General Patch's first wave to chug across the Mediterranean gave the Germans ample time to puzzle over their intelligence reports and ship sightings. During that time, if General Johannes Blaskowitz, Hitler's commander in southern France, realized for sure that the tidal wave of Allied troops would soon break on his shores, he would order a ruthless and devastating counterattack.

As things stood, Blaskowitz's three hundred thousand men in the south, spread thinly over two long shorelines, the Atlantic and the Mediterranean, presented little danger to the Seventh Army's planned invasion, which was centered at Saint-Tropez. The German commanders had already pulled the best fighters north to face Overlord, and only one hundred thousand of the remaining southern forces tucked themselves into the folds of coast around Dragoon's planned landing beaches.

Even this weakened force, however, if too quickly reinforced, would present an overwhelming fusillade of cannon, tank, and gun fire. This danger concerned General Patch more than any other. He worried particularly about the 11th Panzer Division and its couple of hundred tanks now spread around the region near Toulouse. He wanted them and any other German reinforcements kept away from his beachhead. Patch assigned to the air forces the task of bombing the major bridges over the rivers and the forward German positions.

To southern France's seventy-seven thousand shadow army fighters, he gave the jobs of cutting German telecommunications; harassing German garrisons; protecting the port facilities at Toulon, Marseille, and Sète; and, most important, blocking enemy troop movements by road and rail. General Patch particularly wanted German movement along a route from Bordeaux via Toulouse across the Rhône to Marseille stopped. It was along this route that, just as Patch feared, the 11th Panzer Division suddenly began to travel.

"Enemy mobile reserves reported moving from area Toulouse to Rhône delta," the shadow bosses urgently radioed Aaron Bank on August 11. Bank's Team Packard and Ted Baumgold's Team Collodion had parachuted to Lozère and Aveyron, respectively, on the west side of the Rhône in the first week of August. The maquis working with the two teams stood directly in the path not only of the 11th Panzer but also of the 198th Infantry Division. "You will take maximum harassing action," Packard and Collodion's orders now said. The rest of the Jed teams in southern France got similar orders.

Meanwhile, General Patch also worried that the commander of Hitler's Italian forces, Field Marshal Albert Kesselring, had six divisions stationed in northern Italy who could spoil everything with a surprise thrust across the Alps. Patch wanted the alpine passes to southern France plugged up. "Block all passes and routes on Franco-Italian frontier at once if you are in the position to do so," said an August 13 radio message to Jedburgh Team Chloroform.

Team Chloroform's Henry McIntosh and Jean Sassi, with sixty maquisards, began a long trudge by foot, lugging explosives and equipment over a nine-thousand-foot snowcapped ridge that was too treacherous even for mules. Nearby, Bill Thompson's Team Novocaine, which arrived in France on August 7, also received orders to help stop a German incursion from Italy. Team Novocaine rumbled up the icy mountain slopes toward the Italian border more luxuriously, however, with the help of a gasogene truck.

At the same time, maquis groups, including those working with Jed Teams Veganin and Packard, set up ambushes along the routes on both sides of the Rhône to Lyon, where Patch wanted to block German reserves. On the eve of the Dragoon invasion, Resistance groups protected its intended beachhead from the north, east, and west. Nearly eighty thousand Resistance in the south of France now waited for the landing of the Dragoon forces, an order for all-out guerrilla warfare, and the chance to liberate themselves at last.

## CHAPTER THIRTY-THREE
# LEAVING A MAN TO DIE

In Brittany's Ille-et-Vilaine, the early-morning mist rolled in from the sea on a gray, somber day. Team Gavin's Bill Dreux and his fifteen-strong patrol of maquisards stepped quietly and cautiously forward through the woods near the northern Breton coast. From the distance came the thunderous rumble of far-off shelling, probably the 83rd Infantry fighting its slugging match with the Germans, who were besieged in the fortress port of Saint-Malo.

Squinting through the fog, Dreux and his group could not see the tops of the trees, let alone any distance ahead. Finally, at the far edge of the forest, they came to a stone cottage with a thatched roof. An old farmer with bushy eyebrows and leathery wrinkles sat on a bench with his back against the wall.

"*Bonjour*," Dreux said.

"*Bonjour*," replied the farmer. "More fighting, eh?" he grumbled. "When will it end?"

A shy, skinny little girl in a black dress came out of the door. One hand held a slice of bread; the other had been amputated at the elbow. Her face had a long ugly scar that twisted her lips into a permanent grin. Nearby, a brown puppy chased some chickens, and the girl laughed. The Germans had mined the shore against invasion, but no warning could be made sternly enough to keep the children away from the beach. The little girl was the only survivor of four children blown up by the same mine.

"That's my dog," she told Dreux, pointing with the stump of her arm. With her good hand, she took three small seashells from her dress pocket and gave one to Dreux. "It will bring you luck," she said. This early in the day, Dreux did not even know he needed luck. After all, he was just leading a scouting patrol to confirm reports that the Germans had taken over a group of farm-houses known as La Bastille as part of their defense of Saint-Malo. He said good-bye to the farmer, thanked the girl for the seashell, and waved his group forward.

The maquis moved out across the fields and through the hedgerows. Four or five of them, North African veterans of the French army, had dug up old khaki uniforms. One of them lugged along an MG-42, a German machine gun that could fire at the rate of twelve hundred rounds per minute. Ambling across the foggy Breton fields, teenage boys carrying Stens made up the rest of the patrol.

One of the boys wore an old French helmet into which he had drilled holes for relief from the heat. It made him look as if he had survived a murderous gun battle. Another boy, named Pierre, tall and lank with a long, thin face and a sharp nose, wore a dirty blue sweater so small that the sleeves came only halfway down his forearms. Beside Dreux walked the boys' leader, Pépin.

A short, well-built seventeen-year-old with a pug nose, tousled red hair, and blue eyes, Pépin had been orphaned by the war. His style of leadership more resembled that of a school prefect than an officer, and he had a habit of silencing the other boys by announcing that he and Captain Dreux were having "a serious conference."

"Holy God," Bill Dreux had thought when he first met this group. "These are Boy Scouts and I am the Scoutmaster." They chatted so enthusiastically and grabbed their guns so eagerly that Dreux wondered if he should just take them "for a nice walk in the fields and then sit around a fire and toast weenies." "*Ces sacrés gosses,*" those damn kids, older members of the maquis often said of such boys.

They should have been at home playing marbles. Leading these barely trained youngsters, Dreux consoled himself with the thought that they did not go to battle at La Bastille, but only to see if the Germans had occupied it and whether Allied troops should be sent to secure it. Dreux's mission with his teenagers should have been nothing more than a nice country walk.

It was the middle of August. Task Force A had finished its sweep along the more difficult northern shore route and joined the 6th Armored Division in its siege on Brest. On Brittany's southern coast, the 4th Armored had cornered eleven thousand Germans in Lorient.

With the help of Jedburgh Teams Frederick and Hilary, their maquis, and the SAS, Task Force A had successfully kept all three important railway viaducts around Morlaix undamaged by the Germans. The Resistance, the 6th Armored reported, had turned over to the Americans thirty thousand prisoners, as many as the division itself had captured in Brittany. The FFI provided more than 90 percent of the useful intelligence in Brittany, according to the American liberators. Patton's VIII Corps, with the help of thirty thousand maquisards, had destroyed four German divisions stationed in Brittany and two divisions that came from Normandy. But isolated groups of dangerously frightened Germans still roamed the woods and countryside between the axes of the Allied advance.

On August 10, while the military forces pounded away at enemy resistance in the Breton coastal fortresses, the Third Army gave the maquis the jobs of mopping up the interior of the peninsula, assisting in the fortress sieges, and guarding the supply lines. The Jeds and their maquis were no longer true guerrillas in Brittany, but a sort of poor man's infantry that assisted Patton's VIII Corps.

Bernard Knox and Team Giles worked to help defeat a rabble of Germans holed up in the Crozon peninsula, across the bay from Brest, who were pouring artillery fire on American forces fighting for the city. Bob Kehoe and Team Frederick and their maquis fought alongside the regular military to liberate the towns of the Paimpol peninsula. Bill Dreux's Team Gavin got orders to sweep up Germans in the area around Combourg and assist in the battle for Saint-Malo, which was why Dreux now patrolled with his boys.

The mist lifted a little and a fine drizzle descended from the slate gray skies. Dreux's group reached an empty farmhouse near a narrow road. Jagged shards of glass hung from the window frames, and bullets had chipped away at the stone wall. The door hung desolately open. A wagon lay smashed on its side. Pieces of a broken American rifle littered the ground.

Dreux nearly stumbled over a body. Sprawled on his back, the U.S. soldier was so bloated with the gasses of decomposition that he looked like he would burst. His face puffed yellowish green and he smelled of rot. Tiny drops of rain rolled off his forehead and cheeks. Dried blood peeled from a deep gash across his throat. In one hand, he held an unused gauze pad. In the other, he had a rosary, as though, in the end, the American realized a bandage would do no good.

Dreux's boys dug a trench, lifted the body into it, and buried the soldier, his rosary beads still in his hand. They wired two boards together to make a cross. The boys gathered around the grave. Dreux struggled to remember the Lord's prayer, but could not. *"Endormi dans la paix du Seigneur,"* he said instead. At rest in the peace of the Lord.

Now Dreux crossed to a long, chest-high stone wall and looked over it. At the far end of a bare field where nothing grew, he saw row after row of German barbed wire. Behind them stood a small cluster of farmhouses: La Bastille. Dead cows rotted on their sides with their stiff legs sticking out. On Dreux's side of the barbed wire sat another farmhouse with a tall stone wall enclosing it.

Dreux motioned to his boys. With their hearts pounding loudly, they ran in a crouch across the field, toward the barbed wire, and threw themselves against the farmhouse wall. Everyone made it. No shots had been fired. Dreux began to think that maybe La Bastille contained no Germans after all.

"You stay here," he told Pépin. "I'm going ahead to the wire. I'll be back." He stepped out from behind the wall. A sudden gust of wind carried with it the odor of the dead cows. He crossed the hundred yards to the barbed wire and crouched behind a bush. La Bastille seemed deserted. There wasn't a sound. Dreux lit a cigarette and studied the terrain. "When you lit the cigarette under their nose," his partner Major Carbuccia would later say, "you were asking for it."

Dreux was taking his last puff when he heard a noise behind him. He jerked around. Pépin and Pierre, the boy in the blue sweater, had come forward and now crouched beside him. "Get back!" Dreux said. "I told you to stay behind." That's when it happened.

A sharp burst of shots came from the other side of the wire. Little puffs of dirt kicked up around their feet. Dreux and the boys jumped up and ran. Another burst of the machine gun sounded. The hundred yards to the back of the farmhouse seemed endless. At last, they threw themselves on the ground. Dreux's pulse pounded in his throat. "Jesus Christ," he gasped. "That was close. Holy Jesus Christ. The bastards are there."

Everybody began shouting at Dreux. We should retreat, they all said. "That's what I'm thinking about," Dreux answered. The Germans must have seen us from the very beginning, Dreux realized. They might have sent out a flanking squad to circle around and get us from behind. It might be closing in on us now, Dreux thought. He had to get his boys out of here, but to plan his withdrawal, he needed to know where the firing came from. He had to take a look around the wall. "Stay back. That's an order," he barked. He looked at Pierre and Pépin. "Understand?" They both nodded.

Since the Germans would be aiming at chest height at the corner of the wall, Dreux got down on his hands and knees and poked out his head. A burst of fire came, followed immediately by screams. Pierre pitched forward, from behind the wall, out into the open. Dreux reached and dragged him back as bullets hammered chips of stone from the wall above him. Now Dreux saw that Pépin clutched his wrist. Blood poured from his hand and his thumb dangled delicately by little more than a piece of skin. The Algerian with the machine gun cowered against the wall.

Holy God, Dreux suddenly thought. To hit the boys, those shots must have come from behind. The Germans had sent a flanking squad. We're surrounded. We have only seconds to live! Calm yourself. Think. Calm. He kneeled down by Pierre, cutting his bloodied sweater away with his combat knife. Blood flowed from a hole in Pierre's chest, but it did not spurt. No artery had been hit. Dreux pushed a gauze compress over the wound, then realized the bullet had entered from the front, not the back.

The boys had been shot leaning out over Dreux when he looked out. They had disobeyed Dreux's order because they did not understand fundamental infantry tactics. This was the problem of drafting barely trained civilians into war. It may have saved some soldiers' lives, but it put the civilians in the position of fighting hardened, well-trained soldiers when they knew hardly anything about fighting at all.

The good news for Dreux was that since Pierre had been shot from the front, there were no Germans behind them, at least not yet. They might still come up the road, charging around the wall with their Schmeissers blazing. How could he save these kids?

"Cover the road, man," Dreux shouted at the Algerian with the machine gun. "Cover the road."

"I can't. I can't," the Algerian shrieked with quivering lips.

Dreux finished his work on Pierre and turned to Pépin.

"It's only my thumb, Captain," the boy said, trying to be matter-of-fact.

It looked like his thumb would drop off if he shook his hand. Dreux wrapped his handkerchief around the hand and carefully tucked in the thumb. Pierre now stood with one boy supporting him under each arm.

The group walked as quickly as Pierre could toward the wall they had climbed over. Faster, Pierre, faster, Dreux thought. All it would take now was one burst of machine-gun fire and Dreux would lose all his boys. Finally, they eased Pierre over the wall and watched him grow weaker as they crossed several fields.

Just as they reached what Dreux thought would be safety, a middle-aged peasant women came running toward them waving her arms. *"Au secours!"* she cried. "Help. My husband. My husband."

She stopped in front of Dreux, out of breath. She tried to speak. "His legs . . . half torn off . . . bleeding . . . come right away . . . help." Dreux guessed that he must have been caught in the shelling he had heard earlier. The woman sobbed. Her husband was near to death. But, as far as Dreux could tell, so was Pierre. What could Dreux do? He wasn't about to take his boys within range of enemy artillery or to trade the possibility of saving Pierre's life for that of the woman's husband.

"Try to get a doctor, madam," Dreux said and began to move on.

"A doctor! Where? No. You come . . . I beg you." She pulled hard on Dreux's arm.

*"Je suis désolé,"* he told her, I am sorry. The woman dropped his arm and began to sob again uncontrollably. She looked at Dreux with reproach.

"Let's go," he said to his boys.

*"Au secours!"* The woman begged behind him. *"Au secours."*

They walked slowly along the road, and, before long, they heard the rumble of an American jeep, which got Dreux's boys to the doctor. They would be fine. Again and again, though, Dreux would go over that day at La Bastille in his mind, wondering if he had unnecessarily put his boys in danger.

Why had he lit that cigarette? He had been too blasé. Perhaps if he had just turned around at the barbed wire, the shooting would not have started. His boys would not have been shot. But this was war. Eventually, he forgave himself.

What troubled him, however, was the woman and her husband. "Help me," she had begged. The words echoed through Dreux's mind. As he mulled it over, without a boy bleeding to death in front of him, he admitted to himself the real reason he turned his back on the woman: he had seen enough of death and blood and panic and heard enough screams and groans. He did not want to deal with any more. Perhaps he really couldn't have done anything for her. But for the rest of his life, he would grapple with the memory that he hadn't even tried.

# PART VII
# STOPPING THE GERMAN ESCAPE

# CHAPTER THIRTY-FOUR
# SOUTHERN UPRISING

On the evening of August 14, nearly 900 ships and landing craft loaded with 151,000 invasion troops and 21,400 tanks, trucks, and other vehicles rendezvoused at the Mediterranean island of Corsica, off the southern coast of France. They turned their bows toward Operation Dragoon's forty-mile beachhead centered on Saint-Tropez and steamed forward full speed ahead. Ashore, only four German divisions waited for them. The Germans did not definitively realize that General Patch and his forces were coming until the night before.

At 7:10 the following morning, Patch's naval guns and air forces began blasting apart the German coastal gun emplacements, troop concentrations, and radar stations between Nice and Cannes. At 8:00, the first troop-laden landing craft forged through the curtain of smoke and dust that hovered in the air and plowed into the sand.

At the two beaches on the western end of the invasion area, the entire 3rd Division came easily ashore on the Saint-Tropez peninsula by 10:15 in the morning. In the center, near the town of Sainte-Maxime, a naval destroyer plopped a couple of last-minute shells onto the beach and silenced the remaining opposition to the 45th Division's scramble up its four assigned beaches. On the eastern flank, the 36th Division skirted the only heavy Germany artillery fire along the whole forty-mile stretch of beachhead by diverting its landing craft to another beach.

American infantrymen raced up the beaches, onto the coastal roads, and through the seaside towns and villages, quickly overwhelming weak German resistance. The 3rd Division reached Saint-Tropez at 3:00. Half an hour later, the 45th secured Sainte-Maxime. Compared to Overlord, the Dragoon invasion looked like a walkover. So far.

Meanwhile, Hitler's commander in southern France, General Johannes Blaskowitz, had barely pinpointed the invasion's location. Allied air bombing and sabotage by paratroopers and the French Resistance incapacitated German direction finders, cut their telephone lines, and raised havoc with their radio communications. Blaskowitz could not get up-to-date news from the coast or quickly issue orders to his units. His forces on the coast badly needed backup, but thanks to the shadow armies and Allied air forces, his reinforcements could hardly move.

On the far side of the Rhône River, the maquisards fighting with Aaron Bank's Team Packard in Lozère and Ted Baumgold's Team Collodian in Aveyron turned bridges into useless mangles of iron and steel and tunnels into collapsed mounds of stone rubble. The two Jed teams and their Resistance fighters bombed, sniped, and ambushed the feared 11th Panzer Division along every step of their march toward the southern beachhead. Because the Allied air force and French Resistance had cut the bridges over the Rhône, Blaskowitz's weak attempt at a counterattack from the west dribbled across the river by ferry.

A second puny counterattack from the east, by about five hundred soldiers of the German 148th Division based at Nice, got blasted to pieces by the Resistance, paratroopers, and Jedburgh Team Sceptre, who had dropped into France only one day earlier.

Farther north, Sassi's Team Chloroform and Thompson's Team Novocaine, having climbed into the Alps with their explosives, sent crucial bridges over the Durance River tumbling into the water. Field Marshal Kesselring's Italian troops would now have a tough slog if they intended to interfere with the Allied assault. From the north, attempts at movement by remnants of the 9th Panzer and the 157th Reserve Divisions, near Grenoble, were blocked by maquisards working with Sassi's Team Chloroform, and hundreds of others working with additional agents and leaders, who kept the road to the coast severed.

The Dragoon forces soon discovered that the Resistance had taken control of virtually all of southern France, except the regions of special importance to the Germans—between Toulouse and the southern coast, in the Rhône Valley, and along narrow strips of the Mediterranean and Atlantic coasts. But even in these areas, the Resistance made the Germans' life difficult.

Maquis cut the rail routes between Toulouse and the Mediterranean and along the Rhône more than forty times. They destroyed or damaged thirty-two railway and highway bridges leading to the bridgehead. "The continual harassing by the Maquis weakened the enemy to the extent that he was unable to put up organized resistance," a report of the 180th Infantry Division said.

By nightfall of Dragoon's first day, the invasion force had cleared the entire Saint-Tropez peninsula of the enemy, sealed in the strong German position at Fréjus, and shrugged off the two haphazard counterattacks, one from the east and one from the west. One hundred fifty thousand of the eventual 450,000 Dragoon troops had piled ashore. Only 95 were killed and 385 wounded. And the Resistance in southern France had just warmed up.

Prior to General Patch's landing, the shadow bosses had stopped parachute drops of Jed teams in order to defuse German suspicions that the invasion was coming. But now the brakes were off, and between August 13 and 17 ten more Jed teams arrived in southeastern France to assist Patch's invasion. On August 14, meanwhile, the BBC had transmitted a message, à la "Napoleon's hat," that launched the seventy-seven-thousand-strong Resistance into the guerrilla phase all over southern France.

Powerful German machine guns spewed lead into the masonry stone above Jack Singlaub's head. Orange tracer bullets streaked everywhere. Shards of glass and sharp stone splinters tinkled to the ground. The brick and stone houses crumbled into heaps.

Singlaub and his Team James partner, Jacques de Penguilly, along with some members of an SOE mission and a group of SAS, had converged on the Corrèze town of Egletons to help shape a haphazard maquis attack on the German garrison into a well-executed battle. Team James had arrived in France just a few days earlier; there had been no time for training the maquis. Now, Singlaub and Penguilly crouched behind a garden wall, listening and waiting.

They heard the thud of the German antitank cannons, the hiss of their shells, the blast and crumbling of bricks and stone. Then came the drawn-out, chattering reply of the Resistance's Bren guns, fired at nothing but the walls that the Germans hid behind. The bullets killed no one. Why must these Frenchmen waste their precious ammunition?

Singlaub and Penguilly threw themselves over the wall and into another house garden, then crouched low again. Fighters of the Armée Secrète (AS) emerged from behind their guns and kicked over the rubble to shake the

Jedburghs' hands. The maquis' faces beamed as proudly as if Singlaub and Penguilly had been personally dispatched to them by Dwight D. Eisenhower himself.

Don't fire unless you can see a live target, Singlaub told the Frenchmen huddling around him. Shoot in short bursts. If he's not dead after the first few rounds, he's taken cover. Don't waste your bullets.

The weak early-morning sunlight still cast long shadows. A few hundred miles to the south, the Dragoon invasion had only just begun. Hardly twelve hours had passed since the BBC transmitted the code phrase triggering southern France's guerrilla action phase, and already all hell had broken loose. The battle at Egletons was only one of hundreds that raged in southern France that day.

In Egletons, the fighting began when two companies of the Gaullist and seven companies of the Communist Francs-Tireurs et Partisans (FTP) encircled three hundred Germans. But then the FTP, hoping to win all the glory, launched an attack without warning the AS, and the haphazard action gave the Germans time to take thirty civilian hostages and fall back into the nearly impregnable, fortress-like École Nationale Professionelle, a massive three-story complex of reinforced concrete on the eastern edge of town.

Safely ensconced inside, the stranded German soldiers radioed for help. In response, a two-thousand-strong, specially trained antimaquis force began marching the winding route toward Egletons from less than sixty miles up the road at Clermont-Ferrand. Singlaub's maquisards would never win that battle, but that wasn't the point. While the two thousand German soldiers busied themselves rescuing their Egletons comrades, they weren't attacking General Patch or escaping. The strategy, reproduced hundreds of times all over France, kept many tens of thousands of Germans distracted.

In the meantime, at the stone houses where the Egletons Resistance had taken positions, the Germans besieged in the school pounded away with fourteen cannons, three mortars, and all the rifles, machine guns, and ammunition they could find. The Resistance, with their Stens and Brens, might as well have been blowing spitballs. But, if the maquis couldn't beat the Germans in the school outright, they could keep them trapped inside until a swarm of Allied mosquito fighter-bombers could be summoned.

———

Moving from one Resistance position to another, Singlaub and Penguilly carefully surveyed the positions of the German defenses and helped with the battle planning. After giving a last hint to an AS squad, they sprinted, under the dusty trees, across a street toward one of the FTP groups.

"*Qui passé là?*" Who goes there? a bearded man growled, blocking their path.

"Two officers of the FFI," Penguilly answered, angry at the challenge.

In another sector, Singlaub and Penguilly felt the unwelcoming stares of the fanatically brave fighters of the red-shirted FTP. These men saluted with the defiant clenched fist of the Communists. It was their leader, "Colonel" Antoine, a onetime army corporal who had elevated his title, who prematurely launched the Egletons attack. The race to be seen as liberator became a problem all over France.

"Where is your commander?" Penguilly asked the bearded sentry. The man scowled and pointed toward a bullet-riddled house near the school.

FTP troops shouted unfriendly epithets out of shattered windows as Singlaub and Penguilly passed. Sixty miles away, near Clermont-Ferrand, three German Heinkel 111 medium bombers floated off the runway and banked steeply toward Egletons, intending to blast Singlaub's maquis to pieces.

Singlaub and Penguilly scrambled through the back door of the house closest to the fortressed school. Penguilly kept guard; Singlaub climbed narrow wooden stairs to the attic. Under the low, dusty beams, he carefully pushed open a small square window, lifted his head, and peeked out. The Germans had barricaded the school windows with furniture. Their machine-gun crews moved like shadows through the shrubbery.

"*Merde, alors!* Shit, look out!" Singlaub heard Penguilly shout. Two FTP men had been dumb enough to point up at Singlaub in the window. Singlaub dropped instantly. He rolled across the floor and scuttled toward the stairs. The jackhammer sound of bullets on the slate roof began just as Singlaub's boots hit the second floor. He flew out the back door. The FTP men who pointed up at Singlaub might as well have phoned the Germans and told them exactly where to fire their machine guns.

"Let's get the hell out of here in case they have mortars," Singlaub shouted at Penguilly. As they began to run, a metallic clang echoed from the school and, with a huge bang, a cloud of smoke mushroomed from the house. Fragments of slate and wood showered down. In the wall, just where Singlaub had been crouching, the clearing smoke now revealed a huge hole.

Next, the twin-propeller Heinkels buzzed loudly out of the sky and over the rooftops. They roared over the valley, turned, and dove in. FTP troops ran out in the road and blazed with their machine guns at the planes. Germans in the school opened fire. Nine bombs fell from the planes on the maquis positions. Men shouted and ran and dove for the side of the road as the pounding explosions blasted a lane of rubble through the stone houses. Three FTP fighters fell to the ground. Shouts and moans came from every direction. Flames mingled with black smoke.

Civilians and men of both the AS and the FTP ran about with buckets of water; suddenly everyone cooperated. The German bombs had done Singlaub the favor of uniting the AS and FTP against one common enemy.

Penguilly rounded up four Bren gunners from the FTP; Singlaub gathered four from the AS. The planes will be passing directly overhead on their next run, Singlaub told them. As the next one approaches, I will judge its altitude and speed and hold up fingers to show you how far ahead of the planes to fire. One finger meant one plane length, two meant two, and so on. A clenched fist meant no lead at all.

The first Heinkel lined up on the road and flew in below two hundred feet. Singlaub could see the two pilots with their leather helmets in the plane's glass nose. He stepped into the middle of the road and held up one finger.

"Fire!" he shouted.

The gunners raised their Brens and shot five quick bursts. A few rounds hit the wingtip, but the plane banked right at the last moment and most of the fire missed. Singlaub's men jumped for cover as the tail gunner sprayed the road with bullets.

The next plane came in even lower. Singlaub could clearly see the pilot's face. It roared straight at the Jed and his men. Penguilly waved his closed fist. "No lead," Singlaub shouted. The glass in the plane's nose shattered and fell on the road. Holes tore open its green belly. Dark oil poured from the right engine. The men howled with pleasure. Later, they heard that the plane had crashed.

Like a pack of hunting dogs, a platoon of SAS in red berets took up positions around the school, ignoring the German machine guns firing at them. Their plan was to lay down a mortar barrage, drive the Germans indoors, and use the opportunity to move the maquis machine-gun positions forward. That way, when the bombers arrived, all the Germans would be in their bull's-eye, inside the building.

The SAS set up their mortar tubes. Singlaub crept up the stairs to the attic of the same house where he had earlier been fired upon. He slid onto the floor and stayed as low as he could. He planned to act as a spotter for the mortars.

With a hollow thwap, the first mortar arched overhead and dropped in the center of the courtyard. Germans scurried into their rifle pits. Correct by twenty meters right, Singlaub shouted down the stairs. The next shell blasted apart a timber barricade. More enemy dashed for cover. Singlaub enjoyed the spectacle so much that he forgot that the Germans would be anxiously searching for the forward position of the mortar spotter.

A few more adjustments, and the mortars exploded right on the German machine-gun positions, just as planned. Now, Singlaub directed the fire at the roof of the school to drive the machine gunners on the top floors downstairs. Incendiary phosphorous rounds followed, starting fires in the smashed school roof. "That would give the bastards something to think about," Singlaub thought.

One SAS man took a bullet in the head. Another was hit in the right eye. But the ploy to move the maquis' machine-gun positions ahead to cover the school courtyard had been a success.

Singlaub had no time to gloat. Machine-gun rounds suddenly slammed into the slate tiles and began ricocheting around the attic. Singlaub sprawled on his back with his skull ringing like a gong. The blast had thrown him back from his crouching position at the window. He felt as if someone had thrown a bucket of rocks in his face. Thick drops of blood dripped onto the floor from his right cheek. Pain came in waves. But there was no spurting arterial blood. He realized he only had a gouge on his chin and ear, but a fraction of an inch to the left and the round would have gone through his brain.

The machine gun stopped firing, and Singlaub took one last look. Suddenly, he saw the barrel of a 37mm antitank gun moving beneath a camouflage net only seventy-five yards away. Like a madman, Singlaub rushed down the stairs and sprinted into the back garden.

What the FTP soldiers saw was a bloody mess who seemed to be running around crazed. They tried to treat Singlaub's wound, but instead, he grabbed their Bren gun, shouted "le cannon boche," and made a run for it. He sprinted to a tree within fifteen yards of the German cannon, took cover behind it, and fired four long bursts at its crew. Men fell to the ground. Singlaub changed his ammo clip. One German raised his rifle and then flew backward with his arms splayed out.

Singlaub turned around and ran back to the maquis, who grabbed the Bren gun away from him and washed his bloody face with water from a bucket. Twenty-three years old, his first time under fire, and Singlaub killed or wounded all seven members of the gun crew. In the heat of battle, he didn't give it a second thought.

# CHAPTER THIRTY-FIVE
## WITHDRAWAL

For the Overlord forces in the north, things went even more spectacularly than in the south. Omar Bradley's plan to surround the counterattack at Mortain had trapped eighty thousand German fighters in a nearly complete encirclement, and the Allies did not intend to let the Germans survive long enough to escape. Allied artillery shells and air force bombs pounded anything that moved inside the Falaise gap.

Hitler's commanders begged him to order a retreat, but he refused to face the reality of his army's annihilation. He insisted that the troops stay put, reorganize, and renew their attack. It was suicide.

German bodies rotted on the ground. The legs of dead horses were splayed stiffly in the air. Countless French civilians, whole families clutching each other in terror, including women and children, lay dead beside their broken prams and discarded dolls. The stench of rotting human and animal flesh rose so high that pilots flying above vomited. After touring the battlefield, Eisenhower wrote, "It was literally possible to walk for hundreds of yards, stepping on nothing but dead and decaying flesh."

Nearly eight of Hitler's infantry and two of his panzer divisions had been snared in the Allied trap—ten thousand dead and fifty thousand captured. Of the fifty German divisions active in Normandy in June, barely ten were left as fighting units. The battle for France neared its end.

The Allies now sent Patton racing to the banks of the Seine. They had bombed out the bridges and hoped to capture another seventy-five thousand German troops and 250 tanks before they could ferry across. Until now, the Overlord plan had been to stop at the river and build up a supply base before beginning the thrust into Germany. But when Patton's forces discovered the Germans were too weak to prevent an Allied crossing, Eisenhower decided to barrel forward to the German border.

He ordered Montgomery to lead his British and Canadian forces through a northeastern strip along the French coast, aiming for a route into Germany through Belgium and part of the Netherlands, while the American First Army covered his right flank. Farther south, Patton charged straight east on routes both north and south of Paris toward the city of Metz and the Vosges Mountains on the French-German border. There, the battle for France would end when Patton's Third Army linked up with Patch's Sixth Army Group, charging up from the south.

Just as when Patton had charged along the Loire, he again needed someone to protect his extended southern flank, bring intelligence from behind enemy lines, and harass German troops attempting to block his advance, this time in the northeast and east of France. That someone, as Patton said, was still the "other son of a bitch," the Resistance. Bill Colby's Team Bruce and a group of teams including Paul, Arthur, Bunny, Anthony, and Alan dropped in a band below Patton's intended right flank to prepare the maquis to protect him from the south.

Protection of Patton's flank would eventually extend all the way to the German border, but not yet. That far east, the Resistance had hardly been organized or armed. The northeast was so built up, and there were so many Germans flowing through it, that there was nowhere for maquis to hide. In the east, the long distance from England made parachute drops in the short summer nights difficult, not to mention the fact that with so much going on in the rest of France, the shadow chiefs felt unable to spare the planes. To do the jobs of organizing and arming the two regions, the shadow chiefs now relied on their "strategic reserve"—the Jeds—and more than thirty new teams now dropped from the sky.

By the afternoon of August 16, one day after they landed, General Patch's Dragoon forces had already linked up their forty-mile beachhead and pushed twenty miles inland. Two American divisions now struck west to Avignon, intending to fly up the banks of the Rhône River. A column of tanks known as Task Force Butler sped straight north from the beachhead toward the cities of Grenoble and Gap along the Route Napoléon. Another American division hugged France's Italian border to protect Patch's right flank against a possible counterattack from Field Marshal Kesselring's forces in Italy.

Back on the coast, the French First Army now hit the beaches, a day ahead of schedule, and zoomed twenty-five miles west toward the valuable ports of Toulon and Marseilles. As the plan went, the French troops would capture the ports and then follow the Americans who drilled northward. Together, they would knock Hitler's last leg out from under him, meet the Overlord forces, and squeeze closed the lower jaw of Ike's long-planned strategic vise.

General Blaskowitz tried first to stop both the French and the American thrusts by building a defensive line running north from Toulon. When the Allies toppled it, his men erected another futile line, originating at Marseille. That, too, collapsed. With so many troops drained away by the Normandy fight, and the Jeds, Allied agents, and maquis blocking movement of German reserves across the Rhône and toward the coast from Lyon and Grenoble, the German army in the south barely offered a defense. General Patch's forces continually knocked down those of Blaskowitz before they restored their balance.

A slew of surprising radio messages suddenly piled in from Jeds and agents around France. "Boche evacuating our region," wrote Jed Team Ivor from Cher, just south of the Loire. "Big convoys daily from Bordeaux," wrote Jed Team Harold from the northern part of France's Atlantic coastline.

German soldiers in the southwest suddenly began making their way north, mostly on foot, toward the Loire, where they turned east toward the Fatherland's border. In the southeast, the units fighting the Allies suddenly stopped firing and began to disappear in a steady stream up the Rhône. The German 148th Division, near Nice, and the 9th Panzer and 157th Reserve Divisions, near Grenoble, fled east toward the Alps, intending to escape into Italy. Most shockingly, the mass of Hitlerite troops fighting in Normandy began to disengage. The tide of German movement had rapidly changed.

On August 16, the obstinate Führer finally admitted that his forces in France were collapsing. He listened to the pleading and reasoning of his commanders. Lest he lose hundreds of thousands of men and their tanks and equipment to the Allied armies of the Overlord and Dragoon invasions, Hitler ordered the withdrawal from France.

# CHAPTER THIRTY-SIX
# LIKE SHOOTING QUAIL

Eisenhower's northern forces surged east. Patch's southern forces swept north. Hitler's troops just wanted to get the hell out. The quicker Ike's and Patch's armies linked up in the northeast, the greater the number of Hitler's troops who would be cut off. The battle for France had turned into a race. To help the Allies win it, the maquis were assigned the jobs of delaying the German exodus.

"Harass enemy withdrawal on roads. Maximum effort required of you" came the radioed orders to Captain Vuchot, the leader of Jed Team Veganin who had recently given the ill-fated Cy Manierre explosives. Vuchot's maquis sat astride the Rhône, the main escape route along which Blaskowitz's 110,000 troops withdrawing from the southeast now streamed.

Vuchot's groups and many others took positions on the high grounds above the main highway on the east bank of the Rhône. They halted convoys with gammon grenades, blew trucks apart with bazookas, and riddled German soldiers with Stens until the whole valley echoed with gunfire. A little south of Vuchot, Team Monocle, one of a number of Jed teams that had dropped just as Dragoon began, blew a bridge over the Drôme River, where it flowed into the Rhône at Livron. That forced the Germans to ford the Drôme, slowing the north-south traffic from one hundred trucks an hour to four.

Another one hundred thousand of Blaskowitz's forces packed up and fled for Germany from the southwest of France, near Bordeaux and Toulouse. Patch and Eisenhower wanted to force Hitler's defeated troops to follow only two major routes: along the Rhône from the southeast and up the Atlantic and then along the Loire from the southwest. This way, both Allied fighter-bombers, diving out of the sky, and the growing maquis ambush squads, hosing the roads with gunfire, knew just where to find their targets.

What Patch and Eisenhower did not want was the Germans veering off these routes and disappearing into the mountains of the Massif Central. Jack Singlaub's Team James, along with Teams Lee and Alexander, helped block entrance to the Massif Central from the Atlantic coast. The northerly route into the mountains from the Mediterranean also had to be closed. "Counting on your all out effort to impede any German effort from coast north" went the messages to Aaron Bank's Team Packard and Ted Baumgold's Team Collodion nearby.

On the southwest corner of the mountain range, Team Quinine's Tommy Macpherson and his maquis sent a dozen bridges over the Lot and Dordogne rivers tumbling into the water, further blocking the German shortcut through the Massif Central. Stone rubble made by two of Macpherson's bombs trapped a couple of hundred occupation troops and Milice in a mile-long tunnel northeast of Aurillac, at Le Lioran.

At the same time, to keep stray squads of German soldiers in the southwest from attempting to slip over the border into Spain, Teams Bugatti and Chrysler, in the foothills of the Pyrenees, helped close off the routes over the frontier. To keep whole German divisions in the southeast from disappearing into Italy over France's eastern border, Bill Thompson's Team Novocaine, Jean Sassi's Team Chloroform, and the recently dropped Teams Ephedrine and Sceptre blasted away at German columns trying to force a route through the alpine mountain passes near Grenoble.

Turned back from escaping through the mountains of central France, either across the Alps into Italy or across the Pyrenees into Spain, the Germans had no choice but to frantically hopscotch between the big cities and towns along the Atlantic and Rhône, which they knew the Allies would not bomb. But along the stretches between these concentrated populations of civilians, the Allied air forces and Resistance ambush squads blasted the Germans to pieces.

In the southwest, some German commanders decided that the safest thing for them and their troops would be to sandbag their garrison windows, roll out the barbed wire, and wait. Eisenhower's headquarters had other plans. Since no regular troops were scheduled to march through the region, SHAEF ordered the Resistance on August 17 to liberate the towns and cities of the southwest and send the remaining Germans packing. Four more Jed teams parachuted into the region. Not that the swelling hordes of armed, angry French fighters needed or waited for encouragement.

On August 16 and 17, Jack Singlaub accepted the surrender of two garrisons: one at Brive and one at Tulle, the town where two months earlier Das Reich had hanged ninety-nine hostages from the balconies and lampposts. On August 20, as a platoon of Task Force Butler tanks approached the alpine town of Gap from one direction, Henry McIntosh and Jean Sassi of Team Chloroform led squads against the Germans from two other directions and captured the town. On August 24, Aaron Bank's Team Packard and their maquis occupied the southern coastal city of Nîmes.

On August 27, fifty maquisards, working with Stewart Alsop and Dick Franklin's Team Alexander, sneaked through the sewers into the town of Angoulême, fifty miles northeast of Bordeaux. The curé of the nearby village of Torsac brought them weapons by leading fake funeral processions past the German sentries and into the Angoulême cemetery, chanting Latin incantations over coffins filled with guns. On August 31, the infiltrated maquis took the guns from the coffins and, in concert with others surrounding the town, rose up against the Germans. By midnight the Tricolor flew over the Hôtel de Ville, illuminated by automobile headlights.

By now, the Resistance had almost completely swept the enemy from the southwestern departments of Indre, Corrèze, Creuse, Haute-Vienne, and Dordogne, and also occupied cities including Mauriac, Aurillac, Montluçon, Castres, Auch, Tarbes, and Toulouse. In the southeast, they cleared all of Haute-Savoie and much of Ain. In fact, the entire swath of France south of the Loire and west of the Rhône was liberated entirely by the work of the Resistance, aided by the threat of German entrapment posed by the advancing Allied armies in the north and the south.

Crowds belting out the Marseillaise and waving American, British, and French flags marched through the streets of southern France. They lifted Jeds onto their shoulders and carried them through the cities. People danced in the streets. Maquisards marched in long parades. Wine flowed everywhere.

At Nîmes, Aaron Bank made a speech from the balcony of the city hall to a huge crowd who shouted, *"Vive les américains!"* Then he made his way to the local whorehouse. He wanted to celebrate with the women of the "intelligence cell" who had garnered information from drunken Germans whose jaws flapped while their underwear dangled at their ankles. Bank drank so much in the whorehouse barroom that he couldn't remember if he ever went upstairs with one of the ladies.

In a restaurant in the recently liberated town of Périgueux, Team Alexander's Dick Franklin drank champagne with Stewart Alsop. Two twenty-year-old blond twins kissed and fawned over Franklin. They begged for mementos and tried to cut buttons from his uniform. They even tried to pull him away by the arm to take him to bed—he didn't go.

North of the Loire, all of Paris was one gargantuan celebration. On August 25, fifty thousand Resistance fighters, together with a column of French tanks attached to Patton's Third Army, liberated the city. Two divisions of Allied troops paraded past the Arc de Triomphe to the cheers of ecstatic crowds.

Meanwhile, Patton's Third Army still pushed east, and Dragoon's Seventh Army and French First Army pushed north. The gap between the armies of Overlord and Dragoon had narrowed to less than 250 miles. They would soon meet. The Germans still in France desperately raced to squeeze through a narrowing escape hatch in the vicinity of the Belfort Gap, the region roughly northeast of Dijon.

From the southeast, Germans racing up the Rhône Valley struggled through tens of thousands of maquis working with the nine Jed teams that now straddled the river. When Jed Team Jude found they had more maquis than weapons, they raided a sporting rifle factory at Saint-Étienne—two thousand more Frenchmen now shot at the Germans. When constantly being shot at wasn't enough to stop the enemy, Team Anthony blew up a canal lock that flooded the main northward route with water twenty feet deep.

The road north was a "veritable quail shooting station, where daily ambushes yielded results we were never able to keep track of," wrote one agent working in the region. In the last days of August, three thousand Resistance fighters, armed partly by Jed Team Jude, rose up in Lyon, France's second largest city. Faced with the approach of the Allied armies, the five thousand Germans there packed up and left. Patch's Dragoon forces entered the liberated city on September 3.

Across the country, the Germans withdrawing from the southwest continued their desperate northward leapfrog, from one well-populated town to the next.

A few thousand would rush north from Bordeaux or Toulouse first to Poitiers, forty miles below the Loire, where they could rest in the knowledge that the Allies would not subject the civilian population to bombing. They then turned east and rushed next to the safety of Châteauroux, while a succeeding group charged up to Poitiers.

The Germans had no choice but to make this eastward turn, because Patton, worried about his southern flank, had assigned to the Resistance the job of blowing most of the bridges across the Loire, guarding other potential crossings, and trapping the Germans below. From the Atlantic coast to over two hundred miles east at Châtillon, twenty-five thousand armed Resistance, including those working with Paul Cyr's Team George, blocked German crossings of the Loire.

Forced to stay below the south bank of the river, the Germans had to drill through the punishing ambushes of more than nine thousand Resistance fighters working with Jed Teams Hugh, Hamish, Julian, Alec, and Ivor. To avoid the Allied fighter-bombers, the Germans tried to move at night. To protect themselves from Resistance ambushes, a special screening force of five thousand seasoned German troops, acting as escorts to the forces withdrawing from the southwest, tried to guard the escape corridor along the Loire. They had very limited success.

RAF planes swooped in and strafed the German columns. When the desperate Germans ran off the road to avoid the bombs, the Resistance slaughtered them in the woods. Maquis working with Team Alec counted fifty dead Germans each day. Team Ivor estimated that its Resistance killed fifteen thousand Germans and destroyed seventy-five vehicles in the four weeks beginning on August 20. "Whole companies would sit in ambush at different points and just shoot until they were tired of shooting," wrote one American agent.

The Resistance ambushes just south of the Loire notched up a scoreboard of burnt trucks, blocked convoys, and enemy dead, but they could not entirely halt the mass migration of two hundred thousand Germans from the west and southwest. In the last week of August, William Crawshay of Team Hugh and Bob Anstett of Team Hamish hitched a plane ride back to London. At headquarters, they made a desperate case for U.S. Major General Robert Macon to send a column of his 83rd Infantry to block the last eighty thousand Germans still headed east. If you won't do that, Anstett and Crawshay said to their chiefs, at least send more airpower.

In the southwest, a partisan leader code-named Christian tore into Tommy Macpherson's command post and made a desperate plea for his help. Christian, a former French navy man complete with full beard and mustache, led a small maquis that surrounded the German garrison occupying a hydroelectric dam in Sarrans, southeast of Aurillac. The cornered Germans threatened to flatten it.

Since most of the area's Germans had withdrawn toward the Loire, there was little to do in southern France except mop up small groups and prevent their mayhem. Twenty-three thousand Germans still barricaded themselves in Bordeaux, waiting for their turn to crowd their way up the withdrawal route. But until they did, the region's Resistance could only wait to attack them. The 370-foot-tall dam, meanwhile, retained nearly eighty billion gallons of water that would flood fifty square miles of inhabited and agricultural land in a matter of minutes. Macpherson rushed to Sarrans.

Inside the dam waited 120 Germans, fully armed and equipped with ten Bofors 40mm antiaircraft guns to blow apart any attackers. Macpherson had one French officer in full uniform and a small crew of about twenty maquisards armed only with Sten guns. The squad wrapped wet cloths around the Sten muzzles, which made their report sound like machine-gun fire, and ran around the dam firing the guns into the air.

"You are surrounded" warned the message Macpherson sent with a village girl to the garrison commander. Macpherson "demanded" surrender. The Germans responded with a rude gesture. Thousands of maquisards might soon arrive to overwhelm the small garrison force at the dam, the German commander knew, but the spectacle of tons of explosives wired to the dam and the threat of the resulting devastation would keep them at bay.

With no way to end the standoff, and a tense moment likely to spark a kamikaze action by the Germans that might kill hundreds, Macpherson and the French officer Christian approached the dam to parlay with the Germans. Their commander, it turned out, knew how some maquis dealt with German prisoners and refused to surrender to them. Seeing the uniforms of Macpherson and the French officer, however, reassured him. He agreed to dismantle his bombs, abandon his cannons, and climb aboard a convoy of trucks with his men and return to a makeshift POW camp at the Aurillac football stadium.

Macpherson had now captured ten 40mm cannons, but, like the rest of the Jeds, agents, and maquis in the southwest, he had no one to shoot them at. Then he discovered that the last of the Germans, a motley column of twenty thousand troops under the command of Major General Botho Elster, had marched north from Bordeaux on August 28. In exchange for safe passage out of the district, they had been persuaded not to destroy the city. That didn't mean that Elster's column couldn't be attacked elsewhere.

Macpherson raced for Toulouse, where a staff of regular French officers had arrived from the Mediterranean coast. Most of them busied themselves in trying to restore some semblance of order to France, but they spared a somewhat deaf, elderly officer, Colonel Schneider, to command the region's sixteen thousand maquis.

Macpherson appointed himself Schneider's de facto chief of staff. Together, Macpherson, his Team Quinine partner Michel de Bourbon, and their main Resistance colleague, Commissar Georges, rushed around contacting the region's maquis groups and preparing them to follow the Germans north, along with the captured antiaircraft guns and mortars.

The gap between the northern and southern armies was rapidly closing, and shadow headquarters had begun dropping the last of the Jeds into easternmost France, where the battle still raged. In a last hurrah for the Resistance's role in the battle for France, Macpherson chased after Elster's column of twenty thousand.

Sadly, meanwhile, in the chaos of the German withdrawal, Frenchmen had started to fight Frenchmen.

# CHAPTER THIRTY-SEVEN
## "PURIFICATION"

With all possibility of a German victory finally gone, last-minute maquisards, men who had never had the courage to join the fight, rummaged in their closets and pulled out their rusty shotguns and moth-eaten army uniforms. Like vultures joining the feast once the real hunt had finished, they ran for the roads, joined the ambushes, and fired their potshots. *Maquis d'octobre,* some who had been fighting since June called the latecomers.

In Brittany, frenzied crowds of men and women suddenly roved through the streets brandishing their weapons and shouting excitedly. "Warriors who march proudly on the field of battle only after the enemy has been routed," Bill Dreux wrote of them. Even some former collaborators went out on the turkey shoot, hoping a few days of puff-chested heroics might convince their countrymen to forgive their years of treachery.

In Périgueux, just as Dick Franklin, sitting on the banquette in the restaurant with the twins, began to reconsider their offer to sleep with him, the roar of a crowd came from the street. Franklin and his Team Alexander leader Stewart Alsop went outside and found a sorry-looking group of five hundred German soldiers, too young or too old to have ever been anything other than administrators, being guarded by maquis carrying Stens.

The roar came from the rabble of townspeople who crowded around the Germans. A woman spat in the face of one of the soldiers. She held up her child to see and said, "Look at the dirty Boches who are already dead." The maquisards grinned.

They herded the Germans down to the rail yard, where they planned to execute them against the boxcars. Many Germans in France deserved such a fate, Alsop and Franklin thought, but this group of clerks in uniform did not. These men should be treated as prisoners of war, Alsop said to the maquis leader. In return, he got a lecture on German atrocities.

But these men massacred no one, Alsop countered.

Such trifling details did not matter to the maquis or the crowd.

At Coublanc, British Captain Stanley Cannicott of Team Alan watched the maquis "interrogate" a platoon of POWs before executing them. The Germans were forced to kneel with their arms stretched out before them. If they dropped their tired arms, a maquisard hit them on the head with a hammer. Cannicott and the village priest tried to intervene, but it soon became clear that persistence might mean their being shot, too.

In the Vosges Mountains, Lucien Lajeunesse of Team Norman, one of the twenty or so teams recently dropped into eastern France, close to the German border, assigned a fourteen-year-old boy to guard five or six prisoners. Shots suddenly rang out and Lajeunesse discovered the German prisoners dead on the ground. He looked at the fourteen-year-old, who, still holding his Sten, smiled. Let's just say they tried to escape, the boy said to Lajeunesse.

Nor was it just Germans in convoys, in trucks, and on bicycles who had to watch out. As Team Chloroform's Jean Sassi, a Frenchman, drove to Nice to see his family for the first time in years, he was stopped and pulled from his car. The men who ambushed him threatened to slit his throat. "I am a parachutist," Sassi screamed. "I am a Frenchman just like you." He came closer to being killed by fellow Frenchmen than he had by Germans.

When Michel de Bourbon, Team Quinine's French officer, got stopped, he was told, "You are a German parachutist dropped here to make trouble." The last-minute maquisards arrested Bourbon and threw him into a barn. Eventually, he and a comrade overpowered the sentry and escaped.

As the Germans withdrew and the former Vichy officials abandoned their posts and ran for their lives, no one stayed behind to keep order. France was complete anarchy, and the rejoicing and celebration gave way to a vindictive and hysterical bloodlust.

Powerless to stop the execution of the five hundred Germans in Périgueux, Stewart Alsop refused to have the massacre take place under the Stars and Stripes. He grabbed every flag he could see, stuffed his equipment and his team in an old Citroën, and drove away.

During the storm that wrecked the harbors at Normandy in mid-June, SHAEF ordered the SFHQ to redouble efforts to keep German reinforcements from reaching Normandy. The Jeds, Allied agents, and Resistance all over France blew bridges, cut rails, and attacked troop columns. On June 19, Team Quinine's Michel de Bourbon sent a German troop train like this one careening off the tracks.

German reprisals for French interference were vicious. On June 10, 1944, elements of Das Reich Panzer Division rolled into Oradour-sur-Glane. When they left, 642 men, women, and children were dead, and the town had been burned to the ground.

*"Alles kaputt,"* a German soldier said when a parent got up the nerve to ask why the children had not come home from Oradour that afternoon. This picture shows some of the charred bodies recovered from the town.

In addition to waiting for arms drops, the Jeds also spent their July nights maintaining the sabotage program that disrupted German momentum in Normandy. Here a bridge north of Limoges has been destroyed.

Most July nights in 1944 the Jeds and their maquis waited in a dark drop zone.
When the rumble of engines approached, someone ran onto the field, poured kerosene
onto piles of wood, threw matches on top, and watched three towers of flame rise in
a whoosh to greet the four-engine bombers. While the Jeds and maquis took cover
in the woods to protect themselves from the heavy containers that would fall from the
sky, the bombers banked around in a circle and swept in.

Parachutes snapped open in the moonlit sky, and the shadow warriors' black-painted planes lumbered around for one more pass over the drop zone before flying back toward the Channel and home. Weapons containers, under their canopies, came crashing through the tree branches.

At mealtimes, the Jeds and maquis tucked their legs under a makeshift dining table, if there was one: a plank or two, perhaps, nailed between two tree stumps. In this scene, the maquisards in the mountains near Saint-Bertrand in southwestern France celebrate the birthday of Jedburgh Team Bugatti's leader, Hod Fuller.

In Loir-et-Cher, a maquis who intended to slit the throats of two injured Germans instead knocked a grenade from his own belt and blew himself up. The clowning in this life-and-death circus act had to end. Jeds all over France tried to force an alien discipline and obedience on boys and men who had never actually volunteered to be Resistance fighters. The maquisard in this photograph holds two German grenades and two Allied grenades as though he were carrying juggling clubs.

All over France, the Jeds and agents attended interrogations and bush trials—of German POWs, of men claiming to be Allied pilots shot down over France, of French collaborators—as observers in case information emerged that was important to their mission. This Frenchman was executed by firing squad for working with the Gestapo.

While the Jedburgh officers armed and trained the Resistance, the Jedburgh radiomen carefully scouted new locations from which to send their messages. Transmitting more than once from the same spot risked exposure if German direction finders were able to triangulate the signals.

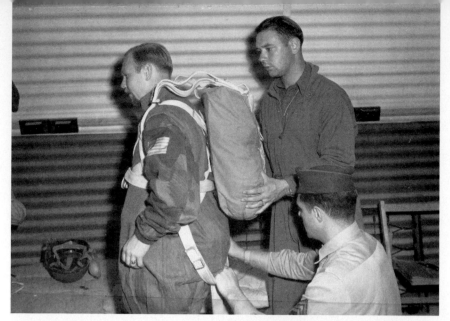

When the Allied breakout from Normandy came, the black-painted bombers at last began dropping large numbers of Jeds into France. Radio operator Lou Goddard had a dream about home. "It was sure good while it lasted," he wrote of the dream to his parents. This photograph of Goddard *(left)* was taken hours before he was killed in a parachuting accident, as he dropped into France.

As Patton's tanks tore into Brittany, ambushes led by Jed-trained maquis slowed the counterattack by Hitler's 2nd Parachute Division. A typical Breton squad of maquisards is pictured standing among the debris of their attack on a group of passing Germans.

After their first attacks, the maquis sang the Marseillaise and congratulated each other, but no one ever really talked about what happened. It was too much to comprehend. On the road behind them lay the twisted bodies of dozens of dead German soldiers in their gray uniforms. Their eyes were still open in their greenish white faces, and their hands still clutched their rifles.

The German troops in Brittany were trapped and desperate. As they struggled past the same ambushes they had earlier fought out of, they became furiously violent. In return, the maquis began executing captured German prisoners. "Even if we had wished to prevent this shooting, we would have been powerless," Bernard Knox wrote in his report. "These men had burned farms and farmers with their wives and children all the way along the road."

The battle between the German soldiers and the French maquis fighters became a vicious circle of violence for violence, where terror avenged terror. In the Morbihan village of Kerhoaden, the Germans hammered the flesh of a captured maquis into rags on an anvil. At Vannes, Wehrmacht soldiers castrated the patriots they captured.

As the date for the southern invasion approached, its commander, General Alexander Patch, assigned to southern France's seventy-seven thousand shadow army fighters the jobs of cutting German telecommunications; harassing German garrisons; protecting the port facilities at Toulon, Marseille, and Sète; and, most important, blocking enemy troop movements by road and rail. Team Bugatti's maquis are seen decamping to do some fighting.

After the Operation Dragoon forces landed, the Germans began withdrawing to avoid the threat of entrapment posed by the advancing Allied armies in the north and the south. The area of France south of the Loire and west of the Rhône was liberated entirely by the Resistance. Team Bugatti's maquis are shown just after liberating Saint-Bertrand.

Crowds marched through the streets of southern France belting out the Marseillaise and waving American, British, and French flags. The hordes lifted Jeds onto their shoulders and carried them through the cities. Hod Fuller of Team Bugatti salutes during one parade.

Once the Germans were gone, Frenchmen started to fight Frenchmen, "purifying" France of former collaborators. Some of the first victims were the so-called *collabos horizontals*, the horizontal collaborators. Public shaving began with prostitutes, then women who had German boyfriends, and finally just any attractive woman who happened to be nabbed.

There were still Germans to fight in France. Larry Swank's Team Ephedrine worked in the Alps with their maquis and a detachment of American troops to close off the passes and helped block between five and fifteen thousand Germans trying to escape over the border. Swank, pictured here in Algiers before dropping in, was killed by a shot through the chest from a maquisard's accidentally dropped rifle.

Field Marshal Kesselring, Hitler's commander in Italy, sent a huge force of seasoned troops into the Alps from Italy to clear a path for their comrades stranded in southern France. During the German attack from Italy, this squad of young maquis boys, who were friends and colleagues of Bill Thompson of Team Novocain, was surrounded. One by one, the Germans wiped them out.

The other dangerous concentrations of Germans fleeing from France were those chased by Eisenhower's troops through the northeast. On August 30, 1944, Team Augustus, working in that region, was intercepted by a group of Germans. Local villagers heard first shouts, then seven shots. Two Team Augustus officers lay dead in puddles by the side of the road. Roger Coté's body was found a few yards away. This photograph was taken just before he parachuted into France.

"The majority of [the Jeds] would, perhaps, return to normal life with relative ease, leaving the war behind like some unlived nightmare," wrote a senior OSS administrator. "But what of the few in whom the real killer instinct had been fostered and aroused?" These photographs of Jean Sassi, before *(left)* and after his Jed experience, demonstrate how much war had changed the Jeds.

General Donovan congratulates Lou Lajeunesse for his work.

In the southeast, Jean Sassi and a comrade sat in a café in Valence celebrating the end of his mission by drinking coffee with two pretty women. A posse of armed men burst in, grabbed the women, and began to drag them away. Sassi drew his pistol.

"Don't lay another hand on them," he said. "They are with us."

"They have been sleeping with Germans," the gang leader said.

"Maybe so, but now they are going to be sleeping with us," replied Sassi.

The gang left, but ten minutes later they returned with more men and weapons of their own. There was nothing Sassi could do for the women but follow behind. Eventually, he found himself at police headquarters, where the gang took the women. The building was filled with crying women, some holding their children, all of whom had been dragged there.

In the middle of the melee stood a group of barbers who shaved the women's heads. A carpet of hair covered the floor. Blood streamed down some women's faces. *Collabos horizontals,* the French called the women, horizontal collaborators. For supposedly giving comfort to the enemy, they got what Parisians called *la coiffure de '44.* Now that the roving gangs of Resistance, blinded by their fury, had finished with the Germans, they began to prey on their fellow French, both actual collaborators and innocent bystanders. Thus began what came to be called the *épuration,* or "purification," of France.

In Amancey, in eastern France, Lou Lajeunesse watched in horror as the maquis paraded two young girls through the streets. Their brothers had once been arrested by the Germans as "terrorists." The girls traded sex for their brothers' release. Now, as punishment for their consorting with the enemy, the maquis shaved their heads, stripped them, made them walk through the town naked, and then urinated on them.

In Marseille, the public shaving began with prostitutes, then women who had German boyfriends, and finally just any attractive woman who happened to be nabbed. Some of the *plumées,* the plucked, as they came to be called, got swastikas branded on their scalps or between their breasts with red-hot pokers.

When the crowds got particularly frenzied, others faced accusations of denouncing resisters. In Marseille, as a *chef de maquis* directed a firing squad against such a woman, a regular French soldier saved her when he walked up to the *chef* and shot him dead. "In the late summer of 1944," Team Quinine radio operator Arthur Brown wrote, "France was a disgusting place to be."

Throughout the country, roving bands of bloodthirsty witch-hunters dragged denounced wretches out of hiding for all manner of crimes, real and imagined. To many minds, Milice and informants deserved what they got. But as the logic went, you could be killed either for having been a black marketeer or for having denounced a black marketeer. In Dordogne, one woman who had joined the Milice when it was formed but then immediately resigned was dragged from her wedding and shot by maquis. They then sat down and ate her wedding breakfast.

The diary of a maquisard in Haute-Savoie recorded the fate of one captured Milicien: "Aged twenty-nine, married three months ago. Made to saw wood in the hot sun wearing a pullover and jacket. Made to drink warm salted water. Ears cut off. Covered with blows from fists and bayonets. Stoned. Made to dig his grave. Made to lie in it. Finished off with a blow to the stomach from a spade. Two days to die."

Near Angoulême, Stewart Alsop and Dick Franklin of Team Alexander discovered a Communist group milling about the courtyard of a country house. The maquis were about to execute the owner because he was a "collaborator." It turned out he was a French count, an aristocrat, and that his wealth and position were his only crimes. In some parts of France, some factions of the Communist FTP had declared class war against the aristocracy, the bourgeoisie, and the Catholic Church.

"If the defeated enemy succeeds in making us forget the very principles in whose names we have stood up to them," de Gaulle's spokesman, Maurice Schumann, said over the BBC, "they will have taken away from us the moral victory, which when all is said and done is the only thing that counts." No one apparently listened. Thirty thousand people died in the "purification" of France, almost exactly the same number shot and executed by the Germans during their four years as occupiers.

This was the dark shadow of the Resistance triumph. It was the problem with dropping weapons in the hundreds of tons to anyone willing to shoot at the enemy. It was a sad but natural fact that after four years of German occupation, the brutalized had themselves become brutal. There was no controlling how the French used the weapons once the enemy was gone.

France was on the verge of liberation, but Team Alexander's Dick Franklin felt sickened and saddened instead of joyful. "I wanted my army, my government, my maquis to be better than that, above the tactics used by the enemy; otherwise we were no better than them," he wrote. "Having liberated France,"

Team Giles's radio operator Gordon Tack said, "I now wonder whether it was worth the trouble."

In northeast France, Hitler had launched thousands of fresh troops into the region, both to watch the backs of his broken units running home and to reinforce a new defensive position, known as the Kitzinger Line, about sixty miles west of the French border with Belgium and Germany. The battle there had become far too heated to be able to work behind the lines in uniform.

The three Jeds of Team Aubrey volunteered to parachute in civilian clothes and cut the rails to the battlefront southeast of Paris. Team Alfred agreed to work in plainclothes to prevent German attempts to stop Patton by blowing bridges over the Oise River. And on August 16, Roger Coté's Team Augustus had thrown themselves out of a low-flying plane over the northeastern department of Aisne, near the Belgian border. Team Augustus, like the ten other Jed teams that dropped in the northeast around them, had agreed to simultaneously accost both the retreat from Falaise and the new German advance.

As the Germans rushed past, Roger Coté safely dodged in and out of the forests and skulked across the rocky landscape of Aisne for two weeks after Team Augustus's chutes had rustled the five hundred feet from sky to ground. Working with the American team leader, Major John Bonsall, and the French second in command, Captain Jean Delviche, Coté radioed intelligence reports on German movements for use by the advancing Allies and arranged airdrops of arms and ammunition to the department's six thousand *résistants.*

As the Allied forces to the west knocked down one German defensive obstacle after another, Team Augustus and their maquis shot up columns of enemy troops and, on one particularly successful day, derailed a German train and its valuable cargo of more than eight hundred trucks. They made hell for the Germans fleeing from the north of France.

Meanwhile, when they ran out of Germans to fight in the south, maquis working with Jack Singlaub's Team James and Charlie Brown's Team Lee followed the Germans north. Joining the Jeds and Resistance in the corridor south of the Loire, they blasted away at the Germans withdrawing from the southwest. Aaron Bank's Team Packard trucked their maquis across the south of France from west to east and joined the Jeds and maquis in the Alps, fighting to keep the Germans from escaping over the border from Italy. These maquisards proved there were still many Frenchmen in France more interested in killing the enemy than in murdering one another.

Meanwhile, Hitler's last defense in France, the Kitzinger Line, the blockade he tried to establish about sixty miles west of France's eastern border, collapsed. The entire Overlord invasion force now plowed east in the direction of Germany. The Dragoon troops moved north to meet them. The Germans remaining in France were more desperate than ever to get out.

Coté's Team Augustus, Lajeunesse's Team Norman, and twenty-five or so other teams working in northeastern and eastern France operated smack in the middle of the corridor of roads and villages along which many tens of thousands of dirty and exhausted German troops, chased by the advancing Allied troops, force-marched their hasty retreat. Some rode in trucks or tanks, but most walked, drove cars, or rode bicycles stolen from French civilians. The Germans went to the towns and simply snatched bicycles from women in the street, often stealing their wedding rings, too. When the bicycle tires went flat, the soldiers simply pulled them off and road on the rims. Vicious treatment awaited anyone who slowed them down.

Of the Jed teams working in the same dangerous region as Coté's Team Augustus, British Sergeant Ken Seymour of Team Jacob was captured, French Captain Chaigneau of Team Aubrey died when he was shot in a firefight, and French Lieutenant d'Oultremont of Team Andrew took a hit from German mortar fire.

In Jura, in eastern France, Team Norman's radio operator, Lou Lajeunesse, saw a whole village massacred after a maquisard dropped a grenade into a German tank turret. From a hiding place in the woods, Lajeunesse watched helplessly while the Germans cut a maquisard's fingernails out with a knife, one at a time, until a soldier disemboweled the poor boy with a bayonet. Other of Lajeunesse's maquis had their eyes gouged out; some had their nipples cut off; one was bayoneted hundreds of times before being put out of his misery. Lajeunesse watched horrified when the boy who cranked the generator to his radio was shot and killed. He was fourteen years old.

One night, as Lajeunesse transmitted from the third floor of a farmhouse, he heard a column of vehicles pull up out front. A number of officers got out of the trucks and barged inside. Two shots killed the farmer and his wife. Lajeunesse quietly tapped out the coordinates of the house, explained that high-level German brass dwelled within, and in the dark climbed down vines that had grown up the building's stone wall. He just made it behind a garden wall when two U.S. P-38s swept in and blew the house and the Germans inside to pieces.

In the Alps, Larry Swank of Team Ephedrine was killed by a shot through the chest from a maquisard's accidentally dropped rifle. Swank's teammates, along with Teams Novocaine, Chloroform, and Sceptre, worked in the Alps with their maquis and a detachment of American troops. They closed off the passes and helped block between five and fifteen thousand Germans trying to escape over the border.

Finally, Field Marshal Kesselring, Hitler's commander in Italy, sent a huge force of seasoned troops into the Alps from Italy to clear a path for their comrades stranded in France. As artillery came pounding into the town of Briançon, even U.S. troops threw away their weapons and ran. "Get us out of here," Team Novocaine's Bill Thompson heard the Americans scream.

If trained American soldiers had no chance against these German warriors, Bill Thompson's maquis were certainly doomed. During their march from Italy, the Germans surrounded an entire company of young maquis boys who were friends and colleagues of Thompson's. One by one, the Germans wiped them out.

Sixty miles east of the Belgian border, near the town of Soissons on the Aisne River, Roger Coté and Team Augustus suddenly found that the tanks that charged past on the roads around them were no longer German panzers but American Shermans. Augustus had been overrun by the 3rd Armored Division of the First Army. The Allies had nearly swept the breadth of France.

In the north, the only hot spot that remained for the Resistance was the sixty-mile strip east of the Aisne. With the Germans largely gone from Brittany, Bob Kehoe's Team Frederick and Bill Dreux's Team Gavin slipped anticlimactically aboard a ship to England, along with Teams Guy, Felix, Gerald, Daniel, and Douglas. The only German forces of any substance in France now were east of the Somme River, barricaded in the fortress ports of Brittany and the Atlantic coast, or on the roads just south of the Loire, where Elster's column of twenty thousand Germans still marched east toward Germany. The barricaded Germans in the ports were harmless; Elster's column and Hitler's forces east of the Somme, however, were not.

To protect the Dragoon invasion's French First Army, which was marching up the east of France, from being broadsided by Elster and any other stray Germans from the west of France, Tommy Macpherson organized his sixteen-thousand-strong maquis force and moved northward up the east side of the Massif Central as a flank-protecting buffer. As Elster's twenty thousand

Germans approached the last leg of their march along the Loire, Macpherson persuaded a French general to loan him a squadron of tanks, took up a position right in Elster's path, and waited for the last—and what might shape up to be the biggest—battle between the Resistance and the Germans.

Meanwhile, to help thwart German threats on the east of the Somme, on August 30, Coté's Team Augustus received orders from the SFHQ to infiltrate behind the lines. The British Second Army wanted the bridges over the Somme near the town of Amiens protected. Once the last of the retreating Germans had crossed, they would try to demolish these overpasses. The Germans' success would turn the river into a dead end, leaving Montgomery's forces stranded on one bank while their quarry on the other side escaped. "This is an important task," the SFHQ message said. "Count on you for fullest cooperation." The Resistance fight in France was close to finished.

# CHAPTER THIRTY-EIGHT
## SURRENDER

On August 30, Coté and his teammates John Bonsall and Jean Delviche slipped through the Allied lines and past the Germans, back into enemy territory. Team Augustus's new mission meant tracking down Resistance fighters near Amiens, arming them, and, in a very short period, organizing them into hidden squads around the Somme River crossings. The Resistance would rain machine-gun fire on any Germans who tried to demolish the bridges. But first Augustus had to haul its cache of arms to Amiens.

Since the British Second Army was only a matter of days away and the mission was urgent, traipsing secretly and in relative safety through the woods was not an option. With their incriminating cargo of weapons and radios, Team Augustus would have to travel on the open road.

Coté and his teammates contacted their old Resistance colleagues and asked them to find a vehicle. German troops, desperate to escape, had grabbed nearly everything with wheels—cars, trucks, bicycles, even horse carriages. A broken-down cart and near-lame horse was all Team Augustus could find. Not even the Germans wanted it.

At nine o'clock that night, with the guns in the cart and hay piled on top, the three Jeds departed, guided along the back roads by a member of the Resistance. He stayed with Team Augustus for an hour, until they assured him they could navigate on their own, begging him to go home—it was already the dangerous time after curfew. The men continued on in the pitch-dark, moonless night toward the village of Barenton-sur-Serre, where they planned to meet a Resistance contact who would help them recruit their volunteers.

Team Augustus rode the horse-drawn cart along a potted dirt road through the backcountry of northeastern France, desperately hoping to evade the Nazi patrols. Since the sun had long set and the curfew hour had passed, Coté and his comrades were automatically suspect. Though German patrols were unlikely on this ill-kept dirt track, Team Augustus had to cross a major road that, at least by day, was crowded like a city avenue with the retreating Germans.

In their civilian clothes and with their forged paperwork, Coté and his teammates might be able to talk their way out of an encounter with the Germans. A thorough inspection, though, would lead the Nazis to the back of the cart, where the radio and boxes of Sten guns and ammo lay beneath the hay.

A downpour began around a quarter past ten. Team Augustus could not see even a few feet in front of them or hear suspicious sounds. They couldn't see the intersection with the major road. They didn't hear the German tank engines idling. They simply rolled forward, blind and deaf, trusting their fate entirely to their old horse.

Suddenly, bright light blinded them. Frightened German voices shouted. The muzzles of a dozen Nazi weapons pointed at Team Augustus. They had rolled right into the middle of the intersection of the main road to Barenton, where two German tanks and an infantry platoon had stopped. *Warum sind Sie unterwegs nach der Ausgangssperre?* the Germans shouted. Why are you out after curfew? *Wo sind Ihre Papiere?* Where are your papers?

Coté had had his papers inspected before and he'd been trained to be quick on his feet with his answers. He handed over his forged identity cards, which he knew would hold up to inspection especially well in this downpour and darkness. Villagers, looking out from behind their curtains, watched Team Augustus climb down from their wagon and stand with their hands up by the side of the road. An officer examined their papers with his flashlight. The shouting stopped. The tension dissipated. They might get away with their lives.

But then a soldier casually walked over to the back of the cart. He began pushing the hay aside with his gun muzzle. It was now only a matter of time. Coté, petrified, turned and ran. First there were shouts; then the local villagers heard seven shots, followed, half an hour later, by the sound of two tanks rumbling off. In puddles by the side of the road lay the two dead bodies of the Team Augustus officers John Bonsall and Jean Delviche. A few yards away lay Coté. He died only four days before the Allied tanks approached the Belgian border and chased the last of the Germans from northeastern France.

---

On September 6, the five thousand Germans defending the withdrawal corridor below the Loire pulled out before it was too late to escape through the narrowing gap between Patton's Third Army moving east and the French First Army moving north. Major General Elster and his column of men now became the only remaining formation of Germans of any importance outside the Vosges Mountains in easternmost France. With the German protective force on the run, Elster's column faced the punishment of the Resistance and their Jed teams and Allied agents tucked into the curve of the Loire alone.

Suddenly, the major general's forward forces halted at the Allier River, just south of where it merged with the Loire at the town of Decize. In the Germans' path stood Column Schneider, the sixteen thousand maquisards Macpherson had helped pull together. Macpherson had mined the one remaining bridge across the Allier in case the Germans should try to cross. Elster's and Schneider's groups faced each other like growling dogs, lobbing artillery shells back and forth across the river. This was the last standoff between the Germans and the Resistance.

An urgent message arrived for Macpherson from British Captain John Cox of Team Ivor, who was operating in the bend of the Loire. Various Resistance chiefs had demanded General Elster's surrender, but he refused, fearing the maquis would cut his men's throats. Elster insisted he would wait until American forces contacted him.

"Will you come and see what you can do?" Cox asked Macpherson. Cox thought Macpherson might be able to persuade Elster that a bloodbath would result if he attempted to cross the Allier. Meanwhile, the leader of nearby Team Julian, Major A. H. Clutton, contacted an American squad patrolling between the Loire and the Cher, and asked them to send a representative to the meeting, which had been set for ten o'clock the following morning at Arçay, a town on the Cher.

In the four years since Churchill first promoted his secret army concept and demanded that the Special Operations Executive "set Europe ablaze," Allied agents had been parachuting into France and black-painted bombers had dropped weapons by the ton. An estimated three hundred thousand Frenchmen had taken to the woods and the mountains all over the country to fight in the Resistance. Many of them had died for one purpose: to help the Allied armies win the war while keeping the body count as low as possible.

Now, Tommy Macpherson faced the biggest testament yet to the good work of the French Forces of the Interior. The surrender of a German major general and the twenty thousand men under him to a force of maquis was a victory of incredible proportions for the French Resistance and for those who had armed and directed them: the SOE, the OSS, the Allied agents in France, and the Jedburghs. It meant the end of the battle for France—victory. But Macpherson faced a big obstacle: to get to Arçay, he had to travel forty miles through twenty thousand German troops.

He and a representative of the French, Major Sarassin, piled into a captured German Red Cross vehicle with its white body and blood-red crosses. Hoping to be taken for a speeding ambulance, they tore across the bridge at Decize and straight through the German lines with their headlights on high beam. They belted across the territory through the night and twice ran roadblocks as machine guns blared at them.

In Arçay the following morning, September 10, during the minutes that ticked toward the ten o'clock meeting, Macpherson fidgeted nervously in a nearly bare, wood-floored room of the *mairie,* the mayor's office. He had arrived there unscathed. Not one bullet had touched the passengers in the ambulance.

Beside Macpherson on one side of a long table sat Major Sarassin, Team Ivor's Captain Cox in full battle dress, Cox's French partner, Lieutenant Colin, and a number of Resistance chiefs. The other side of the table remained empty, except for the mayor of Arçay, who wore his red, white, and blue sash of office. Ten o'clock came and went. They waited nervously. No security had been arranged. They lived at the mercy of the thousands of Germans who crawled over the area.

At 10:02, the sound of slamming car doors drifted into the school. Boots crunched on the gravel. For all Macpherson knew, a few German soldiers might be approaching to machine-gun his group. The door flew open. There, framed in the doorway, stood a short, sharp-faced man wearing the peaked hat and crisp green uniform of a German Wehrmacht officer. It was General Elster. An SS colonel in his black uniform, an aide, and an interpreter accompanied him.

Macpherson and Cox stood up as the German officers came in. No one shook hands. The Germans wordlessly clicked their heels and bowed. The chairs scraping across the floor made the only sound. For a few moments, the group sat in silence.

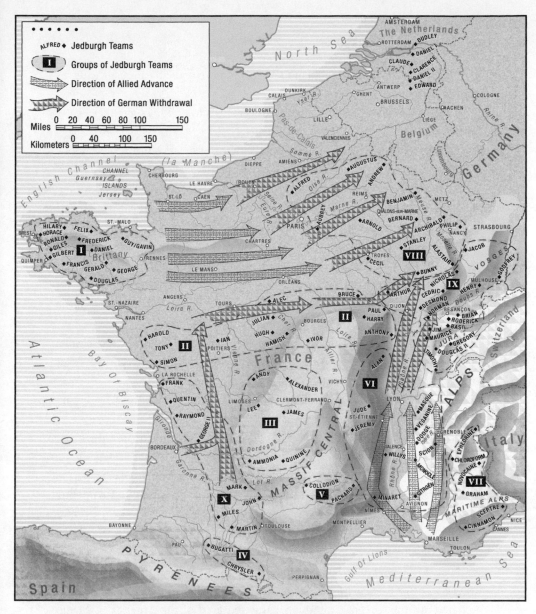

## JEDBURGHS IN FRANCE AND THEIR ROLES IN THE ALLIED ADVANCE

I. Assisted with the liberation of Brittany. II. Guarded Patton's southern flank as he advanced across France. Later harassed the German withdrawal along the Loire. III. Prevented Germans withdrawing from the southwest from traveling northeast through the Massif Central. IV. Helped prevent movement from the southwest toward the southern beachhead and later stopped Germans escaping into Spain. V. Helped prevent movement toward the southern beachhead and later stopped Germans in the south from moving into the Massif Central. VI. Delayed German movement along the Rhône, first during Overlord and later during the German withdrawal. VII. Protected the right flank of the Dragoon forces and then slowed the German withdrawal into Italy. VIII. Harassed German attempts to block the Allied eastward advance and later German withdrawal. IX. Harassed enemy reinforcement of battle areas and harassed withdrawal. X. Assisted in mopping up Germans in the southwest.

"General," Macpherson said in French, "we have come to discuss the terms of your surrender."

"We may discuss," Elster replied, "but certainly not about surrender."

No one else spoke.

"I'm afraid you don't understand, General. You are completely at our mercy, and our terms are unconditional surrender."

"Don't be silly. I have many experienced troops. We want to avoid loss of life. We simply ask you to open the barrier and let us go peaceably through and we will take no action until we are in Germany."

"Nuts to that," Macpherson said very quietly. "You have misunderstood the difficulty . . ."

"You have only disorganized Resistance!" Elster interrupted.

"Surely your scouts have reported our tanks? And you must know that the First French Army is only a short distance behind me."

Elster now asked for a break. He and the SS colonel went outside. Inside, Macpherson, Cox, and the others drummed their fingers nervously. After forty-five minutes, the general finally returned.

"We cannot possibly surrender. If we lay down our arms the French barbarians will come and massacre us," Elster said.

Macpherson knew he had won. The general now looked only for some sort of reassurance.

"Your men may keep their personal arms until American regular forces arrive," Macpherson told the general. Elster haggled for a while, but someone brought a piece of paper, and he signed it. As a gesture, the general gave Macpherson the metal pennant from the front of his staff car. The SS colonel handed Macpherson his Luger.

Just as Elster walked down the steps, Lieutenant Samuel Magill, the American officer Team Julian had invited, skidded up in a jeep. Macpherson sketched out the agreement and what was required of the Americans. Magill swung into action. American troops were called in, and after the Germans piled their arms into weapons dumps they were transported to prison camps. Elster's entire column of twenty thousand Germans would vanish across the Loire and into the U.S. Army pens within two or three days.

The next day, September 11, 1944, armored units of the French First Army physically linked up with Patton's Third Army north of Dijon. The Overlord and Dragoon forces joined, and any Germans remaining in France were cut off. Thanks in part to the Resistance forces and the Jeds and Allied agents who assisted them, only 130,000 out of the nearly 210,000 German troops who had left southern France made it to the Kitzinger Line.

It would take a few weeks, still, for the last of the Jeds to complete their missions in the Vosges Mountains in the east and around the few German coastal fortresses in the west. But, for the most part, Operation Jedburgh's role in the battle for France was over.

Team by team, the Jeds dribbled first into Paris, then London, and on to Milton Hall, their old training base turned holding area. Team Novocaine's Bill Thompson arrived in Paris in his grubby battle dress with a light machine gun slung over his shoulder. He toured the city, looking ready for a fight. When Jean Sassi lost his wallet in a Paris café, he brandished his .45 and held the entire clientele hostage until he had searched everyone's pockets. Some Jeds, for entertainment, threw themselves into any scrap that broke out between soldiers.

"We had brought out the jungle instincts in these men," wrote a senior OSS administrator. "The majority of them would, perhaps, return to normal life with relative ease, leaving the war behind like some unlived nightmare. But what of the few in whom the real killer instinct had been fostered and aroused?" The OSS sent the returning American Jeds on a three-day program to "de-activate these human time bombs," as an OSS administrator put it. The Jeds had become a law unto themselves.

Tired of carrying around their weapons, Lou Lajeunesse and a couple of his chums tried to turn them in at a British supply station in London, but got rebuffed because of chickenshit army regulations. The Jeds walked halfway across London Bridge and dumped the military equipment into the Thames. Then they exchanged their money belts full of counterfeit French francs for pounds at the local bank and started to party. London was full of whiskey and girls.

"Our war, screwed up or not, was fun," wrote Team Alexander's Dick Franklin, but that wasn't the whole truth. Bill Thompson put eight hundred dollars of his newly exchanged francs in an envelope, licked it closed, and mailed it home. He would later use the money to buy his first car. He bought a fifth of scotch with some of the rest and started to drink. He had been having nightmares about his friends, thirty-five maquis the Germans had wiped out in the Alps. He woke up three days later in a Red Cross club. "I suppose I had some sort of a breakdown," he later said. Things had changed since the days when the gung-ho Jedburghs couldn't wait to get to war.

As the summer of 1944 turned the corner into fall, and Allied armies around the globe still scrambled for the defeat of Germany and Japan, the London-based shadow chiefs turned their attention to operations in northern Europe and Germany. Eight Jed teams who had never dropped into France now jumped out of the black-painted bombers into Holland, in support of Montgomery's Operation Market Garden.

Meanwhile, as the war in Europe progressed, Odette Sansom was found, in Buchenwald, the German extermination camp, still clinging to life. Authors and filmmakers would later make her story famous; Odette would receive Britain's highest noncombatant honor, the George Cross. The captured Jedburgh Cy Manierre was liberated from a German POW camp by the Russians in May 1945.

Of the remaining Jeds, most went on to other behind-the-lines operations: the British in Southeast Asia, the Americans in China, and the French in Indochina. Tommy Macpherson and Bernard Knox both worked with the partisans in Italy.

But all that was in the future.

In Arçay, on the day General Elster surrendered, Tommy Macpherson stood in the town square on the bank of the Cher River. Three carloads of American newspaper reporters suddenly pulled up from the U.S. Third Army headquarters. They surrounded Macpherson and Lieutenant Magill, the American who had arrived at the end of Macpherson's negotiations with Elster.

The press began shouting questions. They wanted to know all about the capture of the largest single formation of Germans during the battle for France. Macpherson, of course, had been trained to not even give them his name. Lieutenant Magill did the talking.

Whether Macpherson wanted to or not, he said nothing about how three nonarmy shadow warriors—Jedburghs—had parlayed with General Elster. He slipped away and, for the first time since he had parachuted behind the lines into occupied France three months earlier, found he had nowhere special to go.

Suddenly, a tall blonde from the press walked up to Macpherson. The rest of the news corps surrounded Magill, and it would not be long before General

Robert Macon of the 83rd Infantry praised Magill for single-handedly taking Elster's surrender. But the woman who approached Macpherson said she sensed there was more to the story. Macpherson shrugged. The woman persisted. Macpherson said nothing. For thirty-five more years his presence in France and that of all the Jeds would remain top secret. He said good-bye to the reporter and walked away across the square.

# EPILOGUE

By the end of autumn 1944, 276 Jedburghs had forced their frightened bodies to jump into the French night from black-painted bombers. They joined a group of 389 other SOE and OSS special operations agents working behind the lines that summer.

There were, of course, many hundreds of other Allied personnel causing mayhem for the Germans in France in the weeks following the Normandy invasion—the American Operational Groups and British Special Air Service squads alone numbered over three thousand. But the role of the OGs and the SAS was limited to attacking important behind-the-lines targets deemed too technically or militarily difficult for the less well-trained secret armies of the Resistance. The actual arming, organizing, and directing of the Resistance uprising itself was the job of the Jeds and the Allied agents. It was a job spectacularly done.

Eisenhower wrote, "Without the great assistance of the Resistance, the liberation of France and the defeat of the enemy in western Europe would have consumed a much longer time and meant greater losses to ourselves." Eisenhower's headquarters estimated that the value of the Resistance to the Overlord campaign amounted to the equivalent of fifteen military divisions. The most important Resistance contributions, according to a SHAEF report, included forcing the Germans to chase after maquis groups instead of fighting the Allies; delaying German troop movement to the battlefronts; disrupting German telecommunications; providing military intelligence; and taking over military precautions, such as flank protection and mopping up, so that the Allied armies could advance at greater speed.

After four years of vicious Nazi oppression, many thousands of Frenchmen and Frenchwomen would have wreaked vengeance on the Germans without an ounce of provocation from any outsider. But the Jedburghs' leadership ensured that French Resistance fighters did not waste their lives attacking the Germans haphazardly and that their tremendous bravery and sacrifices assisted in the Allies' overall strategy toward Hitler's ultimate defeat.

"In no previous war," Eisenhower wrote to General Colin Gubbins, the head of SOE, "and in no other theater during this war, have resistance forces been so closely harnessed to the main military effort. . . . I must express my great admiration for the brave and often spectacular exploits of the agents and special groups under control of Special Force Headquarters."

Without the Allied agents and Jedburghs who dropped into France, the maquis would not have had the technical know-how to blow bridges and derail trains. Nor would they have known what bridges and rails were important to the military commanders. Nor would they have had any guns. The Jedburghs and agents in France distributed about twenty-five million pounds of weapons and equipment to the Resistance in 1944. This amounted to 350,000 Sten guns, 150,000 pistols, 80,000 rifles, and other munitions.

What distinguished the Jeds, who made up more than 40 percent of the special ops personnel organizing the Resistance in France, was their long and detailed paramilitary training, which the Allied agents lacked. For the four years before the Jeds arrived in France, F and RF Section agents began the arduous and dangerous clandestine work of organizing a rabble of ill-disciplined Frenchmen into a secret army. They set the stage for D-Day.

The job of leading the Resistance in guerrilla warfare, however, belonged to the Jeds, who reconciled Resistance factions, suggested targets, brought in supplies, and instilled good guerrilla doctrine. The Jedburgh principle was one of leverage—by using the Resistance to launch attacks and sabotage operations, the efforts of a handful of soldiers ballooned into huge assistance in the liberation of France.

Bob Kehoe, Bernard Knox, Tommy Macpherson, Jean Sassi, and the rest of the Jeds have ample reason to be proud of their contributions to the Allied victory in the "Good War." Just as important, the Jedburghs' unprecedented behind-the-lines success has influenced the history of special operations ever since.

In the British election of 1945, the Labour Party won a landslide victory over Churchill's Conservative Party at the polls, and Clement Attlee became prime minister. Lord Selbourne, the political master of the Special Operations Executive under Churchill, suggested to Attlee that the SOE might be turned into an important postwar intelligence tool. Attlee replied that he had no interest in presiding over an entity like Comintern, the Soviet organization whose goal was to spread Communism around the world. The SOE was closed with only two days' notice.

In the United States, OSS head General William Donovan brainstormed plans to make peacetime use of the service's intelligence and covert operations capabilities. The *Chicago Tribune* ran a story in February 1945 that helped seal the fate of OSS: "New Deal Plans to Spy on World and Home Folks, and Super Gestapo Agency Is Under Consideration." After Roosevelt died in April 1945, Donovan got in to see President Truman in May. Donovan handed Truman his proposal. The president thanked him for his service to the country and then, as Donovan looked on, tore the plan in two.

On September 20, 1945, Truman issued an executive order disbanding the OSS. OSS men from around the world, including my grandfather, who was then the chief of the OSS Special Operations London branch, went home. For a couple of years, my grandfather and World War II's other shadow war chiefs observed international events—particularly the mounting tensions between the United States and the Soviet Union—from afar.

But in 1947, amid growing conviction that war with the Soviets would soon come, Truman about-faced on his decision to disband the OSS and established the Central Intelligence Agency, an organization that, like its predecessor, combined intelligence collection with covert operations. However, the United States had demobilized its massive World War II army, lost its taste for conflict, and lived in a nuclear era where war between the superpowers meant atomic suicide. The American public would not be willing to go to war again to protect Europe or Asia at that time. The CIA was charged with preventing Soviet expansionism without letting hostilities break out into a full-scale conflict.

To shadow chiefs like my grandfather, who were now at the CIA and still energized with the excitement of World War II successes like Operation Jedburgh, the natural idea was to prepare to defend Europe and other parts of the world coveted by the Soviets through covert operations. But to use special operations without regular armies fighting nearby was a massive and untested change of paradigm.

Throughout the war in Europe, operations like Jedburgh had been used not in place of standing armies but as an adjunct to support them. But now policy makers saw Jedburgh-like operations as a chance to use foreign nationals to fight for American interests. Using the same principle of leverage as in Operation Jedburgh, the special operations seemed inexpensive and did not require the commitment of American armies; it occupied a place in the middle of the spectrum between diplomacy and outright war. The age of the proxy war had begun.

As one of the first attempts at arming and supporting foreign revolutionaries, Operation Jedburgh therefore became the prototype for dozens of operations in which non-American guerrillas happily fought an enemy they shared with the United States as long as America supplied the money and the guns. The CIA began its shadow war program by supplying potential European Resistance fighters with money and weapons in advance of a potential Soviet invasion. In an adaptation of the Jedburgh concept, the CIA supported revolutions against perceived anti-American governments around the world—from Asia to Africa. Many thousands of foreign lives were lost in CIA-sponsored battles approved by neither the U.S. Congress nor the voters.

Even two of the CIA's most criticized operations—the Bay of Pigs, which attempted to use Cuban nationals to overthrow Castro, and Phoenix, which armed South Vietnamese villagers to root out and execute "suspected" subversive elements from the north—had their origins in the principles of Jedburgh-like operations in World War II. Indeed, two former Jedburghs, Lou Conein of Team Mark and William Colby of Team Bruce, headed CIA operations in Vietnam.

In 1961, after a postmortem of the failed Bay of Pigs invasion, a high-ranking CIA official observed that large-scale CIA operations went sour "because the system kept calling on us for more even when it should have been obvious that secret shenanigans couldn't do what armies are supposed to do."

The CIA continued its proxy-war practices into the eighties with its support of the Afghan rebels against the Soviet occupation. "Afghan freedom fighters have made it as dangerous for a Russian soldier or a Soviet convoy to stray off a main road as it was for the Germans in France in 1944," CIA Director William Casey said. But when the Soviets finally withdrew, there was no friendly army in place as there was in France to bring stability. A situation not unlike the period of *épuration* in France was allowed to continue unfettered and expanded into full-scale civil war. Twenty years later, some of the same Islamic extremists the United States weighed down with weapons in Afghanistan now call themselves al Qaeda. Though the shadow warriors took away tremendous enthusiasm from Operation Jedburgh, perhaps they had not learned some of its cautionary lessons.

During World War II, even the arming of the French Resistance had its "collateral damage"—the thirty thousand deaths of the *épuration*. In the case of Operation Jedburgh, those regrettable deaths were balanced by protection of the Allied armies pursuing a "noble war." Operation Jedburgh had saved many thousands of Allied lives. As an author, I feel proud to have met the men of Operation Jedburgh and to tell their story. Theirs was an amazing feat. But even the Jedburgh experience shows that special operations are not a cost-free panacea to be used whenever the United States wishes to exert its will without committing its forces. As the United States moves increasingly toward a special operations paradigm, the question must be asked, Will the unintended costs of subversive warfare be worth paying?

As for the Jeds themselves, Bill Colby became the Central Intelligence Agency's most controversial director. Appointed by President Nixon, he attempted to pacify the CIA's detractors by cooperating with congressional investigations and disclosing information about previously unknown covert activities, including the assassination of foreign leaders. Colby's harshest critics inside the agency believed that he could not have done it more harm had he himself been a Soviet agent. But since Congress would learn the CIA's secrets one way or another, Colby was convinced he could best protect it by divulging wrongdoing and controlling how the story got out.

John "Jack" Singlaub went on to fight in Korea and Vietnam, achieve the rank of major general, and become the highly decorated chief of staff for U.S. forces in South Korea. After being forced to retire for publicly criticizing President Carter's national security policies, he became the chairman of the World Anti-Communist League.

In this role, and cooperating with National Security Council Deputy Director Oliver North and CIA Director William Casey, Singlaub worked to raise funds for, and was involved with the sales of weapons to, the Nicaraguan Contras. This so-called private aid program was widely criticized as an attempt by the Reagan White House to circumvent a congressional ban on "directly or indirectly" aiding the Contras militarily. Nevertheless, Singlaub remains a living legend in the special forces community and is honored as a hero.

Aaron Bank earned the rank of colonel and in 1952 founded the U.S.

Army Special Forces. He is widely considered to be the "Father of the Green Berets." Lou Lajeunesse became a clockmaker and settled in Connecticut, largely refusing to talk about the war. Bob Kehoe became an analyst at the CIA; Dick Franklin worked there as a communications expert. Jean Sassi stayed in the French army and retired as a colonel. Tommy Macpherson became a businessman and was later knighted for his assistance in reorganizing the British armed services. Stewart Alsop became an influential national columnist, first at the *Saturday Evening Post* and then at *Newsweek*. Bernard Knox became one of the world's foremost classical scholars.

By Eisenhower's estimate, the Resistance force these Jeds helped to arm and train eventually engaged the Germans with the strength of fifteen divisions— three hundred thousand men. Yet the number of days by which the Jeds helped shorten the battle for France and the resulting number of lives that were saved remain untallied and unheralded. When they volunteered, the Jeds were warned that, though their missions were considered especially hazardous, there would be no fame or glory. Operation Jedburgh, they were told, would probably remain top secret for the rest of their lives. There would be no accolades in the newspapers, no stories for the grandchildren, and, for Roger Coté and the other twenty-two Jedburgh who were killed, no explanations for their families.

Though the surviving Jeds quietly received commendations and medals fifty years ago, their only lasting rewards are their private memories of their successes. Many have stayed in touch—writing letters, attending reunions— drawn together by a common secret they could discuss with no one but each other. Many of the forty or so still-surviving Jeds have not even told their stories to their children. They have grown so used to keeping the secrets that they don't know how to begin telling them now that the records have been declassified and the veil has been lifted.

Proud of their contribution to the war effort and humbled by the excesses they witnessed, the Jeds are uncommonly aware of the moral ambiguities of war. Many of them gained a new confidence and determination through their Jedburgh experience. Tommy Macpherson became self-reliant to the point of seeming remote to his friends and family. Michel de Bourbon has spent his life feeling a certain restlessness. Bill Dreux never felt the same sense of purposefulness that he felt as a Jed. Lou Lajeunesse was simply horrified by the whole experience and never wanted to talk about it again.

Some former Jeds have bookshelves crammed with any volume that makes even the most obscure reference to their work—they need to make sense of the most daring, dangerous acts of their lives. Others have done their best to forget about what they weren't allowed to discuss. Some think of Operation Jedburgh as the bravest thing they had ever done; others think of it as the most terrifying nightmare. But all of them marvel that, when the green light blinked on in their black-painted bombers, they'd actually jumped.

## ACKNOWLEDGMENTS

This project grew out of curiosity about my grandfather's secret career, first in the OSS and then in the CIA. In the preface I explained in depth why it was that my family and I became so interested in the work that my grandfather always refused to talk about. What I didn't express in the preface was my gratitude to him and his wife for, well, being my grandparents—and good ones at that—and of course for leaving enough curled-up papers and photos in their basement to whet my appetite for this project.

There must be a hundred other people of their generation to whom I also owe thanks—old friends of my grandparents who have helped with my CIA and OSS research over the years. Perhaps more important, I owe thanks to the octogenarian former members of Operation Jedburgh along with one or two OSS London branch headquarters staff who so generously gave of their time.

Joe De Francesco of Team Jim, who sadly has passed away, acted as my Jedburgh-research traffic cop. Because of the top secret nature of Operation Jedburgh, it was some thirty years before the Jeds had their first reunion. Some time after that, Joe became a kind of alumni organizer of the Jeds in the United States, and he gave me dozens of addresses and phone numbers of Jeds and their widows. He also put me in touch with Ron Brierley and Albert de Schonen, both of Team Daniel, who had kept tabs on all the British and French Jeds over the years.

Bob Kehoe, the Team Frederick radio operator, was the first of my week-long interview victims. I arrived in Boulder, Colorado, on a Monday, but it was not until around Thursday that he first asked when I might be going home. At that stage I knew barely a thing about Jedburgh, and Bob patiently explained even its most basic aspects to me. He also very kindly spent hours helping me to understand the mind-set of young men in the 1940s and what could possibly persuade them to volunteer first for the army and second for even more hazardous duty behind enemy lines.

Retired Major General Jack Singlaub of Team James was the first of the Jedburgh team leaders I met with. Like Kehoe, he patiently brought me up to speed from the officers' perspective, during both many days in his study and many phone calls over the three and a half years I have been at work on this book. His long experience in the military and in special operations also provided me with important insight. On a personal level, Jack taught me that holding vastly different political views need not stand in the way of developing a deep affection for someone. His wife, Joan, by the way, is one of the world's best cooks. Jack's James teammate Jacques de Penguilly kindly put me up in his home in Brittany and provided me with valuable French perspective.

Sir Thomas Macpherson of Team Quinine, in spite of the fact that he splits his time between homes in London and Scotland and travels extensively in connection with his still very active business interests, also spent days with me. By nature, I think, a rather private man, he happily endured some intensely personal questions about his childhood and family life. He also provided me with some of the most swashbuckling anecdotes in this book.

Jean Sassi of Team Chloroform, who retired from a career in the French army to his home in Tavergny, north of Paris, regaled me and my translator over the course of six days. He waved his arms in the air, jumped up from his chair to enact the shooting of Germans, laughed, shouted, and brought his Jedburgh story to life in a way that inspired me throughout the writing of this book.

Bernard Knox of Team Giles enthusiastically narrated both hilarious and tragic stories of his time in Brittany. When I couldn't visit, Bernard eked out his stories over a series of hour-long phone calls. His wife, Betty, very patiently put up with my visits and phone calls, though Bernard's attention was sometimes more urgently required elsewhere.

This list of Jedburghs who began by agreeing to speak with me for an hour or two and then found themselves press-ganged into feeding me and spending days with me goes on: Lou Lajeunesse of Team Norman, one of the most sensitive of the men connected with Jedburgh I met, recalled war experiences he found painful to remember and talk about. Michel de Bourbon and Arthur Brown, Macpherson's Quinine teammates, spent days with me, too.

Arthur very kindly allowed me to read and quote from his unpublished memoir of the war, and spoke to me very frankly about life at that time. Michel, at his Florida home, helped me to understand both the French perspective on Operation Jedbugh and the complex range of emotions and factors that motivated the various factions in France during the occupation. He also gave me a ride in his antique Rolls-Royce—and then made me push it when it broke down!

Dick Franklin of Team Alexander and Bill Thompson of Team Novocaine also welcomed me into their homes for days on end. Like Arthur Brown, Dick very kindly let me read his touching unpublished manuscript. Bill showed me round his town of Leavenworth, Kansas, and included me in his regular dinner and lunch engagements with his friends. Bill also had a personal album of some of the best candid pictures of the Jeds I've seen and gave me permission to reproduce a few in this book.

During the days on end I spent tapping away on my laptop while these Jeds so kindly searched their memories for stories, I developed strong feelings of affection for these men. I would like to say here that it is my most fervent hope that nothing I have written in this book offends them, for I truly like and respect all of them.

Other Jeds and family members of deceased Jeds to whom I own my gratitude but who were subjected to my questions for only hours instead of days include Ted Baumgold, Jacob Berlin, John Cox, Elmer Esch, Camille Lelong, Bob Lucas, Henry McIntosh, Roger Pierre, Jack Poché, Dick Rubenstein, Donald Spears, Mason Starring, David Stern, Gordon Tack, Ray Trumps, Patricia Alsop, Elizabeth Winthrop, Daphne Friele, Violette Desmarais, Louise Queinnec, Kay Strong, and Christopher Wise.

I also owe particular thanks to the late Paul van der Stricht, former chief of Western European Operations of OSS Special Operations in London, who had outlasted all other London branch senior staff. He entertained me regularly in his Greenwich, Connecticut, home and provided me with invaluable insights not only into the relationships between the American, British, and French shadow chiefs but also into the means by which behind-the-lines operations were linked to the needs of the main military commanders fighting in northern France.

Many other Jeds and family members of deceased Jeds kindly took the time to write sometimes very lengthy letters to me: Ron Brierley, Audrey Brown, Lura May Dillow, Anne Ellis, Donald Gibbs, Maurice Geminel, Roger Leney,

Nancy Manierre, E. Mautaint, Maurice Pirat, John Sharp, John Smallwood, Sylvia Thomson, Amanda Todd, A. A. E. Trofimov, René de la Tousche, and Robert Toussaint.

I apologize to those who gave of their time but do not find their stories mentioned in this book. The Jedburgh story is so rich that it could fill several volumes, and I regret that not all the great tales could be included. I do not in any way wish to imply that the men and stories that I have written about are somehow more valuable than others.

I also sadly regret that too many of the Jeds I talked to and corresponded with, who would have very much enjoyed seeing their stories in print, passed away before the publication of this book. To their families, I offer my condolences and apologies for taking so much time to complete this complicated work.

Two people provided me with indispensable editorial assistance, reading and rereading draft after draft. Michelle Conlin, my beautiful wife and an incredibly talented writer and editor, took time out from work to listen as I recited sections to her over the phone, even when she had her own deadlines. After giving birth, she maneuvered our new baby in one arm and this manuscript in the other to make it so much better than I could have on my own. My father, Keith Beavan, a former journalist and diplomat, caught most (I hope) of the historical and grammatical blunders that would have embarrassed me if my editor had seen them.

Writers Joanna Hershon and Matt Bai read early drafts and provided indispensable encouragement.

My assistant Allie Spiro-Winn made coming to the office tons more fun. To her goes the credit for formating the copious notes and entering probably thousands of handwritten corrections. Karen Heinzman did a wonderful job of contemporaneous translation for me during interviews with French Jedburghs and Resistance and has become a friend. Blair Morris kindly helped with translation of French correspondence.

My thanks to Wayne Fuhrman at the Humanities and Social Science Branch of the New York Public Library, Polina Ilieva of the Hoover Archives, Larry McDonald at the College Park annex of the National Archives, Carole MacCormack of the Public Records Office at Kew Gardens, Mark Seaman, formerly of the Imperial War Museum, along with the rest of the staffs at these institutions and also at the U.S. Army Center of Military History.

Clive Bassett of the Carpetbaggers Museum in Harrington, England, from where some of the black-painted bombers flew, helped bring the Jed story to life for me by driving me around old training bases and airfields.

Two little boys—or should I say young men?—Samuel and Hugo Douglas-Freeman, put me up in their home, with the permission of their parents and my lifelong friends Sarah and Michael, during trips to London. Michelle Rockler gave me a place to stay in Palo Alto.

Wendy Wolf, my editor at Viking, has been patient, kind, and—sometimes most important—funny. It was her careful use of the red pen that brought this story into focus and made it much better than I ever could have done alone. Her assistant, Clifford Corcoran, with wonderful efficiency shuffled this manuscript, together with its maps and photos, around the various Viking departments until, somehow, it emerged as a book.

I am forever grateful to my agent, Eric Simonoff, for having faith in me from the beginning, sharing my vision, and being my friend.

Finally, my heartfelt thanks to the publishing professionals at Viking who so wonderfully designed, produced, and marketed this book: production editor Bruce Giffords, jacket designer Jesse Reyes, interior designer Daniel Lagin, production director Carrie Ryan, copy editor Maureen Clark, marketing director Nancy Sheppard, and publicity director Carolyn Coleburn.

# THE JEDBURGH TEAMS AND THEIR MEMBERS

Members of each team are given in the following order: team leader, second in command, radio operator. A best effort has been made to ensure correct spelling of individual names. However, spellings of different names often vary from one official document to the next.

**ABBREVIATIONS**

CE  Captured and executed
CS  Captured and survived
K    Killed in action
W    Wounded in action
WD  Wounded in action and later died

| TEAM | MEMBERS | NAT. | NOM DE GUERRE |
|------|---------|------|---------------|
| Alan | Capt. S. R. Cannicott (W) | Br. | |
| | Lt. R. Toussaint | Fr. | A. Gairaud |
| | Lt. R. Clause | Fr. | F. de Heysen |
| Alastair | Maj. O. H. Brown | Br. | |
| | Lt. R. Karriere | Fr. | R. Maitre |
| | Sgt. G. N. Smith | Br. | |
| Alec | Lt. G. C. Thomson | U.S. | |
| | Lt. A. Bordes (WD) | Fr. | B. Allett |
| | Sgt. J. White | U.S. | |
| Alexander | Lt. S. J. O. Alsop | U.S. | |
| | Lt. R. de la Tousche | Fr. | R. Thouville |
| | Sgt. N. R. Franklin | U.S. | |

| TEAM | MEMBERS | NAT. | NOM DE GUERRE |
|---|---|---|---|
| Alfred | Capt. L. R. Macdonald | Br. | L. D. MacDougal |
| | Lt. J. Herenguel | Fr. | G. de Wavrant |
| | Sgt. A. W. Key | Br. | |
| Ammonia | Capt. B. McD. Austin | U.S. | |
| | Lt. R. Lecompte | Fr. | R. Conte |
| | Sgt. J. B. Berlin | U.S. | |
| Andrew | Maj. A. H. S. Coombe-Tennant | Br. | |
| | Lt. E. d'Oultrement | Belg. | |
| | Sgt. F. Harrison | Br. | |
| Andy | Maj. R. A. Parkinson (W) | Br. | |
| | Cdt. J. Verneuil (W) | Fr. | J. Vermeulen |
| | Sgt. G. Loosmore | Br. | |
| Anthony | Capt. M. Stasse | Fr. | C. Deprez |
| | Lt. M. B. Starring | U.S. | |
| | Sgt. J. L. Bradner | U.S. | |
| Archibald | Maj. A. du P. Denning (W) | Br. | |
| | Lt. F. Costes (W) | Fr. | A. Montlac |
| | Sgt. R. L. Pierre | U.S. | |
| Arnold | Capt. M. de Carville | Fr. | M. Coudray |
| | Capt. J. F. H. Monahan | Br. | |
| | Sgt. A. de Ville | Br | |
| Arthur | Capt. Cecil F. Mynatt (W) | U.S. | |
| | Lt. X. Humblet | Fr. | L. Hache |
| | Sgt. A. V. Bacik | U.S. | |
| Aubrey | Capt. G. Marchant | Br. | |
| | Capt. A. Chaigneau (K) | Fr. | J. Telmont |
| | Sgt. I. Hooker | Br. | |
| Augustus | Maj. J. H. Bonsall (K) | U.S. | |
| | Capt. J. Delviche (K) | Fr. | J. Decheville |
| | Sgt. R. E. Coté (K) | U.S. | |
| Basil | Capt. R. Riviere | Fr. | R. Raincourt |
| | Capt. T. A. Carew | Br. | |
| | Sgt. J. L. Stoyka | U.S. | |

| TEAM | MEMBERS | NAT. | NOM DE GUERRE |
|---|---|---|---|
| Benjamin | Maj. H. O'Bryan-Tear (W) | Br. | A. J. Forrest |
| | Lt. P. Moniez | Fr. | P. Marchand |
| | Lt. H. Kaminski (W) | Fr. | J. Camouin |
| Bernard | Capt. J. de W. Waller | Br. | |
| | Capt. E. Nasica (W) | Fr. | E. Prato |
| | Sgt. C. M. Bassett (W) | Br. | |
| Brian | Maj. F. P. C. Johnstone | Br. | |
| | Cdr. R. Cretin (W) | Fr. | R. Francomte |
| | Sgt. N. A. Smith | Br. | |
| Bruce | Maj. W. E. Colby | U.S. | |
| | Lt. C. M. Lelong | Fr. | J. P. Favel |
| | Lt. R. Villebois | Fr. | L. Giry |
| Bugatti | Maj. H. W. Fuller | U.S. | |
| | Capt. G. de la Roche | Fr. | G. Rocher |
| | Lt. M. Sigaud | Fr. | M. Guillemot |
| Bunny | Capt. J. F. D. Radice (WD) | Br. | |
| | Lt. M. Geminel (W) | Fr. | M. Gerville |
| | Sgt. J. Chambers | Br. | |
| Cecil | Maj. D. J. Nielson | Br. | |
| | Capt. A. Keser | Fr. | A. Frayant |
| | Sgt. R. Wilde | Br. | |
| Cedric | Capt. D. D. Bazata (W) | U.S. | |
| | Lt. L. Lesne | Fr. | F. Chapel |
| | Sgt. R. C. Floyd | U.S. | |
| Chloroform | Capt. J. Martin | Fr. | J. Martino |
| | Lt. H. D. McIntosh | U.S. | |
| | Lt. J. Sassi | Fr. | J. H. Nicole |
| Chrysler | Capt. C. H. Sell | Br. | |
| | Lt. P. Aussaresses | Fr. | J. Soual |
| | Sgt. R. E. Chatten | Br. | |
| Cinnamon | Capt. R. Harcourt (W) | Br. | |
| | Capt. H. Lespinasse-Fonsegrive | Fr. | F. L. Ferrandon |
| | Lt. J. Morineau | Fr. | J. Maurin |

| TEAM | MEMBERS | NAT. | NOM DE GUERRE |
|---|---|---|---|
| Citroën | Capt. J. E. St. C. Smallwood | Br. | |
| | Capt. P. Bloch | Fr. | R. Alcée |
| | Sgt. F. Bailey | Br. | |
| Clarence | Capt. A. J. Bestebreurtje (W) | Neth. | |
| | Lt. G. M. Verhaeghe (W) | U.S. | |
| | Sgt. W. W. Beynon | U.S. | |
| Claude | Lt. A. H. Todd (CS) | U.S. | |
| | Capt. H. A. Groenewoud (K) | Neth. | |
| | Sgt. C. Scott (K) | U.S. | |
| Collodion | Capt. H. Hall | Br. | |
| | Lt. H. Marsaudon | Fr. | P. Morgan |
| | Sgt. T. Baumgold | U.S. | |
| Daniel | Capt. K. D. Bennett | Br. | |
| | Lt. A. de Schonen | Fr. | |
| | Sgt. R. Brierley | Br. | |
| Daniel II | Maj. R. K. Wilson | Br. | |
| | Sgt. G. W. Mason | Br. | |
| Desmond | Capt. W. H. Pietsch Jr. | U.S. | |
| | Lt. L. G. Maunoury | Fr. | H. Bourriot |
| | Sgt. R. R. Baird | U.S. | |
| Dicing | Maj. R. Harcourt (CS) | Br. | |
| | Capt. C. J. Ruysch van Dugteren | Neth. | |
| | Capt. A. J. Bestebreurtje | Neth. | |
| | Sgt. C. C. Somers | Br. | |
| Dodge | Maj. C. E. Manierre (CS) | U.S. | |
| | Sgt. L. T. Durocher | Can. | |
| Douglas | Capt. R. A. Rubinstein | Br. | |
| | Lt. J. Roblot | Fr. | J. Ronglou |
| | Sgt. J. D. Raven | Br. | |
| Douglas II | Capt. R. A. Rubinstein | Br. | |
| | Lt. J. Roblot (K) | Fr. | J. Ronglou |
| | Sgt. J. T. Van Hart | U.S. | |

| TEAM | MEMBERS | NAT. | NOM DE GUERRE |
|---|---|---|---|
| Dudley | Maj. J. M. Olmsted | U.S. | |
| | Capt. H. Brinkgreve (K) | Neth. | |
| | Capt. J. P. Austin (CE) | Br. | |
| Edward | Capt. McC. Sollenberger | U.S. | |
| | Capt. L. Staal | Neth. | |
| | Sgt. J. Billingsley | U.S. | |
| Ephedrine | Capt. L. Donnart | Fr. | L. Rabeau |
| | Lt. L. E. Swank (K) | U.S. | |
| | Lt. R. Desplechin | Fr. | J. Bourgoin |
| Felix | Capt. J. Souquet | Fr. | J. Kernevel |
| | Capt. J. J. Marchant | Br. | |
| | Sgt. P. M. Colvin | Br. | |
| Francis | Maj. C. M. Ogden-Smith (K) | Br. | |
| | Lt. G. le Borgne | Fr. | G. le Zachmeur |
| | Sgt. A. J. Dallow | Br. | |
| Frank | Capt. A. Martelli | Fr. | A. Massoni |
| | Lt. I. Isaac | Br. | |
| | Sgt. T. Henney | Br. | |
| Frederick | Maj. A. W. Wise | Br. | |
| | Capt. P. Bloch-Auroch | Fr. | P. Aguirec |
| | Sgt. R. Kehoe | U.S. | |
| Gambling | Maj. A. J. Clutton | Br. | |
| | Capt. M. J. Knottenbelt | Neth. | |
| | CQMS* J. S. Menzies | Br. | |
| Gavin | Maj. R. Carbuccia | Fr. | D. Jeanclaude |
| | Capt. W. B. Dreux | U.S. | |
| | Lt. P. Valentini | Fr. | |
| George | Capt. P. Cyr | U.S. | |
| | Capt. P. Ragueneau | Fr. | P. Erard |
| | Lt. P. Gay | Fr. | C. Lejeune |
| George II | Capt. P. Cyr | U.S. | |
| | Capt. P. Ragueneau (W) | Fr. | P. Erard |
| | Lt. P. Gay | Fr. | C. Lejeune |

*Company Quartermaster Sergeant.

| TEAM | MEMBERS | NAT. | NOM DE GUERRE |
|---|---|---|---|
| Gerald | Capt. S. J. Knerly | U.S. | |
| | Capt. C. l'Herbette | Fr. | J. L. Beaumont |
| | Sgt. B. E. Friele | U.S. | |
| Gilbert | Capt. C. G. W. Blathwayt | Br. | |
| | Capt. P. Carron de la Carrière | Fr. | P. Charron |
| | Sgt. N. Wood | Br. | |
| Giles | Capt. B. M. W. Knox | U.S. | |
| | Capt. P. Grall | Fr. | P. Lebel |
| | Sgt. G. H. Tack | Br. | |
| Godfrey | Lt. I. Forbes | U.S. | |
| | Lt. P. Laval | Fr. | J. Morhanges |
| | Sgt. F. Hanson | U.S. | |
| Graham | Maj. M. G. M. Crosby | Br. | |
| | Capt. P. Gavet | Fr. | P. Gouvet |
| | Sgt. W. H. Adams | U.S. | |
| Gregory | Capt. K. D. Bennett (W) | Br. | |
| | Lt. P. E. A. de Schonen (W) | Fr. | |
| | Sgt. R. Brierley | Br. | |
| Guy | Capt. A. Duron | Fr. | A. Dhomas |
| | Capt. A. A. E. Trofimov | Br. | |
| | Lt. R. Groult | Fr. | J. Deschamps |
| Hamish | Lt. R. M. Anstett | U.S. | |
| | Lt. R. Schmitt | Fr. | L. Blachere |
| | Sgt. L. J. Watters | U.S. | |
| Harold | Maj. V. E. Whitty | Br. | |
| | Lt. P. Jolliet | Fr. | P. Rimbaut |
| | Sgt. H. Verlander | Br. | |
| Harry | Capt. D. D. Guthrie | Br. | |
| | Lt. P. Rousset | Fr. | P. E. Dupont |
| | Lt. R. Couture | Fr. | R. Legrand |
| Henry | Capt. S. Jean-Montcler | Fr. | S. Montcler |
| | Lt. R. E. Moore | U.S. | |
| | Sgt. V. M. Rocca | U.S. | |

| TEAM | MEMBERS | NAT. | NOM DE GUERRE |
|---|---|---|---|
| Hilary | Lt. E. Mautaint | Fr. | E. Marchant |
|  | Lt. P. H. Chadbourne | U.S. |  |
|  | Lt. R. Hervouet | Fr. | R. Pariselle |
| Horace | Capt. J. Summers | U.S. |  |
|  | Lt. G. Leclerq | Fr. | G. Levalois |
|  | Sgt. W. Zielski | U.S. |  |
| Hugh | Capt. W. R. Crawshay | Br. |  |
|  | Capt. L. l'Helgouach | Fr. | D. Legrand |
|  | Lt. R. Meyer | Fr. | R. Mersiol |
| Ian | Maj. J. J. Gildee | U.S. |  |
|  | Capt. A. Desfarges | Fr. | Y. Delorme |
|  | Sgt. L. J. Bourgoin (K) | U.S. |  |
| Isaac | Lt. Col. J. R. H. Hutchison | Br. | J. Hastings |
|  | Lt. Col. F. G. Viat | Fr. |  |
|  | Sgt. J. Sharp | Br. |  |
| Ivor | Capt. J. H. Cox | Br. |  |
|  | Lt. R. Colin | Fr. | Y. M. Dantec |
|  | Sgt. L. F. Goddard (K) | U.S. |  |
| Jacob | Capt. V. A. Gough (CE) | Br. |  |
|  | Lt. M. Boissarie (K) | Fr. | G. Baraud |
|  | Sgt. K. Seymour (CS) | Br. |  |
| James | Lt. J. K. Singlaub | U.S. |  |
|  | Lt. J. le Bel de Penguilly | Fr. | D. Leb |
|  | Sgt. A. J. Denneau | U.S. |  |
| Jeremy | Capt. G. M. Hallowes | Br. |  |
|  | Lt. H. C. Giese | Fr. | H. Fontcroise |
|  | Sgt. R. A. Leney | Br. |  |
| Jim | Capt. P. W. Donovan | U.S. |  |
|  | Lt. J. A. de Francesco | Fr. | J. Lavige |
|  | Sgt. M. F. Heneley | U.S. |  |
| John | Capt. D. L. Stern | Br. |  |
|  | Lt. M. de Galbert | Fr. | J. Lerocher |
|  | Sgt. D. Gibbs | Br. |  |

| TEAM | MEMBERS | NAT. | NOM DE GUERRE |
|---|---|---|---|
| Jude | Capt. W. L. O. Evans | Br. | |
| | Capt. J. Larrieu | Fr. | J. Lavisme |
| | Sgt. A. E. Holdham | Br. | |
| Julian | Maj. A. H. Clutton | Br. | |
| | Lt. J. Vermot | Fr. | J. Brouillard |
| | CQMS J. S. Menzies | Br. | |
| Julian II | Capt. J. P. Souquet | Fr. | J. Kernevel |
| | Lt. P. Scherrer | Fr. | P. Sauvage |
| | Lt. R. Meyer | Fr. | R. Mersiol |
| Lee | Capt. C. E. Brown | U.S. | |
| | Capt. P. Angoulvent (K) | Fr. | N. Viguier |
| | Lt. M. Pirat | Fr. | A. Chevalier |
| Mark | Capt. L. E. Conein | U.S. | |
| | Lt. J. Thevenet | Fr. | F. G. Thevemet |
| | Sgt. J. J. Carpenter | U.S. | |
| Martin | Capt. T. A. Mellows (WD) | Br. | |
| | Lt. G. Redonnet | Fr. | G. Remond |
| | Sgt. N. E. S. Carey | Br. | |
| Masque | Capt. N. E. Guillot | U.S. | |
| | Lt. J. Bouvery | Fr. | J. Gramont |
| | Sgt. F. M. Poche | U.S. | |
| Maurice | Capt. C. M. Carman | U.S. | |
| | Lt. H. Reveilhac | Fr. | H. Humesnil |
| | Sgt. F. J. Cole | U.S. | |
| Miles | Capt. E. T. Allen | U.S. | |
| | Lt. R. Estève | Fr. | P. Fourcade |
| | Sgt. A. Gruen | U.S. | |
| Minaret | Maj. L. C. M. Hartley-Sharpe | Br. | |
| | Capt. P. Cros | Fr. | P. Muton |
| | Sgt. J. W. Ellis | Br. | |
| Monocle | Capt. J. Fiardo | Fr. | J. Tozel |
| | Lt. R. H. Foster | U.S. | |
| | Sgt. R. J. Anderson | U.S. | |

| TEAM | MEMBERS | NAT. | NOM DE GUERRE |
|------|---------|------|---------------|
| Nicholas | Capt. J. C. C. Maude | Br. | |
| | Lt. H. Penin | Fr. | H. Puget |
| | Sgt. M. A. Whittle | Br. | |
| Norman | Lt. M. Lautier | Fr. | F. Bataille |
| | Lt. K. C. Dillow | U.S. | |
| | Sgt. L. E. Lajeunesse | U.S. | |
| Novocaine | Lt. C. J. Gennerich | U.S. | |
| | Lt. J.-Y. Pronost | Fr. | J. Lelann |
| | Sgt. W. Thompson | U.S. | |
| Packard | Capt. A. Bank | U.S. | |
| | Lt. H. Denis | Fr. | C. Boineau |
| | Lt. F. Montfort | Can. | |
| Paul | Maj. E. M. H. Hood | Br. | |
| | Lt. M. Vallée | Fr. | P. Cormier |
| | Sgt. K. J. W. Brown | Br. | |
| Philip | Capt. C. J. Liberos | Fr. | J. G. de Rouen |
| | Lt. R. A. Lucas | U.S. | |
| | Sgt. J. M. Orgat | U.S. | |
| Quentin | Capt. R. S. Fenton | Br. | |
| | LT J. Raux | Fr. | J. Lassere |
| | Sgt. D. Rawson | Br. | |
| Quinine | Maj. R. T. S. Macpherson | Br. | |
| | Lt. M. de Bourbon-Parme | Fr. | M. Bourdon |
| | Sgt. O. A. Brown | Br. | |
| Raymond | Capt. R. Dehosses | Fr. | R. Waguet |
| | Lt. H. Cadilhac | Fr. | H. Chaulais |
| | Sgt. W. Adams | Br. | |
| Roderick | Capt. J. Preziosi | Fr. | J. Paoli |
| | Lt. W. C. Boggs | U.S. | |
| | Sgt. C. P. Mersereau | U.S. | |
| Ronald | Lt. S. R. Trumps | U.S. | |
| | Lt. G. Deseilligny | Fr. | G. Dartigues |
| | Sgt. E. B. Esch | U.S. | |

| TEAM | MEMBERS | NAT. | NOM DE GUERRE |
|---|---|---|---|
| Sceptre | Lt. W. C. Hanna | U.S. | |
| | Lt. F. Franceschi | Fr. | F. Tevenac |
| | Sgt. H. V. Palmer | U.S. | |
| Scion | Maj. O. P. Grenfell | Br. | |
| | Lt. R. Gruppo | Fr. | G. Revard |
| | Sgt. T. Cain | Br. | |
| Simon | Capt. A. W. C. Coomber | Br. | |
| | Capt. M. Fouere (K) | Fr. | M. Fontaine |
| | Sgt. C. Somers | Br. | |
| Stanley | Capt. O. E. Craster | Br. | |
| | Lt. R. Cantais | Fr. | R. Carliere |
| | Sgt. E. J. Grinham | Br. | |
| Stanley II | Capt. A. J. Bestebreurtje | Neth. | |
| | Capt. P. C. H. Vickery | Br. | |
| | Sgt. W. W. Beynon | U.S. | |
| Timothy | Capt. L. Moutte | Fr. | L. Ambel |
| | Lt. R. G. Mundinger | U.S. | |
| | Lt. R. T. Heyns (W) | U.S. | |
| | Sgt. D. A. Spears | U.S. | |
| Tony | Maj. R. K. Montgomery | U.S. | |
| | Lt. M. Paris | Fr. | M. Devailly |
| | Sgt. J. E. McGowan | U.S. | |
| Veganin | Major N. Marten | Br. | |
| | Capt. G. Vuchot (K) | Fr. | C. L. Noir |
| | Sgt. J. Gardner (K) | Br. | |
| Willys | Capt. G. Marchal | Fr. | P. J. Granier |
| | Capt. J. C. C. Montague | Br. | |
| | Sgt. T. Cornick | Br. | |

# NOTES

Full details of works cited may be found in the sources, beginning on page 365. For abbreviations used in the notes, see page 365.

## PREFACE

xvii. **Gerry Miller:** Except where noted, information about Gerry Miller is derived from personal recollection and private conversations with his family, friends, and former colleagues.

xviii. **"Proud to be":** Inscription in the Miller guest book.

xviii. **"accepted Gerry Miller's":** Colby and Forbath, *Honorable Men*, 455.

xix. **Daniel Schorr:** In *Man Who Kept the Secrets*, 288–92, Powers gives an account of events leading up to Schorr's revelation.

xix. **Church . . . investigated:** See *Interim Report* and *Final Report* of the Church committee.

xix. **assassination attempts:** *Interim Report* of the Church committee, throughout.

xix. **mind-control experiments:** *Final Report* of the Church committee, book 1, 386.

xix. **Salvador Allende:** Ibid., 143, 151, and 154.

xix. **trial for his atrocities:** Associated Press, "Pinochet Indicted on Human Rights Charges"; *New York Times* editorial, "Trial for General Pinochet."

xix. **"crash course":** Powers, *Intelligence Wars*, xvi.

xx. **which he spent in Office of Strategic Services (OSS):** This much he would say, and it is confirmed by numerous documents in the OSS collection, RG 226, NARA.

xx. **medal was awarded in 2004:** Sanger, "War Figures Honored with Medal of Freedom."

xxi. **my grandfather was first:** War Diary, vol. 1, 98.

xxi. **"[W]ithout their great assistance":** Eisenhower, *Crusade in Europe*, 296.

xxi. **Truman disbanded the OSS:** For excellent histories of the OSS, see B. Smith, *Shadow Warriors*, and R. H. Smith, *OSS*.

xxi. **investment banking:** Miller's curriculum vitae.

xxi. **The Soviet army ... the atom bomb:** *Final Report,* book 1, 20–23.

xxii. **one-third staffed:** Ibid., book 4, 28.

xxii. **preeminent activity:** Ibid., 27–29; Powers, *Intelligence Wars,* 18–20.

xxii. **"stay-behind" networks:** Colby and Forbath, *Honorable Men,* 81–84.

xxii. **job of chief:** "Notification of Personnel Action," Sept. 28, 1950.

xxii. **station chief:** Colby and Forbath, *Honorable Men,* 109; "Notification of Personnel Action," Aug. 7, 1956.

xxii. **"CIA's largest":** Colby and Forbath, *Honorable Men,* 109.

xxiii. **chief of operational services:** "Fitness Report" on Gerald E. Miller, Mar. 31, 1965.

xxiii. **support Afghan resistance:** Coll, *Ghost Wars,* 58.

xxiii. **1981:** Ibid., 90.

xxiii. **revived the idea:** "Sufferings of Afghanistan."

xxiii. **jihad sales pitch:** Weaver, "Blowback."

xxiii. **recruited and raised funds:** Beardon, "Afghanistan"; *9/11 Commission Report,* 55.

xxiii. **millions ... training:** "Sufferings of Afghantistan"; Weaver, "Blowback"; Coll, *Ghost Wars,* throughout.

xxiii. **Tora Bora:** Liu, "Fortress Tora Bora."

xxiv. **"Afghan freedom fighters":** Coll, *Ghost Wars,* 97.

xxiv. **The Soviets withdrew ... ending half a century of Communism:** Beardon, "Afghanistan."

xxiv. **1998 car bombing ... 9/11 attacks:** Ibid.; *9/11 Commission Report,* 55–61.

xxv. **Department of Defense:** S. Hersh, "Coming Wars."

xxv. **moral authority:** R. H. Smith, *OSS,* 362.

xxv. **playbook:** Ibid., 361–83.

## CHAPTER ONE: SHADOW WAR SETBACK

3. **Odette Sansom entered:** This account of the incarceration and interrogation of Odette Sansom (later Odette Hallowes) is largely taken from *Odette,* 236–71, by Jerrard Tickell, with whom Odette cooperated, and from the war memoirs of Hugo Bleicher, *Colonel Henri's Story,* 96–103.

3. **"I still have nothing to say":** Quoted in Tickell, *Odette,* 258.

3. *Les souris:* Ibid., 243.

3. **"The Gestapo will send for you":** Ibid., 259.

4. **Bleicher's Abwehr:** Foot, *SOE in France,* 115–20, gives an overview of the German security operations in France. Bleicher, *Colonel Henri's Story,* 48–49 and throughout, details the rivalry between the SD and the Abwehr, and the difference in their interrogation methods.

4. **A mop ... shaped eyes:** P. Churchill, *Duel of Wits,* 225; Tickell, *Odette,* photo at frontispiece.

4. **married ... World War I:** "Odette Hallowes," *Times* obit; Foot, "Odette Hallowes," obit.

4. **"For a friend":** Quoted in Tickell, *Odette,* 258.

5. **"There is no point":** Ibid., 261.

5. **A couple of weeks earlier:** Marks, *Between Silk and Cyanide*, 283.

5. **Station 53:** Ibid., 12; Foot, *SOE in France,* 157; Mackenzie, *Secret History of SOE,* 737.

5. **twenty-year-old-member . . . FANY:** In *Secret History of SOE,* 736, Mackenzie says the radio operators were FANYs; in *Between Silk and Cyanide,* 19, Marks says their average age was twenty.

5. **Five minutes later:** According to Foot, *SOE in France,* 151, transmissions from agents were limited to five minutes to prevent the Germans from zeroing in on them.

5. **dispatch rider:** The procedure for receiving, decoding, and delivering radio messages is taken from Buckmaster, *They Fought Alone,* 59–60.

5. **back door:** Cookridge, *Set Europe Ablaze,* 19.

5. **lift:** Buckmaster, *They Fought Alone,* 11.

5. **64 Baker Street:** The location of the various SOE headquarters is discussed in Foot, *SOE in France,* 35; West, *Secret War,* 30; Cookridge, *Set Europe Ablaze,* 19–20.

5. **"Inter-Services Research Bureau":** Cookridge, *Set Europe Ablaze,* 20. For a discussion of the SOE's cover names, see Foot, *SOE in France,* 11.

5. **British chiefs of staff:** Chiefs of Staff, "Special Operations Executive Directive for 1943," Mar. 20, 1943, reprinted in Stafford, *Britain,* 248–57.

5. **1942 assassination . . . atomic bomb program:** Morris, "Mission Impossible."

6. **thirteen thousand people:** Mackenzie, *Secret Hisoty of SOE,* 719.

6. **Norway to Burma:** Butler, *Amateur Agent,* 75.

6. **most important:** Mackenzie, *Secret History of SOE,* 222–23.

6. **April 17:** Marks, *Between Silk and Cyanide,* 283.

6. **leafing:** This scene is a typical one for Buckmaster, taken from a number of sources, but it is my own assumption that he was in his office at the time that the radio message in question arrived in England.

6. **thirty-seven . . . Ford Motor Company office:** Howarth, *Undercover,* 186–87.

6. **". . . *Vive la France"*:** Buckmaster, *Specially Employed,* 14; W. Churchill, *Their Finest Hour,* 510–11.

6. **Buckmaster searched:** Buckmaster, *Specially Employed,* 14.

6–7. **He had fought . . . in September 1940:** Howarth, *Undercover,* 186–87.

7. **smoked Gauloises:** Tickell, *Odette,* 81.

7. **By September 1941:** Buckmaster, *They Fought Alone,* 20.

7. **"Buck":** Tickell, *Odette,* throughout.

7. **against you:** Cookridge, *Set Europe Ablaze,* 56.

7. **silver compact:** Tickell, *Odette,* 122.

7. **". . . hock it":** Howarth, *Undercover,* 187.

7. **personal attachment:** Cookridge, *Set Europe Ablaze,* 56.

7. **Rabinovitch:** Marks, *Between Silk and Cyanide,* 283; Foot, *SOE in France,* 252.

7. **extraordinary hope:** Stafford, *Britain,* 93.

8. **threw into disarray:** West, *Secret War,* 161: "The sad fact is that for all the sacrifices of 1942 and 1943, F Section [one of two SOE sections working in France]

approached the critical New Year of 1944 with the prospect of an Allied invasion, in a state of disarray, having seen most of its circuits wound up or penetrated by the enemy."

8. *panier à salade:* This continued account of the incarceration and interrogation of Odette Sansom (later Odette Hallowes) is largely taken from *Odette*, 236–71, by Jerrard Tickell, and from Hugo Bleicher, *Colonel Henri's Story*, 96–103.

8. **hid a potato:** Ibid., 264.

8. **I have nothing to say:** Although Tickell's *Odette* discusses this preliminary interview at 84 avenue Foche, it gives only general details of the topics discussed. Therefore, assuming these preliminary interviews of SOE agents at avenue Foche all followed a similar form, I have reconstructed this dialogue from that given in other accounts, most particularly that of Wing Commander F. F. E. Yeo-Thomas in Bruce Marshall, *White Rabbit*, 113, and from other of Odette's interviews described by Tickell.

9. **"I am so hungry":** Quoted in Tickell, *Odette*, 265.

## CHAPTER TWO: RESISTANCE? WHAT RESISTANCE?

10. **scheme to arm:** This discussion about Winston Churchill's decision to form the SOE and the reasons behind it is largely taken from West, *Secret War*, 21–28; Foot, *SOE in France*, 6–10; Stafford, *Britain*, 10–27; Cookridge, *Set Europe Ablaze*, 1–6.

10. **340,000 exhausted men:** Keegan, *Second World War*, 81.

10. **Messerschmitt:** Described to me by Jean Sassi (June 12, 2002), who was there.

10. **Churchill . . . debated:** For an excellent account of this debate, see Lukacs, *Five Days in London*.

11. **"creation of widespread revolt":** Quoted in Foot, *SOE in France*, 6.

11. **keep the German army overextended:** The elements of this strategy were contained in a paper entitled "British Strategy in a Certain Eventuality," presented by the chiefs of staff to Churchill on May 25, 1940; see ibid., 6–7.

11. **"stimulate the seeds of revolt":** Cookridge, *Set Europe Ablaze*, 2.

11. **development . . . two-way radio:** War Diary, vol. 6, i: "The airplane with the help of modern communication has made practical the transfer of large quantities of stores and troops to selected points difficult for the enemy to detect or guard."

11. **reduced conventional force . . . devastating:** Stafford, *Britain*, 10–11.

11. **Churchill established:** For far more detailed histories of the SOE's formation, see Cookridge, *Set Europe Ablaze*, 1–18; West, *Secret War*, 1–28; Foot, *SOE in France*, 1–11; and Mackenzie, *Secret History of SOE*, 1–56.

11. **"set Europe ablaze":** Dalton, *Fateful Years*, 366.

12. **". . . lessen her misfortune":** Ousby, *Occupation*, 59.

12. **". . . le combat":** Ibid., 60.

12. **rebel . . . two-thirds:** Ibid., 63–66.

12. **General Charles de Gaulle:** This discussion of the structure of the SOE's operations into France is taken from Foot, *SOE in France*, 19–22, and Mackenzie, *Secret History of SOE*, 228–34.

12. **". . . defeat final and irremediable":** De Gaulle, *Speeches*, 1.

13. **forbade Free French sabotage:** Vomecourt, *Army of Amateurs*, 22.
13. **SOE's new "independent French":** Foot, *SOE in France*, 20.
13. **When the general . . . secret networks:** Ibid., 21–24.
13. **Buckmaster . . . common enemies notwithstanding:** Ibid., 20.
13. **safely keep its secrets:** De Gaulle led the expedition to Dakar, and it was said that the failure of the expedition resulted from secrets leaking from his headquarters. British officialdom decided that the security of the Free French should not be relied upon; see ibid., xviii.
13. **clandestine army:** The two types of work are discussed in ibid., 149–50.
13. **a chance to crawl up the beaches:** For discussion of the evolution of what the SOE called its "detonator concept," see Stafford, *Britain*, 28–49.
14. **Operation Savanna:** Ibid., 56; Mackenzie, *Secret History of SOE*, 244–45; Foot, *SOE in France*, 154.
14. **Josephine B:** Mackenzie, *Secret History of SOE*, 244–46.
14. **refused to jump:** Foot, *SOE in France*, 50; West, *Secret War*, 56.
14. **disappeared:** Foot, *SOE in France*, 161–62.
14. **air raid:** West, *Secret War*, 41; Foot, *SOE in France*, 161.
14. **foothold:** Foot, *SOE in France*, 161.
14. *attentisme:* Jackson, *France*, 239: "Only a tiny minority of people were actively involved in political collaboration . . . Only a small minority were actively involved in organized Resistance. . . . The large majority . . . were actively involved in neither, and often described as *attentiste*."
14. *"Ils sont corrects":* Ousby, *Occupation*, 103.
15. **Mers el-Kébir:** Ibid., 76–77.
15. **the shadow war . . . had hardly begun:** Foot, *SOE in France*, 161.

## CHAPTER THREE: A SPARK OF REBELLION
16. **shot the Russians dead:** Associated Press reporter Frederick Oeschner, quoted in D. Miller and Commager, *World War II*, 61.
16. **June 22, 1941 . . . balance of the war:** Ibid., 58–59.
16. **Barbès-Rochechouart:** Ousby, *Occupation*, 223.
17. **". . . saboteurs working underground":** Stafford, *Britain*, 68.
17. **Within two weeks . . . end of November:** Ousby, *Occupation*, 225–26.
17. **Germans shot . . . military adviser:** Ibid., 226.
17. **seventy attacks:** Ibid., 225.
18. **October 20, 1941:** Mackenzie, *Secret History of SOE*, 265.
18. **Jean Moulin:** For an excellent account of Moulin's life and work, see Marnham, *Resistance and Betrayal.*
18. **". . . hundreds of thousands":** Moulin's report to de Gaulle entitled "Report on the Activities, Plans and Requirements of the Groups Formed in France with a View to the Eventual Liberation of the Country," reproduced in Foot, *SOE in France*, 489–98.
18. **united Resistance fight:** Mackenzie, *Secret History of SOE*, 273.
18. **spymasters:** Stafford, *Britain*, 72–73.
18. **Vichy France's . . . Armistice Army:** Ibid., 93.
18. **ambassador to . . . the Resistance:** Ibid., 72–73.

18. **twenty-seven new agents:** Ibid., 71.

18. **rate of arms:** Foot, *SOE in France*, 473.

18. **André Girard:** The Carte episode is taken from ibid., 204–11 and 255–57, and Stafford, *Britain*, 92–93.

19. **Carte network:** Mackenzie, *Secret History of SOE*, 254 and 267–68.

19. **Churchill had in mind:** Before Churchill formed the SOE, when he first tried to convince the leaders of the crumbling French government to resist, he suggested that the French army itself should break up into thousands of tiny guerrilla cells around France; see W. Churchill, *Their Finest Hour*, 153.

19. **British chiefs of staff:** Stafford, *Britain*, 92–93.

19. **first priority:** Ibid., 92, and Foot, *SOE in France*, 207.

19. **In July 1942 . . . its skin:** Tickell, *Odette*, 105.

19. **organize Carte's secret army:** For complete histories of the Carte network and its importance to SOE planning, see Foot, *SOE in France*, 204–11 and elsewhere; Cookridge, *Set Europe Ablaze*, 98–114; West, *Secret War*, 138–41; Stafford, *Britain*, 92–93. See P. Churchill, *Duel of Wits*, and Tickell, *Odette*, for firsthand reminiscences of the agents' experiences.

19. **locked their weapons:** Foot, *SOE in France*, 210; Mackenzie, *Secret History of SOE*, 565.

20. **lost a briefcase:** Foot, *SOE in France*, 205 and 251–53; West, *Secret War*, 139; Cookridge, *Set Europe Ablaze*, 106–14; and Bleicher, *Colonel Henri's Story*, 74 onward, discuss the loss of the briefcase by André Marsac (code-named End) in November 1942, and its devastating, far-reaching consequences.

20. **April 15, 1943:** Foot, *SOE in France*, 252.

20. **greatest hope:** Carte's collapse, according to the SOE's official historian, was a "dream which had been broken"; see Mackenzie, *Secret History*, 568.

20. **Allied orders:** For an overview of the Allied plans for the French Resistance, see Casey, *Secret War*, 69–102. The evolution of strategy for use of the Resistance and its coordination with the Allied landings is the entire subject of Stafford, *Britain*.

20. **"You wasted":** The dialogue is a shortened version of what appears in Tickell, *Odette*, 266–68.

## CHAPTER FOUR: UNCLE SAM JOINS IN

23. **Back in July 1940:** This discussion of the events leading up to Bill Donovan's formation of the COI is largely taken from B. Smith, *Shadow Warriors*, 30–68; S. Alsop and Braden, *Sub Rosa*, 10–18; Ford, *Donovan*, 88–109; A. C. Brown, *"C,"* various; and West, *MI6*, various.

23. **if he had not been Catholic:** A. C. Brown, *"C,"* 265.

23. **Pan Am Clipper:** Ibid., 264.

23. **Brits showed:** Ford, *Donovan*, 91.

24. **King George VI:** West, *MI6*, 204.

24. **Churchill expounded:** A. C. Brown, *"C,"* 355.

24. **Churchill also emphasized:** Ibid., 355.

24. **Donovan met . . . Secret Intelligence Service:** West, *MI6*, 140.

24. **endorsed the use of agents provocateurs:** A. C. Brown, *"C,"* 355.

24. **eight separate espionage outfits:** S. Alsop and Braden, *Sub Rosa,* 14.
24. **"Service of Strategic Information":** West, *MI6,* 207.
24. **"unlimited national emergency":** A. C. Brown, *"C,"* 358.
25. **"the spirit of revolt":** West, *MI6,* 209.
25. **Special Operations branch of the COI:** Originally, the SO branch had the name Special Activities Goodfellow (SAG) after the man who headed it. Similarly, Secret Intelligence had the name Special Activities Bruce (SAB); see Ford, *Donovan,* 111.
25. **employed thirteen thousand:** S. Alsop and Braden, *Sub Rosa,* 17.
25. **Donovan-Hambro Accord:** B. Smith, *Shadow Warriors,* 170–73; Jakub, *Spies and Saboteurs,* 49–60 and 79–82; and the War Diary, vol. 1, xiv–xxxiii, set forth the evolving agreements between the OSS's SO and the SOE regarding areas of operation. The two important agreements, the Donovan-Hambro Accord of June 1942 and the operational revisions of January 1943, are reproduced in the War Diary, vol. 12, 16–28 and 29–31.
25. **Britain's backyard:** The collaboration and rivalry of the British and American intelligence and special operations services is the subject of Jakub, *Spies and Saboteurs.*
25. **Roosevelt detested de Gaulle:** Ibid., 151.
25. **independent and open:** Ibid., 91.
26. **Churchill would not have appreciated:** Ibid., 91.
26. **Donovan now wanted his own agents:** War Diary, vol. 1, iii.
26. **Donovan's Special Operations . . . sections of the SOE:** "SOE and SO London (Operational Arrangements)," agreement signed by SOE head Charles Hambro and OSS SO chief Colonel Huntington; see ibid., vol. 12, 30.
26. **Americans arrived at Baker Street:** R. H. Smith, *OSS,* 166; Jakub, *Spies and Saboteurs,* 154.
26. **"jeunes filles":** Casey, *Secret War,* 22.
26. **Franklin Canfield:** A brief biographical sketch of Canfield can be found in War Diary, Special Operations Branch, OSS London, vol. 11, 5.
26. **time to go home:** Canfield, *Memoirs,* 12–15.
27. **I don't want to drown:** Ibid., 14–15.
27. **Canfield joined . . . Special Operations branch:** Ibid., 17–18.
27. **cold winter morning:** Donovan, in fact, originally sent Canfield, via London, to Gibraltar to go into North Africa with the invasion, but the State Department blocked the plan, and Canfield returned to London to take his place there; see ibid., 22–23.
27. **two similarly inexperienced Donovan envoys:** R. H. Smith, *OSS,* 166; Bross, *Secret Operations,* 12–13; Canfield, *Memoirs,* 23–24; van der Stricht, author interview, Dec. 28, 2001.
27. **nearly 120 agents in France:** Buckmaster, *They Fought Alone,* 55.
27. **But the war experiences . . . only weeks old:** Canfield, *Memoirs,* 10; Bross, *Secret Operations,* 88; van der Stricht, author interview, Dec. 28, 2001.
27. **cum laude degree:** Canfield, *Memoirs,* 7 and 9.
27. **God save everyone:** The discussion of the tension between American and British staff officers of the OSS SO and the SOE in London is taken from a wide va-

riety of sources, but it is most succinctly put by Canfield's OSS SO colleague
John Bross in *Secret Operations,* 55–56: "With one or two exceptions, Americans assigned to work in the [SOE] country sections felt . . . generally unhappy.
This was partly the fault of the Americans themselves with little preparation for
their assignments. . . . It was difficult for the Americans to pick up these responsibilities nor . . . were they encouraged to do so by their English colleagues who
made their impatience with what they regarded as ignorant and incompetent
American interference abundantly clear. Moreover it was clearly British policy
to restrict American access to and influence over France and Scandinavian resistance groups.

28. **had little desire to supervise:** Ibid., 12–30 and 42–59; van der Stricht, letter to
R. Harris Smith, Apr. 14, 1971, Charles Carman Collection, Hoover. Back-and-
forth memos between van der Stricht and his opposite number in the SOE,
Robin Brook, demonstrate how difficult it was for the SO and SOE staffs to settle on mutually agreeable arrangements; see War Diary, vol. 3, vi–vii.

28. **by circling them through:** Bross, *Secret Operations,* 16.

28. **"O double S":** Ibid., 15.

28. **the Americans could do better:** Van der Stricht, author interview, Dec. 28,
2001.

28. **Mike Rowlandson:** Canfield, *Memoirs,* 24.

28. **Control and Dispatch:** War Diary, vol. 2, xxii.

28. **Canfield observed:** Ibid.; Bross, *Secret Operations,* 31.

28. **Exercise Spartan:** Historical Officer—Canadian Military Headquarters, "Report No. 94," para. 1.

28. **for the first time in World War II:** Ibid., para. 5.

28–29. **largest offensive military exercise:** Ibid.

29. **invited not only Canfield:** SOE, History of Jedburghs, part I, 9.

29. **Spartan scenario:** Historical Officer, "Report No. 94," para. 10; A. Brown, *Jedburghs,* 3; War Diary, vol. 4, x–xi.

29. **As this faux battle . . . military effort:** SOE, History of Jedburghs, part I, 7; War
Diary, vol. 4, x.

29. **But Rowlandson . . . D-Day uprising:** Use of the fusiliers in Spartan is described in War Diary, vol. 4, x–xi.

29–30. **Canfield and his . . . toward the front:** Ibid.

30. **"indoctrinated":** SOE, History of Jedburghs, part I, insert between 4 and 5.

30. **Operation Sledgehammer:** The origin of the Jedburgh concept and the adop-
tion of its code name is described in ibid., part I, 1–5; A. Brown, *Jedburghs,* 1–2;
and War Diary, vol. 4, i–ii.

30. **given the name:** Anonymous, "Jedburgh." There has been much, probably
erroneous, speculation about the origin of the Jedburgh code name. Most
likely, an SOE security officer chose the name randomly from a preapproved list
of code names, according to common practice, from a random list of words; see
War Diary, vol. 4, i.

30. **Operation Jedburgh:** SOE, History of Jedburghs, part I, 1–9; War Diary, vol. 4,
xii–xvi.

31. **six hundred men:** A. Brown, *Jedburghs,* 6. Detailed breakdowns of the various

duties of the large force can be found in SOE, History of Jedburghs, and War Diary, vol. 4.

31. **fished dry:** A. Brown, *Jedburghs,* 8.

31. **the largest ... operation:** This is my own assertion, but given that, according to Foot, *SOE in France,* 20, a total of about sixteen hundred agents dropped into France, and since the group discussed in this book amounted to just under three hundred, or about 18 percent of the total, I think it is fair.

31. **very backbone of the Resistance:** One of the officers in charge of overseeing the new group of agents wrote that they "may be the backbone of the Resistance movement after D-Day, by which time . . . many of the present leaders will be 'blown' "; see "Jedburghs," OSS memo.

## CHAPTER FIVE: A SLIM CHANCE

35. **balanced a rifle:** Lou Lajeunesse told me the story of his recruitment on the first of my visits with him (May 28, 2002) and again on Aug. 12, 2002.

35. **Fort Wadsworth:** Ibid.; National Park Service, "Fort Wadsworth."

35. **sweltering summer:** The summer of 1943 was New York City's second hottest in thirty years; see National Climatic Data Center, "New York Climate Summary."

35. **five hundred warships:** Meany, "Port in a Storm."

35. **U-boat "wolf packs":** Anonymous, "Nazi U-Boats Attack New York Shipping."

35. **technical network:** Lajeunesse, author interview, May 28, 2002; Anonymous, "Fort Tilden's Harbor Entrance Control Post."

36. **Lajeunesse strong-armed him:** Lajeunesse, author interviews, May 28 and Aug. 12, 2002.

36. **"We have orders":** Ibid. Dialogue from recollections of Lajeunesse.

37. **"How did . . . speak French?":** Ibid. Dialogue between Lajeunesse and the colonel in the glass room from recollections of Lajeunesse.

37. **Like many French Canadians ... out of reach:** Ibid.

37. **pitched their vital plan:** War Diary, vol. 4, xvii.

37. **highest priority:** R. H. Smith, *OSS,* 174.

37. **personnel quotas:** K. Roosevelt, *War Report of the OSS,* vol. 1, 210.

37. **Lajeunesse's temperament:** Lajeunesse, author interviews, May 28 and Aug. 12, 2002.

38. **the phone rang:** Ibid., May 28, 2002.

38. **Altoona:** Ibid., Aug. 12, 2002.

38. **The interview was over:** Ibid., May 28 and Aug. 12, 2002.

39. **Knox would have risked anything:** This story and Bernard Knox's biographical information are taken from his conversations with me (Feb. 15, Mar. 21, and May 3, 2002), from his *Essays,* xi–xxiii, and from his lecture "Premature Anti-Fascist."

40. **unemployment stood at 23 percent:** Knox, *Essays,* xvi.

40. **Knox became a Communist:** The British traitors Donald Maclean and Kim Philby were also Communist activists at Cambridge during Knox's time there, though he never met them. Knox told me, Feb. 15, 2002, that the FBI interviewed him about his activities at Cambridge after Philby's exposure in 1961.

41. **cost half a million lives:** *Microsoft Encarta Online Encyclopedia,* s.v. "Spanish Civil War," http://encarta.msn.com/text_761580634_0/Spanish_Civil_War.html (accessed Apr. 20, 2005).

41. **"I've moved heaven":** Quote related to me by Bernard Knox (May 3, 2002).

42. **"Miss King":** Knox, *Essays,* xxii.

43. **fifty speedy radio operators:** War Diary, vol. 4, xix.

43. **uniquely qualified . . . officers:** Ibid., xviii.

43. **"Success of the plan":** Ibid., xvii.

43. **Prosper network:** The destruction of Prosper is discussed in Cookridge, *Set Europe Ablaze,* 133–53; Foot, *SOE in France,* 307–22; West, *Secret War,* 141–54.

43. **massacred . . . fifteen hundred:** West, *Secret War,* 154.

43. **arrested him and fourteen other key leaders:** Mackenzie, *Secret History of SOE,* 590–91; Foot, *SOE in France,* 238–40.

43. **Lieutenant General Frederick Morgan:** War Diary, vol. 4, xiv.

44. **"I have agreed in principle":** Ibid., xiv.

44. **Lieutenant General Jacob Devers:** Ibid., xv.

44. **September 4, 1943:** Ibid., xvii.

44. **flew to Washington:** A recruitment drive among American forces in the United Kingdom had turned out to be useless; see ibid., vol. 2, xviii.

44. **on August 11:** Ibid., xiii.

44. **no later than New Year's Day:** Ibid., vol. 12, 120; R. H. Smith, *OSS,* 175, and others give credit for the recruitment of the American Jedburghs to George Sharp, the Washington-based Area Operations Officer for Western Europe, but Smith wrote his book long before the declassification of the OSS War Diary. While the War Diary pages pertaining to Jedburgh recruitment (vol. 4, xvi–xxii) make clear that Sharp was involved in Jedburgh recruitment, it also demonstrates that Canfield had been appointed the U.S. officer responsible in all matters concerning Jedburghs and that he took overall charge of the recruitment drive.

## CHAPTER SIX: ANYONE HERE SPEAK FRENCH?

45. **Fort Monmouth:** This description of conditions and the mood at Fort Monmouth is taken from my interview with Ted Baumgold (Aug. 21, 2002) and from Dick Franklin's memoir, "Jedburg," 137.

45. **"Any of you guys":** I quote the lieutenant's words as Ted Baumgold remembered them (Aug. 21, 2002).

45. **New York family:** Ibid.

46. **obsolete hangars:** Reed, "Evaluation of Selected Cultural Resources at Fort Monmouth, New Jersey"; Patterson Army Health Clinic, "Fort Monmouth Landmarks."

46. **". . . smoke a cigarette":** Baumgold, author interview, Aug. 21, 2002.

46. **one hundred:** War Diary, vol. 4, xxii.

46. **"pianists":** Cookridge, *Set Europe Ablaze,* 32.

46. **double the . . . radio contact:** As of D-Day, before these new radio recruits began dropping in, the SOE's main radio station maintained contact with 137 radio operators in France; see Mackenzie, *Secret History of SOE,* 602.

46. **bulletin boards:** Berlin, author interview, Sept. 22, 2002.

46. **dispatched letters:** Singlaub, author interview, Feb. 7, 2002.

46. **"We are looking":** N. Smith, oral history, IWM.

46. **Royal Armoured Corps:** A. Brown, *Jedburghs,* 8; Tack, author interview, June 24, 2002.

47. **"Qui veut obtenir":** Sassi, author interview, June 11, 2002.

47. **among the Free French:** Irwin, "Special Force," 101; War Diary, vol. 2, xxxi.

47. **Monmouth in New Jersey:** "Disposition of Officers Interviewed in Connection with the Jedburgh Plan," OSS memo.

47. **last drags:** Baumgold, author interview, Aug. 21, 2002; Kehoe, author interview, Nov. 26, 2001; Kehoe, "An Allied Team."

47. **emphasized the danger:** "Selection of Agents," OSS memo: "The exact nature of the work will not be revealed to the individual other than the fact that it is to be a special mission in enemy occupied territory. However, individuals will be fully informed in regard to the penalties that may be imposed in the event they are captured."

47. **lunatics:** For discussions of the types of men who volunteered for this kind of work, see Hutchison, *That Drug Danger,* 83, and Foot, *SOE in France,* 40–41.

48. **Corporal Bill Thompson:** Thompson, author interview, Sept. 3, 2002; Thompson, "Autobiography," 20–23.

48. **Private First Class Jack Poché:** Poché, author interview, Oct. 15, 2002.

48. **fifty push-ups . . . knife and fork:** This description of early army training is taken largely from Franklin, "Jedburg," 129–32.

48–49. **Other men . . . stood in their way:** I am grateful to Bob Kehoe for his patient and introspective explanation of young men's mentalities during World War II (Nov. 26, 2001).

49. **stevedore:** Thompson, author interview, Sept. 3, 2002; Thompson, "Autobiography," 20–23.

49. **"stereololiphosis":** Poché, author interview, Oct. 15, 2002.

49. **casualty rates:** Foot, *SOE in France,* 20; Sassi, author interview, June 11, 2002.

49. **Hitler's order:** For information on Hitler's infamous "Commando Order," see Foot, *SOE in France,* 186–87.

49. **tanker Gordon Tack:** Tack, author interview, June 24, 2002.

49. **Glyn Loosemore:** Loosemore, oral history, IWM.

49. **Jean Sassi . . . native Nice:** Sassi, author interviews, June 11 and 12, 2002.

50. **SS St. Louis:** United States Holocaust Memorial Museum, "SS St. Louis."

50. **"If not me":** Baumgold, author interview, Aug. 21, 2002.

## CHAPTER SEVEN: WE JUST WANT TO FIGHT

51. **Second Lieutenant Jack Singlaub:** The story of Jack Singlaub's recruitment into the Jeds is taken mostly from several daylong interviews at his home (Jan. 9, Feb. 7, and Dec. 4, 2002).

51. **Singlaub's job:** Ibid., Jan. 9, 2002.

51. **good looks:** Impressions of Singlaub's handsomeness come from various photographs taken of him at the time. The impressions of his character are my own, having spent several days in conversation with him and knowing his personal history.

52. **First Lieutenant Aaron Bank:** Bank, *From OSS*, 11. Note that although most Jeds were recruited during the large recruitment drive in the late summer and fall of 1943, some, like Bank, were transferred to the Jeds after being recruited by similar means some weeks earlier, to be either an instructor or a part of an OSS "Operational Group"; see Irwin, "Special Force," 94. Bank was recruited as an instructor; see "Disposition of Officers Interviewed in Connection with the Jedburgh Plan," OSS memo.

52. **Second Lieutenant Mason Starring:** Starring, author interview, Oct. 14, 2002.

52. **military installations:** The nonexclusive list of bases from which the recruiters collected officers included Camps Hood, Fannin, and Wolters in Texas; Camp Edwards, Massachusetts; Fort Benning, Georgia; Fort Bragg and Camp Mackall, North Carolina; Camp Shelby, Mississippi; Fort Sill, Oklahoma; Camp Blanding, Florida; Camp McClellan, Alabama; Fort Riley, Kansas; Camp Croft, South Carolina. The greater number of officers came from Benning, Bragg, and Mackall; see "Extension of Temporary Duty," OSS memo, and "Assignment of Officers," OSS memo.

52. **unimpeachable orders:** Irwin, "Special Force," 92; War Diary, vol. 2, xxx.

52. **disgruntled COs:** Arthur Brown, in his monograph *Jedburghs: A Short History,* 9, writes that British commanding officers were "sick to death of having their best men taken through special trawls." I have assumed that the same attitude prevailed among American commanding officers.

52. **paratroopers would be the least likely:** Irwin, "Special Force," 94.

53. **His plans . . . had all fallen apart:** All Singlaub background told to me by Jack Singlaub (Jan. 9 and Dec. 4, 2002).

53. **Captain William Crawshay:** Crawshay, oral history, IWM.

53. **Major Adrian Wise:** Singlaub, author interview, Mar. 19, 2002.

53. **Tommy Macpherson:** Macpherson related the story of his childhood and ultimate POW escape to me (Jan. 20 and June 22 and 23, 2002).

56. **Major William Colby:** Colby's background taken from Colby, *Honorable Men,* 29–33.

56. **"wanted to get involved":** Ibid., 74.

56. **First Lieutenant William Dreux:** Like Aaron Bank, Dreux was recruited as an instructor, somewhat earlier than the other Jeds but by similar means; see "Disposition of Officers Interviewed in Connection with the Jedburgh Plan," OSS memo.

56. *gueules cassées . . .* **dead Frenchmen:** Dreux, *No Bridges Blown*, 1–10.

57. **Singlaub was devastated:** Singlaub, author interview, Dec. 4, 2002.

57. **"Shut the door" . . . "Well?":** Quotations by memory of Singlaub (Jan. 9 and Dec. 4, 2002).

57. **André Grandclément:** Discussions of Grandclément's treachery can be found in Foot, *SOE in France,* 279–80; West, *Secret War,* 157; and Cookridge, *Set Europe Ablaze,* 206–8.

58. **Roger Bardet:** Bardet's becoming Bleicher's agent is discussed in Foot, *SOE in France,* 273–74; Cookridge, *Set Europe Ablaze,* 113–14; and Bleicher, *Colonel Henri's Story,* 109–10.

58. **thirty-two thousand German agents:** Marshall, *White Rabbit,* 65.

58. **complete disarray:** West, *Secret War*, 161: "The sad fact is that for all the sacrifices of 1942 and 1943, F Section approached the critical New Year of 1944 with the prospect of an Allied invasion, in a state of disarray, having seen most of its circuits wound up or penetrated by the enemy."

58. **"Army jargon":** Dreux, *No Bridges Blown*, 2.

## CHAPTER EIGHT: SHRINKS WITH NOTEPADS

59. **flipped his cabbie:** Singlaub discusses his arrival at OSS headquarters in his *Hazardous Duty*, 25–27. He also related the account to me (Feb. 7, 2002).

59. **Munitions Building:** Naval Historical Center, "Main Navy and Munitions Buildings."

59. **about a hundred:** War Diary, vol. 4, xix.

59. **Jedburgh recruits:** The experience of the prospective Jedburghs on their arrival in Washington is taken from accounts cited below and from "Special Recruitment, Jedburgh Plan," an OSS memo.

59. **Officers' Suicide Society:** Hall, *You're Stepping*, 11–12.

60. **Que:** Some references refer to "Q" Building. I have chosen the spelling used in K. Roosevelt, *War Report of the OSS*, vol. 1, 86.

60. **scent of malt:** The description of Que Building is taken from Hall, *You're Stepping*, 13.

60. **"tempo" buildings:** K. Roosevelt, *War Report of the OSS*, vol. 1, 86.

60. **Decrepit wooden structures:** Hall, *You're Stepping*, 13–14.

60. **OSS expansion:** K. Roosevelt, *War Report of the OSS*, vol. 1, 86.

60. **halfway between:** Hall, *You're Stepping*, 13–14.

60. **struck by the shades of people:** The description of the interior of Que Building is taken from Dreux, *No Bridges Blown*, 11.

60. **An escort shuffled:** Hall, *You're Stepping*, 19.

60. **sunglasses:** Dreux, *No Bridges Blown*, 14.

60. **apologized for "losing" it:** Morgan, *Spies and Saboteurs*, 15–17.

60. **OSS security officer:** Hall, *You're Stepping*, 20.

61. **"... kept secret":** Bank, *From OSS*, 13.

61. **the interview:** War Diary, vol. 4, xix.

61. **attacked like a district attorney:** Singlaub with McConnell, *Hazardous Duty*, 26.

62. **"... I have initiative":** Ibid.

62. **Congressional Country Club's pool:** Hall, *You're Stepping*, 23–25; Singlaub and McConnell, *Hazardous Duty*, 27–28; Bank, *From OSS*, 14–15; and Manierre, *Pop's War*, chapter 2.

62. **khaki-clad members:** This description of Area F is taken from ibid.

62. **dubbed Area F:** K. Roosevelt, *War Report of the OSS*, vol. 1, 241.

63. **"Oh So Social":** Singlaub and McConnell, *Hazardous Duty*, 27.

63. **Hod Fuller:** Colby with Forbath, *Honorable Men*, 36.

63. **René Dussaq:** Ibid.

63. **Douglas Bazata:** Ibid.

63. **"You have been brought here":** Singlaub and McConnell, *Hazardous Duty*, 28.

63. **For the next fourteen days:** The field exercises, tests, and training regime at

Area F are described in "Outline of Training Programs at Areas 'A' and 'F,' " OSS memo, and also in Hall, *You're Stepping,* 25–43; Singlaub and McConnell, *Hazardous Duty,* 27–28; Bank, *From OSS,* 14–15; and Manierre, *Pop's War,* chapter 2.

64. **"A small bridge":** "Outline of Training Programs at Areas 'A' and 'F,' " OSS memo.

64. **Bank lost his temper:** Bank, *From OSS,* 16.

64. **Jack Gildee:** Singlaub and McConnell, *Hazardous Duty,* 29–30.

64. **morning milk truck:** Hall, *You're Stepping,* 38–39.

64. **numbered only fifty-five:** Fifty-five American Jedburgh officers eventually shipped to England; see War Diary, vol. 4, xx. I have assumed the same number survived the Area F selection process.

65. **". . . You do understand that":** Dialogue and the description of Donovan's office is taken, with kind permission, from Singlaub and McConnell, *Hazardous Duty,* 30–31.

## CHAPTER NINE: KILLING LESSONS

69. **sixty-one other radio operators:** War Diary, vol. 4, xxi.

69. **RESTRICTED:** The receipt of the "restricted" envelopes and the instructions on their opening is related in Franklin, "Jedburg," 140.

69. **anonymous civilians:** Bank, *From OSS,* 13.

69–70. **Fending off nosy . . . getting himself into:** Kehoe, author interviews, Nov. 26 and 29, 2001.

70–71. **Maryland glided . . . dust rose:** Truck ride description is from Singlaub, author interview, Feb. 7, 2002.

71. **creek bubbled:** Description of Area B is from ibid., and Kehoe, "An Allied Team."

71. **nine thousand acres:** National Park Service, "Catoctin Mountain Park."

71. **OSS appropriated one camp:** K. Roosevelt, *War Report of the OSS,* vol. 1, 241.

71. **Camp David:** White House Military Office, "Camp David."

71. **no clear sense:** Various Jedburgh interviews.

71. **"A guerrilla":** This quote is taken from notes for a lecture entitled "Guerrilla Warfare" in "Outline of Training Programs at Areas 'A' and 'F,' " OSS memo. I have assumed that Area B instructors followed scripts similar to those at Areas A and F.

72. **The survival . . . killed as a paramilitary:** Ibid.

72. **old feeling of futility:** Kehoe, author interview, Nov. 26, 2001.

72. **five o'clock reveille:** Lajeunesse, untitled memoirs; Bank, *From OSS,* 16.

72. **two-story platforms:** Kehoe, author interview, Nov. 26, 2001.

72. **treacherous course:** Franklin, "Jedburg," 143.

72. **leisurely hour:** From timetables included in "Outline of Training Programs at Areas 'A' and 'F,' " OSS memo.

72. **Kehoe joked:** Kehoe, author interview, Nov. 26, 2001.

72. **Canfield's posse crowded:** From timetables included in "Outline of Training Programs at Areas 'A' and 'F,' " OSS memo.

72. **camouflage . . . use compasses:** Examples of subjects studied taken from ibid.

73. **assistant instructor:** Singlaub, author interview, Feb. 7, 2002.

73. **play with everything:** From lecture notes entitled "Explosives and Demolitions—Lesson No. 1" in "Outline of Training Programs at Areas 'A' and 'F,' " OSS memo.
73. **Larry Swank:** Singlaub, author interview, Feb. 7, 2002.
73. **practiced designing bombs:** From lecture notes entitled "Explosives and Demolitions—Lesson No. 1" in "Outline of Training Programs at Areas 'A' and 'F,' " OSS memo.
73. *never* **run:** Michel de Bourbon (Feb. 20–23, 2002) told me that the Jeds were told not to run during demolitions training in England. I have assumed the instruction was standard and given at Area B.
73. **lightning storm:** From lecture notes entitled "Explosives and Demolitions—Lesson No. 2" in "Outline of Training Programs at Areas 'A' and 'F,' " OSS memo.
73. **". . . geef a dem":** Quote from Franklin, "Jedburg," 142.
73. **Bill Thompson:** Thompson, "Autobiography," 24.
73. **Dick Franklin again found himself:** Franklin, "Jedburg," 141.
74. **former assistant commissioner:** Singlaub and McConnell, *Hazardous Duty,* 31.
74. **wore a collar:** Franklin, "Jedburg," 142.
74. **lethal maneuvers:** From lecture notes entitled "Close Combat" in "Outline of Training Programs at Areas 'A' and 'F,' " OSS memo.
74. **Franklin kept one eye:** Franklin, "Jedburg," 142.
74. **". . . kill or be killed":** From lecture notes entitled "Close Combat" in "Outline of Training Programs at Areas 'A' and 'F,' " OSS memo.
74. **"stirring like hell":** Franklin, "Jedburg," 142.
74. **sentry system . . . run like hell:** From various lecture notes in "Outline of Training Programs at Areas 'A' and 'F,' " OSS memo.
74. **". . . SOME SHIT!":** Franklin, "Jedburg," 143, and many other Jedburgh memoirs.
75. **brand-new communications center:** For details of the establishment of the new communications base, see War Diary of the Communications Branch, OSS London.
75. **new packing station:** For details of the establishment of the new packing station and the reassignment of U.S. bombers, see ibid., vol. 1, xxxvii.
75. **November 28, 1943:** Ibid., vol. 4, xxi.

**CHAPTER TEN: GIVE HER A RING AND SAY GOOD-BYE**
76. **Jeds assembled:** Kehoe, author interview, Nov. 26, 2001; Lajeunesse, author interview, May 28, 2002.
76. **Kehoe caught the train . . . his father again:** Kehoe, author interviews, Nov. 26 and 29, 2001.
76. **Up in Connecticut:** Lajeunesse, author interview, May 28, 2002.
77. **". . . married virgin":** Kehoe, author interview, Nov. 26, 2001.
77. **Jack Singlaub . . . finally got down on one knee:** Singlaub and McConnell, *Hazardous Duty,* 32; Singlaub, author interview, Dec. 4, 2002.
77. **Bob Kehoe left:** Kehoe, author interviews, Nov. 26 and 29, 2001.

77. **snow covered . . . their feet:** Singlaub, author interview, Feb. 7, 2002.
77. **smashed the record:** Franklin, "Jedburg," 143.
77. **". . . real McCoy":** Bank, *From OSS,* 16.
77. **". . . alive *as yet*":** L. F. Goddard, letter to his parents, Dec. 2, 1943.
77. **". . . make our wills":** L. F. Goddard, letter to his parents, Dec. 2, 1943.
78. **Intrepid:** For a biography of Stephenson, see Stevenson, *Man Called Intrepid.*
78. **Stephenson left in disgust:** Singlaub and McConnell, *Hazardous Duty,* 33.
78. **". . . ashamed to cry":** C. J. Goddard, letter to L. F. Goddard, Feb. 4, 1944.
78. **Area B roll call:** The officers left in time to arrive in England on December 23 and the radio operators on December 31; see War Diary, vol. 4, xxii.
78. **thirty-five cents:** The description of the routine at Fort Hamilton and the cost of a ride to New York City come from Hall, *You're Stepping,* 114.
78. **arms of his wife:** Franklin, "Jedburg," 144.
78. **eloped to Hoboken:** Ibid., 125.
78. **cleavage:** Thompson, author interview, Sept. 3, 2002.
79. **fighting knife:** Thompson, "Autobiography," 24.
79. **under guard:** Franklin, "Jedburg," 144.
79. ***Queen Mary:*** Ibid., 144.
79. **winter storm soon blew up:** Kehoe, "An Allied Team."
79. **no menial work:** Ibid.; Kehoe, author interview, Nov. 26, 2001; Franklin, "Jedburg," 147.
79. **Dick Franklin . . . guarding the brig:** Franklin, "Jedburg," 147.
79. **nurse's nipple:** Pierre, author interview, Dec. 2001.
79. **Franklin retrieved his toothbrush:** Franklin, "Jedburg," 147.
79. **gymnast's spotter:** Kehoe, "An Allied Team"; Kehoe, author interview, Nov. 26, 2001.
80. **fireside chat:** F. D. Roosevelt, fireside chat, Dec. 24, 1943.
80. **newsreel announcers:** Pathe Gazette, "The Big Three in Teheran": "Students of war are already forecasting a crushing, all-out offensive involving many millions of men."
80. **time . . . carefully chosen:** F. D. Roosevelt, fireside chat, Dec. 24, 1943.
80. **"My friends":** Ibid.
80–81. **"We agreed . . . the compass":** F. D. Roosevelt, fireside chat, Dec. 24, 1943.
81. **". . . command Overlord":** Eisenhower, *Crusade in Europe,* 207.
81. **nearly four million . . . ten million soldiers:** F. D. Roosevelt, fireside chat, Dec. 24, 1943.
81. **". . . loved ones at home":** Ibid.

## CHAPTER ELEVEN: HAPPY NEW YEAR!

82. **During the *Queen* . . . boiled apricots:** Pierre, author interview, Dec. 2001; Lajeunesse, author interview, May 28, 2002.
82. **Bob Kehoe finally descended:** Kehoe, "An Allied Team"; Kehoe, author interview, Nov. 26, 2001.
82. **". . . I miss her":** Singlaub, letter to his parents, Jan. 16, 1944.
83. **"He was convinced" . . . "knock it off":** Dialogue is condensed from version in Dreux, *No Bridges Blown,* 23.

83. **before Christmas Eve:** War Diary, vol. 4, xxii.

83. **In the cold drizzle . . . conveyor-belt fashion:** Singlaub and McConnell, *Hazardous Duty*, 34.

83. **An OSS training . . . "Well, boys":** Manierre, *Pop's War,* chapter 8.

83. **One week later . . . docked in Glasgow:** War Diary, vol. 4, xxii.

84. **doughnut after doughnut:** Franklin, "Jedburg," 149.

84. **crisscrossed with Glasgow's laundry:** Description of steaming through Glasgow is taken from Dreux, *No Bridges Blown*, 24.

84. **the SOE had installed:** A. Brown, "Jedburghs," 8.

84. **quick-marched:** Tack, oral history, IWM.

84. **stately seventeenth-century home:** Marian Fathers, "Fawley Court."

84. **Special Training School 54:** A. Brown, "Jedburghs," 8; War Diary, vol. 4, xxii.

84. **fifteen words a minute:** War Diary, vol. 4, xix.

84. **their girlfriends:** A. Brown, "One Bright," 122.

84. **a party:** The New Year's Eve party is described in Franklin, "Jedburg," 149–50.

84. **tried to steal their girls:** "The punch served with our cakes was mildly spiked"; see Franklin, "Jedburg," 149. "We were joined by sixty or so American OSS sergeants . . . only too ready to steal our girls"; see A. Brown, "One Bright," 124. I've relied here on Fussell's discussion of typical relations between American GIs and British Tommies in his *Boys' Crusade*, 15–23.

84–85. **Brown sneaked . . . body part:** A. Brown, "One Bright," 72; A. Brown, author interview, Jan. 17, 2002.

85. **Norman Smith watched:** N. Smith's oral history, IWM.

85. **Glyn Loosemore . . . ran around:** Loosemore, oral history, IWM.

85. **smell of burning:** N. Smith, oral history, IWM.

85. **Sixty thousand civilians:** Knight, *Short Guide to Great Britain*, 5.

85. **Gordon Tack's father:** Tack, author interview, June 24, 2002.

85. **neither rational nor fair:** I have relied on Fussell's *Doing Battle*, 105–8, for its excellent description of the demoralization that occurs when a soldier faces the realities of war.

85. **". . . question to arise":** Loosemore, oral history, IWM.

85. **Yanks pranced around:** Fussell, *Boys' Crusade*, 16: "The American soldier dolled up for a date looked like a gentleman, the British soldier . . . looked like a slob."

85. **"deodorant":** Ibid.

86. **soap had been rationed:** Knight, *Short Guide to Great Britain*, 21–22.

86. **girlfriends laughed a little too hard:** This is my assumption based on Arthur Brown's assertion in "One Bright," 124, that the Americans were only "too glad to steal the girls."

86. **"One Yank":** Joke appears in Fussell, *Boys' Crusade*, 17.

86–87. **To be fair . . . party soon broke up:** Franklin, "Jedburg," 150–52.

87. **not started well:** A. Brown, "One Bright," 124: "We were joined by sixty or so American OSS sergeants, fresh from the States; a scruffy crowd, already bemedalled without a shot fired in anger, unable to drill to save their lives, overpaid and only too ready to steal our girls."

CHAPTER TWELVE: CLOSE TO MUTINY

88. **half-frozen bog:** Singlaub describes this scene in *Hazardous Duty,* 36.

88. **stomach had been hurting:** Singlaub suffered from repeated bouts of chronic appendicitis during this period. His several treatments in hospital and the initial misdiagnosis of his pain as gastroenteritis are discussed in his letters to his parents (Jan. 29, Feb. 3, Mar. 5, Apr. 16, and June 4, 1944) and in his "Team James" file. It is my own supposition, however, that he had pain on this particular day.

88–89. **"What a nasty" . . . lagged far behind:** Singlaub and McConnell, *Hazardous Duty,* 36.

89. **an SOE paramilitary school:** For more on the SOE commando training in the West Highlands, see Mackenzie, *Secret History of SOE,* 729, and Foot, *SOE in France,* 55–56.

89. **Jed officers had arrived:** The *Queen Elizabeth* anchored on December 23 in Glasgow; see War Diary, vol. 4, xxii). The Jed officers spent one night there before going to Inverness-shire the following day; see Manierre, *Pop's War,* chapter 8.

89. **". . . Righto!":** Dreux, *No Bridges Blown,* 31.

89. **location of your ambush:** The elements of an ambush are described in S. Alsop and Braden, *Sub Rosa,* 116–18, and the Public Record Office, *SOE Syllabus,* throughout.

89. **Jeds practiced this scenario:** Conditions described in Dreux, *No Bridges Blown,* 33.

89. **"Snoop and poop":** Singlaub, author interview, Feb. 7, 2002.

90. **". . . caught a packet":** Dreux, *No Bridges Blown,* 33.

90. **An ambush . . . bat for singles:** Elements of a good ambush taken from the Public Record Office, *SOE Syllabus,* throughout.

90. **thirty shillings:** Foot foreword to Mackenzie, *Secret History of SOE,* xx.

90. **parachuted by the tens of thousands:** Mackenzie, *Secret History of SOE,* 602.

90. **most common weapon:** Lorain, *Clandestine Operations,* 118–21.

90. **Bren light machine gun:** Ibid., 136–37.

90. **they could load, fire, clean:** Sten and Bren training described to me by Singlaub (Feb. 7, 2002).

90. **learned to swim . . . spring-loaded plunger:** Ibid.; Dreux, *No Bridges Blown,* 30–31; P. Churchill, *Of Their Own Choice,* 14.

90. **". . . real McCoy" . . . Yugoslavia, Greece, or France:** Bank, *From OSS,* 19–20.

91. **black leather glove:** Singlaub, author interview, Feb. 7, 2002.

91. **one big game:** Dreux, *No Bridges Blown,* 34–35.

91. **New Year's Eve:** Manierre, *Pop's War,* chapter 8.

91. **jumped off their train . . . Special Training School 3:** Stern, author interview, Oct. 18, 2002; War Diary, vol. 9, 8.

91. **Dreux quickly felt like a tiny bacillus:** Dreux's metaphor; see *No Bridges Blown,* 37.

91. **commanding officer, Major Sinclair:** Stern, author interview, Oct. 18, 2002.

91. **"You will be tested . . . call 'assessment' ":** This speech is attributed to the

commanding officer of another SAB by Morgan, *Spies and Saboteurs*, 22. I have assumed that a similar speech was given by Sinclair.

91. "... flunk out": Dreux, *No Bridges Blown*, 37.

91. officers grumbled angrily: Crosby, *Irregular Soldier*, 89.

91. "booby hatch": Olmsted, memoir, 13.

91. wetting the bed: According to Crawshay, oral history, IWM; Dreux, *No Bridges Blown*, 39, and others, questions about bed-wetting were posed by the psychiatrists.

91. radio aptitude tests: Morgan, *Spies and Saboteurs*, 112.

91. ink blobs: Dreux, *No Bridges Blown*, 37.

92. "fuck your buddy test": Fussell, *Doing Battle*, 88.

92. graded the men: Dreux, *No Bridges Blown*, 37.

92. eleven testing stations: War Diary, vol. 9, 8.

92. "delicate radio equipment": The list of situations is discussed in Morgan, *Spies and Saboteurs*, throughout.

92. matched or exceeded . . . But then came the interviews: Crosby, *Irregular Soldier*, 91.

92. "girls": Schonen, author interview, June 10, 2002.

92. psychotic maniac: Singlaub, author interview, Feb. 7, 2002.

92. "... danger pay": Morgan, *Spies and Saboteurs*, 116.

92. "... after a rodeo": "Report on Seventy-Five SO Agents," OSS report.

92. serve their country: Morgan, *Spies and Saboteurs*, 116.

92. boastful: "Report on Seventy-Five SO Agents," OSS report.

92. rejected . . . nearly one-third: War Diary, vol. 9, 24.

93. training area was still not complete: "Jedburgh Training," OSS memo; War Diary, vol. 9, 16.

93. roll calls: S. Alsop and Braden, *Sub Rosa*, 148.

93. promise . . . had been broken: War Diary, vol. 9, 16.

93. To top it all off . . . "neutralize the Luftwaffe": "Jedburgh Training," OSS memo.

93. "violently insulting": "Misconduct of an American Officer," OSS memo.

93. pulled the chain: De Francesco, author interview, Oct. 5, 2002.

93. canceling their leave: "Jedburgh Training," OSS memo.

93–94. "Never has so little" . . . "SOME SHIT!": Manierre, *Pop's War*, chapter 9.

94. close to falling apart: "I am frankly worried about the Jedburgh plan," wrote Henry B. Coxe, one of the Americans now in charge of Operation Jedburgh; see "Jedburghs," OSS memo.

## CHAPTER THIRTEEN: EISENHOWER'S PLAN

95–96. Dwight Eisenhower . . . France to the border: I have distilled my short discussion of the strategy for the invasion of France from the much more detailed treatments in Eisenhower, *Crusade in Europe*, 220–53; Ambrose, *Victors*, 51–68; Hastings, *Overlord*, 19–68; Keegan, *Second World War*, 373–78; Hammond, "Normandy," 3–19; and Harrison, *Cross-Channel Attack*, 158–97.

95. January 15, 1944: Harrison, *Cross-Channel Attack*, 158.

95. **Overlord's 175,000 men:** Ambrose, *Victors*, 66.

96. **tons of daily supplies:** Eisenhower, *Crusade in Europe*, 235.

96. **Anvil:** Operation Anvil is discussed in great detail in J. Clarke and R. R. Smith, *Riviera to the Rhine.*

96. **Overlord armada:** Figures taken from Ambrose, *Victors*, 66.

96. **Hitler had dotted:** For more detailed discussions of the German defense system, see Hastings, *Overlord*, 58–68; Harrison, *Cross-Channel Attack*, 231–67; "Interference by Resistance Groups with the Movement of German Local Armoured Reinforcements," SOE planning memo.

96. **consider moving men:** Hastings, *Overlord*, 35; Keegan, *Second World War*, 376.

96. **"The crux of the operation":** Morgan is quoted in Hastings, *Overlord*, 27.

98. **The two preconditions for victory:** Casey, *Secret War*, 76.

98. **three ways to keep the Germans at bay:** Keegan, *Second World War*, 376.

98. **bull's-eyes:** For discussions of the pre–D-Day bombing and sabotage targets, see Harrison, *Cross-Channel Attack*, 198–230, and Casey, *Secret War*, 76–91.

98. **"simply have to go home":** Ike is quoted in Harrison, *Cross-Channel Attack*, 220.

98. **"bonus":** Ibid., 202; Stafford, *Britain*, 153.

100. **keep Hitler away from his men in Normandy:** For a detailed discussion of the combined use of the Resistance and the air forces in the Transportation Plan, see Harrison, *Cross-Channel Attack*, 198–230.

100. **"We are going to need":** Ike is quoted in Lyon, *Eisenhower*, 282.

100. **four hundred thousand . . . Resistance fighters:** "Potentialities of Resistance Groups in France," OSS memo; Mackenzie, *Secret History of SOE*, 602.

100. **SOE and OSS Special Operations . . . was coordinated:** Stafford, *Britain*, 153; War Diary, vol. 1, 1–4 and 13; "Operational Directive to SOE/SO," SHAEF, Mar. 23, 1944.

100. **187 other agents:** War Diary, vol. 3, 6.

100. **In the first few months of 1944:** Stafford, *Britain*, 153–54.

100. **671 locomotives:** War Diary, vol. 1, 20.

100. **SHAEF's orders:** Ibid., 17.

100. **in the last few days before D-Day:** Stafford, *Britain*, 154; War Diary, vol. 1, 17.

101. **First, individual German units . . . cut the tracks:** "Interference by Resistance Groups with the Movement of German Local Armoured Reinforcements," SOE planning memo.

101. **"colored" plans:** War Diary, vol. 3, 57; "SOE/SO Planning Review," May 9, 1944.

101. *messages personnels:* The system of BBC messages is described in Foot, *SOE in France*, 110–11.

103. **no one left to hear them:** See chapter 1.

103. **fifty thousand potential new fighters:** Mackenzie, *Secret History of SOE*, 602.

103. **maquis:** For a good précis of the history of the maquis, see ibid., 591–93, and S. Alsop and Braden, *Sub Rosa*, 144.

104. **the strategic reserve of agents:** The Jedburghs were "the 'strategic reserves' for the Resistance all over France: a comparatively small number would go at once

to the battle area, and the rest would be held ready to reinforce any other district which needed them"; see Mackenzie, *Secret History of SOE,* 603–4.

104. **mutiny:** According to O. Brown, oral history, IWM, "They almost threatened at one stage to mutiny," one Milton Hall training officer later said.

104. **the Jeds hated:** "Jedburgh Training," OSS memo.

104. **"There seems to be a general impression":** "Comments on Major Dodderidge's Paper," OSS memo.

104. **arrests and executions:** Mackenzie, *Secret History of SOE,* 596.

104. **captured by D-Day:** "Jedburghs," OSS memo.

104. **"I am frankly worried":** Ibid.

## CHAPTER FOURTEEN: SOME SHIT

105. **window of a railway ticket office:** Hutchison, *That Drug Danger,* 86.

105. **Ringway:** For descriptions of Ringway and the training there, see Foot, *SOE in France,* 77–79, and Hall, *You're Stepping,* 134–47.

105. **"Please, sir":** Anecdote related to me by Knox (Mar. 21, 2002). A similar instance of being shamed into action at another SOE school by a beautiful FANY is related by Oliver Brown in his oral history, IWM.

105. **"... top of a stepladder":** Lajeunesse, author interview, May 28, 2002.

105. **helium-filled balloon:** Description of the barrage balloon used at Ringway comes from Franklin, "Jedburg," 177, and Dreux, *No Bridges Blown,* 43.

106. **Brown watched horrified:** O. Brown, oral history, IWM.

106. **"squashed":** Dreux, *No Bridges Blown,* 43.

106. **"... tie up the ends for burial":** Langelaan, *Masks of War,* 78–79.

106. **one inauspicious day:** De Francesco, author interview, Oct. 5, 2002.

106. **one in nine hundred jumps:** Foot, *SOE in France,* 79.

106. **big wet stains:** Kehoe, author interview, Nov. 26, 2001.

106. **Every one ... "like a guardsman":** Dreux, *No Bridges Blown,* 40–42, including quotes.

106. **Teeth marks:** Teeth marks are mentioned in Hall, *You're Stepping,* 137.

106. **tethered himself to the gondola:** Description of the inside of the gondola is from Franklin, "Jedburg," 177.

107. **good hard punch:** Anecdote from Langelaan, *Masks of War,* 78–79.

107. **"It's the goddamned way I do it":** Dialogue recalled by Starring, author interview, Oct. 14, 2002.

107. **René Dussaq:** Knox, author interview, Mar. 21, 2002.

107. **"Four one thousand":** Dialogue recalled by Knox, author interview, Aug. 22, 2002.

107. **Jack Singlaub:** Singlaub and McConnell, *Hazardous Duty,* 37.

107. **"Would it break His Majesty's government":** Quoted in Hall, *You're Stepping,* 141.

107. **"... had it, chum":** Quoted in Dreux, *No Bridges Blown,* 41.

107. **"Jesus Christ!":** Knox, author interview, Aug. 22, 2002.

107. **fourteen-foot wall:** Foot, *SOE in France,* 78.

107. **"... you know what":** Quoted in Dreux, *No Bridges Blown,* 42.

108. **"... son of a bitch!":** Attributed to Gildee by Knox, author interview, Aug. 22, 2002.

108. **five- or six-man group:** Hall, *You're Stepping,* 123.

108. **125 miles an hour:** Dreux, *No Bridges Blown,* 41.

108. **Back at Milton Hall:** See Singlaub and McConnell, *Hazardous Duty;* Dreux, *No Bridges Blown;* and Bank, *From OSS.*

108. **"Every effort should be made":** "Jedburghs," OSS memo.

108. **"... been made sergeants":** N. Smith, oral history, IWM.

108. **radiomen forgave the theft:** A. Brown, "One Bright," 124.

108. **"... merde!":** Singlaub and McConnell, *Hazardous Duty,* 39.

108. **a buzz went through the corridors:** "Role of Jedburghs," SOE, History of Jedburghs, part 5, 1.

109–11. **As you can all see ... capture more likely:** I have reconstructed Mockler-Ferryman's speech from ibid., and from accounts of the speech in S. Alsop and Braden, *Sub Rosa,* 143–44, and Bank, *From OSS,* 24–26.

109. **dropped to such maquis:** "Advantage of Jedburgh Teams Arriving in the Field in Uniform," SOE policy paper.

109. **In some cases:** "Jedburgh Procedure," SOE, History of Jedburghs, appendix I.G.

109. **"The bearer of this document":** Quoted in Dreux, *No Bridges Blown,* inside front cover.

109–10. **Once with their maquis ... Jedburgh team might be sent:** SOE, History of Jedburghs, part 5, 2.

110. **In the coming weeks ... against the Germans:** "Role of Jedburghs," SOE, History of Jedburghs.

110. **provide liaison:** "Procedure for the Dispatch of Jedburgh Teams," SFHQ briefing paper.

110. **SAS and OGs:** Casey, *Secret War,* 75.

110–11. **When a Jed team ... into Spain:** "Role of Jedburghs," SOE, History of Jedburghs, appendix I.G.

111. **in full uniform:** "Advantage of Jedburgh Teams Arriving in the Field in Uniform," SOE policy paper.

111. **most definitely parachute in uniform:** Ibid.

111. **"Oh, that's all?":** Dialogue quoted in S. Alsop and Braden, *Sub Rosa,* 144.

### CHAPTER FIFTEEN: IN CASE OF DEATH

112. **"operational training":** War Diary, vol. 4, 9–10.

112. **last of a group of new American officers:** Ibid., 5–6.

112. **Lieutenant Stewart Alsop:** S. Alsop, *Stay of Execution,* 35–36 and 282–87.

112. **"animals":** Knox, author interview, Mar. 21, 2002.

112. **"You chaps go ahead":** Musgrave is quoted in Dreux, *No Bridges Blown,* 62. For the method of team formation see S. Alsop and Braden, *Sub Rosa,* 149–51, and Dreux, *No Bridges Blown,* 62–64.

113. **scar-faced captain:** Knox, author interview, Mar. 21, 2002.

113. **Paul Grall ... Jacques de Penguilly:** In the official records, only the Frenchmen's noms de guerre are recorded. I have taken their real names, used here, from A. Brown, *Jedburghs.*

113. **Macpherson . . . report to Milton Hall:** Macpherson, author interview, Jan. 20, 2002.

113. **teams now trained . . . bridge in Greece:** SOE, History of Jedburghs, part 3, 3–5.

113–14. **shot his Gestapo captor . . . reeked of doom:** Millar, *Maquis,* 5–6, including quotes.

114. **terrorizing farmers:** N. Smith, oral history, IWM.

114. **invited to stay:** Bank, *From OSS,* 32–33.

114. **hopping aboard:** N. Smith, oral history, IWM.

114. **More than a million and a half Americans:** Hammond, "Normandy," 14.

114. **one huge enclave of army tents:** Hastings, *Overlord,* 46.

114. **"get their affairs in order":** A. Brown, "One Bright," 128.

115. **sailed to Algeria:** Ibid.; SOE, History of Jedburghs, part 3, 5.

115. **travel became so restricted:** Kehoe, author interview, Nov. 26, 2001.

115. **the priest reassured him:** Lajeunesse, author interview, Aug. 12, 2002.

115. **"You aren't by chance Captain Knox":** Dialogue recalled by Knox, author interview, Mar. 21, 2002.

115. **Paul Cyr . . . got similar messages:** For the composition of Jed teams and dates of insertion, see "Index to SO Reports," OSS paper, and A. Brown, *Jedburghs.*

115. **write their final letters:** Kehoe, author interview, Nov. 26, 2001.

115. **write a will:** Dreux, *No Bridges Blown,* 72.

115. **make confession:** Ibid., 90.

116. **French-language broadcast:** For accounts of the transmission of warning and action messages by the BBC, see Aron, *France Reborn,* 84–95, and Foot, *SOE in France,* 110–11 and 387–89.

116. **Four nights earlier . . . nothing unusual:** Ibid.

116. **At 9:15 p.m.:** Foot, *SOE in France,* 388.

116. **"Et voici":** Knox, *Essays,* 26.

116. **The first part . . . rail sabotage:** Aron, *France Reborn,* 87–89.

116. **". . . most ghastly disaster of the war":** Brooke is quoted in Casey, *Secret War,* 101.

116. **Churchill had gone to bed:** Ibid.

116–17. **announcer read hundreds of *messages personnels:*** Aron, *France Reborn,* 88; Foot, *SOE in France,* 387–89.

117. **wish list:** "Delay of Enemy Reinforcements Action," SOE memo.

117. **Dick Franklin slept:** Franklin, "Jedburg," 182.

117. **Jack Singlaub:** Singlaub and McConnell, *Hazardous Duty,* 40.

## CHAPTER SIXTEEN: SUICIDE PILLS

121. **On the Normandy beaches:** For my account of D-Day, I have relied on D. Miller and Commager, *World War II;* Hammond, "Normandy"; Eisenhower, *Crusade in Europe;* Keegan, *Second World War;* Hastings, *Overlord.*

122. **lost 96 percent of its men:** D. Miller and Commager, 290.

122. **Only a little more than a third . . . within half an hour:** Hammond, "Normandy," 29.

123. **Annihilation of V Corps . . . busy for half a day:** For accounts of the two

British deception teams, see Casey, *Secret War,* 102, and Foot, *SOE in France,* 386–87.

123. **thirty-four thousand Americans had inched their way forward:** Hammond, "Normandy," 32.

123. **"sustained a most annoying artillery fire":** Eisenhower, *Crusade in Europe,* 251.

124. **SFHQ sent its first seven Jed teams:** The list of the Jed teams, their areas of operation, and their dates of insertion can be found in "Index to SO Reports, WE Section," OSS paper.

124. **light oil and tinny smell:** Cowburn, *No Cloak,* 10.

124. **Roaring down:** The account of Bob Kehoe's parachuting into France is taken from his interviews with me (Nov. 26–29, 2001) and his "An Allied Team."

124. **eight thousand feet:** Dreux, *No Bridges Blown,* 87.

124. **"What's the matter with him":** Dialogue recalled by Kehoe, author interview, Nov. 26, 2001.

124. **Back at Milton Hall . . . see these Jeds again:** Knox, "Premature Anti-Fascist."

125. **jumpmaster switched off . . . a torch, a flashlight:** Cowburn, *No Cloak,* 11.

125. **three German paratroop and two other mobile divisions:** There were five mobile German divisions in Brittany; see Harrison, *Cross-Channel Attack,* map 6.

125. **sixty thousand fewer Germen cutthroats:** Team Frederick report; Team George report; Casey, *Secret War,* 93–94; SOE, History of Jedburghs, part 6, 1.

126. **a team of dressers . . . hobble to the plane:** Dreux, *No Bridges Blown,* 85–86.

126. **"Good luck . . . Good luck":** Dialogue according to Knox, author interview, Mar. 21, 2002.

126. **gap in his teeth:** O. Brown, oral history, IWM.

126. **chewing gum:** Lajeunesse, author interview, May 28, 2002.

126. **". . . shoot myself like a soldier":** According to Knox, author interview, Mar. 21, 2002.

126. **shadow chiefs urgently dispatched:** The list of the Jed teams, their areas of operation, and their dates of insertion can be found in "Index to SO Reports, WE Section," OSS papers.

126. **Team Quinine and . . . Team Ammonia:** Team Ammonia report; Team Quinine report; "Outline Plan for the Use of Resistance in Immediate Support of Overlord."

127. **Team Harry:** Team Harry report, 26.

127. **Team Hugh:** Team Hugh report; Casey, *Secret War,* 93–94.

127. **Team Veganin:** The size of a typical panzer division is taken from "Interference by Resistance Group with the Movement of German Local Armoured Reinforcements," SOE planning memo. Team Veganin's mission statement is found in its mission report. The priority of action for Jedburgh teams and Resistance in southeast France can be found in "Resistance in South-East France," OSS paper, and "Outline Plan for the Use of Resistance in Immediate Support of Overlord."

127. **"I'm not doing that":** N. Smith, oral history, IWM.

127. **"Running in!":** Dreux, *No Bridges Blown,* 92.

129. **Jesse Gardner's body:** List of Jedburgh casualties in SOE, History of Jedburghs, appendix X.C; Team Veganin's report.

129. **surviving Jeds:** Various interviews.

## CHAPTER SEVENTEEN: FORGET ABOUT VENGEANCE

130. **In a field in . . . carry for miles:** Team George report; Paul Cyr film.

130–31. **Jacob Berlin . . . "I was just about to blow your head off":** Dialogue recalled by Jacob Berlin, author interview, Sept. 22, 2002; Berlin, "Behind Enemy Lines"; Team Ammonia report.

131. **Arthur Brown and Team Quinine . . . ammunition, explosives, and detonators:** A. Brown's "One Bright," 133; Team Quinine report; Bourbon, author interview, Feb. 20, 2002.

131. ***"J'ai un Français ici . . . Il est venu avec son épouse!":*** Dialogue recalled by Bourbon, author interview, Feb. 20, 2002.

131. **descended into a battle:** Team Frederick report; Kehoe, "An Allied Team"; Kehoe, author interview, Nov. 26, 2001.

131. **terribly wrong:** Team Veganin report.

131. **taught to receive a parachute drop:** A. Brown, "One Bright," 134.

132. ***Silence!:*** Paul Cyr film; Team George report.

132. **"It was like a regular circus":** Paul Cyr film.

132. ***S'il vous plaît:*** Ibid.; Team George report.

132. **"Ça ne risque rien":** This was the response always given to SOE agent George Millar; see his *Maquis*, 40.

132. **"About a mile":** Paul Cyr film.

132. **In May . . . slave labor:** This incident was reported by POWs from the 4th SS Panzer Grenadier Regiment; see "Maquis—Excerpts from POW Interrogations."

132–33. **In Cantal . . . freak shows:** A. Brown, "One Bright," 134.

133. **Tommy Macpherson . . . he said:** Dialogue recalled by Macpherson, author interview, Jan. 20, 2002.

133–34. **In Brittany . . . do with his life:** Kehoe, author interview, Nov. 26, 2001; Kehoe, "An Allied Team."

134. **"Is it true":** This question was asked of the SOE's George Millar; see his *Maquis*, 37.

134. **We found a body!:** Team Frederick report; Kehoe, "An Allied Team"; Kehoe, author interview, Nov. 26, 2001.

134. **Gardner's chute remained folded:** Team Veganin report.

134. ***Allons!* . . . no evidence of agent activity:** Team Frederick report; Kehoe, "An Allied Team"; Kehoe, author interview, Nov. 26, 2001.

134. **"Are you crazy?":** Millar, *Maquis*, 40.

135. **Bob Kehoe's march:** Team Frederick report; Kehoe, "An Allied Team"; Kehoe, author interview, Nov. 26, 2001.

135. **man who had hanged himself:** A. Brown, "Jedburgh Quinine."

135. **sautéed omelets:** Berlin, "Behind Enemy Lines."

135. **Farm de la Nouée:** Paul Cyr film; Team George report.

135. **It took some negotiating . . . requisite cigarettes:** Ibid.; S. Alsop and Braden, *Sub Rosa*, 155.

136. **A beautiful young Frenchwoman:** Paul Cyr film.
136. **body odor and garlic:** Kehoe, author interview, Nov. 26, 2002.

## CHAPTER EIGHTEEN: BOYS VS. PANZERS

137. **Tommy Macpherson ... bumped his way:** Macpherson recounted this story of his maquis group and of blowing the bridge to me (Jan. 20, 2002), but I have also relied on accounts he gave in his oral history recording and quoted in Stafford, *Secret Agent,* 215–16, and R. Miller, *Behind the Lines,* 150.
137. **shot on sight:** For details on Hitler's Commando order, see Foot, *SOE in France,* 186–87.
138. **crowd of Breton men:** Paul Cyr film; Team George report.
138. **"We have not come here to enjoy ourselves":** Quote is taken from Macpherson, oral history, IWM.
139. **"The Cantal Resistance":** Macpherson, author interview, Jan. 20, 2002.
139. **Macpherson's bridge-blowing strategy had worked:** Ibid.
139. **To Team George's camp:** Team George report.
140. **Ike needed the Resistance "bonus":** This summary of the problems in Normandy is taken from Ambrose, *Victors,* 190–95; Keegan, *Second World War,* 390; and D. Miller and Commager, *World War II,* 306–39.
140. **Montgomery tried again ... on June 13:** Hastings, *Overlord,* 333.
140. **fourteen hedgerows per kilometer:** Ambrose, *Victors,* 194.
140–41. **strategists had hoped ... five miles inland:** Eisenhower, *Crusade in Europe,* 262–66.
141. **2nd SS Panzer Division began snaking its way:** Hastings, *Das Reich,* 1.
141. **Hitler ordered ... Hungary, Denmark, and Norway:** Casey, *Secret War,* 107.
141. **General Pierre Koenig:** War Diary, vol. 1, 34.
142. **With five or six maquisards:** The anecdote of the ambush of the panzer division was related to me by Macpherson (Jan. 20, 2002).

## CHAPTER NINETEEN: *"ALLES KAPUTT"*

144. **In the week after D-Day ... derailed at least once:** Foot, *SOE in France,* 389; Casey, *Secret War,* 104.
144. **"Railway movement in area now nil":** Team Quinine report.
144. **hardly a train could move:** "Rail Communications."
144. **French children dropped ... outriders:** Macpherson, author interview, June 21, 2002.
144. **removed road signs:** "French Resistance, 4 June to 31st July," SHAEF.
144–45. **Near Jasseron ... with the maquis:** Activity report of Lieutenant Leon F. Ball, Western Europe, 1411–25.
145. **two soldiers ... were assassinated:** This incident was reported by a POW from the 897th Infantry Regiment; see "Maquis—Excerpts from POW Interrogations."
145. **In Morbihan:** Paul Cyr film; Team George report.
145. **"... five slugs in the belly":** Team Frederick report.
145. **Hitler ordered his commanders:** "OKW War Diary," 25.
145. **Thirty-five "generals" ... were arrested:** Ibid.

146. **". . . burnt to the ground":** Quoted in "French Resistance, 4 June to 31st July," SHAEF.

146. **tat tat tat of sporadic gunfire:** The story of the attack on Team Frederick was related to me by Bob Kehoe (Nov. 26, 2001), and is detailed in Kehoe, "An Allied Team," and the Team Frederick report.

146. **"What are we going to do?":** Dialogue recalled by Kehoe, author interview, Nov. 26, 2001.

147. **annihilate the maquis:** The account of the attack on Base Dingson is taken from Paul Cyr film; Team George report; Aron, *France Reborn*, 122–25. For the attack on Oradour, see Hastings, *Das Reich*, 162–78; for the attack on Tulle, see ibid., 118–26, and "Testimony of the Abbé of Tulle."

147. **two companies . . . north of Limoges:** Ousby, *Occupation*, 287–88.

148. **"If that is not sufficient":** Schoenbrun, *Soldiers of the Night*, 377.

148. **"I name myself":** Hastings, *Das Reich*, 123.

149. **". . . We good Algerians":** "Testimony of the Abbé of Tulle."

149. **". . . and I will give you absolution":** Ibid.

149. **"Don't be foolish":** Paul Cyr film; Team George report.

150. **killed . . . 642:** The number is given in numerous sources.

150. **six hundred Resistance boys:** Paul Cyr film; Team George report.

150. **In Tulle . . . gave them clemency:** Hastings, *Das Reich*, 126.

150. **children did not return:** Ibid., 178.

150. **"All persons of the male sex":** Kehoe, author interview, Nov. 26, 2001.

150. **"This happens to any man":** This incident was reported by a POW from the 5th Parachute Regiment; see "Maquis—Excerpts from POW Interrogations."

150–51. **"You don't say":** Kehoe, author interview, Nov. 26, 2001.

151. ***"Alles kaputt":*** Hastings, *Das Reich*, 178.

## CHAPTER TWENTY: BLOWING TRAINS TO BITS

152. **Beginning on D-Day plus thirteen . . . savaged by the storm:** Hammond, "Normandy," 35–37; Casey, *Secret War*, 108.

153. **". . . prophesied a gloomy fate for Overlord":** Eisenhower, *Crusade in Europe*, 263.

153. **Bourbon . . . snipped the phone lines:** This story of the derailing of a train was related to me by Michel de Bourbon (Feb. 20–24, 2002).

153. **SHAEF had ordered the SFHQ:** "SHAEF Directive to SOE/SO," June 15, 1944.

153. **"What are you doing!":** Dialogue recalled by Bourbon, author interview, Feb. 20–24, 2002.

154. **a crane to move the train cars:** Millar, *Maquis,* 221.

154. **"Have blown rail":** Team Quinine report.

154. **". . . south Maurs":** Ibid.

154. **two more Jed teams:** "Index to SO Reports, WE Section," OSS paper.

154. **disabled the Bordeaux-Paris rail line:** Team Ian report.

154. **"It's fun":** Team Hamish report.

154. **forty-five miles a day:** Casey, *Secret War,* 108.

155. **In the north of France . . . less than five days:** "French Resistance, 4 June to 31st July," SHAEF report.

155. **three weeks to get only four hundred miles:** Casey, *Secret War,* 104.
155. **The 271st Infantry Division . . . at Normandy's Saint-Lô seventeen days later:** "French Resistance, 4 June to 31st July," SHAEF report.
155. **they might have pushed Operation Overlord:** Foot, *SOE in France,* 397.
155. **". . . success beyond expectation":** "Rail Communications," June 23, 1944.
155. **"The terrorist movement crippled":** "OKW War Diary."
155–56. **". . . simply killed off":** Foot, *SOE in France,* 356.
156. **". . . comparable to the Air Forces' ":** Ibid., 387.
156. **"Every effort must be made to supply the Maquis":** Casey, *Secret War,* 124.
156. **Operation Zebra:** "OSS Massive Supply Drops," OSS paper.
156. **13,500 and 7,000 tons of daily supplies:** Hammond, "Normandy," 36.
156. **By June 27:** Hastings, *Overlord,* 163–65.
156. **breakout attack:** This section discussing the lead-up to Operation Cobra is taken from ibid., 244–50; Eisenhower, *Crusade in Europe,* 266–72; D. Miller and Commager, *World War II,* 306–17; Blumenson, *Breakout,* 185–241; and Hogan, "Northern France," 3–7.
156. **thirty-five miles from the beach:** Eisenhower, *Crusade in Europe,* 266.
156. **more than a million men and 177,000 vehicles:** Hammond, "Normandy," 37.
157. **"prevent or delay movement . . . Brittany Peninsula":** "SHAEF Directive to SOE/SO," June 15, 1944.
157. **". . . containing Resistance":** "SHAEF Directive to SOE/SO," July 7, 1944.
158. **In the north and northeast of France . . . 30,500 men by the beginning of August:** War Diary, vol. 3, 283–84 and 1368–69.

## CHAPTER TWENTY-ONE: BACK IN ACTION

159. **Team Frederick had . . . barely escaped:** The story of Kehoe's escape from the Forêt de Doualt and rescue by Simone Le Göeffic is taken from the Team Frederick report; Kehoe, "An Allied Team"; and Kehoe, author interview, Nov. 26–29, 2001.
159. **overcast sky:** I have assumed the day was overcast since it was the day before the storm that wreaked havoc in Normandy began.
160. **In central France . . . were not Germans:** Team Hugh report; William Crawshay, oral history, IWM.
161. **hollow handlebars or seat stem:** Method of hiding messages described by Macpherson, author interview, June 21, 2002.
161. **"The area is crawling with enemy patrols":** Dialogue recalled by Kehoe, author interview, Nov. 26–29, 2001.
161. **". . . shot them through the head":** Activity report of agent Lieutenant Leon F. Ball, Western Europe.
161. **". . . forged your enlistment papers":** Dialogue recalled by Kehoe, author interview, Nov. 26–29, 2001.
161. **". . . team's savior":** Ibid.; Kehoe, "An Allied Team"; Team Frederick report; Kehoe, author interviews, Nov. 26–29, 2001.
162. **return . . . to the scene of the German attack:** The story of Bob Kehoe's retrieval of the radio is taken from ibid.

163. **nailed a five-year-old boy to a farmhouse door . . . stabbed his wife and children:** Team George report; Paul Cyr film.

164. **about twenty-five Jed teams:** SOE, History of Jedburghs, insert at part 3, v.

164. **medical permission:** Singlaub, author interview, Mar. 19, 2002.

164. **The Jeds scanned . . . sent to the back:** For discussions of the Jeds' frustrations, see S. Alsop and Braden, *Sub Rosa,* 151–52, and Marks, *Between Silk and Cyanide,* 528 and 534–37.

164. **More Jed teams had not yet been needed:** SOE, History of Jedburghs, part 6, 11.

164. **"Boche communications . . . morale terrific":** Team Frederick report.

**CHAPTER TWENTY-TWO: NAPOLEON'S HAT**

166. **Bill Dreux followed a Resistance worker:** The story of Team Gavin's stay in a rectory is taken from Dreux, *No Bridges Blown,* 80–109, and the Team Gavin report.

167. **". . . Good Lord knows what else":** Dialogue quoted in Dreux, *No Bridges Blown,* 98–99.

167. **Henry McIntosh and his French teammates:** The story of Team Chloroform's journey through German-infested territory is taken from the Team Chloroform report and Jean Sassi, author interview, June 13, 2002.

168. **". . . burn our village":** Dialogue recalled by Sassi, author interview, June 13, 2002.

168. **Bill Dreux and his team:** Team Gavin's journey is taken from Dreux, *No Bridges Blown,* 151–64, and the Team Gavin report.

169. **"No, don't move":** Dialogue recalled by Sassi, author interview, June 13, 2002.

169. ***"Was ist los?":*** Dialogue adapted from Dreux, *No Bridges Blown,* 164.

170. **". . . bon Dieu":** Quoted ibid., 167.

170. **". . . not a little worried":** Team Giles report.

170. **wine barrels:** Team Horace report.

170. **cargo of charcoal:** Team Gilbert report, 425.

171. **transport full of pigs:** Team George report, 177.

171. **twenty-one others:** "Index to SO Reports, WE Section," OSS paper.

171. ***"Le chapeau de Napoléon":*** Team Giles report, 339, and many other sources.

**CHAPTER TWENTY-THREE: MANNA OF WEAPONS**

175. **dispatched a detail to guard the drop zone:** Major Wise of Team Frederick wrote in his report, "We arranged for a cadre of FFI leaders to watch parachutings in order to learn the procedure of a Reception Committee." Bernard Knox and Team Giles followed the same procedure, which Knox describes in *Essays,* xxvi–xxvii, and in the Team Giles report. This scene is my own reconstruction of a drop-zone reception based on Knox's description to me (Feb. 15, 2002) and other accounts. The responsibilities of a reception committee are described in Foot, *SOE in France,* 83.

175. **did not panic them:** Millar, *Maquis,* 308.

175. **jars of kerosene:** Ibid., 303. Millar discusses the building of fires to be lit at the last moment using paraffin.

176. *"La lune brille sur le dolmen":* Knox, *Essays,* xxvi.

176. **arm groups throughout France directly by airdrop:** "We took the decision to stay in the center of Finistère from which the arming of coast areas could be carried on"; see Team Giles report.

176. **jug of strong cider:** Kehoe reported in "An Allied Team" that there was bread and cider at the drop ground where he was received. In *Maquis,* 302, Millar also wrote of bringing food to a drop zone.

176. **reception committee work maquis hated :** Activity report of Captain Victor J. Layton.

176. **seventy planeloads of weapons:** War Diary, vol. 3, 1370–72.

176. **three hundred German paratroops:** Team Giles report.

177. **a *bergerie:*** "When it rained we found a shepherd's hut," said Sassi, author interview, June 19, 2002.

177. **dirt floor:** Kehoe, "An Allied Team": "It was sheer luxury to have a dry place to work and sleep."

177. **under the fading stars:** "When it was nice, we slept on the ground, no problem," said Sassi, author interview, June 19, 2002.

177. **refused to sleep inside:** Knox, author interview, May 22, 2002.

177. **haystack:** Tack, author interview, June 24, 2002.

177. **Twenty or so of the maquis:** According to the Team Giles report, "Captain Lebel and Knox organized a defense system around the CP." The first thing agents were trained to do when setting up camp was to post a sentry; see Millar, *Maquis,* 151.

177. **hundred-strong group:** Team Giles report.

177. **more cavalier:** Knox, author interview, May 22, 2002.

177. **wrapped his arms around his gun:** "When in France we always slept with weapons," said Sassi, author interview, June 13, 2002.

177. **stealthily warn the Jeds:** Franklin, "Jedburg," 198.

178. **suspicious shadows:** Dreux, *No Bridges Blown,* 133.

178. **resting on its barrel:** Franklin, "Jedburg," 193.

178. **often did not:** According to the activity report of Captain Owen Denis Johnson, "We often didn't sleep especially during moon periods. We were perpetually alert and from that point of view the life was a strain."

178. **formed a cordon . . . questioning civilians:** The method of German Resistance sweeps was explained to me by Macpherson (June 23, 2002) and Tack (June 24, 2002).

178. **French telephone operators:** Macpherson, author interview, June 23, 2002.

178. **tips from the gendarmes:** Team Gilbert report.

178. **runners stationed:** Knox, author interview, Feb. 15, 2002.

178. **position circled in red:** Team Giles report.

178. **captured Milicien escaped:** Ibid.

178. **marched ten to fifteen miles:** Ibid.; Tack, author interview, June 24, 2002.

179. **3:30 each morning:** Knox, author interview, Feb. 15, 2002.

179. **subdued melodies:** Musical passwords are discussed in Hutchison, *That Drug Danger,* 121.

179. **chocolate to the farmer's children:** Knox, author interview, May 22, 2002.
179. **single ammunition cartridge:** Tack, author interview, June 24, 2002.

## CHAPTER TWENTY-FOUR: WHAT WOULD DAD THINK?

180. *Mon capitaine:* I have constructed this scene from many sources and many discussions with various Jedburghs. Though the events and details are accurate, the sequence of some events in this scene are the result of informed reasoning. I do not mean to imply that every single Jed got bowls of coffee handed to them, or that all Jeds shaved in the morning, or that the personal letters that arrived were always handed out at the breakfast table.
180. **if they had lost their bags:** According to the activity report of Captain Owen Denis Johnson, a parachute canopy was one way to stay warm if the sleeping bag was lost.
180–81. **In western Normandy . . . week of the invasion:** Eisenhower, *Crusade in Europe,* 267–72; Hammond, "Normandy," 37.
181. **"dogged doughboy fighting":** Eisenhower, *Crusade in Europe,* 269.
181. **". . . most sanguinary of the war":** Ibid., 271–72.
181. **fake coffee . . . toasted wheat:** Millar, *Maquis,* 161, mentions wheat coffee; Berlin mentioned acorn coffee to me (Sept. 11, 2002); Morgan, *O.S.S. and I,* 179, discusses chicory coffee.
181. **No one noticed . . . a drowned gnat or hornet:** Morgan discusses the filth of the crockery and cutlery in *O.S.S. and I,* 179–80.
181. **Men began . . . daily routine:** Bob Anstett reported the typical pattern and schedule of a day in the life of a Jedburgh in the Team Hamish report. In writing this and subsequent chapters, I have assumed that all the Jedburgh teams followed similar daily schedules, although there must obviously have been variation among teams and from place to place.
182. **". . . laugh his head off":** Sassi, author interview, June 13, 2002.
182. **dig his own grave:** Tack, author interview, June 24, 2002.
182. **double-edged razor . . . resembling a shower:** Bathing habits are discussed by Knox, author interview, Mar. 21, 2002; Dreux, *No Bridges Blown,* 131; and A. Brown, "Jedburgh Quinine," 13.
182. **"There are no officers and men here":** Dialogue in Millar, *Maquis,* 45.
182. **If the Jeds and Allied agents hoped . . . looking for water himself:** The principle was explained to me by Sassi (June 19, 2002): "You would not ask someone else to get water or tea."
182. **left Team Giles's Bernard Knox with only his paratroop boots:** Knox, "Glory."
183. **maquis often spirited away:** Tack, author interview, June 24, 2002.
183. **women's knickers:** Kehoe, author interview, Nov. 26, 2001; the underwear was actually dropped to nearby Team Gerald, according to their report, and brought to Kehoe by a member of the maquis.
183. **captain's bars:** Knox, "Glory."
183. **differentiate him among his men:** Knox, author interview, Mar. 21, 2002.
183. **a plank or two:** Crosby describes such a dining table in *Irregular Soldier,* 102.

183. **condemned cow:** Pierre, author interview, Dec. 2001.
183. **More maquis were killed:** Millar, *Maquis,* 166.
183. ***"en braquant les bureaux de tabac":*** Phrase used in the activity report of American agent Second Lieutenant Roger Henquet.
183. **reported rumors:** Described in Morgan, *O.S.S. and I,* 180, and Knox, author interview, Mar. 21, 2002.
183. **personal letters . . . different life:** Kehoe, author interview, Nov. 26, 2001.
183. **breakfast arrived:** The sequence of events is my own surmise. The containers were generally emptied in the morning, so I have assumed that Kehoe was handed his letters around breakfast time.
183. **William Morgan got a chunk of . . . pork:** Morgan, *O.S.S. and I,* 179–80.
183. **Team Frederick got big wedges:** Kehoe, author interview, Nov. 26, 2001.
183. **eggs for breakfast:** Tack, author interview, June 24, 2002, and Knox in various discussions with me.
184. **baked in a hole:** Lajeunesse, author interview, Aug. 11, 2002.
184. **picking off rabbits:** Berlin, author interview, Sept. 11, 2002.
184. **grudgingly accept IOUs:** Sassi, author interview, June 19, 2002: "They would say to the merchants that they would be paid after the liberation."
184. **fake . . . francs:** Knox, author interview, Mar. 21, 2002.
184. **"I like your butter very much":** Dialogue recalled ibid.
184. **When a letter arrived . . . worked there:** Kehoe, author interview, Nov. 29, 2001.
184. **sister's marriage:** A. Brown, "Jedburgh Quinine," 12.
184. ***Boches* or *schleuhs* or *stols, shlocks,* or Fritz:** Millar, *Maquis,* 87.
184. ***Mort à les boches!:*** Sassi, author interview, June 13, 2002.
185. **"We've been lucky until now":** Kehoe, author interview, Nov. 26, 2001.

## CHAPTER TWENTY-FIVE: INSUBORDINATION

186. **Jean Sassi kicked:** Sassi, author interview, June 13, 2002.
186. **distant forest clearings:** Activity reports of Second Lieutenant Andre Studler and Second Lieutenant Robert A. Cormier.
186. **show of rebelliousness:** According to Sassi, author interview, June 13, 2002, "He was one of these guys who was really respected by his men because people respect people who do what they want to do."
186. **"It was a matter of extreme urgency":** Team Veganin report.
186. **"We insisted on discipline":** Team Hamish report, 284.
187. **Martin and Henry McIntosh had manhandled their unsubmissive leader:** Sassi, author interview, June 13, 2002.
187. **Tommy Macpherson . . . who left through the front:** Macpherson, author interview, Jan. 20, 2002.
187. **stolen black Citroën:** Ibid., June 22, 2002.
187. **Teams Felix and Francis:** Team Felix report, 362; Team Francis report, 383.
187. **Team Giles organized doctors:** Team Ian report, 302; Team Giles report, 345.
187. **Team Veganin assembled:** Team Veganin report, 8; Team Gilbert report, 423; Team Giles report, 346.
187. **Some of the Jed-organized groups . . . were most needed:** Team Hugh report.

188. **"Where is our chief?":** Dialogue recalled by Sassi, author interview, June 13, 2002.

188. **"le Chicago gangster":** Morgan, *O.S.S. and I*, 186–87.

188. **"Captain Bazooka":** Activity report of First Lieutenant René Dussaq, 805.

188. **The problems came when the Jeds began to press:** "Weapons training was not a problem," Sassi told me (June 13, 2002). "The military discipline was what they resisted."

188–89. **We are tired . . . the next morning:** "They tired very easily when they had to make long marches and couldn't carry heavy packs," said Knox, author interview, Mar. 21, 2002.

189. **Rust and grime filled . . . gun barrels:** "The barrels and working parts almost invariably filled with filth and rust," according to the activity report of Second Lieutenant William B. Macomber, 896.

189. **"Why should we obey you?":** Sassi, author interview, June 13, 2002.

189. **In Loir-et-Cher:** Activity report of Second Lieutenant Paul Martineau, 1027.

189. **John Alsop's orders:** J. Alsop, "Memoirs," 111.

189. **the manner of men Sassi and the rest of the Jeds tried to shape:** Ford and MacBain, *Cloak and Dagger*, 78; Team Veganin report, 3: "The origin of these men varied: workmen, farmers, business men."

189. **Many had ended up in the woods:** Morgan, *O.S.S. and I*, 183; Team Veganin report, 5.

189. **In Brittany, the entire male population:** Louise Queinnec, the woman who took in the injured men at Peumerit-Quintin, told me this story (June 16, 2002).

190. **Often, maquis crowded:** According to the Team Veganin report, 8, "It was the maquis where one ate the best that was the most prosperous and the chief the most famous."

190. **"We don't want to be soldiers":** Sassi, author interview, June 13, 2002.

190. **"Why are we waiting":** Ibid.

190. **Very few believed they could have any influence:** "Morale was low . . . they had no fighting spirit . . . they hated the enemy but feared him"; see Morgan, *O.S.S. and I*, 183.

190. **Some hoped to hide:** Macpherson, author interview, Jan. 20, 2002; Sassi, author interview, June 19, 2002; Team Veganin report.

190. **Others burned with a desperate need:** "Each wanted to run his own little band at his own will and pleasure," according to the Team Veganin report, 8.

190. **They simply wanted to make other men scared:** "They were seeking to avenge a member of their family who had been tortured or killed by the Germans"; see Morgan, *O.S.S. and I*, 183.

190. **In Finistère, a young maquis:** Tack, author interview, June 24, 2002.

190. **"Alphabetical Resistance":** Macpherson, author interview, Jan. 20, 2002.

190. **The largest organizations of the maquis:** Kedward, *In Search of the Maquis*, 47.

190. **now-dissolved French army regiments:** Macpherson, author interview, Jan. 20, 2002.

190. ***naphtalines,* or mothballs:** Buckmaster, *They Fought Alone*, 206.

191. **The *naphtalines* . . . planned to hide:** Macpherson, author interview, Jan. 20, 2002.

191. **Some FTP groups around France:** For a detailed discussion of Communists' plotting for the eventual takeover of France, see Marnham's *Resistance and Betrayal.*

191. **Other maquis groups plotted a return to the monarchy:** Knox, "Glory."

191. **There were even Spanish Communists:** Sassi, author interview, June 13, 2002; J. Alsop, "Memoirs," 103.

191. **Convincing the leaders:** "I could only exercise any form of command by consent and the use of considerable tact"; see Crosby, *Irregular Soldier,* 112.

191. **The Jeds attended one diplomatic dinner:** Ibid.: "Small things like this were of great value in ensuring I was accepted"; J. Alsop, "Memoirs," 103 and 113.

191. **In Lot, the regional commander:** Team Quinine report.

191. **"We are in agreement":** Team Giles report, 344.

191. **FTP group ambushed:** Starring, author interview, Oct. 14, 2002.

191. **Team Harry contended with a group:** Team Harry report, 120–21.

191–92. **After all these long weeks . . . Allies finally reached:** Eisenhower, *Crusade in Europe,* 264–65.

192. **"If you do not obey":** Morgan, *O.S.S. and I,* 245.

192. **"We decided we would get rid of 'Napoleons' ":** Team George report, 192.

192. **Team Hamish shot a maquis:** Team Hamish report, 284.

192. **Team Veganin's group surrounded a house:** Team Veganin report, 9.

192. **"You will choose a new chief":** Dialogue recalled by Sassi, author interview, June 13, 2002.

192. **Was their leader killed, was he kidnapped:** The fate of the rebellious leader is an open question. Sassi seemed to imply to me without saying directly (June 19, 2002) that the leader was executed, but when I mistakenly expressed shock, Sassi backtracked and suggested that the leader was simply warned to go away.

192. **Word of what . . . the rapist was shot:** Ibid., June 13, 2002; Team Vega-nin report, 9; Team Hamish report, 284–85.

192. **In Côtes-du-Nord . . . next to him, sobbing:** Kehoe, "An Allied Team"; Team Frederick report, 144; Kehoe, author interview, Nov. 26, 2001.

192–93. **Jean Sassi . . . himself to his knees:** Kehoe, author interview, Nov. 26, 2001; Sassi, author interview, June 19, 2002.

193. **"I'm innocent," he cried. "I'm innocent":** Dialogue recalled by Sassi, author interview, June 19, 2002.

193. **Team Hamish had to set aside a part of every afternoon:** Team Hamish included interrogations in the part of each day it set aside for planning ambushes and receptions; see Team Hamish report, 285.

193. **"It was not for us":** Ibid., 284.

193. **Vichy militia:** Millar, *Maquis,* 279–80.

193. **"Miliciens!":** Quoted ibid.

194. **In Yonne . . . misery with a shot:** Défourneaux, *Winking Fox,* 33; activity report of René Défourneaux, 1233–34.

194. **"How do you know he is guilty?":** Dialogue recalled by Kehoe, author interview, Nov. 26, 2001.

194. **"I am a German officer":** Buckmaster, *They Fought Alone,* 120.

194. **"The Germans would have killed my family":** Sassi, author interview, June 19, 2002.

194. **whose eyes the Germans removed with forks and whose testicles they shoved in their mouths:** Activity report of Captain Owen Denis Johnson, 432.

194. **In Aube . . . blood splattered over everyone:** Activity report of Seaman Third Class James La Rosee, 1115.

195. **". . . like a mailman delivering letters":** Sassi, author interview, June 19, 2002.

195. **It was a sham:** Ibid.

195. **In Brittany, Bob Kehoe said nothing:** Kehoe, author interview, Nov. 26, 2001.

195. **In Yonne, agent Défourneaux:** Défourneaux, *Winking Fox,* 33.

195. **Sassi made no comment:** Sassi, author interview, June 19, 2002.

195. **throw up:** Ibid.

195. **he would regret not stopping the torture:** Kehoe, author interview, Nov. 26, 2001.

195. **Paincheau . . . ordered them to dig:** Anecdote comes from Millar, *Maquis,* 281–82.

195–96. **"I have tried for a long time":** Dialogue quoted ibid., 282–83.

### CHAPTER TWENTY-SIX: THE BREAKOUT APPROACHES

197. **inexperienced French officers:** War Diary, vol. 1, 34–40 and 75–77.

197. **". . . collaborator translate your French":** Team Horace report, 515.

197. **"Very surprised no instructions received":** Team Andy report, 455.

198. **"We could never understand":** Team George report, 207.

198. **twelve lamp shades:** Activity report of Captain Victor Layton, 1526.

198. **letter from the Scottish woman:** Millar, *Maquis,* 129.

198. **On July 14 . . . southeastern France:** "OSS Massive Supply Drops."

198. **2,100 tons of weapons and supplies:** Foot, *SOE in France,* 473.

198. **Team Ian, working in central France:** Team Ian report, 308.

198. **Team Felix armed three thousand:** Team Felix report, 375.

198. **Team Hugh, another six thousand:** Team Hugh report, 95.

198. **"Sabotaged 46 locomotives":** Radio message from Team Quinine, July 5, Team Quinine report; Macpherson, author interview, Jan. 20, 2002.

198. **"Coordinated attack":** Radio message from Team Quinine, July 24, Team Quinine report; Macpherson, author interview, Jan. 20, 2002.

198. **"360 rail cuts":** Radio message from Team Quinine, July 20, Team Quinine report; Macpherson, author interview, Jan. 20, 2002.

198. **". . . price of one million francs":** Radio message from Team Quinine, July 5, Team Quinine report.

198. **"Consider your head undervalued":** Radio message to Team Quinine, July 6, Team Quinine report.

198–99. **Farther south . . . Mediterranean coasts:** Team Bugatti report.

199. **"Sabotage blown 3 bridges":** Team Hamish report, 265.

199. **"12 wagons on petrol train":** Team Dodge report.

199. **spirit downed Allied aircrews:** See reports of Teams Hugh, Hamish, and Chloroform, for example.

199. **steal their cigarettes:** Knox, author interview, Feb. 15, 2002.
199. **sent his maquisards to assassinate members of the Milice:** Activity report of Second Lieutenant Roger B. Henquet.
199. **"... so much butter":** Team Hamish report, 284.
199. **The German 271st Infantry Division . . . kept from the fighting in Normandy:** "French Resistance, 4 June to 31st July," SHAEF report; J. Clarke and R. R. Smith, *Riviera to the Rhine,* 96.
200. **"... evolved into an organized army":** J. Clarke and R. R. Smith, *Riviera to the Rhine,* 96.
200. **played poker . . . drank the local pub dry:** S. Alsop and Braden, *Sub Rosa,* 152.
200. **Jack Singlaub charged:** Singlaub, author interview, Mar. 19, 2002.
200. **ninety-three Jed teams:** SOE, History of Jedburghs, part 10, 1.
200. **mood was mutinous:** Marks, *Between Silk and Cyanide,* 528.
200. **Omar Bradley's American forces . . . thirty miles short of that goal:** Hammond, "Normandy," 41; Eisenhower, *Crusade in Europe,* 272.
200. **snouts of about 60 percent of their . . . tanks:** Zaloga, "Normandy Legends."
201. **audacious new plan code-named Cobra . . . slew of German defenders:** Hastings, *Overlord,* 250.

## CHAPTER TWENTY-SEVEN: "IN GRAVE DANGER"

203. **Kehoe . . . sat with his radio receiver:** The story of Aïde and the massacre of Team Frederick's reception committee was related to me by Bob Kehoe (Nov. 28, 2001) and is discussed in his "An Allied Team."
203. **On July 9, Team Frederick had relocated:** Team Frederick report, 139.
204. **On the morning of July 20 . . . their own success:** Ibid., 152; Kehoe, author interview, Nov. 28, 2001.
205. **on July 7, the German high command had ordered:** "OKW War Diary," 54 and 57.
205. **On July 21 . . . the occupiers finally launched:** Ousby, *Occupation,* 331.
205. **In Vienne . . . coast and into Angoulême:** Team Ian report, 313.
205. **But nothing had alerted . . . who passed to see:** Kehoe, author interview, Nov. 28, 2001; Kehoe, "An Allied Team."
205. **"We have information":** Radio message to SFHQ, July 28, 1944, Team Giles report, 330.
205. **The machine guns opened up:** The story of the July attack on Team Frederick's command base was related to me by Bob Kehoe (Nov. 28, 2001); also see Kehoe, "An Allied Team" and the Team Frederick report.
206. **German 2nd Parachute Division burned farms . . . suspend men by their feet:** Team Francis report, 402.
206. **In Team Ian's area:** Team Ian report, 314.
206. **trenches filled with the decomposed bodies:** Team Francis report, 402.
206. **"In grave danger":** Radio message to SFHQ, July 26, 1944, Team Giles report, 330.
206. **"The FTP are reaching boiling point":** Radio message to SFHQ, July 27, 1944, ibid.

206. **"You must avoid":** SFHQ radio message to Team Giles, July 28, 1944, ibid., 331. "HQ 21 Army Group did not wish resistance activity in Brittany to have the effect of drawing into Brittany German troops from other parts of France"; see "Brittany Plan," SFHQ internal memo.

206. **He now commanded about two thousand armed men:** French Forces of the Interior—1944, 590.

206. **"We repeat":** Radio message to SFHQ, July 29, 2003, Team Giles report, 331.

207. **At 9:10 p.m. . . . his four clips of ammo:** Team Francis report, 403–7.

207. **In Vienne . . . sneak past the outposts to safety:** Team Ian report, 316–17.

207–8. **Back in Côtes-du-Nord . . . dined on boiled potatoes:** Kehoe, author interview, Nov. 28, 2001; Kehoe, "An Allied Team"; Team Frederick report, 147.

208. **"You need not be afraid":** Dialogue appears in Team Francis report, 406.

208. **They shot him first . . . laughed and joked:** Ibid., 403–7. The killing of the SAS man was witnessed by the Team Francis radio operator.

208. **Back at Bernard Knox's command post:** Knox, author interview, May 3, 2002.

208. **"Major Ogden-Smith killed":** Radio message to SFHQ, Aug. 2, 1944, Team Giles report, 332.

208. **In Vienne, John Gildee . . . of the nineteen who would die:** A full accounting of the Jedburgh casualties can be found in A. Brown, *Jedburghs.*

## CHAPTER TWENTY-EIGHT: COBRA STRIKE

211. **After days of torrential rain:** This account of Operation Cobra is taken from Hastings, *Overlord,* 344–66; Hogan, "Northern France," 6–10; D'Este, *Decision in Normandy,* 400–407; Eisenhower, *Crusade in Europe,* 266–74; D. Miller and Commager, *World War II,* 317–21; and Fussell, *Boys' Crusade,* 43–52.

211. **"Looks as if they've got cold feet":** Hastings, *Overlord,* 253.

211. **"Bombing attacks":** Ibid.

212. **140,000 artillery shells and over eight million pounds of bombs:** Casey, *Secret War,* 111.

212. **"My grenadiers and the pioneers":** Quoted in Fussell, *Boys' Crusade,* 51.

212. **"We stood tensed in muscle":** Pyle is quoted in Hastings, *Overlord,* 254, and elsewhere; Fussell gives a particularly detailed account of this short bombing in *Boys' Crusade,* 266–74.

212. **"The attack goes ahead":** Hastings, *Overlord,* 255.

213. **"It's always slow going":** Eisenhower, *Crusade in Europe,* 272.

214. **"We shall continue attacking":** D'Este, *Decision in Normandy,* 405.

214. **A horseman who came up through the cavalry:** See ibid., 404–5, for a brief discussion of Patton's character and travails.

214. **"a yellow son of a bitch":** Long, "Mistreatment of Patients in Receiving Tents."

215. **"murder those lousy Hun bastards":** Speech delieverd by Patton to the troops in England, June 5, 1944.

215. **As the compromise plan . . . deep in enemy territory:** Blumenson, *Breakout,* 344–70.

216. **"Soon you'll get to greet your compatriots":** Carbuccia is quoted in Dreux, *No Bridges Blown,* 207.

216. **The first tanks of Patton's advance:** The story of Team Gavin and Patton's tanks related in Dreux, *No Bridges Blown,* 207–9, and Team Guy/Gavin report, 484.

216. **At the other end of Brittany:** Radio message to SFHQ, Aug. 2, 1944, Team Giles report, 332; Knox, author interview, June 1, 2002.

216. **They stoked locomotive engines:** "They were on foot, on bicycles and in horse-drawn carts," according to Team Giles report, 351; Knox, author interview, June 1, 2002.

216–17. **In the early hours of August 1 . . . Patton's unconventional assault:** Blumenson, *Breakout,* 341–72.

217. **Surely you don't expect:** The protests of the maquis can be found throughout the Jed reports; Knox, author interview, June 1, 2002.

217. **Knox and the rest . . . sympathized with the maquis:** Knox, author interview, June 1, 2002.

217. **In Morbihan:** Team Gerald report, 569.

217. **Bernard Knox and the other Jeds:** Knox, author interview, June 1, 2002.

217. **"Allied forces advancing into Britanny":** SFHQ radio message to Team Francis, Aug. 2, 1944, Team Francis report, 387.

217. *Merde!***:** The wording is mine; the sentiment supplied by Knox, author interview, June 1, 2002.

218. **"*Le chapeau de Napoléon*":** Dreux, *No Bridges Blown,* 209.

**CHAPTER TWENTY-NINE: "A MESSAGE OF THE HIGHEST IMPORTANCE"**

219. **In planning his audacious Brittany campaign:** This discussion of Patton's plans is synthesized from D'Este, *Decision in Normandy,* 408–10; Blumenson, *Breakout,* 343–51; and Hogan, "Northern France," 14.

219. **". . . grease the treads of our tanks":** Patton's speech to the troops, June 5, 1944.

220. **"stagecoaches":** William M. King of the 6th Armored Division quoted in Blumenson, *Breakout,* 354.

220. **". . . nothing but a map of Brittany":** General Grow is quoted ibid., 372.

220. **rabble of thirty thousand:** French Forces of the Interior—1944, 561.

220–21. **On August 1 . . . exciting new orders:** See ibid., 557–69, for a discussion of SFHQ's liaison with Patton's Third Army.

221. **Jed Team Horace:** Radio message to SFHQ, July 28, 1944, Team Horace report, 514.

221. **"Advancing Allied troops":** SFHQ radio message to Team Gilbert, Aug. 4, 1944, Team Gilbert report, 413.

221. **In the north . . . on the coast road:** SFHQ radio messages to Teams Frederick, Felix, and Hilary, Aug. 2, 1944, Team Frederick report, 140; Team Felix report, 366; and Team Hilary report, 543.

221. **In central Finistère:** Team Giles report, 351.

221. **Farther south, Teams Gilbert and Francis:** Team Francis report, 397; Team Gilbert report, 429.

223. **air force refused:** SFHQ radio message to Team Horace, Aug. 2, 1944, Team Horace report, 514.

223. **Team Horace begged headquarters:** Ibid., 521.

223. **". . . important enough to risk planes":** Radio message to SFHQ, July 31, 1944, ibid., 514.

223. **A thousand miles farther south . . . renamed Dragoon for security reasons:** For discussions of the southern invasion plans, see J. Clarke and R. R. Smith, *Riviera to the Rhine,* 75–85, and J. Clarke, "Southern France," 5–9.

224. **"Let the other son of a bitch":** Singlaub and McConnell, *Hazardous Duty,* 48.

224. **Patton gave the shadow armies:** Casey, *Secret War,* 130.

224. **Patch gave them the similar job:** J. Clarke and R. R. Smith, *Riviera to the Rhine,* 81; J. Clarke, "Southern France," 9; "Plan for the Use of Resistance in Support of Operation Anvil."

224. **In those first days of August:** SOE, History of Jedburghs, vol. 6, 7–8.

224. **Each afternoon at Milton Hall:** The description of the Jeds coming down from Musgrave's office is taken from S. Alsop and Braden, *Sub Rosa,* 152.

224. **Radioman Roger Coté . . . waving good-bye to him:** Author interview with Coté's sister, Violette Desmarais, Oct. 2, 2002.

224–25. **"This evening I am . . . our son who loves you very, very much":** Coté, letter to his parents, Aug. 9, 1944.

225. **"It was sure good while it lasted":** L. F. Goddard, letter to his parents, Apr. 2, 1944.

225. **"Even if you don't hear from me":** Singlaub, letter to his parents, Aug. 2, 1944.

225. **In all of June and July . . . floated through the night:** SOE, History of Jedburghs, appendices XA and XB; "Index to SO Reports, WE Section."

225. **"And now a message":** Knox, author interview, Feb. 15, 2002.

225. **August 2 at 6:00 p.m.:** French Forces of the Interior—1944, 555; radio messages to a number of Brittany Jed teams.

225. **"I have only one thing to say to you":** Aron, *France Reborn,* 130; Team Gilbert report, 429.

225. **Two clips is all you get:** Morgan, *O.S.S. and I,* 204–5.

226. **Remember . . . do not fire:** Knox, author interview, May 3, 2002.

226. **When you hear the whistle:** Whistles mentioned in S. Alsop and Braden, *Sub Rosa,* 117, and Team Hilary's report, 554.

226. **"How can the Germans hit you":** Morgan, *O.S.S. and I,* 216.

### CHAPTER THIRTY: FLYING BODY PARTS

227. **To ambush a German convoy:** This section is an amalgamation from ambushes described in S. Alsop and Braden, *Sub Rosa* (116–18); Dreux, *No Bridges Blown* (204–6); Morgan, *O.S.S. and I* (212–26); Foot, *SOE in France* (395); the agent reports of William Morgan (1254–58), Captain Owen Denis Johnson (430–32), Lieutenant Maurice Bassett (627), and Second Lieutetant William B. Macomber (900); the reports of Jedburgh Teams Gerald (569–70), Hilary (552–54), Gilbert (432), and others; and author interviews with Sassi (Sept. 21, 2002), Knox (May 3, 2002), and Trumps (Mar. 18, 2002). For the tactics of an ambush, see Morgan, *O.S.S. and I,* 212–25, and the agent report of William Morgan, 1254–58.

228. **They had fought on the Russian front:** For the history of Hitler's 2nd Parachute Division, see Blumenson, *Breakout,* 341.

228. **In Morbihan, the blast:** Team Gerald report, 570.

228. **In Finistère, orange flames leapt:** Knox, author interview, May 3, 2002.

228. **"Bits and pieces":** Ibid., Mar. 21, 2002.

228. **A lonesome, torn-away arm:** For the gore witnessed by men in battle, see Fussell, *Doing Battle*, 112.

229. **worry if they would fire at all:** According to Morgan, *O.S.S. and I*, 219, whether maquisards would actually engage the enemy was a major concern of Jeds and agents; only 15 percent of trained U.S. soldiers could be induced to fire at the enemy in combat; see Baum, "Price of Valor."

229. **"Concentrate first on the drivers":** Morgan, *O.S.S. and I*, 200–210.

229. **Short experience as soldiers:** This, anyway, was the experience of regular soldiers; see Fussell, *Doing Battle*, 100.

229. **most of the soldiers collapsed:** According to Morgan, *O.S.S. and I*, 206, "When a gammon hits the side of a truck, the truck and all its occupants are done for."

229. **Unable to see the hidden maquis:** See ibid., 216: "How can the Germans hit you with mortar fire if they don't know where you are?"

229. **Do not draw fire:** Kehoe, author interview, Nov. 26, 2001.

229. **Jean Sassi knocked over maquisards:** Sassi, author interview, June 13, 2002.

229. **"Though their trucks might be shot up":** Team Hilary report, 553.

230. **"He who fights and runs away":** Berlin, author interview, Sept. 11, 2002.

230. **Unlike in regular battle:** "You cannot afford to lose men or equipment"; see Morgan, *O.S.S. and I*, 208.

230. **The maquis rifle teams . . . flankers from giving chase:** Ibid., 200–210.

230. **their hands still clutched their rifles:** "They were all very young," according to the Team Giles report, 352.

230. **Now that it was over:** The maquis' reactions to battle are taken from Fussell, *Doing Battle*, 106.

230. **After the ignominy:** "Fear of killing, rather than fear of being killed, was the most common cause of battle failure," wrote U.S. Army historian S. L. A. Marshall (quoted in Baum, "Price of Valor").

230. **refused to tell their wives about these battles:** Louise Queinnec, the wife of a Breton Resistance fighter, told me that her husband refused to talk about his experiences (June 15 and June 16, 2002).

231. **brains to sprout out of a corpse's nose:** The various dispositions of German corpses come from Fussell, *Doing Battle*, 106.

231. **"The shooting of the German":** Dreux, *No Bridges Blown*, 205.

231. **Tens of thousands . . . as it roared toward Lorient:** French Forces of the Interior—1944, 576–96.

231. **In central Finistère:** Team Giles report, 351–52.

231. **Following the guidance of Jed Team Gerald:** Team Gerald report, 572; Blumenson, *Breakout*, 379.

231. **Knox's maquis mounted:** Detailed discussions of the maquis' successes against the Germans in Brittany can be found in French Forces of the Interior—1944, 535–616; Aron, *France Reborn*, 110–42; and various Jed team reports.

232. **"Bren gun and rifle fire":** Team Hilary report, 553.

232. **At the village of Cléder:** Aron, *France Reborn,* 137–38.

232. **Frustrated by a Team Felix ambush:** Team Felix report, 376.

232. **"Ahead," he replied. "It's our duty":** Aron, *France Reborn,* 133.

232. **By August 4 . . . short of Brest:** Blumenson, *Breakout,* map VIII.

232. **"In view of rapid Allied advance":** Radio message from SFHQ to Team Gilbert, Aug. 4, 1944, Team Gilbert report, 414.

233. **Team Frederick quickly reported the occupation:** French Forces of the Interior—1944, 577.

233. **Team Francis, in southern Finistère:** Radio message to SFHQ, Aug. 10, 1944, Team Francis report, 388.

233. **"to the last man, the last cartridge":** Blumenson, *Breakout,* 339–43.

233. **"Elements of German forces":** Radio message to SFHQ, Aug. 5, 1944, Team Giles report, 335.

233. **they killed everyone they saw:** Aron, *France Reborn,* 137.

233. **In Châteauneuf, fifty massacred civilians:** Team Giles report, 353.

233. **"People being tortured and killed":** Team Hilary report, 552.

233. **their interpretation of the rules of war:** French Forces of the Interior—1944, 568.

233. **"Even if we had wished":** Team Giles report, 352.

234. **Germans hammered the flesh . . . castrated the patriots:** Aron, *France Reborn,* 137.

## CHAPTER THIRTY-ONE: ARRESTED

235. **Cy Manierre froze:** The story of Manierre's encounter with the German patrol near Serves-sur-Rhône is taken from his Team Dodge report, 13–19.

235. **Germans had taken to patrolling:** Activity report of Captain Owen Denis Johnson.

235. **suggested negotiating for peace:** D'Este, *Decision in Normandy,* 413–15.

236. **Hitler intended to throw every available piece of armor:** Blumenson, *Breakout,* 457.

236. **already hobbled movement of German forces:** "The FFI had become so aggressive that *Army Group G* was able to move only large, well-protected convoys along the highways and rails of southern France"; see J. Clarke and R. R. Smith, *Riviera to the Rhine,* 97.

238. **More important than ever were the groups:** For missions of the southern Jed teams, see SOE, History of Jedburghs, vol. 6, 6–9; the individual team reports; and "Plan for the Use of Resistance in Support of Operation Anvil." For disposition of German divisions around southern France, see J. Clarke and R. R. Smith, *Riviera to the Rhine,* 65–70.

238. **The other two teams:** Reports of Teams Ivor, Alec, and Julian.

238. **With the exception of VIII Corps . . . German forces in the south:** Blumenson, *Breakout,* 433–35; D'Este, *Decision in Normandy,* 412–14; Hogan, "Northern France," 14–15.

238. **Paul Cyr's Team George:** Team George report.

238. **At the same time, Teams Ian and Harold:** SOE, History of Jedburghs, Part 6, 14.

239. **Lou Goddard . . . Captain John Cox:** Team Ivor report, 629.

239. **Goddard . . . a cheerful hard worker:** Captain John Cox, letter to Mr. & Mrs. C. J. Goddard, Oct. 6, 1944.

239. **his high-school hiking club . . . exploring a cave:** Barbara Goddard, *Memoirs of Lewis Frelan Goddard.*

239. **the heavy canister whipped dangerously:** According to Captain Cox's letter to Goddard's parents (Oct. 6, 1944), Team Ivor's leader believed this to be the cause of Goddard's death.

239. **the tangled canister detached itself:** Ibid. The tangled container "whisked to the rear by the slip stream of the plane must have hit him and probably killed him instantly."

239. **The pilot had mistakenly dropped them:** Team Ivor report, 635; Gaujac, *Special Forces,* 231.

240. **Two hundred townspeople attended:** Gaujac, *Special Forces,* 231.

240. **"It is with regret":** Adjutant General's Office, letter to Mr. C. J. Goddard, Aug. 21, 1944.

240. **Manierre . . . climbed into the cab:** Manierre's arrest is related in his Team Dodge report, 15–19; "Casualty reports;" OSS memo; "Arrest of Major Manierre," OSS memo.

## CHAPTER THIRTY-TWO: JEDS RAIN DOWN

243. **Knox and his men moved in to investigate:** Knox related his discovery of the dead Americans to me (Aug. 15, 2002) and in his *Tragic Sense,* 16–20.

243. **"It's all right soldier":** Dialogue appears in Knox, *Tragic Sense,* 16–20.

244. **It was August 7 . . . penning thirty thousand Germans within:** Blumenson, *Breakout,* 414; "11th Special Forces Detachment Operations Report," 237.

244. **"that their way had been made clear for them":** Mackenzie, *Secret History of SOE,* 619.

244. **Singlaub and the rest of Team James listened intently:** Singlaub, author interview, Mar. 19, 2002; Singlaub and McConnell, *Hazardous Duty,* 42–43.

244–45. **Hitler's northern France forces . . . many tens of thousands of Germans:** For discussions of the Falaise Pocket encirclement, see Blumenson, *Breakout,* 457–556; D'Este, *Decision in Normandy,* 418–35; Eisenhower, *Crusade in Europe,* 274–79.

245. **he also built a new defensive line:** "OKW War Diary," 65–66.

245. **making preparations to withdraw:** "By the middle of August it was quite evident that the enemy was preparing to evacuate field forces from that part of France lying south of the Loire"; see War Diary, vol. 13, 119.

245. **Team Lee would drop into Haute-Vienne . . . Team James into Corrèze:** "Index to SO Reports, WE Section."

245. **The Allies wanted to force them to travel north:** Macpherson, author interview, Jan. 20, 2002: "The Allies didn't see Germans coming through the Massif Central because if they came up those roads they wouldn't be visible to RAF."

246. **"This is the main German escape route":** Singlaub and McConnell, *Hazardous Duty,* 42.

246. **Tommy Macpherson's Team Quinine:** Macpherson, author interview, Jan. 20, 2002.

246. **Team Lee would do similar work:** Team Lee report.

246. **the Germans had concentrated nearly eighteen hundred troops:** Team James report, 748.

246. **at the Italian ports of Naples and Salerno:** J. Clarke and R. R. Smith, *Riviera to the Rhine*, 91.

246. **On August 10 . . . and Taranto in southern Italy:** Ibid., 91; Casey, *Secret War*, 132.

246. **Undercover Nazi agents . . . weren't sure where:** For a discussion of German intelligence reports on the impending southern invasion, see "OKW War Diary," 99–102.

247. **Each of his convoys . . . devastating counterattack:** J. Clarke and R. R. Smith, *Riviera to the Rhine*, 70–95.

247. **As things stood . . . planned landing beaches:** See ibid., 65–70, for a discussion of German preparedness against the southern invasion.

247. **Even this weakened force . . . near Toulouse:** "The most dangerous threat was the ability of the German defenders to assemble enough forces for an effective counterattack"; see ibid., 81.

247. **To southern France's . . . Rhône to Marseilles:** "Summary of Allied Aid," War Diary, vol. 13, 116; "Plan for the Use of Resistance in Support of Operation Anvil."

247. **the 11th Panzer Division suddenly began to travel:** "OKW War Diary," 102.

247. **"Enemy mobile reserves":** Special Projects Operation Center message to Team Packard, Aug. 11, 1944, Team Packard report.

248. **The maquis working with the two teams:** SOE, History of Jedburghs, part 6, 6–9, and map at Appendix VI. B; the individual team reports; and "Plan for the Use of Resistance in Support of Operation Anvil."

248. **Meanwhile, General Patch also worried:** J. Clarke, "Southern France," 15; J. Clarke and R. R. Smith, *Riviera to the Rhine*, 64.

248. **Patch wanted the alpine passes:** "Report of Special Force Unit No. 4," War Diary, vol. 3, 338; a map of the crucial routes Patch wanted blocked can be found in "Plan for the Use of Resistance in Support of Operation Anvil."

248. **"Block all passes":** Special Projects Operation Center message to Team Chloroform, Team Chloroform report, E101.

248. **Team Chloroform's Henry McIntosh:** Team Chloroform report #2, 3; Sassi, author interview, June 19, 2002.

248. **Bill Thompson's Team Novocaine:** Team Novocaine report, E101.

## CHAPTER THIRTY-THREE: LEAVING A MAN TO DIE

249. **Dreux and his fifteen-strong patrol:** The story of Dreux's reconnaissance of La Bastille is taken from his *No Bridges Blown*, 237–57. All dialogue is quoted from these pages.

249. **probably the 83rd Infantry:** Blumenson, *Breakout*, 414.

249. **"Bonjour":** Dialogue quoted in Dreux, *No Bridges Blown*, 238.

250. **Task Force A had finished its sweep:** Blumenson, *Breakout*, 413–14.

251. **important railway viaducts:** French Forces of the Interior—1944, 569.
251. **thirty thousand prisoners:** Actions of the Free French forces captured or led to the capture of approximately 50 percent of German troops taken in Brittany, according to a report by the assistant chief of staff, G1 of 6th Armored Division on Aug. 29, 1944, quoted ibid., 568. "An American corps, supported by 30,000 maquisards, took 60,000 prisoners"; see Aron, *France Reborn,* 129.
251. **90 percent of the useful intelligence:** According to a Sept. 9, 1944, report of the intelligence officer of the Ninth Army, which took over from the Third in Brittany; see Aron, *France Reborn,* 130.
251. **Patton's VIII Corps, with the help:** Ibid., 129.
251. **On August 10 . . . guarding the supply lines:** French Forces of the Interior— 1944, 561–62; 11th Special Force Detachment, Third U.S. Army, "Plan for Resistance Movements in Brittany," in "11th Special Forces Detachment Operations Report."
251. **Bernard Knox and Team Giles:** Team Giles report.
251. **Bob Kehoe and Team Frederick:** Team Frederick report, 150.
251. **Bill Dreux's Team Gavin:** "11th Special Forces Detachment Operations Report," 270.

### CHAPTER THIRTY-FOUR: SOUTHERN UPRISING

257. **landing craft loaded with 151,000 invasion troops:** The discussion of the Dragoon landing is taken from J. Clarke and R. R. Smith, *Riviera to the Rhine,* 92–117; "OKW War Diary," 95–105; Casey, *Secret War,* 136–40; and J. Clarke, "Southern France," 13–16.
258. **On the far side . . . toward the southern beachhead:** SOE, History of Jedburghs, part 6, 6–9 and map at Appendix XVI. B; individual team reports; and "Plan for the Use of Resistance in Support of Operation Anvil."
258. **dribbled across the river:** "OKW War Diary," 103.
258. **A second puny counterattack . . . one day earlier:** J. Clarke and R. R. Smith, *Riviera to the Rhine,* 107; Team Sceptre report, E101.
258. **Farther north . . . road to the coast severed:** Team Chloroform report; Team Novocaine report; SOE, History of Jedburghs, part 6, 8.
258–59. **The Dragoon forces . . . leading to the bridgehead:** J. Clarke and R. R. Smith, *Riviera to the Rhine,* 96–97.
259. **"The continual harassing":** Quoted in A. L. Funk, *Hidden Ally,* 253.
259. **By nightfall . . . and 385 wounded:** J. Clarke and R. R. Smith, *Riviera to the Rhine,* 122.
259. **ten more Jed teams:** "Index to SO Reports, WE Section."
259. **BBC had transmitted a message:** The prearranged BBC messages for intensified guerrilla action in the southern zone were sent on the evening of August 14; see "Summary of Allied Aid," 116.
259. **Powerful German machine guns:** The story of the mid-August siege at Egletons is taken from conversations with Jack Singlaub (Jan. 9 and Mar. 19, 2002) and Jacques de Penguilly (June 17, 2002); the Team James report, 748–57; the report of Major de Guelis of Mission Tilleul; and Singlaub and McConnell, *Hazardous Duty,* 45–66. All dialogue is quoted from *Hazardous Duty.*

260. **maquis' faces beamed:** "We should like to emphasize the joy of the troops when they saw us among them"; see Team James report, 752.

260. **Don't waste your bullets:** "They didn't know to fire in bursts," said Singlaub, author interview, Mar. 19, 2002. "We could be of greatest value by giving technical advice and leading the troops actually engaged in the fight"; see Team James report, 751.

260. **Hardly twelve hours:** The prearranged BBC messages for intensified guerrilla action in the southern zone were sent out in the evening of August 14 (Summary of Allied Aid, 116).

261. **The race to be seen as liberator:** See, for example, the Team Packard and Team Alexander reports.

**CHAPTER THIRTY-FIVE: WITHDRAWAL**

265. **trapped eighty thousand German fighters:** D'Este, *Decision in Normandy,* 430.

265. **German bodies rotted . . . flying above vomited:** Fussell, *Boys' Crusade,* 62–63; Eisenhower, *Crusade in Europe,* 279–80.

265. **"It was literally possible":** Eisenhower, *Crusade in Europe,* 279.

265. **eight of Hitler's infantry and two of his panzer divisions:** Ibid.

265. **ten thousand dead . . . ten were left as fighting units:** D'Este, *Decision in Normandy,* 430–31.

265. **seventy-five thousand German troops and 250 tanks:** Blumenson, *Breakout,* 573.

266. **He ordered Montgomery . . . charging up from the south:** The plan for the charge to the German border is described ibid., 657–60; Eisenhower, *Crusade in Europe,* 291–93; and Hogan, "Northern France," 23–25.

266. **the Resistance had hardly been organized . . . maquis to hide:** SOE, History of Jedburghs, part 6, 10.

266. **In the east, the long distance . . . spare the planes:** Ibid., 12.

266. **By the afternoon of August 16:** J. Clarke, "Southern France," 14.

266–67. **Two American divisions . . . forces in Italy:** For a more detailed discussion of the Sixth Army Group's movement, see J. Clarke and R. R. Smith, *Riviera to the Rhine,* 126–42.

267. **Back on the coast:** Ibid., 80. The French had planned to land on D-Day plus three.

267. **Blaskowitz tried . . . at Marseille:** J. Clarke, "Southern France," 15.

267. **With so many troops . . . from Lyon and Grenoble:** "FFI Before and After D-Day," 32.

267. **"Boche evacuating our region":** Team Ivor report.

267. **"Big convoys daily from Bordeaux":** Team Harold message, Aug. 19, 1944, Team Harold report, 498.

267. **German soldiers in the southwest:** "OKW War Diary," 110.

267. **The German 148th Division . . . escape into Italy:** J. Clarke, "Southern France," 14.

267. **On August 16:** Ibid., 16; "OKW War Diary," 104.

CHAPTER THIRTY-SIX: LIKE SHOOTING QUAIL

268. **To help the Allies win it:** For missions assigned to the Resistance during Operation Dragoon, see J. Clarke and R. R. Smith, *Riviera to the Rhine*, 81; "Plan for the Use of Resistance in Support of Operation Anvil"; and SOE, History of Jedburghs, vol. 6, 6–9.

268. **"Harass enemy withdrawal":** Special Projects Operating Center message to Team Dodge, Aug. 18, 1944, Team Dodge report.

268. **Blaskowitz's 100,000 troops:** "OKW War Diary," 108 and 110.

268. **Vuchot's groups ... echoed with gunfire:** Team Veganin report.

268. **A little south of Vuchot ... from one hundred trucks an hour to four:** Team Monocle report.

268. **Another one hundred thousand of Blaskowitz's forces:** "OKW War Diary," 110.

269. **What Patch and Eisenhower did not want ... also had to be closed:** "Report of Special Force Unit No. 4," War Diary, vol. 3, 338.

269. **"Counting on your all out effort":** Special Projects Operating Center message to Team Packard, Aug. 23, 1944, Team Packard report; individual team reports; SOE, History of Jedburghs, part 6, 15; "Summary of Allied Aid," 120–23.

269. **On the southwest corner ... at Le Lioran:** Macpherson, author interview, Jan. 20 and June 21, 2002.

269. **At the same time ... passes near Grenoble:** Individual team reports; SOE, History of Jedburghs, part 6, 8; "Summary of Allied Aid," 116–23.

269. **Since no regular troops:** Casey, *Secret War*, 146.

270. **Four more Jed teams parachuted:** The teams were John, Mark, Martin, and Miles; see SOE, History of Jedburghs, part 6, 16.

270. **On August 16 and 17:** Singlaub and McConnell, *Hazardous Duty*, 62; Team James report, 755.

270. **On August 20:** Team Chloroform report #1, 7; J. Clarke and R. R. Smith, *Riviera to the Rhine*, 145; A. L. Funk, *Hidden Ally*, 123–30.

270. **On August 24:** Team Packard report, E101, 2; Bank, *From OSS*, 69–70.

270. **On August 27 ... automobile headlights:** Team Alexander report, 810–12.

270. **By now, the Resistance:** Western Europe, vol. 3, 394.

270. **In the southeast:** "Summary of Allied Aid," 117.

270. **the entire swath of France south of the Loire:** Casey, *Secret War*, 146.

270–71. **At Nîmes ... one of the ladies:** Bank, *From OSS*, 72.

271. **In a restaurant ... he didn't go:** Franklin, Jedburg, 200.

271. **all of Paris:** For a full discussion of the liberation of Paris, see Foot, *SOE in France*, 413–15; French Forces of the Interior—1944, 1234–73; "Summary of Allied Aid," 118–19.

271. **Jed Team Jude:** Team Jude report.

271. **blew up a canal lock:** Team Anthony report.

271. **"veritable quail shooting":** Report of the American agent Captain Owen Denis Johnson, 430.

271. **In the last days of August ... entered the liberated city on September 3:** Team Jude report; report of American agent First Lieutenant Andred E. Paray, 1471–74.

272. **A few thousand would rush north ... charged up to Poitiers:** According to

the Team Alex report, 673, "Germans came from south and southwest through Poitiers, Châteauroux to Vierzon and Bourges."

272. **The Germans had no choice ... German crossings of the Loire:** "11th Special Forces Detachment Operations Report," 257; Team George report, 189.

272. **nine thousand Resistance:** Team Hugh report, 101.

272. **To protect themselves from Resistance ambushes:** Team Alec report, 674.

272. **RAF planes swooped in:** French Forces of the Interior—1944, 1067.

272. **fifty dead Germans:** Team Alec report, 674.

272. **killed fifteen thousand Germans:** Team Ivor report, 659.

272. **"Whole companies would sit in ambush":** Report of the American agent Captain Owen Denis Johnson, 430.

272. **The Resistance ambushes just south of the Loire:** Team Hugh report, 105.

272. **In the last week of August ... at least send more airpower:** Ibid., 102; Team Hamish report, 293.

273. **The 370-foot-tall dam:** Janberg, "Barrage de Sarans."

273. **would flood fifty square miles:** Macpherson's estimation, author interview, Jan. 20, 2002.

274. **In exchange for safe passage:** Casey, *Secret War,* 147.

274. **Macpherson raced for Toulouse ... Elster's column of twenty thousand:** Macpherson, author interviews, Jan. 20 and June 21, 2002; Macpherson quoted in Stafford, *Secret Agent,* 220–21.

**CHAPTER THIRTY-SEVEN: "PURIFICATION"**

275. *Maquis d'octobre:* S. Alsop and Braden, *Sub Rosa,* 180.

275. **"Warriors who march":** Dreux, *No Bridges Blown,* 217.

275. **Even some former collaborators:** J. Alsop, "Memoirs."

275. **In Périgueux, just as Dick Franklin:** The anecdote about the execution of Germans at Périgueux comes from Franklin, "Jedburg," 200–201; S. Alsop and Braden, *Sub Rosa,* 178–80.

275. **"Look at the dirty Boches":** Quoted in S. Alsop and Braden, *Sub Rosa,* 179.

276. **At Coublanc ... their being shot, too:** Cannicott, *Journey,* 38.

276. **In the Vosges ... boy said to Lajeunesse:** Lajeunesse, author interview, May 28, 2002.

276. **"I am a parachutist":** Sassi, author interivew, Sept. 22, 2002.

276. **"You are a German parachutist":** Bourbon, author interview, Feb. 20, 2002.

276. **As the Germans withdrew:** Aron, *France Reborn,* 138.

277. **"Don't lay another hand on them":** Dialogue recalled by Sassi, author interview, Sept. 22, 2002.

277. *Collabos horizontals:* Ousby, *Occupation,* 305.

277. *la coiffure de '44:* Ibid., 306.

277. *épuration:* For excellent discussions of the *épuration,* see Ousby, *Occupation,* 303–14, and Marnham, *Death of Jean Moulin,* 204–20.

277. **In Amancey ... urinated on them:** Lajeunesse, author interview, May 30 and Aug. 12, 2002.

277. **In Marseille ... with red-hot pokers:** Marnham, *Death of Jean Moulin,* 211.

277. *plumées:* Ousby, *Occupation,* 306.

277. **In Marseille, as a *chef de maquis*:** Marnham, *Death of Jean Moulin,* 211.

277. **"In the late summer of 1944":** A. Brown, "One Bright," 162.

278. **ate her wedding breakfast:** Marnham, *Death of Jean Moulin,* 206.

278. **"Aged twenty-nine":** Quoted in Ousby, *Occupation,* 304.

278. **Near Angoulême ... his only crimes:** Franklin, "Jedburg," 202.

278. **"If the defeated enemy suceeds":** Quoted in Ousby, *Occupation,* 307.

278. **Thirty thousand people died:** Marnham, *Death of Jean Moulin,* 203.

278. **exactly the same number shot:** The Germans shot and massacred thirty thousand; see Aron, *France Reborn,* 465.

278. **"I wanted my army":** Franklin, "Jedburg," 205.

278–79. **"Having liberated France":** Tack, author interview, Apr. 16, 2002.

279. **In northeast France ... Belgium and Germany:** Blumenson, *Breakout,* 419, 575–76, and 662; "OKW War Diary," 96.

279. **too heated to be able to work behind the lines:** "The few teams that were sent to reinforce Resistance in the north were volunteers to work in civilian clothes"; see SOE, History of Jedburghs, part 6, 10.

279. **on August 16, Roger Coté's Team Augustus:** Team Augustus report.

279. **Team Augustus, like the ten other Jed teams:** See Lewis, *Jedburgh Team Operations,* for a detailed study of the teams who were dropped in northeast France.

279. **As the Germans ... fleeing from the north of France:** Radio messages, Aug. 20–24, 1944, Team Augustus report.

279. **ran out of Germans to fight ... withdrawing from the southwest:** Team Ivor report, 651; Team Lee report, 687; Team James report.

279. **Aaron Bank's Team Packard:** Team Packard report, 3.

280. **many tens of thousands ... anyone who slowed them down:** Millar, *Maquis,* 330–41.

280. **British Sergeant Ken Seymour:** Team Jacob report.

280. **French Captain Chaigneau:** Team Aubrey report.

280. **French Lieutenant d'Oultremont:** Team Andrew report.

280. **In Jura ... blew the house and the Germans inside to pieces:** Lajeunesse, letter to the author, n.d.; Lajeunesse, author interviews, May 30 and Aug. 11, 2002.

281. **Larry Swank of Team Ephedrine:** Team Ephedrine report.

281. **between five and fifteen thousand Germans:** SOE, History of Jedburghs, part 6, 8; activity report of Leon F. Ball, 1424.

281. **Finally, Field Marshal Kesselring:** "OKW War Diary," 96.

281. **"Get us out of here":** Thompson, "Autobiography," 33.

281. **One by one, the Germans wiped them out:** Ibid., 33–34; Thompson, author interview, Sept. 4, 2002.

281. **Sixty miles east of the Belgian border:** Gaujac, *Special Forces,* 183.

281. **Bob Kehoe's Team Frederick ... and Douglas:** Team Frederick report, 143; Team Guy report, 488; Team Felix report, 369; Team Gerald report, 564; Team Daniel report, 582; Team Douglas report, 618.

281–82. **To protect the Dragoon invasion's French First Army ... battle between the Resistance and the Germans:** Macpherson, author interview, Jan. 20, 2002.

282. **"This is an important task":** SFHQ radio message to Team Augustus, Aug. 30, 1944, Team Augustus report.

## CHAPTER THIRTY-EIGHT: SURRENDER

283. **Coté and his teammates . . . slipped through Allied lines:** The story of the death of Coté and his teammates is taken from an OSS investigative report included in the Team Augustus report and from Gaujac, *Special Forces,* 183–84.

285. **On September 6, the five thousand Germans:** Team Ivor report, 652; Team Alex report, 681; "OKW War Diary," 111.

285. **Suddenly, the major general's forward forces . . . back and forth across the river:** Macpherson, author interviews, Jan. 20 and June 21 and 23, 2002; Macpherson, oral history, IWM.

285. **An urgent message . . . American forces contacted him:** Team Ivor report, 653–55; French Forces of the Interior—1944, 1067–69; Team Julian report, 728–29. A chronology of the development of negotiations with Elster can be found in French Forces of the Interior—1944, vol. 7, and Team Julian report, 731.

285. **"Will you come":** Macpherson, oral history, IWM.

285. **Major A. H. Clutton:** Team Julian report, 729.

286. **He and a representative of the French . . . blared at them:** Macpherson, author interview, Jan. 20, 2002; Macpherson related the tale of the ambulance in Stafford, *Secret Agent,* 221.

286. *the mairie,* **the mayor's office:** Team Ivor report, 654.

286. **Beside Macpherson . . . crawled over the area:** Ibid., 654–55; Macpherson, author interview, June 23, 2002.

286. **a short, sharp-faced man:** Photo in Graham, "Nazi Cadet's Ardor."

286. **An SS colonel:** Macpherson, author interview, June 23, 2002.

288. **Germans would vanish . . . within two or three days:** Ibid.

288. **north of Dijon:** J. Clarke, "Southern France," 29.

288. **only 130,000 out of nearly 210,000 German troops:** "OKW War Diary," 108.

289. **Team Novocaine's Bill Thompson:** Thompson, author interview, Sept. 4, 2002.

289. **Jean Sassi:** Sassi, author interview, Sept. 22, 2002.

289. **Some Jeds, for entertainment:** Thompson, author interview, Sept. 4, 2002.

289. **"We had brought out the jungle instincts":** Alcorn, *No Bugles,* 199.

289. **"de-activate these human time bombs":** Quoted from ibid. Thompson told me (Sept. 4, 2002) that the Jeds were put on this program.

289. **Tired of carrying around their weapons . . . started to party:** Lajeunesse, author interview, Aug. 11, 2002.

289. **"Our war, screwed up or not":** Franklin, "Jedburg," 197.

289–90. **Bill Thompson put eight hundred dollars . . . he later said:** Thompson, author interview, Sept. 4, 2002.

290. **As the summer of 1944 . . . the French in Indochina:** SOE, History of Jedburghs, part 8; A. Brown, "One Bright," 164.

290. **In Arçay . . . give them his name:** Macpherson, author interview, June 23, 2002.

290. **it would not be long:** Anderson, "20,000 Nazis Give Up."
291. **walked away across the square:** Macpherson, author interview, June 23, 2002.

## EPILOGUE

292. **other SOE and OSS special operations agents:** "Index to SO Reports, WE Section."
292. **"Without the great assistance":** Eisenhower, *Crusade in Europe,* 296.
292. **fifteen military divisions:** Mackenzie, *Secret History of SOE,* 624.
292. **The most important Resistance contributions:** Ibid., 622.
293. **"In no previous war":** Eisenhower, letter to Gubbins, May 31, 1945.
293. **twenty-five million pounds:** "Summary of Allied Aid," 97.
293. **This amounted to 350,000 Sten guns:** Mackenzie, *Secret History of SOE,* 602, gives the number of weapons dropped by May; "Summary of Allied Aid," 97, gives the tonnage dropped per month in 1944. My estimates of the number of weapons are based on these two sources.
293. **The Jedburgh principle:** Mackenzie, *Secret History of SOE,* 606.
293–94. **In the British election of 1945. . . with only two days' notice:** Foot, *History of the Special Operations Executive,* 355–56.
294. **In the United States . . . disbanding the OSS:** B. Hersh, *Old Boys,* 165–67.
295. **Lou Conein of Team Mark and William Colby of Team Bruce:** Colby and Forbath, *Honorable Men,* 141–288.
295. **"because the system":** Quoted in Smith, *Shadow Warriors,* 419.
295. **"Afghan freedom fighters":** Quoted in Coll, *Ghost Wars,* 97.
296. **Bill Colby . . . how the story got out:** *Encyclopedia of World Biography,* 2nd ed., s.v. "William E. Colby."
296. **John "Jack" Singlaub . . . a hero:** Perisco, "His Dog Tags"; Parry and Barger, "Reagan's Shadow CIA"; O. Kelly, "How Americans Help Finance Foreign Wars."
296. **Aaron Bank:** Robinson, "Fighting Behind Enemy Lines"; Glenn, "From the OSS to Special Forces."

# SOURCES

## ABBREVIATIONS

CMH      U.S. Army Center of Military History, Washington, DC
ETOUSA European Theater of Operations, U.S.A.
FOIA      Freedom of Information Act
Hoover   Hoover Institution Archives, Stanford University, Stanford, CA
IWM     Sound Archives, Imperial War Museum, Kensington, London, UK
MORI    Management of Officially Released Information
NARA    National Archives and Records Administration, College Park, MD
PRO      Public Record Office, Kew, Surrey, UK
RG       Registry group
SPOC    Special Projects Operation Center, Algiers

## AUTHOR INTERVIEWS

An asterisk indicates that a conversation took place by telephone. Karen Heinz-man translated during interviews with Jean Sassi and Louise Queinnec.

Patricia Alsop (wife of Stewart Alsop, Jed Team Alexander): Unrecorded date
Ted Baumgold (Jed Team Collodion): Aug. 21, 2002
Jacob Berlin (Jed Team Ammonia): *Sept. 11, *Sept. 12, and *Sept. 22, 2002
Michel de Bourbon (Jed Team Quinine): Feb. 20, Feb. 21, Feb. 22, Feb. 23, and
     Feb. 24, 2002
Ron Brierley (Jed Team Daniel): *Oct. 16, 2001
Arthur Brown (Jed Team Quinine): *Oct. 31, 2001; Jan. 17 and Jan. 18, 2002
John Cox (Jed Team Ivor): *Aug. 22, 2002
Joe De Francesco (Jed Team Jim): *Oct. 19, 2001; *Oct. 4, *Oct. 5, and *Oct. 6, 2002
Violette Desmarais (sister of Roger Coté, Jed Team Augustus): *Apr. 16 and
     *Oct. 2, 2002
Elmer Esch (Jed Team Ronald): *Oct. 15, 2002
Dick Franklin (Jed Team Alexander): Feb. 21, 2002

Daphne Friele (secretary to Colonel Musgrave, Milton Hall): *Unrecorded day in Oct. 2001

Bob Kehoe (Jed Team Frederick): *Oct. 26, Nov. 26, Nov. 27, Nov. 28, and Nov. 29, 2001

Bernard Knox (Jed Team Giles): Feb. 15, Mar. 21, May 3, May 5, *May 22, *June 1, *Aug. 15, and *Aug. 22, 2002; *June 25, 2003; *May 13, 2004

Lucien Lajeunesse (Jed Team Norman): May 28, May 29, May 30, Aug. 11, and Aug. 12, 2002

Camille Lelong (Jed Team Bruce): *Apr. 8 and *May 14, 2002

Bob Lucas (Jed Team Philip): *Oct. 16, 2002

Sir Thomas Macpherson (Jed Team Quinine): *Nov. 14, 2001; Jan. 20, Jan. 21, June 21, June 22, and June 23, 2002

Henry McIntosh (Jed Team Chloroform): Feb. 25 and Feb. 26, 2002.

Jacques de Penguilly (Jed Team James): *Apr. 16, June 17, and June 18, 2002

Roger Pierre (Jed Team Archibald): Unrecorded day in Dec. 2001

Jack Poché (Jed Team Masque): *Oct. 15, 2002

Louise Queinnec (Breton Resistance member): June 15 and June 16, 2002

Dick Rubenstein (Jed Team Douglas): Jan. 24, 2002

Jean Sassi (Jed Team Chloroform): June 11, June 12, June 13, June 19, Sept. 21, and Sept. 22, 2002

Albert de Schonen (Jed Team Gregory): *Apr. 16 and June 10, 2002

Major General John Singlaub (Jed Team James): *Jan. 9, Feb. 7, Mar. 19, and Dec. 4, 2002; *Feb. 28, 2003

Donald Spears (Jed Team Timothy): *Oct. 18, 2002

Mason Starring (Jed Team Anthony): *Oct. 14, 2002

David Stern (Jed Team John): *Oct. 18, 2002

Kay Strong (sister of John Bonsall, Jed Team Augustus): May 20, 2002

Gordon Tack (Jed Team Giles): *Apr. 16 and June 24, 2002

Bill Thompson (Jed Team Novocaine): Sept. 3, Sept. 4, and Sept. 5, 2002

Ray Trumps (Jed Team Ronald): Mar. 18, 2002

Paul van der Stricht (Chief, WE Operations, OSS/SO, London): Dec. 28, 2001; July 2 and Nov. 27, 2002

Elizabeth Winthrop (daughter of Stewart Alsop): Unrecorded dates, 2002

Christopher Wise (son of Adrian Wise, Jed Team Frederick): Jan. 21, 2002

## LETTERS TO THE AUTHOR

Ron Brierley (Jed Team Daniel), Oct. 17, 2001

Audrey Brown (wife of Oliver Brown, Jed Team Alastair), May 20, 2002

Lura May Dillow (wife of Conrad Dillow, Jed Team Norman), June 4, 2002

Anne Ellis (wife of J. W. Ellis, Jed Team Minaret), May 22, 2002

Maurice Geminel (Jed Team Bunny), June 23, 2002

Donald Gibbs (Jed Team John), May 27, 2002

Bob Kehoe (Jed Team Frederick), n.d.

Bernard Knox (Jed Team Giles), Apr. 12, 2002

Lucien Lajeunesse (Jed Team Norman), n.d.

Roger Leney (Jed Team Jeremy), July 10, 2002

Nancy Manierre (wife of Cyrus Manierre, Jed Team Dodge), June 20, 2002
E. Mautaint (Jed Team Hilary), June 12, 2002
Maurice Pirat (Jed Team Lee), Aug. 5, 2002
Louise Queinnec (Breton Resistance member), Oct. 4, 2002
Jean Sassi (Jed Team Chloroform), Apr. 24, 2002
Albert de Schonen (Jed Team Gregory), Apr. 20, 2002
John Sharp (Mission Isaac), May 20, 2002
John Smallwood (Jed Team Citroën), July 8, 2002
Sylvia Thomson (wife of George Thomson, Jed Team Alec), July 20, 2002
Amanda Todd (wife of L. A. Todd, Jed Team Claude), Nov. 1, 2002
René de la Tousche (Jed Team Alexander), n.d.
General Robert Toussaint (Jed Team Alan), July 11, 2002
A. A. E. Trofimov (Jed Team Guy), June 17, 2002

## JEDBURGH TEAM REPORTS

Extensive after-action reports exist for nearly every one of the Jedburgh teams sent into France. They amount to several thousand pages. Some team leaders, after completing their work, wrote preliminary reports at temporary military head-quarters in France. Some wrote more extensive reports when they returned to London. Some did both. For this and other reasons, a number of team reports ex-ist in several versions. Some team reports exist in only one of the following loca-tions. Others can be found, in their various versions, in more than one or all locations. Citations in the notes with page numbers refer to versions in the War diary. Citations without page numbers refer to unpaginated versions in records of Jedburgh teams.

CIA History of OSS Aid to the French Resistance. Boxes 740–41, entry 190, RG 226, NARA.

Jedburghs. War Diary of the Special Operations Branch—OSS London. Vol. 4. Boxes 24–26, entry 91, RG 226 (also available in microfilm from NARA). For more on the War Diary, see page 368.

Records of Jedburgh Teams. Boxes 1–3, entry 101, RG 226, NARA.

SOE (Special Operations Executive) Jedburgh Reports. Folders 471–564, HS6, PRO (also available in microfilm from Adam Matthew Publications, Ltd., Marl-borough, Wiltshire, United Kingdom).

## ALLIED AGENT ACTIVITY REPORTS

Like the Jeds, the hundreds of other British and American agents working in France wrote extensive after-action reports totaling several thousand pages. The reports of the American and British agents are held at the NARA and PRO, re-spectively. All agent report citations in the notes refer to those found in Western Europe, except the de Grelis report, which is in SOE.

SOE (Special Operations Executive) Agent Reports. Folders 566–84, HS6, PRO (also available in microfilm from Adam Matthew Publications, Ltd., Marlbor-ough, Wiltshire, United Kingdom).

Western Europe. War Diary of the Special Operations Branch—OSS London. Vol. 3. Boxes 19–24, entry 91, RG 226 (also available in microfilm from NARA). For more on the War Diary, see below on this page.

## PUBLISHED OFFICIAL HISTORIES AND REPORTS

Foot, M. R. D. *SOE in France. An Account of the Work of the British Special Operations Executive in France 1940–1944*. London: HMSO, 1966. This comprehensive history of the SOE's F Section was commissioned by the British government, which gave Foot unfettered access to restricted SOE files. This account is the single most important overview of special operations in France.

*Interim Report* and *Final Report of the Select Committee to Study Governmental Operations with Respect to Intelligence Activities*. Report of Senator Frank Church's committee on its 1975–1976 investigation into the illegal operations of the Central Intelligence Agency. Published by the U.S. Government Printing Office in 1976 and available on the Web site of the Assassination Archives and Research Center at http://www.aarclibrary.org/publib/church/reports/contents.htm (accessed Apr. 15, 2005).

Mackenzie, W. *The Secret History of SOE. Special Operations Executive 1940–1945*. London: St Ermin's Press, 2000. This official overview of the SOE's establishment and operations around the world remained classified for many years. It is an indispensable reference for students of World War II special operations.

*The 9/11 Commission Report: Final Report of the National Commission on Terrorist Attacks Upon the United States*. Published by W. W. Norton in 2004 and available on the Web site of the National Commission at http://www.9-11commission.gov/report/index.htm (accessed Apr. 15, 2005).

## UNPUBLISHED OFFICIAL HISTORIES AND REPORTS

French Forces of the Interior—1944. File no. 8–3 FR, acc. no. 419–1, CMH. A one-thousand-page history in manuscript of the contribution to the liberation of France of the French Resistance and the Allied agents and Jedburghs who worked with them. Produced by the Historical Division of ETOUSA.

History of Jedburghs in Europe. Files 17 and 18, HS7, PRO. The official Special Operations Executive history of the Jedburghs, including summaries of each team's accomplishments.

History of Special Operations MED. Entry 427, RG 407, NARA. The history of OSS special operations run from Algiers, including the use of Jedburgh teams dropped into southern France.

War Diary, OSS, London. Entry 91, RG 226, NARA. Declassified in 1979, the War Diary is perhaps the most important document for serious research into OSS special operations in Europe during World War II. In fourteen volumes and close to ten thousand pages, it records the work of the SO in London from the inception of the London branch in 1942.

## OTHER ARCHIVAL DOCUMENTS

Because the documents consulted are too numerous to list, only those relied upon most heavily are presented here.

"The Advantage of Jedburgh Teams Arriving in the Field in Uniform as Opposed to Arrival in Civilian Clothes." SOE policy paper, SOE Folder 288, HS8, PRO.

"Appreciation of the Potentialities of the French Resistance in Eastern, Central and Southern France." SFHQ planning paper, June 13, 1944. Folder 265, box 349, entry 190, RG 226, NARA.

"Arrest of Major Manierre." Memo, F. E. Rosell to Col. Joseph F. Haskell, Aug. 16, 1944. Folder 18, box 11, entry 126, RG 226, NARA.

"Assignment of Officers." Memo, E. F. Connely to the Adjutant General, Officers' Branch, Nov. 6, 1943. Folder 1, box 280, entry 92, RG 226, NARA.

"Brittany Plan." SFHQ internal memo, July 7, 1944. Folder 30, box 330, entry 190, RG 226, NARA.

"Casualty Reports." Memo, Frederick W. McKinnon Jr. to Archibald van Beuren, Jan. 8, 1945. Folder 18, box 11, entry 126, RG 226, NARA.

"Close Combat." In "Outline of Training Programs at Areas 'A' and 'F' for Operational Groups." Folder 3629, entry 146, RG 226, NARA.

"Comments on Major Dodderidge's Paper on Jedburgh Training." Memo, Henry Coxe to the Commanding Officer, SO Branch, OSS, London, Feb. 14, 1944. OSS file Paris-SO-OP-19, folder 1077, box 450, entry 190, RG 226, NARA.

"Coordination of Activities Behind the Lines with the Actions of Allied Military Forces Invading N.W. Europe." SOE paper, Apr. 6, 1943. Folder 288, HS8, PRO.

"Coordination of SF Activities in France with Plan Neptune for First U.S. Army." Memo, AC of S (assistant chief of staff), HQ First U.S. Army to SFHQ, May 15, 1944. Folder 31, box 330, entry 190, RG 226, NARA.

"Delay of Enemy Reinforcements Action by Resistance Groups." E. Mockler-Ferryman, Apr. 7, 1944. Folder 16, box 329, entry 190, RG 226, NARA.

"Development of Resistance in Northeast France." SFHQ planning paper, Aug. 20, 1944. Folder 265, box 349, entry 190, RG 226, NARA.

"Disposition of Officers Interviewed in Connection with the Jedburgh Plan." Memo, C. S. Williams to Mr. Scribner, Nov. 11, 1943. Folder 339, box 355, entry 190, RG 226, NARA.

"11th Special Forces Detachment Operations Report." Folder 4, box 294, entry 92, RG 226, NARA.

"Explosives and Demolitions—Lesson No. 1" and "Lesson No. 2." In "Outline of Training Programs at Areas 'A' and 'F' for Operational Groups." Folder 3629, entry 146, RG 226, NARA.

"Extension of Temporary Duty." Memo, E. F. Connely to the Adjutant General, Officers' Branch, Nov. 5, 1943. Folder 1, box 280, entry 92, RG 226, NARA.

"FFI Before and After D-Day." Manuscript #B-035, Historical Division, Headquarters, United States Army, Europe, Foreign Military Studies Branch. Box 9, RG 338, NARA.

"Fitness Report" on Gerald E. Miller, Central Intelligence Agency, Mar. 31, 1965. MORI Document ID 1145758 (provided to the author via FOIA office, Nov. 17, 2004).

"French Resistance, 4 June to 31st July." SHAEF report. Box 147, entry 30A, RG 331, NARA.

"French Resistance—Brittany." Collection of documents related to the use of Jeds, Allied agents, and Resistance in conjunction with the Third Army advance. Folder 30, box 330, entry 190, RG 226, NARA.

"French Resistance—Parts I and II." SHAEF evaluation of contributions of the French Resistance to the liberation of France. Folder 265, box 349, entry 190, RG 226, NARA.

"Guerrilla Warfare." In "Outline of Training Programs at Areas 'A' and 'F' for Operational Groups." Folder 3629, entry 146, RG 226, NARA.

"Index to SO Reports, WE Section." Folder 1, box 14, entry 168A, RG 226, NARA.

"Interference by Resistance Groups with the Movement of German Local Armoured Reinforcements." Aug. 3, 1943. Folder 16, box 329, entry 190, RG 226, NARA.

"Jedburgh Training." Memo, Major Dodderidge to the Commanding Officer, SO Branch, OSS, London, Feb. 11, 1944. Folder 1077, box 450, entry 190, RG 226, NARA.

"Jedburghs." Memo, Henry B. Coxe to the Commanding Officer, SO Branch, OSS, London, Feb. 14, 1944. Folder 1077, box 450, entry 190, RG 226, NARA.

"Jedburghs." SOE paper, Dec. 20, 1943. Folder 288, HS8, PRO.

"Maquis—Excerpts from POW Interrogations." Folder 26, box 330, entry 190, RG 226, NARA.

"Misconduct of an American Officer." Memo, Captain Cyrus E. Manierre to the CO, Training Detachment, ME 65, Apr. 15, 1944. Folder 73, box 9, entry 128, RG 226, NARA.

"Notification of Personnel Action" regarding Gerald E. Miller, Central Intelligence Agency, Sept. 28, 1950. MORI Document ID 1145722 (provided to the author via FOIA office, Nov. 17, 2004).

"Notification of Personnel Action" regarding Gerald E. Miller, Central Intelligence Agency, Aug. 7, 1956. MORI Document ID 1146620 (provided to the author via FOIA office, Nov. 17, 2004).

"OKW War Diary." Manuscript, Historical Division, Headquarters, United States Army, Europe, Foreign Military Studies Branch. RG 338, NARA.

"Operational Directive to SOE/SO." Supreme Headquarters Allied Expeditionary Force, SHAEF (44) 25, Mar. 23, 1944. Folder 16, box 329, entry 190, RG 226, NARA.

"OSS Massive Supply Drops to the French Resistance." Manuscript in CIA History of OSS Aid to the French Resistance. Folder 1476, box 740, entry 190, RG 226, NARA.

"Outline of Training Programs at Areas 'A' and 'F' for Operational Groups." Folder 3629, entry 146, RG 226, NARA.

"Outline Plan for the Use of Resistance in Immediate Support of Overlord." May 24, 1944. In History of Special Operations MED.

"Plan for Resistance Movements in Brittany, Aug. 10, 1944." In "11th Special Forces Detachment Operations Report." Folder 4, box 294, entry 92, RG 226, NARA.

"Plan for the Use of Resistance in Support of Operation Anvil." Aug. 1, 1944. Folder 12, box 329, entry 190, RG 226, NARA.

"Post D-Day Activity Behind the Enemy Lines in France." SFHQ planning paper, June 4, 1944. Folder 32, box 331, entry 190, RG 226, NARA.

"Post D-Day Resistance Activities." Memo, G3 (Operations) Division, SHAEF to SFHQ, May 31, 1944. Folder 32, box 331, entry 190, RG 226, NARA.

"Potentialities of Resistance Groups in France." Memo, John Bross to the Chief, SO Branch, London, Feb. 10, 1944. Folder 16, box 329, entry 190, RG 226, NARA.

"Procedure for the Dispatch of Jedburgh Teams." SFHQ briefing paper, SOE folder 288, HS8, PRO.

"Rail Communications." Excerpts from 21st Army intelligence report, June 23, 1944. Folder 1, box 17, entry 99, RG 226, NARA.

"Rapport sur l'Activité de la mission Augustus." In file titled "Augustus," box 10, entry 128, RG 226, NARA.

"Rapport sur la Fin Tragique de la Mission Interalliée Augustus." In file titled "Augustus," box 10, entry 128, RG 226, NARA.

"Recommendation for Award of Bronze Star to Bernard Knox." Folder 57, box 9, entry 128, RG 226, NARA.

"Recommendation for Award of Distinguished Service Cross to Robert Kehoe." Folder 57, box 9, entry 128, RG 226, NARA.

"Report on Seventy-Five SO Agents (Mostly Jedburghs) Dropped by Parachute into France." OSS report. Carmen Collection, Hoover.

"Resistance in South-East France." Mar. 22, 1944. Folder 12, box 329, entry 190, RG 226, NARA.

"Resistance Movement in the West." Manuscript #B-022, Historical Division, Headquarters, United States Army, Europe, Foreign Military Studies Branch. Box 8, RG 338, NARA.

"Role of Jedburghs." Summary of the speech given by Brigadier Mockler-Ferryman to Jedburgh students on Feb. 24, 1944. In SOE, History of Jedburghs in Europe.

"Role of Resistance Groups in the South of France." SHAEF Directive, May 21, 1944. Folder 12, box 329, entry 190, RG 226.

"Selection of Agents." Brigadier General David G. Barr, Order to the Commanding General, First U.S. Army, by command of Lieutenant General Devers. Nov. 6, 1943. Folder 339, box 355, entry 190, RG 226, NARA.

"SHAEF Directive to SOE/SO." June 15, 1944. In War Diary, vol. 12.

"SHAEF Directive to SOE/SO." July 7, 1944. In War Diary, vol. 12.

"A Short History of EMFFI." A history of the État Major (Headquarters) of the French Forces of the Interior, Sept. 21, 1944. Folder 265, box 349, entry 190, RG 226, NARA.

"SOE/SO Planning Review." May 9, 1944. Folder 31, box 330, entry 190, RG 226, NARA.

"Special Force Headquarters Operational Procedure." SFHQ paper outlining procedures for the dispatch and coordination of activities of Jedburgh teams and agents, May 1944. Folder 381, HS8, PRO.

"Special Recruitment, Jedburgh Plan." OSS memo. Folder 339, box 355, entry 190, RG 226, NARA.

"Summary of Allied Aid to the French Resistance." In War Diary, vol. 13, 90–126.

"Team James." Folder 4, box 9, entry 128, RG 226, NARA.

"Testimony of the Abbé of Tulle." In French Forces of the Interior—1944.

## AUDIOTAPES AND FILM

Robin Brook (SOE Director of Western Europe and SFHQ representative to SHAEF), accession #9805, IWM.

Oliver Brown (Jed Team Alastair), accession #12423, IWM.

Thomas Carew (Jed Team Basil), accession #18357, IWM.

William Crawshay (Jed Team Hugh), accession #12521, IWM.

Paul Cyr (Jed Team George), film in the motion picture archives, RG 226, NARA.

Robert Ferrier (SOE instructor), accession #18559, IWM.

Duncan Guthrie (Jed Team Harry), accession #12354, IWM.

Selwyn Jepson (SOE recruiting officer), accession #9331, IWM.

Glyn Loosemore (Jed Teams Andy and Ivor), accession #17949, IWM.

Sir Thomas Macpherson (Jed Team Quinine), accession #17912, IWM.

John Smallwood (Jed Team Citroën), accession #17998, IWM.

Norman Smith (Jed Team Brian), accession #17741, IWM.

Gordon Tack (Jed Team Giles), accession #16699, IWM.

## UNPUBLISHED AND PRIVATELY PUBLISHED MANUSCRIPTS, LETTERS, DIARIES

Materials are privately held unless otherwise noted.

Adjutant General's Office. Letter to Mr. C. J. Goddard, Aug. 21, 1944.

Alsop, John. "John Alsop's Memoirs of His Experiences in World War II." Unpublished manuscript.

Alsop, Stewart. Letters to his parents, Apr. 8, Apr. 23, Apr. 25, Sept. 14, Sept. 21, 1944.

Bross, John A. *Secret Operations: Some Reminiscences.* Privately printed, 1980.

Brown, Arthur. "Jedburgh Quinine." Unpublished manuscript.

———. *Jedburghs: A Short History.* Privately printed. Available at http://www.freespace.virgin.net/arthur.brown2 (accessed June 17, 2004).

———. "One Bright Summer's Day." Unpublished manuscript.

Canfield, Franklin. *Memoirs of a Long & Eventful Life.* Privately printed, 1996.

Cannicott, Stanley. *Journey of a Jed.* Privately printed, undated.

Coté, Roger. Letter to his parents, Aug. 9, 1944. Translated by Violette Desmarais.

Cox, Captain John. Letter to Mr. & Mrs. C. J. Goddard, Oct. 6, 1944.

Dillow, Konrad. "My Journey." Unpublished manuscript.

Eisenhower, General Dwight D. Letter to General Colin Gubbins, May 31, 1945.

Franklin, D. "Jedburg." Unpublished manuscript.

Goddard, C. J. Letter to Lewis Frelan Goddard, Feb. 4, 1944.

Goddard, Lewis Freelan. Letters to his parents, Dec. 2, 1973, and Apr. 2, 1944.

Knox, Bernard. Letter to R. Harris Smith, Mar. 4, 1971. Hoover.

Lajeunesse, Lucien. Untitled memoir of participation in Operation Jedburgh. Unpublished manuscript.

Loosemore, Glyn. "A Postscript to Arthur's Brown's 'The Jedburgh's: A Short History.' " Privately printed, undated.

Manierre, Cyrus. *Pop's War: The War Memoirs of Cyrus E. Manierre.* Edited and compiled by Carter Manierre. Privately printed, undated.

Miller, Gerry. Curriculum vitae held by Colin Beavan.

————, and Dorothy Miller. Guest book held by Colin Beavan.

Olmsted, John. Memoir of his work as a Jed supporting Operation Market Garden. Hoover.

Queinnec, Louise. "Resistance Pendant l'Occupation allemande de 1940 à 1944." Unpublished manuscript.

Schonen, Albert de. *Les Jedburgh et les Maquis.* Privately printed, undated.

Singlaub, John. Letters to his parents, Jan. 16, Jan. 29, Feb. 3, Mar. 5, Apr. 16, June 4, June 28, and Aug. 2, 1944.

Thompson, Bill. "Autobiography." Unpublished manuscript.

————. "My WW2 Memories." Unpublished manuscript.

Todd, Harvey. "Harvey Allan Todd, June 1939 to Dec 30, 1946." Unpublished manuscript.

Van der Stricht, Paul. Letter to R. Harris Smith, Apr. 14, 1971. Charles Carman Collection, Hoover.

## PUBLISHED FIRST-PERSON ACCOUNTS

Alcorn, Robert. *No Banners, No Bands; More Tales of the O.S.S.* New York: David McKay, 1965.

————. *No Bugles for Spies; Tales of the O.S.S.* New York: David McKay, 1962.

Alsop, Stewart. *Stay of Execution.* Philadelphia: J. B. Lippincott, 1973.

————, and Thomas Braden. *Sub Rosa: The OSS and American Espionage.* New York: Reynal and Hitchcock Publishers, 1946.

Applegate, Rex. *Kill or Be Killed.* Military Service Publishing Company, 1943.

Aussaresses, Général Paul. *Pour la France.* Paris: Éditions du Rocher, 2001.

Bank, Aaron. *From OSS to Green Berets: The Birth of Special Forces.* Novato, CA: Presidio Press, 1986.

Beevor, J. G. *SOE. Recollections and Reflections 1940–1945.* London: The Bodley Head, 1981.

Berlin, Jacob, as told to C. Tom Sutherland. "Behind Enemy Lines." *Official Journal of the Richmond County Historical Society,* vol. 29, no. 1, Summer 1998.

Bleicher, Henri. *Colonel Henri's Story.* London: William Kimber, 1954.

Bruce, David K. E. *OSS Against the Reich: World War II Diaries of Colonel David K.E. Bruce.* Edited by Nelson Lankford. Kent, OH: Kent State University Press, 1991.

Buckmaster, Maurice. *Specially Employed.* London: Batchworth Press, 1952.

————. *They Fought Alone.* London: Odhams Press, 1959.

Butler, Ewan. *Amateur Agent.* New York: Norton, 1963.

Casey, William J. *The Secret War Against Hitler.* London: Simon & Schuster, 1988.

Churchill, Peter. *Duel of Wits.* London: Hodder & Stoughton, 1953.

———. *Of Their Own Choice*. London: Hodder & Stoughton, 1952.

———. *The Spirit in the Cage*. London: Hodder & Stoughton, 1954.

Churchill, Winston. *Their Finest Hour*. Boston: Houghton Mifflin, 1949.

Colby, William, and Peter Forbath. *Honorable Men: My Life in the CIA*. New York: Simon & Schuster, 1978.

Copeland, Miles. *Without Cloak or Dagger*. New York: Simon & Schuster, 1974.

Cowburn, Benjamin. *No Cloak, No Dagger*. London: The Adventurers Club, 1960.

Crosby, Bing. *Irregular Soldier*. Guernsey: XB Publications, 1993.

Dalton, Hugh. *The Fateful Years: Memoirs 1931–1945*. London: Muller, 1957.

Davidson, Basil. *Partisan Picture*. Bedford, England: Bedford Books, 1946.

———. *Special Operations Europe: Scenes from the Anti-Nazi War*. London: Gollancz, 1981.

Défourneaux, René. *The Winking Fox: Twenty-two Years in Military Intelligence*. Indiana: Indiana Creative Arts, 1998.

Dodds-Parker, Douglas. *Setting Europe Ablaze: Some Account of Ungentlemanly Warfare*. Windlesham, England: Springwood Books, 1983.

Dourlein, Pieter. *Inside North Pole*. London: William Kimber, 1953.

Dreux, William B. *No Bridges Blown (OSS Officer Behind Enemy Lines in France)*. Notre Dame, IN: University of Notre Dame Press, 1971.

Eisenhower, Dwight D. *Crusade in Europe*. New York: Doubleday, 1948.

Evans, Captain Jack. *The Face of Death*. New York: William Morrow, 1958.

Frenay, Henri. *The Night Will End*. New York: McGraw-Hill, 1976.

Fussell, Paul. *Doing Battle*. New York: Little, Brown, 1996.

Gaulle, Charles de. *The Speeches of General de Gaulle*. London: Oxford University Press, 1949.

Goldsmith, John. *Accidental Agent*. New York: Scribner, 1971.

Hall, Roger. *You're Stepping on My Cloak and Dagger*. New York: Norton, 1957.

Hamilton-Hill, Donald. *SOE Assignment*. London: William Kimber, 1973.

Heslop, R. *Xavier*. London: Rupert Hart-Davies, 1970.

Hunt, Howard E. *Undercover: Memoirs of an American Secret Agent*. New York: Berkley, 1974.

Hutchison, John. *That Drug Danger*. Montrose, CO: Standard Press, 1977.

Kehoe, Robert. "Jedburgh Team Frederick—1944: An Allied Team with the French Resistance." *Studies in Intelligence*, Winter 1998–99. Available on the Web site of the Central Intelligence Agency, http://www.cia.gov/csi/studies/winter98_99/art03.html (accessed Oct. 8, 2004).

Kemp, Peter. *No Colours or Crest*. London: Cassell, 1958.

Knox, Bernard. *Essays Ancient and Modern*. Baltimore: Johns Hopkins University Press, 1989.

———. "Glory." Review of Patrick Marnham's *Resistance and Betrayal*. *New Republic*, June 17, 2002.

———. Introduction. In *The Iliad*, translated by Robert Fagles. New York: Penguin Classics, 1990.

———. "Premature Anti-Fascist." Abraham Lincoln Brigade Archives—Bill Susman Lecture Series. King Juan Carlos I of Spain Center, New York University, 1998. Available at the Web page of the Abraham Lincoln Brigade Archives, http://www.alba-valb.org/lectures/1998_knox_bernard.html (accessed Oct. 8, 2004).

———. *The Tragic Sense and the Pursuit of Happiness*. Washington, DC: George Washington University Press, 1977.

Kramer, Rita. *Flames in the Field: The Story of Four SOE Agents in Occupied France*. London: Penguin, 1995.

Langelaan, George. *The Masks of War*. New York: Doubleday, 1959.

Le Chene, Evelyn. *Watch for Me by Moonlight—A British Agent with the French Resistance*. London: Eyre Methuen, 1973.

Lovell, Stanley. *Of Spies and Stratagems*. New Jersey: Prentice Hall, 1963.

Marks, Leo. *Between Silk and Cyanide*. London: HarperCollins, 1998.

Millar, George. *Maquis*. London: Heinemann, 1945.

Morgan, William J. *The O.S.S. and I*. New York: Norton, 1957.

———. *Spies and Saboteurs*. London: Gollancz, 1955.

Obolensky, Serge. *One Man in His Time*. New York: McDowell, 1958.

Passy, Colonel (Andre Dewavrin). *Souvenirs, II, 10 Duke Street Londres*. 3 vols. Monte Carlo: Raoul Solar, 1947–51.

Singlaub, John, Maj. Gen., with Malcolm McConnell. *Hazardous Duty: An American Soldier in the Twentieth Century*. New York: Summit Books, 1991.

Stevenson, William. *A Man Called Intrepid*. 1976. Reprint, London: Sphere Books, 1981.

Sweet-Escott, B. *Baker Street Irregular*. London: Methuen, 1965.

Verity, H. *We Landed by Moonlight*. London: Ian Allan, 1978.

Vomécourt, Philippe de. *An Army of Amateurs*. Garden City, NY: Doubleday, 1961.

Walters, Anne-Marie. *Moondrop to Gascony*. London: Macmillan, 1947.

Wilkinson, Peter. *Foreign Fields: The Story of an SOE Operative*. London: I. B. Tauris, 1997; New York: St. Martin's Press, 1997.

## SECONDARY PUBLICATIONS

Ambrose, Stephen. *The Victors*. New York: Simon & Schuster, 1998.

Amery, Julian. *Sons of the Eagle: A Study in Guerilla War*. London: Macmillan, 1948.

Anderson, David. "20,000 Nazis Give Up As Plea for Token Battle Is Denied." *New York Times*, Sept. 18, 1944.

Aron, Robert. *France Reborn: The History of the Liberation, June 1944–May 1945*. New York: Scribner, 1964.

Associated Press. "Pinochet Indicted on Human Rights Charges." *New York Times*, Dec. 14, 2004.

Baker, Richard Brown. *The Year of the Buzz Bomb: A Journal of London, 1944*. New York: Exposition Press, 1952.

Baum, Dan. "The Price of Valor." *New Yorker*, July 12 and 19, 2004.

Beardon, Milton. "Afghanistan, Graveyard of Empires." *Foreign Affairs*, Nov./Dec. 2001.

Blacker, Irwin R. *Irregulars, Partisans, Guerrillas*. New York: Simon & Schuster, 1954.

Blumenson, Martin. *Breakout and Pursuit*. Washington, DC: U.S. Army Center of Military History, 1961.

Braddon, Russell. *Nancy Wake*. London: Cassell, 1956.

Brown, Anthony Cave. *Bodyguard of Lies*. New York: Harper & Row, 1975.

———. *"C": The Secret Life of Sir Stewart Menzies: Spymaster to Winston Churchill*. New York: Macmillan, 1987.

———. *The Last Hero: Wild Bill Donovan*. New York: Times Books, 1982.

———, ed. *Secret War Report of the OSS*. New York: Berkley, 1976.

Brunner, John W. *OSS Weapons*. Williamstown, NJ: Phillips Publications, 1991.

Burke, Michael. *Outrageous Good Fortune*. New York: Little, Brown, 1984.

Calmette, Arthur. *Les Équipes Jedburgh dans la Bataille de France*. Paris, 1966.

Calvi, Fabrizio. *OSS: Le Guerre Secrète en France, 1942–1945*. Paris: Hachette, 1990.

Chaloou, George C., ed. *The Secrets War: The Office of Strategic Services in World War II*. Washington, DC: National Archives and Records Administration, 1992.

Christenson, Christian E. "Underground Management: An Examination of World War II Resistance Movements." Master's thesis, Naval Postgraduate School, Monterey, CA, 1994.

Clarke, Jeffrey J. "Southern France." Washington, DC: U.S. Army Center of Military History, n.d.

———, and Robert Ross Smith. *Riviera to the Rhine*. Washington, DC: U.S. Army Center of Military History, 1993.

Clarke, R. W. *The Carpetbaggers*. Harrington, England: Carpetbagger Aviation Museum, 1997.

Coll, Steve. *Ghost Wars*. New York: Penguin, 2004.

Collier, Basil. *Hidden Weapons: Allied Secret or Undercover Services in World War II*. London: Hamish Hamilton, 1982.

Cookridge, Edward Henry. *Set Europe Ablaze: The Story of Special Operations in Western Europe, 1940–1945*. New York: Crowell, 1966.

———. *They Came from the Sky*. New York: Crowell, 1965.

Dear, Ian. *Sabotage and Subversion: The SOE and OSS at War*. London: Cassell, 1999.

D'Este, Carlo. *Decision in Normandy*. 1983. Reprint, New York: HarperCollins, 1994.

Doneux, Jacques. *They Arrived by Moonlight*. London: Odhams, 1956.

Dunlop, Richard. *Donovan, America's Master Spy*. Chicago: Rand McNally, 1982.

Ehrlich, Blake. *Resistance: France 1940–1945*. Boston: Little, Brown, 1965.

Fiske, Donald W., et al. *Selection of Personnel for Clandestine Operations: Assessment of Men*. Laguna Hills, CA: Aegean Park Press, 1997.

Foot, Michael. R. D. "Odette Hallowes." Obituary. *Independent*, Mar. 17, 1995.

———. *Resistance*. London: Paladin Books, 1978.

———. *Six Faces of Courage*. London: Eyre Methuen, 1978.

———. *SOE. An Outline History of the Special Operations Executive 1940–46*. London: BBC, 1984.

Ford, Corey. *Donovan of OSS*. Boston: Little, Brown, 1970.

———, and Alastair MacBain. *Cloak and Dagger: The Secret Story of OSS*. New York: Grosset & Dunlap, 1945.

Funk, Arthur. "American Contact with the Resistance in France, 1940–1943." *Military Affairs*, Feb. 1970.

———. *Hidden Ally. The French Resistance, Special Operations, and the Landings in Southern France, 1944.* Westport, CT: Greenwood Press, 1992.

Fussell, Paul. *The Boys' Crusade.* New York: Modern Library, 2003.

———. *Wartime.* New York: Oxford University Press, 1990.

Gardner, John, et al. *Assessment of Men: Selection of Personnel for the Office of Strategic Services.* New York: Rinehart, 1948.

Gaujac, Paul. *Special Forces in the Invasion of France.* Translated by Janice Lert. Paris: Histoire & Collections, 1999.

Gildea, Robert. *Marianne in Chains: Daily Life in the Heart of France During the German Occupation.* New York: Holt, 2002.

Giskes, Herman. J. *London Calling North Pole.* London: Kimber, 1953.

Glenn, John M. "From the OSS to Special Forces." *Military History,* Feb. 1998.

Goddard, Barbara. *Memoirs of Lewis Frelan Goddard, a Jedburgh, Killed in Action on August 7, 1944, in France as a Member of Team IVOR.* Privately printed, 1994.

Graham, Frederick. "Nazi Cadet's Ardor Cools Under Fire." *New York Times,* Sept. 20, 1944.

Gutjahr, Robert. "The Role of Jedburgh Teams in Operation Market Garden." Master's thesis, U.S. Army Command and General Staff College, Fort Leavenworth, KS, 1990.

Hammond, William M. "Normandy." Washington, DC: U.S. Army Center of Military History, 1994.

Harrison, Gordon A. *US Army in World War II: European Theater of Operations: Cross-Channel Attack.* Washington, DC: Office of the Chief of Military History, U.S. Army, 1962.

Hastings, Max. *Das Reich: Resistance and the March of the 2nd SS Panzer Division through France, June 1944.* New York: Holt, Rinehart & Winston, 1982.

———. *Overlord.* New York: Simon & Schuster, 1984.

Heilbrunn, Otto. *Partisan Warfare.* New York: Praeger, 1962.

Hemingway, Ernest. *For Whom the Bell Tolls.* 1940. Reprint, New York: Scribner, 1995.

Hemingway, Jack. *Misadventures of a Fly Fisherman: My Life With and Without Papa.* New York: McGraw-Hill, 1987.

Henoeffer, William. "If Donovan Were Here Today." Address delivered at CIA Headquarters to the Second International Jed Reunion, May 14, 1988.

Hersh, Burton. *The Old Boys.* New York: Scribner, 1992.

Hersh, Seymour. "The Coming Wars." *New Yorker,* Jan. 24 and 31, 2005.

His Britannic Majesty's Stationery Office. *Combined Operations: The Official Story of the Commandos.* New York: Macmillan, 1943.

Hogan, David W. "Northern France." Washington, DC: U.S. Army Center of Military History, n.d.

———. *U.S. Army Special Operations in World War II.* Washington, DC: U.S. Army Center for Military History, 1992.

Howarth, Patrick. *Undercover. The Men and Women of the Special Operations Executive.* London: Routledge and Kegan Paul, 1980.

———, ed. *Special Operations.* London: Routledge and Kegan Paul, 1955.

Hymoff, Edward. *The OSS in World War II: The True Story of American Agents Behind Enemy Lines.* New York: Richardson and Steirman, 1986.

Irwin, Major Wyman W. "A Special Force: Origin and Development of the Jedburgh Project in Support of Operation Overlord." Master's thesis, U.S. Army Command and General Staff College, Fort Leavenworth, KS, 1991.

Jackson, Julian. *France—The Dark Years.* Oxford: Oxford University Press, 2001.

Jakub, Jay. *Spies and Saboteurs: Anglo-American Collaboration and Rivalry in Human Intelligence Collection and Special Operations, 1940–1945.* New York: St. Martin's Press, 1998.

Jones, Benjamin F. "Looking for Bernard Knox: Warrior, Ancient and Modern." *War, Literature and the Arts,* vol. 15, 1 and 2.

———. "The Moon Is Down: The Jedburghs and Support to the French Resistance." Master's thesis, University of Nebraska, 1999.

Kedward, H. Roderick. *In Search of the Maquis: Rural Resistance in Southern France, 1942–1944.* Oxford: Oxford University Press, 1993.

———. *Occupied France: Collaboration and Resistance, 1940–1944.* Oxford: Blackwell, 1985.

Keegan, John. *The Second World War.* New York: Viking, 1989.

Kelly, Orr. "How Americans Help Finance Foreign Wars." *U.S. News & World Report,* Sept. 23, 1985.

Kelly, Richard. "Jedburgh Mission Hamish." *Blue Book,* July 1946.

King, Major Michael R. "Jedburgh Operations: Support to the French Resistance in Central France from June through September 1944." Master's thesis, U.S. Army Command and General Staff College, Fort Leavenworth, KS, 1991.

Knight, Eric. *Short Guide to Great Britain.* Washington, DC: War and Navy Departments, c. 1941.

Lankford, Nelson D. *The Last American Aristocrat: The Biography of David K. E. Bruce.* Boston: Little, Brown, 1996.

Levy, Bert. *Guerrilla Warfare.* Washington, DC: Infantry Journal Press, 1942.

Lewis, Samuel J. *Jedburgh Team Operations in Support of the 12th Army Group, August 1944.* Fort Leavenworth, KS: Combat Studies Institute, 1991.

Liu, Melinda, et al. "Fortress Tora Bora." *Newsweek,* Dec. 10, 2001.

Lorain, P. *Clandestine Operations. The Arms and Techniques of the Resistance, 1941–1944.* New York: Macmillan, 1983.

Lukacs, John. *Five Days in London, May 1940.* New Haven, CT: Yale University Press, 1999.

Lyon, Peter. *Eisenhower.* Boston: Little, Brown, 1974.

Macksey, Kenneth. *The Partisans of Europe in World War II.* London: Hart-Davis, MacGibbon, 1975.

Marnham, Patrick. *The Death of Jean Moulin.* London: Pimlico, 2001.

———. *Resistance and Betrayal.* New York: Random House, 2000.

Marshall, Bruce. *The White Rabbit: The Secret Agent the Gestapo Could Not Crack.* 1952. Reprint, London: Cassell, 2000.

Mattingly, Major Robert E. *Herringbone Cloak—GI Dagger: Marines of the OSS.* Washington, DC: History and Museums Division, U.S. Marine Corps, 1989.

Maxwell, Major David S. "Special Forces Missions: A Return to the Roots for a Vision of the Future." Master's thesis, U.S. Army Command and General Staff College, Fort Leavenworth, KS, 1995.

Melton, H. Keith. *O.S.S. Special Weapons & Equipment: Spy Devices of World War II*. New York: Sterling, 1991.

Michel, Henri. *The Shadow War: Resistance in Europe, 1939–1945*. New York: Harper & Row, 1972.

Miller, Donald L., and Henry Steele Commager. *The Story of World War II*. New York: Simon & Schuster, 2001.

Miller, Russell. *Behind the Lines*. London: Secker & Warburg, 2002.

Minnery, John. *OSS Sabotage and Demolition Manual*. Boulder, CO: Paladin Press, 1974.

Moon, Tom. *This Grim and Savage Game: O.S.S. and the Beginning of U.S. Covert Operations in World War II*. Los Angeles: Burning Gate Press, 1991.

Murrow, Edward R. *In Search of Light: The Broadcasts of Edward R. Murrow*. Edited by Edward Bliss Jr. New York: Knopf, 1967.

Nichols, Major Ralph D. "Jedburgh Operations: Support to the French Resistance in Eastern Brittany from June–September 1944." Master's thesis, U.S. Army Command and General Staff College, Fort Leavenworth, KS, 1993.

Nixon, Captain James C. "Combined Special Operations in World War II." Master's thesis, U.S. Army Command and General Staff College, Fort Leavenworth, KS, 1993.

"Odette Hallowes." Obituary. *London Times*, Mar. 17, 1995.

Ousby, Ian. *Occupation: The Ordeal of France*. 1997. Reprint, London: Pimlico, 1999.

Overton Fuller, Jean. *Double Agent? Light on the Secret Agents' War in France*. London: Pan Books, 1961.

———. *The German Penetration of SOE. France 1941–1944*. London: Kimber, 1975.

Parnell, Ben. *The Carpetbaggers; America's Secret War in Europe (Air Force Support to OSS and Resistance)*. Austin, TX: Eakin Publications, 1987.

Parry, Robert, and Brian Barger. "Reagan's Shadow CIA: How the White House Ran the Secret 'Contra' War." *New Republic*, Nov. 24, 1986.

Pawley, Margaret. *In Obedience to Instructions*. London: Pen and Sword Books, 1999.

Paxton, Robert O. *Vichy France: Old Guard and New Order, 1940–1944*. New York: Knopf, 1972.

Persico, Joseph. "His Dog Tags Don't Come Off." *New York Times Book Review*, Aug. 4, 1991.

———. *Piercing the Reich*. New York: Viking, 1979.

Pinck, Dan C., Geoffrey M. T. Jones, and Charles T. Pinck, eds. *Stalking the History of the Office of Strategic Services: An OSS Bibliography*. Boston: OSS/Donovan Press, 2000.

Powers, Thomas. *Intelligence Wars*. Revised and expanded edition. New York: New York Review of Books, 2004.

————. *The Man Who Kept the Secrets*. New York: Knopf, 1979.

Prados, John. *Lost Crusader: The Secret Wars of CIA Director William Colby*. Oxford: Oxford University Press, 2003.

Public Record Office. *SOE Syllabus: Lessons in Ungentlemanly Warfare*. Richmond, England: PRO, 2001.

Robinson, Linda. "Fighting Behind Enemy Lines." *U.S. News & World Report*, Feb. 10, 2003.

Rochester, Devereaux. *Full Moon to France*. New York: Harper & Row, 1977.

Roosevelt, Kermit. *The Overseas Targets: War Report of the OSS*. Vol. 2. New York: Walker, 1976.

————. *The War Report of the OSS*. Vol. 1. New York: Walker, 1976.

Rosner, Major Elliot J. "The Jedburghs: Combat Operations Conducted in the Finistère Region of Brittany, France, from July–September, 1944." Master's thesis, U.S. Army Command and General Staff College, Fort Leavenworth, KS, 1990.

Ruby, Marvel. *F Section SOE. The Story of the Buckmaster Networks*. London: Leo Cooper, 1988.

Sanger, David E. "War Figures Honored with Medal of Freedom." *New York Times*, Dec. 15, 2004.

Schoenbrun, David. *Soldiers of the Night: The Story of the French Resistance*. New York: Dutton, 1980.

Seaman, Mark. *Bravest of the Brave*. London: Michael O'Mara, 1999.

Shaver, John W., III. "Office of the Strategic Services; Operational Groups in France During World War II, July–October 1944." Master's thesis, U.S. Army Command and Staff College, Fort Leavenworth, KS, 1993.

Smith, Bradley. *The Shadow Warriors: OSS and the Origins of the CIA*. New York: Basic Books, 1983.

Smith, Richard Harris. *OSS: The Secret History of America's First Central Intelligence Agency*. Berkeley: University of California Press, 1972.

Stafford, David. *Britain and European Resistance 1940–1945: A Survey of the Special Operations Executive*. London: Macmillan, 1983.

————. *Secret Agent: The True Story of the Special Operations Executive*. London: BBC Consumer Publishing, 2000.

"The Sufferings of Afghanistan Come to New York." *Economist*, Sept. 15, 2001.

Tebbutt, Roy. *Operation Carpetbagger and Special Operations*. Harrington, England: Carpetbagger Aviation Museum, n.d.

Tickell, Jerrard. *Moon Squadron*. London: Allan Wingate, 1956.

————. *Odette: The Story of a British Agent*. London: Chapman & Hall, 1949.

"A Trial for General Pinochet." *New York Times*, Dec. 15, 2004.

U.S. Department of the Army. *Guerrilla Warfare and Special Forces Operations*. Washington, DC: U.S. Department of the Army, 1961.

Weaver, Mary Anne. "Blowback." *Atlantic Monthly*, May 1996.

West, Nigel. *MI6, British Secret Intelligence Service Operations, 1909–1945*. London: Weidenfeld & Nicolson, 1983.

————. *Secret War. The Story of SOE*. London: Hodder & Stoughton, 1992.

Wilkinson, P., and Astley Bright. *Gubbins and SOE*. London: Cooper, 1993.

Zaloga, Steven. "Normandy Legends." *Osprey Military Journal*, issue 3/4, July 25,

2001. Available at http://www.missing-lynx.com/articles/usa/zaloga_culin_cutter.htm (accessed June 24, 2004).

## OTHER SOURCES

Anonymous. "Fort Tilden's Harbor Entrance Control Post." Page on the Web site "The History of Fort Tilden, NY," posted Jan. 24, 2001, http://www.geocities.com/fort_tilden/hecp.html (accessed Jan. 30, 2003).

Anonymous. "Jedburgh." Page on the Web site of the University of Edinburgh's Department of Geography, post date unknown, http://www.geo.ed.ac.uk/scotgaz/towns/townfirst234.html (accessed May 15, 2003).

Anonymous. "Nazi U-Boats Attack New York Shipping." Page on the Web site "History of Fort Tilden," posted Nov. 14, 1999, http://www.geocities.com/fort_tilden/uboats.html (accessed Jan. 30, 2003).

Clark, John. "The Ball of Kirriemuir." Page on Clark's personal Web site collecting songs sung by servicemen and -women, post date unknown, http://www.squaddiesongs.com/songs/ballofkirriemuir.html (accessed Nov. 14, 2003).

Hampshire City Council. "Hampshire Treasures, Vol 6, Page 220—Liss." Page on the Web site of Hampshire County Council, post date unknown, http://www.hants.gov.uk/hampshiretreasures/vol06/page220.html (accessed Nov. 25, 2003).

Historical Officer—Canadian Military Headquarters. "Report No. 94: GHQ Exercise Spartan, March 1943." Document on the Web site of the Department of National Defense Canadian Forces, post date unknown, http://www.dnd.ca/hr/dhh/Downloads/cmhq/cmhq094.pdf. (accessed May 13, 2003).

Janberg, Nicolas. "Barrage de Sarrans." Page on the Web site of Structurae—International Gallery and Database of Structures, posted June 22, 2002, http://www.structurae.net/en/structures/data/s0003906/index.cfm (accessed Oct. 10, 2004).

Long, Lieutenant Colonel Perrin H. "Mistreatment of Patients in Receiving Tents." Aug. 16, 1943. Quoted on page on the Web site of the Patton Society, post date unknown, http://www.pattonhq.com/unknown/chap08.html (accessed June 30, 2004).

Marian Fathers. "Fawley Court: A History and Present Activities." Page on the Web site of the Congregation of Marian Fathers, post date unknown, http://www.marians-uk.org/fawleycourt.html (accessed Nov. 30, 2003).

Meany, Joseph F., Jr., Ph.D. "Port in a Storm: The Port of New York in World War II." Article on the Web site of the New York State Museum, post date unknown, www.nysm.nysed.gov/hisportofnewyork.html (accessed Jan. 13, 2003).

Morris, Nigel. "Mission Impossible: The Special Operations Executive, 1940–1946." Article on the Web page of the British Broadcasting Corporation, post date unknown, http://www.bbc.co.uk/history/war/wwtwo/soe_03.shtml (accessed Feb. 1, 2005).

National Climatic Data Center. "New York Climate Summary." Page on the Web site of the National Climatic Data Center, posted Dec. 2002, http://lwf.ncdc.noaa.gov/oa/climate/research/cag3/Y8.html (accessed Jan. 31, 2003).

National Park Service (NPS). "Catoctin Mountain Park." Page on the Web site of the NPS, posted July 3, 2003, http://www.nps.gov/cato/ (accessed July 17, 2003).

————. "Fort Wadsworth." Page on the Web site of the NPS, post date unknown, http://www.nps.gov/waysite/way-2g.htm (accessed Jan. 31, 2003).

Naval Historical Center. "Main Navy and Munitions Buildings." Page on the Web site of the United States Navy, post date unknown, http://www.history.navy. mil/photos/pl-usa/pl-dc/nav-fac/mn-mun.htm (accessed June 30, 2003).

Pathe Gazette. "The Big Three in Teheran," Dec. 9, 1943. Archived on the Web site of British Pathe, post date unknown, http://www.britishpathe.com (accessed Oct. 15, 2003).

Patterson Army Health Clinic. "Fort Monmouth Landmarks." Page on the Web site of the U.S. Army's North Atlantic Regional Medical Command, post date unknown, http://www.narmc.amedd.army.mil/patterson/landmark.htm (accessed Feb. 20, 2003).

Patton, General George S., Jr. Speech delivered to the troops in England, June 5, 1944. Archived on the home page of the Web site of the Patton Society, post date unknown, www.pattonhq.com/pdffiles/speech.pdf (accessed June 30, 2004).

Prest, David. "Evacuees in World War II—The True Story." Article on the Web site of the British Broadcasting Corporation, post date unknown, http://www. bbc.co.uk/history/war/wwtwo/evacuees_01.shtml (accessed Oct. 10, 2004).

Reed, Mary Beth, et al. "Evaluation of Selected Cultural Resources at Fort Monmouth, New Jersey," chapter 4. Page on the Web site of InfoAge, June 1996, http://www.infoage.org/chapter-4a-crr.html (accessed Feb. 20, 2003).

Roosevelt, President Franklin D. Fireside chat on the subject of the Cairo and Tehran Conferences, Dec. 24, 1943. Archived on the Web site of Franklin D. Roosevelt Presidential Library and Museum, post date unknown, http://www. fdrlibrary.marist.edu/122443.html (accessed Oct. 15, 2003).

United States Holocaust Memorial Museum. "SS St. Louis: Voyage to Nowhere." Page on the Web site of the museum, post date unknown, http://www.ushmm. org/outreach/louischr.htm (accessed Feb. 20, 2003).

White House Military Office. "Camp David." Page on the Web site of the White House, post date unknown, http://www.whitehouse.gov/whmo/camp-david. html (accessed July 17, 2003).

# PERMISSIONS

# INDEX